AF530534

CENTRE-STATE FINANCIAL RELATIONS

CESS RESEARCH STUDIES

Public Policy and the Rural Poor in India No. 1

The working of the Andhra Pradesh State Road Transport Corporation No. 2

Levels of Living in a State Setting : The case of Andhra Pradesh No. 3

Centre-state Financial Relations : A Study in Levels of Development of States No. 4

CESS RESEARCH STUDIES 4

CENTRE-STATE FINANCIAL RELATIONS

A Study in Levels of Development of States

M. L. SASTRY
G. R. REDDY

Foreword by
Y. VENUGOPAL REDDY

CENTRE FOR ECONOMIC AND SOCIAL STUDIES,
HYDERABAD

And

CONCEPT PUBLISHING COMPANY, NEW DELHI-110059

ISBN 81-7022-210-9

First Published 1988

Published by
Ashok Kumar Mittal
Concept Publishing Company
A-15-16 Commercial Block, Mohan Garden
NEW DELHI-110059 (India)

Photocomposed by
Microtech Advance Printing Systems (P) Ltd.
NEW DELHI-110015

Printed at
Taj Press
A-35/4, Maya Puri
NEW DELHI

FOREWORD

Referring to the Union-State financial relations in India, Lady Hicks had mentioned that financial relations are more complicated in India than in almost any other federation, certainly more than they are in the USA, Canada, Australia or Nigeria. No doubt the problem of coordination is not restricted to financial field in India but it extends to political, economic and administrative fields in the context of Centre-State or Union-State relations. However, the issue of financial relations is not only important but also quantifiable and to a larger extent, menable to analysis.

It is possible to approach the issue of Union-State relations in different ways. Most commonly, the subject is viewed in the context of the erosion of the autonomy of the States and continuous as well as increasing dependence of the State Governments on the Union Government. This sentiment is expressed in varying degrees and tones. For instance the proceedings of the historic debate of the Opposition Leaders in October 1983 on Centre-State Relations resulting in the Srinagar Declaration captures the spirit of this sentiment. Dr Farooq Abdullah summed up the situation when he said that absolute dependence of the units upon the Union and increasing indebtedness as a consequence thereof make the States ineffective with the result that even where one wants to shoulder responsibility it does not become possible.

In a more academic sense the problem is examined as one of fiscal imbalance classified into two segments i.e. problem of vertical fiscal imbalance and the problem of horizontal fiscal imbalance. On the one hand we have the emergence of financial disequilibrium which necessitates the transfer of funds from the Centre to the States and concomitantly there is the issue of differences in the potential and consequently fiscal situation of the different states. A number of studies on the analysis of the Centre-State relations in the context of Finance Commissions observed the persistent dilemma of increasing transfer of resources from the Centre to States and the glaring regional economic disparities.

It should be recognised that the problem of inter-State inequalities, in some form or the other exist in almost all Federations. However, it is said that certain features of inequalities among the states make the problem qualitatively different from that in the developed Federations leading to special justification for treating the issue of fiscal equalisation as part and parcel of the problem of national growth instead of treating it as a problem of income distribution. Thus, discriminatory transfers to less developed States should invariably aim at equalising the opportunities for growth. The point is expressed slightly differently when it is said that an economic or functional approach to equitable distribution of national funds among States should be guided mainly by the consideration of each according to capacity and to each according to its needs

While viewing the Centre-State financial relations in the context of the planned development one should not ignore the impact of planning itself on the fiscal situation in the States. In this context it has been noted that the increasing dependence of States on the Centre is a dynamic problem of inter-governmental financial relations which cannot be solved once and for all.

Following this logic and operationalising the issue, it is sometimes suggested that modifications in the structure and area of operations of Finanace Commission and the Planning Commission should be considered.

The same logic would lead one to argue that the issue of Centre-State financial relations is not something that should be considered purely from the point of view of the State Government demanding greater autonomy and more equitable distribution of sources or the

Union Government insisting on the requirement of cornering resources for national development and discretionary transfers to have the manoeuvrability to assign the source on the basis of uneven position of dirrerent States. In this light, while endorsing the need for a fresh look at the functioning of both Finance Commission and Planning Commission, it is urged by some that the task before the Centre and the States is to outgrow this tradition of each looking at the problem from a partisan spirit, each stressing or even overstressing its own claims, and to develop a spirit of cooperation, mutual trust and solidarity.

If the issue of Union-State financial relations were to be viewed in an overall context, it is necessary to appreciate the overall fiscal situation that prevails in the country as a whole. In this regard, Dr. Thimmaiah explains the Indian fiscal scene in terms of different stages. After the independence, till 1960s, the Indian fiscal scene was characterised by vertical as well as horizontal federal fiscal imbalances. Central Governments was able to raise more resources and distribute it among different states through the mechanisms of Finance Commisions, but relatively better off States received more funds than the poorer states. In the second which started in the late 1960s the vertical federal imbalances became more evident because of the growing expenditure of the State Government under the planning regime. The Planning Commission had to step in with its own mechanisms for transferring of financial resources from the Central Governments to the States to supplement the devolution of finances as per Finance Commision's recommendations through Gadgil Formula. The plan assistance could reduce vertical as well as horizontal imbalances to some extent for about a decade. Dr Thimmaiah adds that, after emergency the political awakening of the pressure groups and their articulation resulted in demands on both the Centre and the State Government to spend more and tax less. According to Dr Thimmaiah during the first two stages of the Indian fiscal evolution, the bargaining was between the State Government on the one hand and the Central Government on the other. But in the third stage of the fiscal evolution which is currently prevailing, the tug of war is going on between both the Central and State Governments on the one hand and various powerful pressure groups on the other.

This would lead us to believe that the problem of Union-state financial relations has to be viewed in the context of what could be called the fiscal crisis in India. The fact that there is a fiscal crisis seems to have been fully recognised in the context of the formulation of the Seventh Five Year Plan. There are a number of distinct steps in public policy recently to demonstrate this. First, a rigid discipline of prohibiting over-drafts by the State Governments has been imposed by the Reserve Bank of India at the instance of Ministry of Finance. Second, long term fiscal policy statement has been made and series of efforts are underway to ease the resource position of the Government of India. Third, the need for generating surpluses from the public enterprises is fully recognised. Fourth, the limits to using adminmistered prices as an instrument for generating resources has been recognised.

Thus we are at cross-roads in terms of the fiscal policies in the country as a whole in general and the Union-State Relations in particular. It would be timely to have a review of the flow of funds to the states with varying levels of development through the variety of instruments that the Union Government has at its command. It should also be recognised that the instruments available for the Union Government are not restricted to the statutory and non-statutory transfers but encompass the allotment of open market borrowings to the State Governments, the poloicies of disposition of funds by the all India financial institutions, etc. This book by Mr M.L.Sastry and Mr G.R. Reddy tries to meet this important requirement at a critical juncture of review of our policies.

The book starts with narrating the levels of development of different States and tries to capture the characteristics of the economies of different States. It is clearly established that the regional imbalances among different States have been accentuated, though a large number of instruments explained in the later chapters were avowedly used to reduce the regional disparities. The net effect of the various financial instruments available through both Finance Commission and Planning Commission on the State plan outlays is sought to be indicated by analysing the per capita State Plan outlays with reference to the levels of development. Essentially the effects of Central Assistance given, acccess to open market borrowings permitted, and the statutory devolution due to the awards of the Finance Commission can be found in the plan outlays. While States' own efforts are admittedly significant, the qualitative impact of flows in terms of additionality to the State should be recognised.

After explaining the formula governing the Central Assistance with special reference to the objectivity and certainty introduced by Gadgil Formula, the authors explain the introduction of some progressivity though the effect on individual States of different groups was not as progressive. The study of market borrowings shows that the Government of India has been increasing its share of the market borrowings at the cost of the State Governments though the trend is sought to be reversed recently. Though the authors have not pointed out, it is necessary to appreciate a trade off in terms of macro policy framework. If the aggregates in the economy are treated as pre-determined, the increased flow of Central Assistance on top of larger share of taxes to the State Governments awarded by the Finance Commission would be possible only if the Government of India is able to have relatively greater access to market borrowings. In this route, the State Governments are in a position to have an opportunity between larger Central Assistance and larger access to open market borrowings and clearly the terms being what they are, the States are better off by opting for larger Central Assistance.

The value of the book is enhanced by the fact that the thrust in the flow of institutional finances to different States is examined. These include credit by Commercial Banks, assistance by all India financial institutions and Central Government investments in States.

The analysis would be incomplete unless evaluation of financial transfers to the States under the recommendations of the successive Finance Commissions, are also explained. The systems as well as the final outcome in terms of per capita transfer of resources to different States are indicated. The uneven economic and financial position of the States gets reflected in the structure of States' own revenues and transfers from the Centre as also the shares of different taxes in States' own tax revenues. Before making an overall assessment of the Centre State financial transfers, the authors examined the debt burden of the States and conclude that the debt servicing burden is not alarming though the outstanding debt is increasing.

It will be evident from the brief narration of what is contained in the book, that it is very comprehensive in its coverage. The value of the book is enhanced by the mass of data that is appended in the second part. In a way the book is an update and an advance over an earlier volume covering somewhat similar ground, viz., the book by Mr K.Venkatraman. While this book appears to be relatively short on analysis, it is more than made good by the amount of informative narration and the statistical tables that have been presented. Even so, there are some relevant areas not covered in this book but requiring deeper understanding and analysis. For instance, the impact on different States, (on incomes and rates of growth) of the huge subsidies on food, fertilisers etc., accorded by Union Government year after year, must be studied since only some States may happen to benefit substantially.

In fact, as one goes through this book the need for exploring further more fundamental issues could be felt. The way the functions or responsibilities have been dilinenated in the Constitution for the Union and the State and the matching of sources of financial resources provided itself may require a review. Such a review would naturally encompass not only the roles of Planning and Finance Commissions but also the items listed under the Union, State and Concurrent lists. Some of the issues such as role of Centrally Sponsored Schemes and the amounts covered by such schemes has become an important bone of contention in the recent meetings of the National Development Council. Further a number of developments have taken place since the adoption of Constitution which were not envisaged at the time the Constitution was drafted. For instance, the extent of importance of the mechanisms of market borrowings which is virtually controlled and allocated by Union Government in financing developmental programmes was perhaps not visualised. The external borrowings and external assistance as an important source of funding public investments which is mainly controlled by Union Government could not have been perceived by the founding fathers of the Constitution. The implications of large scale acceptance of the concept of welfare and consequent larger responsibilities for the State Governments might not have been envisaged by the constitution makers. Finally, the thrust towards all India-norms in regard to social infrastructure might not have been fully captured by the makers of the Constitutions. A quantitative back up for further probe into some of these issues is provided by this book thus enhancing its value. In recognition of the need for an overall review, Sarkaria Commission has been appointed and in this sense the book is also timely.

I would strongly recommend the book to all those who are involved in analysis and policy making of developmental issues in general and financial and planning issues in particular. This can be treated as a guide to the practitioners. Secondly it is useful as an excellent reference document to the students of India's Economic Development. Finally, it provides a wealth of information and raises issues helping in identification of fruitful areas of further research.

I compliment the authors on the painstaking and extremely useful effort and commend the book.

HYDERABAD PROFESSOR Y. VENUGOPAL REDDY
November, 1986

PREFACE

There was a great deal of interest in the later half of the seventies on the issue of Centre-State financial relations. This arose, initially, as one aspect of Centre-State relations in general which had acquired importance and topical interest in the changed political context in the country after the Emergency and was further accentuated by the appointment of a new Finance Commission (the seventh) and later by the initiation of the process of formulation of new Five Year Plan (1978-83). It was in this latter context that the issue came up before the National Development Council in March, 1978 when a Committee of the NDC was appointed. In connection with the work of this Committee and, later, of its working group, the Planning Commission collected and furnished a great deal of information some of which was available for the first time. This information was naturally analysed by different States in different ways with a view to supporting different points of view. Similar analyses had been done by a number of research workers and eminent academicians also. Thus a wealth of data had become available in regard to Centre-State financial relations.

Sri B.P.R. Vithal, former Principal Secretary (Finance & Planning) Govt., of A.P. took very keen intrest in this subject. With his encouragement and guidance, Shri M.L.Sastry, Officer on Special Duty (Finance Dept.) collected, arranged and presented this information in a readily available form, which was published by the State Government as "Centre-State Financial Relation-Certain Relevant Data" in June, 1979. No attempt was made at that time to make any analytical study of the data.

This data book proved to be very useful, but with the passage of time, the need for updating and revising the data was also felt. With the help of Shri G.R.Reddy, Joint director (Finance Department) the data book was revised, updated and expanded in 1985. When it was under consideration for printing, Shri T.L.Sankar, Principal Secretary (Finance and Planning), Shri K. Kosalram, Secretary (Finance) and Dr.Y.Venugopal Reddy, Secretary (Planning) suggested that the data should be arranged and accompanied by some analytical studies. Dr. Venugopal Reddy took a keen interest and devised a Chapter scheme for the analytical notes. He also suggested a broad analytical framework which has been followed in the preparation of this work.

The book is in two parts. Part one contains analytical notes divided into ten chapters and part two contains statistical statements arranged into eleven appendices.

Chapter one presents the broad characteristics of the economy of the States and describes the basis for categorising the States into three groups to represent broadly the different levels of development.

Chapter two deals with the evolution of statutory transfers to the States under the recommendations of the Finance commissions. The components of the transfers as well as the principles governing such transfers have been discussed in detail in this chapter.

The evolution of Central assistance for States' plans and equity in its distribution have been discussed in chapter three.

The growth and distribution of States' plan outlays since the inception of Planning have been analysed in chapter four.

The flow of discretionary transfers to the states is analysed in chapter five.

Chapter six analyses the flow of institutioinal transfers to the States.

Chapter seven analyses the distribution of market borrowings between the Centre and the States and equity in the distribution of market borrowings among the States.

Chapter eight discusses the growth of public debt and debt burden of the States.

The growth in revenue of the States and its structure has been analysed in chapter nine.

The book closes with chapter ten which presents an overall assessment of the financial transfers from the Centre to the States.

In view of the wide coverage of the topics as well as a long time-span, it has not been possible to carry out an exhaustive analysis. No attempt has been made to use any sophisticated tools for the analysis. We have taken the State Domestic Product to roughly and fairly represent the levels of development of different States and tried to see if there is any correlation between the financial flows and levels of development. The brief analysis presented in the chapters is mainly aimed at bringing out the salient features of the datailed date presented in the appendices. Because of the limited nature of the analysis, there may be a number of loose ends which we hope would be taken up for detailed analysis by researchers in the field. We believe that more than the analysis contained in this book, the range of data presented in this book, some of which is published for the first time, will be of immense use to the researchers in the field of Centre-State financial relations.

The book would not have been written but for the keen interest evinced by Dr. Venugopal Reddy right from the formulation of the study. His constant encouragement and goadings have motivated us to complete the work. He has read through the successive drafts with an intense care inspite of his heavy pre-occupations. His searching queries and highly useful suggestions have resulted in a vastly improved manuscript, but the responsibility for the deficiencies is entirely ours.

We are thankful to the Finance and Planning Department, Government of Andhra Pradesh for providing us all the facilities required for completing the book, and permitting its publication. We are particularly thankful to Shri T.L.Sankar in this regard.

Shri E.Suresh Babu nas patiently and accurately typed the manuscript. Shri K.Naga Babu, Deputy Statistical Officer joined us at a later stage and been very useful to us in the preparation of the summary analytical tables. Our thanks are due to both of them.

We express our deep appreciation of the contribution made by Prof.D.Narasimha Reddy of the Central University who read through the entire manuscript with great care and diligence and suggested, some revisions in presentation.

We would like to place on record our deep sense of gratitude to the Centre for Economic and Social Studies, Hyderabad, particularly its Director, Prof. R. Radhakrishna for sponsoring the publication of this book.

Hyderabad, M.L. SASTRY
November, 1986 G.R. REDDY

CONTENTS

PART ONE

STUDY OF FLOWS AND LEVELS OF DEVELOPMENT

ONE

ECONOMIES AND GROUPING OF STATES

This chapter presents the broad characteristics of the States and their present levels of development by certain broad indicators. The purpose of presenting these details is to arrive at a basis for grouping the States by levels of development. The analysis of flow of resource to States presented in the subsequent chapters of this volume is mainly done with reference to the grouping of the states arrived at in this chapter. The information presented in this chapter is also expected to serve as a backdrop for the analysis presented in subsequent chapters. No attempt has been made in this chapter to study the performance of the States either spatially or inter-temporally. The focus in this chapter is mainly on the fourteen major States as the analysis presented in the chapters that follow covers only these States. Wherever necessary only a passing reference is made to the remaining eight states mostly consisting of north-eastern hill States designated by the Government of India as "Special Category States".

DEMOGRAPHIC CHARACTERISTIS

The Indian States vary widely in terms of demographic characteristics. While Uttar Pradesh with a population of 1108.62 lakhs (1981 census) accounts for 16.2 per cent of the total population, Tripura with a population of 7.75 lakhs accounts for only 0.1 per cent of the total population. Out of the 22 states, six major States, viz., Andhra Pradesh, Bihar, Madhya Pradesh, Maharashtra, Uttar Pradesh and West Bengal account for as much as 66 per cent of the total population.

Though the size of the population varies widely among the States, the percentage increase in population between 1971 and 1981 is fairly uniform among the States barring a few states like Kerala and Tamil Nadu where the increase is considerably lower than the national average.

Wide variations are noticed in the density of population among the States. While in Kerala and West Bengal the average density is nearly three times higher than the national average, in Rajasthan, it is half the national average. The density in special category States is generally lower.

There are also variations in the proportion of urban population in the Indian States. The proportion of urban population in the States of Bihar, Kerala, Orissa and Uttar Pradesh is considerably lower than the national average of 23 per cent, while in the States of Karnataka, Gujarat, Maharastra and Tamil Nadu, the proportion is higher. It is interesting to note that the proportion of urban population is relatively higher in the special category States.

The percentage of literate population varies widely among the States from 70 per cent in Kerala to 24 per cent in Rajasthan. Andhra Pradesh, Bihar, Madhya Pradesh, and Uttar Pradesh are among the States with low literacy rates. Among the special category States Jammu and Kashmir, Meghalaya and Sikkim have lower literacy than the national average. Between 1961 and 1981, the relative position of the States in terms of literacy has remained more or less the same. In fact the States with already higher levels of literacy improved their position further. The literate population in kerala increased from 55.1 to 69.17 per cent. There is also considerable increase in the literacy rates in Tamil Nadu, Maharastra and Gujarat over their already higher levels. Though the rates of literacy increased in all the States, the increase in low-literacy States is very much lower than the increase attained in high-literacy States.

The precentage of Scheduled Caste population is higher than the national average of 15.7 per cent in the States of Haryana, Punjab, Rajasthan, Tamil Nadu, Uttar Pradesh and West Bengal. The percentage of tribal population is higher in the States of Bihar, Gujarat, Madhya Pradesh, Orissa and Rajasthan. In some special category States like Meghalaya and Nagaland over 80 per cent of the total population is tribal.

ECONOMIC CHARACTERISTICS:

Per Capita Income: The per capita income of a State represents broadly the levels of development attained. Taking the comparable estimates of per capita domestic products for the year 1979-80, it is noticed that there are wide variations in the levels of per capita income among the States. At one extreme is Punjab with a per capita income of Rs.2,528 and at the other extreme is Bihar with per capita income of only Rs. 785. The difference is over three times. Only the States of Gujarat, Haryana, Karnataka, Maharastra, Punjab and West Bengal have higher per capita incomes than the national average of Rs. 1339 in 1979-80. Another disturbing feature of the distribution of per capita income is low increase of the levels of per capita income attained in the poorer States over time. While the per capita income of Punjab recorded an increase of 560 per cent between 1960-61 and 1979-80, the increase recorded in Bihar is only 263 per cent. In 1960-61, Maharastra had the highest per capita income of Rs. 409 and Bihar had the lowest income of Rs. 216, the difference being less than 2 times. Over the years the difference has increased to over 3 times.

Sectoral Income: The sectoral distribution of Net State Domestic Product (SDP) of States presented in Appendix Table 1.8 reveals that bulk of the States' domestic product is derived from the primary sector consisting of mainly agriculture and allied sectors. On an average, 43.8 per cent of the SDP was derived from the primary sector in 1981-82. Gujarat, Kerala, Maharastra, Tamil Nadu and West Bengal are among the States where the contribution of the primary sector is considerably lower. Next to primary sector, the tertiary sector contributes on an average 33.7 to the SDP. The contribution of tertiary sector is higher in the States of Gujarat, Kerala, Maharastra, West Bengal and Tamil Nadu. In Tamil Nadu as much as 50.9 per cent of the SDP is generated in the tertiary sector. On the average, the contribution of the secondary sector consisting of manufacturing, construction etc., is 22.5 per cent of the total SDP. The contribution of the secondary sector is fairly higher in the States of Gujarat, Karnataka, Maharastra and West Bengal.

As compared to 1971-72. there has been a decline in the contribution of the primary sector and increase in the contribution of tertiary and secondary sectors. This trend is noticeable in all the States. There has been a steep fall in the contribution of primary sector in Punjab from 60.4 per cent in 1971-72 to 44.3 per cent in 1981-82. Only in Maharastra the contribution of the primary sector increased from 25.4 per cent to 29.0 per cent. On an average the contribution of the tertiary sector increased from 29.3 to 33.7 per cent and that of secondary sector from 20.6 per cent to 22.5 per cent between 1971-72 and 1981-82. States like Punjab, Haryana, and Gujarat have recorded higher increase in the share of the tertiary sector. There has been some decline in the share of the secondary sector in the States of Maharastra and Tamil Nadu, while Punjab recorded a substantial increase in its share.

Agriculture: In almost all the States, bulk of the area under cultivation is devoted to the raising of food crops. The all-India area under food crops is 77.3 per cent in 1981-82. Gujarat and Kerala are the only States where the area under nonfood crops either exceeds or equals the area under food crops. There has not been any major change in the percentage of area under food crops between 1971-72 and 1981-82.

The per capita income generated in agriculture including animal husbandary varies widely from Rs. 1400 in Punjab to Rs. 382 in Tamil Nadu. As against the average per capita income of Rs. 611 generated in the agricultural sector in 1981-82, States of Punjab, Haryana, Andhra Pradesh and Orissa record fairly higher levels of per capita agricultural income.

Irrigation: There are wide variations in the percentage of net sown area irrigated among the states. Nearly 50 per cent of the area or more is irrigated in the States of Punjab, Haryana, Uttar Pradesh and Tamil Nadu. The area irrigated in Punjab is as much as 86 per cent in 1981-82. In Maharastra, only 12.3 per cent of the area is irrigated as against the national average of 29.2 per cent.

Industry: Taking the per capita gross value added of industrial output in 1981-82, the States of Gujarat, Haryana, Maharastra, Punjab, Tamil Nadu and West Bengal can be considered to have reached fairly higher levels of industrialisation as compared to other States. The per capita value added in these States is also fairly higher.

Infrastructure: In terms of road length per 100 sq. kms. of area, Kerala occupies the top position with 267 Kms. followed by Punjab and Tamil Nadu with 92 and 95 Kms. respectively. In Madhya Pradesh and Rajasthan the road length is lower than the national average of 49 kms. in 1980-81. In terms of bank offices per lakh population, Punjab and West Bengal occupy the top positions with over 10 offices per lakh population as against the average of 5.8 offices. Gujarat, Haryana, Karnataka and Kerala are the other States, where the number of bank offices is condiderably higher than the national average. Gujarat occupies the first place in the per capita industrial consumption electricity followed by Punjab, Maharastra, Karnataka and Haryana.

Social Services: Among the social service indicators, enrolment of children of the age group 6-11 and hospital beds per lakh of population in the year 1982-83 have been taken into account. In Gujarat, Maharastra, Punjab and Tamil Nadu enrolment of children in primary classes is 100 per cent of the children in the age group 6-11 years. It is interesting to note that enrolment ratios in the special category states are 100 per cent. In terms of hospital beds per lakh of population (December 1982) Kerala occupies the first place with 203 beds as against the national average of 84 beds. The number of beds in Guajrat, Maharastra, Punjab and West Bengal is also considerably higher than the national average. The special category States also rank very high in terms of number of hospital beds.

GROUPING OF STATES:

On the basis of the characteristics of the States presented above, it would be difficult to group them into different levels of development. The construction of a composite index of development involves methodological problems, such as, selection of rational variables, assigning weights to each of these variables, which cannot be above subjectivity. No attempt has been made in this chapter to construct such an index. Out of all the indicators of development presented in the previous section, per capita income of the States can be safely considered as a comprehensive indicator of economic progress. Any progress that takes place in the economy with a few exceptions like Kerala, would get reflected in the per capita income of the States. Therefore, the grouping of the States has been done on the basis of the per capita State Domestic Product (SDP).

The problem that one faces in choosing SDP as the basis for grouping is the likely fluctuations in the SDP on account if aberrations in weather in a single year and the non-comparability of estimates of SDP prepared by different States. To take care of these problems, the comparable estimates of per capita State domestic product prepared by the Central Statistical Organisation (CSO) have been made use of. To offset the yearly fluctuations, if any, the average per capita SDPs of the States for three years from 1977-80, has been used for grouping the States. The average per capita SDP and the deviation in respect of each State from the all-India average are presented in the table below. States are arranged in descending order of per capita SDP.

TABLE 1.1 : **Average Per Capita SDP 1977-78 to 1979-80**

	State	Per capita SDP (Rs)		Deviation from average (%)
1.	Punjab	2409		92.3
2.	Haryana	1983		58.3
3.	Maharastra	1844		47.2
4.	Gujarat	1715		36.9
5.	West Bengal	1337		6.7
6.	Karnataka	1317		5.1
7.	Tamil Nadu	1253		-
8.	Kerala	1239	(-)	1.1
9.	Rajasthan	1131	(-)	9.7
10.	A.P.	1097	(-)	12.5
11.	Orissa	975	(-)	22.2
12.	M. P.	926	(-)	26.1
13.	U.P.	902	(-)	28.0
14.	Bihar	778	(-)	37.9
	All India:	1253		

As may be seen from the table, the per capita SDP of six States exceeds the all-India average in the range of 5.1 to 92.3 per cent.

Tamil Nadu's per capita SDP is found to be the same as the national average. There are 7 States whose per capita SDP falls short of national average ranging from about 1 per cent to 37.9 per cent. At the one extreme is Punjab with per capita SDP exceeding 92.3 per cent of the national average and at the other extreme is Bihar with per capita SDP below the national average by as much as 37.9 per cent.

Corresponding with the three levels of income, viz., high income, middle income and low income, States are categorised into three groups. States with per capita income 10 per cent or more above the national average are categorised as Group-A states. States with per capita income within +- 10 per cent of the natiuonal average are categorised as Group-'B' States and the States with per capita income 10 per cent or more below the average are categorised as Group-C States. Within each group the States are arranged in descending order of the average per capita SDP. The grouping of the States is confined to only 14 Major States and do not include special category States as the analysis in the chapters that follow is intended to cover only major States. Because of their peculiar problems, the special category States have been getting preferential treatment in the determination of plan outlays, allocation of Central assistance, etc., In view of this, inclusion of the special category States in the analysis would distort the all-India average position and makes the comparison of the States with reference to this average less meaningful. Therefore, the analysis presented in the remaining chapters of this volume is done with reference to the average of 14 major States. The distribution of 14 major States into three groups is given below in descending order of their average per capita income.

Group 'A'		*Group 'B'*		*Group 'C'*	
1.	Punjab	1.	West Bengal	1.	Andhra Pradesh
2.	Haryana	2.	Karnataka	2.	Orissa
3.	Maharastra	3.	Tamil Nadu	3.	Madhya Pradesh
4.	Gujarat	4.	Kerala	4.	Uttar Pradesh
		5.	Rajasthan	5.	Bihar

An examination of the Appendix Tables 1.23 to 1.27 giving the ranking of the States based on various indicators of development reveals that Group-A and Group-B States rank fairly higher in respect of a number of indicators. States falling in Group-A are found to share among themselves 1 to 5 ranks in respect of a number of indicators particularly in the agricultural and industrial sectors. This lends support to the classification of States based on per capita income, adopted in this volume.

TWO

STATUTORY TRANSFERS TO STATES

This Chapter deals with the evolution of financial transfers to the States under the recommendations of the successive Finance Commissions. The components of the transfers as well as the principles governing them have been discussed in detail in this chapter. After presenting the evolution of transfers, equity in the inter-state distribution of the transfers has been analysed.

Transfer of resources from the Centre to the States is inherent in the relationship envisaged in the Constitution between the Centre and the States. The intention of the architects of the Constitution to make the Centre strong and pre-eminent in the financial and legislative matters is clearly discernible in the Seventh Schedule which delineates the powers of the Centre and the States. For the promotion of the country's unity and its continued existence as a vast unified market which is essential for rapid economic development of the country as a whole, the levy and administration of taxes with wide economic base, such as, income tax, corporation tax, Union excise duties, customs, etc., have been assigned to the Centre. While the financial power for levying and collecting major sources of revenue rests with the Centre, States are assigned functional responsibilities in the fields of agriculture, education, medical care, public health, irrigation, law and order, etc., requiring resources far in excess of the financial powers assigned to them. The heads of revenue and functional responsibilities were assigned on the basis of whether the Centre or the States were better equipped to deal with the particular head. This had resulted in divergence between financial powers and functional responsibilities. To correct this imbalance, the Constitution embodies both mandatory and enabling provisions for facilitating a wide ranging transfer of resources from the Centre to the States. Briefly stated the Constitution provides for transfer of resources from the Centre to the States in the following forms:

(i) through the levy by the Centre, but assignment in whole of the proceeds of certain taxes (Article 269)
(ii) through mandatory sharing of the proceeds of income tax (Artical 270)
(iii) through permissive participation in the proceeds of Union excise duties (Artical 272)
(iv) through statutory grants-in-aid of the revenues of the States (Article 275)
(v) through grant for any public purpose (Article 282)
(vi) through grant of loan for any public purpose (Article 293)

Besides marking out the channels through which resources can flow from the Centre to the States, the Constitution also provides for a machinery for regulating the flow of resources in the form of the Finance Commission (Article 280). Article 280(1) lays down that the President shall, within two years from the commencement of the Constitution and thereafter at the expiration of every fifth year or at such earlier time as the President considers necessary, constitute a Finance Commission to make recommendations as to the distribution of net proceeds of divisible taxes, to lay down the principles of grants-in-aid and to make recommendations on any other matter referred to the Commission by the President. The purpose of the Finance Commissions is primarily to facilitate a periodical assessment ofthe fiscal needs of the States and make recommendations on an objective basis, for the transfer of resources from the Centre to the States. Generally the Finance Commission have been assigned the task of making recommendations regarding the distribution between the Union and the States of the net proceeds of taxes which are to be divided between them under the Constitution and allocation between the States of the proceeds assigned to the States. The Finance Commissions have been recommending principles which should govern the grants-in-aid of the revenues of the States which are in need of assistance, under Article 275.

Besides the Finance Commission which is a statutory body enshrined in the Constitution, transfer of resources from the Centre to the States is also taking place through the Planning Commission, a body created by an executive order and through the Central Ministries (under Articles 282 and 293). The following table presents the transfer of resources to the States through the above three channels.

TABLE 2.1 : **Transfer of Resources**

(*Rs. Crores*)

	Finance Commission		Planning Commission		Others	
	Amount	% to total	Amount	% to total	Amount	% to total
First Plan (1951-56)	447	31.2	880	61.5	104	7.3
Second Plan (1956-61)	918	32.0	1058	36.9	892	31.1
Third Plan (1961-66)	1590	28.4	2738	48.9	1272	22.7
Annual Plans (1966-69)	1782	33.3	1917	35.8	1648	30.8
Fourth Plan (1969-74)	5421	35.9	4731	31.3	4949	32.8
Fifth Plan (1974-79)	11048	43.1	10565	41.2	4046	15.7
Sixth Plan (1979-84)	22888	38.4	24505	41.1	12238	20.5

Source: Report of the Eighth Finance Commission.

Over the years, the transfers through the Finance Commission and the Planning Commission have tended to become more or less equal. The share of the discretionary transfers from the Central Ministries had increased from 7.3 per cent during 1951-56 to 20.5 per cent during 1979-84. Though the Finance Commission is a statutory body, transfers through it are no more than those effected through the Planning commission. As this Chapter deals with the statutory transfers effected through the Finance Commission, these are discussed in detail in the following.

Composition of Finance Commission Transfers

As indicated earlier, the transfers effected through the Finance Commission consist of shared in taxes and duties and grants-in-aid. The composition of the Finance Commission transfers is presented in Table 2.2.

TABLE 2.2 : **Composition of Finance Commission Transfers**

(*Rs. Crores*)

	Share in taxes and Duties		Grants*		Total Amount
	Amount	% to Total	Amount	% to Total	
First Plan	344	77.0	103	23.0	447
Second Plan	668	72.8	250	27.2	918
Third Plan	1196	75.2	394	24.8	1590
Annual Plan	1282	71.9	500	28.1	1782
Fourth Plan	4562	84.2	859	15.8	5421
Fifth Plan	8275	74.9	2773	25.1	11048
1979-84	21177	92.5	1711	7.5	22888
1984-89	35208	89.2	4244	10.8	39452

* includes grants in lieu of tax on Railway Passenger fares.

Source: Report of the Eighth Finance Commission.

Though the transfers to the States have been taking place mainly through the channel of shares in taxes and duties, the share of taxes and duties in the total transfers increased to a record level of 92.5 per cent only during the period covered by the recommendations of the Seventh commission (1979-84). The states have all along been pressing for transfers to be effected mainly, if not wholly through devolution of taxes and duties. This would obviously help them, since they would be able to share the benefits of buoyancy in the tax receipts of the Centre and of additional taxes by it. The Seventh Finance Commission recognised the strength of the arguments of the States and recommended transfers mainly through the tax devolutions. The commission Stated that,

> We are clearly of the view that grants-in-aid element in the transfer of resources should as far as possible be a residual item and

the attempt should be to make the bulk of the transfers through tax shares.

(Chapter 9, Seventh Finance Commission Roport)

Though the Eighth Finance Commission had followed the policy of the Seventh Commission in according importance to tax devolutions, in the scheme of transfers recommended by the Eighth Finance Commission for the period 1984-89, the share of grants-in-aid had increased to 10.8 per cent. The increase in the share of grants can be attributed to an increase in the annual grant in lieu of the tax on railway passenger fares from Rs.23.12 crores to Rs. 95 crores by the Eighth Finance Commission and grants to some of the States for meeting special problems. The elements constituting tax devolutions and grants-in-aid are discussed in detail below.

Tax devolutions to the States have been taking place through assignment of shares in net proceeds of income tax, Union excise duties, additional excise duties and assignment in whole of the net proceeds of estate duty. The composition of the tax devolutions to the States is presented in Table 2.3.

TABLE 2.3: **Percentage Composition of Tax Devolutions**

	Income Tax	Union Excise	Addl. Excise	Estate duty	Total
First Plan	80.8	18.6	-	0.6	100.0
Second Plan	56.1	22.9	19.2	1.8	100.0
Third Plan	46.4	33.3	18.1	2.2	100.0
Annual Plans	39.5	49.0	10.1	1.4	100.0
Fourth Plan	46.9	40.6	11.7	0.8	100.0
Fifth Plan	39.6	44.8	15.0	0.6	100.0
1979-84	24.5	64.4	10.8	0.3	100.0
1984-89	20.3	66.9	12.5	0.3	100.0

It may be seen from the table that bulk of the tax devolutions is through the share of the States in Union excise duties. While the share of the Union excise duties in total tax devolution had increased from 18.6 per cent during 1951-56 to 66.9 per cent during 1984-89, the share of income tax had declined from 80.8 per cent to 20.3 per cent. In the tax devolutions there are three aspects which need to be discussed here. They are (1) Size of the divisible pool (2) allocation of the divisible pool between the Centre and the States and (3) distribution of States' share among the States. In the case of (1) and (2) the interests of the States are harmonious and run counter to the interests of the Centre. Only in the case of (3) that the interests of States clash with each other. The issues concerning the individual taxes that come under the purview of the Finance Commission are discussed below.

INCOME TAX

Taxes on income other than agricultural income., though levied and collected by the Centre, are compulsorily shareable between the Centre and the State under Article 270(1) of the Constitution. The proceeds attributable to Union territories and taxes payable in respect of Union emoluments as also any surcharge which may be levied for the purpose of the Union are kept out of the divisible pool by the provisions contained in the Articles 270(2),(3),(4) and Article 271 of the Constitution.

The assignment of the net proceeds of income tax to the States which was fixed by the First Finance Commission at 55 per cent was enlarged progressively by the successive Finance Commissions and is now placed at 85 per cent by the Eighth Finance Commission (same as recommended by the Seventh Commission). The distribution of the divisible pool of income tax among the States had been; 90 per cent on the basis of population and 10 per cent on the basis of assessment. This principle was follwed by all the Finance Commissions excepting the First, Third and the Fourth Commissions which gave 80 per cent weightage to population and 20 per cent weightage to assessment. The lesser weightage given to the assessment by the later Finance Commissions has helped the backward States.

The States have been pleading before the successive Finance Commissions for an increase in the size of the divisible pool for two main reasons. One is the continuation on a permanent basis of Union surcharge and its enhancement from time to time, the proceeds of which are not shareable. The other most important reason is the merger of income tax paid by the companies in the corporation tax which under clause IV of Article 270 of the Constitution is not shareable with the States. Till 1959, income tax paid by the companies formed part of the divisible pool. The receipts under corporation tax which amounted to Rs. 54 crores in 1958-59 are placed at Rs. 3120 crores in B.E.1986-87. On the otherhand, the receipts under income tax which were Rs. 173 crores in 1958-59 had increased to only Rs. 2580 crores in the B.E. 1986-87. This shows how the States were deprived of an increasing source of revenue. The surcharge on income tax had been abolished with effect from 1985-86 in response to the demands of the States. But the Centre has not yet responded to the requests of the States for the merger of income tax paid by the companies in the income tax ie., restoring the Pre-1959 position. Though the Finance Commissions have been sympathetic to the pleas of the States, they have refrained from recommending the sharing of corporation tax in view of the explicit provisions of the Constitution making corporation tax not shareable. The Seventh Finance Commission had suggested that the Centre might consider holding discussions with the States in order to settle the point finally. The decline in the role of the income tax in total devolution has been mainly because of the exclusion of tax paid by the companies from the purview of income tax.

UNION EXCISE DUTIES

Under Article 272 of the Constitution, Union Excise duties may be divided between the Union and the States, if Parliament by law so provides. Though sharing of excise duties is of a permissive nature, all the Finance Commissions had found it necessary to include sharing of such duties in varying degrees. The First Commission fixed the share of the States at 40 per cent of the net proceeds of duty on tobacco, matches and vegetable products. Gradually the number of articles considered for the purpose of the divisible pool was increased to 36 and the shares of the States was fixed at 20 per cent by the Third Commissions. The Fourth Commission recommended the inclusion of net proceeds of duties on all commodities other than regulatory duties and special excise duties, in the divisible pool and fixed the share of the States at 20 per cent of the proceeds. The Seventh Commission made a radical departure from the past in stepping up the shares of the States from 20 per cent to 40 per cent of the net proceeds of duties on all commodities excepting the duty on the generation of electricity which was recommended to be passed on to the States 100 per cent. The Eighth Finance Commission raised the share of the States to 45 per cent; 40 per cent to be distributed among all the States and the remaining 5 per cent to be distributed among those States which have deficits after taking into account their share from all taxes and duties including their share in the 40 per cent of the proceeds of excise duties.

Over the periods covered by the various Finance Commissions, the distribution of excise duties among the States has become more progressive. The first three Commissions had recommended the distribution mainly on the basis of population. Fourth, Fifth and Sixth Finance Commissions while giving predominant weightage to population had given some weightage to backwardness of the States. The Seventh Commission made the distribution more progressive by giving equal weightage to (1) Population (2) inverse of per capita State Domestic Product (3) Population below the poverty line and (4) a formula of revenue equalisation. The inclusion of duties on all commodities in the divisible pool as well as the increase in the shares of the States had placed the Union excise duties in a predominant position in the devolution of taxes.

ADDITIONAL EXCISE DUTIES

The National Development Council (NDC) in December 1956 decided on replacement of sales tax on cotton fabrics, woollen fabrics, rayon and artificial silk fabrics, sugar and tobacco including manufactured tobacco, by additional excise duties in the interests of convenience of trade and avoidance of tax evasion. The Second Finance Commission for the first time recommended the distribution of additional excise duties among the States on the basis of guaranteed level of States' revenue from sales tax on these commodities in 1956-57 and on population basis. For the distribution of amounts above the guaranteed level, the successive Finance Commission had recommended varying degrees of weightage to population and sales tax collection. The Sixth Finance Commission recommended the abolition of the guaranteed amounts and recommended the distribution giving a weightage of 70 per cent to population, 20 per cent to State Domestic Product and 10 per cent to collections. The Seventh Commission recommended the distribution of additional excise duties in respect of sugar on the basis of despatches and in respect of textiles and tobacco on the basis of the product of the population and the per capita SDP. The Eighth Finance commission recommended a uniform formula for the distribution of additional excise duties in respect of all the three commodities. After setting apart the portion attributable to the Union Territories, the Commission recommended the distribution by giving equal weightage to SDP and population.

States have been expressing their concern before the successive Finance Commissions not only on the principles of distribution of net proceeds of duties, but also on the manner in which the scheme of replacement of sales tax by additional duties of excise has been operated by the Central Government so far. As a result of the discussions at the meeting of the NDC in March 1970, the Government of India agreed to the following:

(i) conversion of specific duties into ad valorem.
(ii) raising the incidence of additional excise duties as a percentage of value of clearances to 10.8 per cent over a period of two to three years.
(iii) achieving a ratio of 2:1 between the yield of basic and special excise duties on the one hand and the additional excise duties on the other.

It was also agreed that a Standing Review Committee on which the Government of India and the State Governments would be represented, would be set up to meet atleast once a year. While in recent years the first and third assurances have been partly fulfilled, the second assurance remains still unfulfilled. The Standing Review Committee had recommended that the incidence of 10.8 per cent of the value of clearances in respect of additional excise duty might be achieved by 1989-90 in three stages, i.e., 8.5 per cent by 1984-85, 9.75 per cent by 1987-88 and 10.8 per cent by 1989-90. The Eighth Finance Commission expressed the hope that the recommendation made by the Review Committee would be implemented by the Centre within the timeframe contemplated. Non-fulfilment of the assurances even after such a long time has constrained the States in asking for handing over the items of additional excise duties back to them for levy of sales tax.

ESTATE DUTY

Estate duty on property other than agricultural land, is one of the taxes and duties mentioned in Article 269 of the Constitution which is to be levied and collected by the Government of India and the net proceeds of which except to the extent attributable to Union Territories, are to be distributed amongst the States. The Second Finance Commission examined for the first time the question of distribution of net proceeds of estate duty among the States. It had recommended the distribution of estate duty attributable to immovable property on the basis of such property located in a State. Third to Fifth Commissions had recommended the distribution of duty in respect of immovable property on the basis of value of property located in a State and the duty in respect of movable property on the basis of population. The Seventh and Eighth Finance Commissions made no distinction between movable and immovable property and recommended the distribution on the basis of value of property located in a State and brought into assessment. As the net proceeds of estate duty are negligible their distribution is of little consequence to the States. Estate duty on property other than agricultural land was abolished in 1985.

GRANTS-IN-AID

Grants-in-aid play an important role in the scheme of transfer of resources from the Centre to the States. The Constitution makers realised that the scheme of devolution of income tax and Union excise duties might not be adequate to cover the needs of the States. Therefore, Article 275 of the Constitution provides for payment of grants-in-aid of the revenues of such States as Parliament may determine to be in need of assistance. This power is exercised by the President by making an order after considering the recommendations of the Finance Commission. The First Finance Commission formulated a set of principles that should govern the grants-in-aid. Some of these principles related to the manner in which the budgetary needs of the States had to be assessed on a uniform basis, taking into account tax effort and the scope for economy in expenditure. In addition to merely budgetary needs, that Commission recognised that equalising the standards of basic social services in different States was an important purpose to be served by grants-in-aid.

The five Finance Commissions which followed broadly endorsed these principles. Grants are basically serving the purpose of filling the gap of the States on revenue account. The Seventh Finance Commission reformulated the principles which should govern the grants-in-aid. It formulated that grants-in-aid might be given in the first place to enable the States to cover fiscal gaps, if any left after devolution of taxes and duties, in the second place to narrow, as far as possible, disparities in the availability of various administrative and social services between the developed and the less developed States and in the third place to enable the States to meet special burdens on their finances because of their peculiar circumstances. The Seventh Commission recommended grants on the first principle to 8 states and under the second principle to 17 States but confined the grants to nonplan, non-developmental sectors only like Jails, Police, etc. No grants were recommended under the third principle. The Eighth Finance Commission followed broadly the principles enunciated by the Seventh Commission and recommended revenue gap grants to 11 States, upgradation grants to 16 States and grants for meeting the special problems to 10 States. The Eighth Finance Commission also recommended grants towards 50 per cent contribution of the Centre to the margin money for financing relief expenditure of the States. In the total grants-in-aid recommended by the Eighth Finance Commission, the share of revenue gap grants, upgradation grants, margin money grants and special problem grants are 44.9, 24.3, 15.9 and 1.4 per cent respectively. The rest is accounted for by grants in lieu of tax on railway passenger fares.

GRANTS IN LIEU OF TAX ON RAILWAY PASSENGER FARES

Tax on railway passenger fares is one of the taxes mentioned in Article 269 of the constitution, which is levied and collected by the Government of India but assigned to the States. Such a tax was first levied in 1957. The second Finance Commission fixed an amount of Rs. 12.5 crores representing annual collection from this source and recommended its distribution among states in proportion to the net proceeds of actual railway passenger travel in a State. The tax was abolished and merged in the basic fares with effect from 1st April, 1961. The grant was raised to Rs. 16.25 crores per annum from 1966-67. It was stationary at that level until it was, again, raised to

Rs. 23.12 crores for the period 1980-81 to 1983-84 in accordance with the recommendation contained in the Seventh Report of the Railway Convention Committee, 1980. The Eighth Finance Commission recommended that the annual quantum of the grant be raised to Rs. 95 crores and the shares of the States allocated in the same proportion as the average of the non-suburban passenger earnings in each State in the years 1978-79 to 1981-82 bears to the average of the aggregate non-suburban passenger earnings of all States in those years.

PER CAPITA TRANSFER OF RESOURCES

To analyse the equity in the transfer of resources recommended by the Finance commissions, State-wise indices of per capita transfers have been worked out for the periods covered by the awards of each of the Finance Commissions starting from the Second Finance Commission. Because of the reorganisation of the States in November 1956, the State-wise distribution of transfers under the award of the First Finance Commission are not readily available. The indices are presented in Table 2.4.

The indices of per capita transfers to States to Group-A States has come down from 107.0 for the period covered by the Second Commission to 77.6 for the period covered by the Eighth Finance Commission. In respect of Group-B States the index had come down from 110.3 to 100.1. Only in respect of the Group-C States that the index had registered an increase from 91.0 for the period covered by the Second Commission to 109.0 for the period covered by the Eighth Commission. The distribution had become favourable to the backward States roughly from the period covered by the Fourth Commission, during which weightage was given to backwardness in the distribution of Union excise duties and the weightage given to assessment in respect of income tax was reduced from 20 per cent to 10 per cent. The practice of giving weightage to backward states was being continued since then by the successive Finance Commissions. For the entire period 1957-58 to 1988-89 , progressivity is noticeable in the Finance Commission's transfers.

TABLE 2.4 : Indices of Percapita Transfer of Resources to the States Under the Finance Commission Awards

STATES	Second Commn. 1957-58 to 1961-62	Third Commn. 62-63 to 65-66	Fourth Commn. 66-67 to 68-69	Fifth Commn. 69-70 to 73-74	Sixth Commn. 74-75 to 78-79	Seventh Commn. 79-80 to 83-84	Eighth Commn. 84-85 to 88-89	Total transfer II to VIII Commn.
Group 'A' States	**107.0**	**111.9**	**94.1**	**96.5**	**84.4**	**91.4**	**77.6**	**84.5**
1. Punjab	120.0	104.5	87.5	89.3	77.8	84.9	72.5	81.9
2. Haryana	-	-	68.3	80.7	73.6	81.3	64.2	68.7
3. Maharastra	117.7	101.5	102.7	103.6	88.0	92.7	79.1	86.9
4. Gujarat	74.5	138.4	91.1	92.7	84.9	96.0	82.3	87.5
Group'B' States	**110.3**	**105.6**	**115.0**	**103.7**	**107.8**	**98.2**	**100.1**	**101.4**
5. West Bengal	128.1	89.2	87.3	108.7	116.3	99.4	119.2	111.7
6. Karnataka	132.1	115.9	145.3	90.5	80.8	92.0	87.8	90.4
7. Tamil Nadu	89.7	94.0	102.0	96.5	84.0	105.6	96.0	98.1
8. Kerala	94.6	136.2	175.2	117.2	143.2	102.7	95.3	107.8
9. Rajasthan	102.5	115.6	98.8	110.2	131.6	89.4	92.2	96.6
Group 'C' States	**91.0**	**91.9**	**92.9**	**99.0**	**101.3**	**104.6**	**109.0**	**105.4**
10. Andhra Pradesh	104.3	115.3	105.7	101.8	111.9	96.7	102.1	102.4
11. Orissa	114.8	193.8	209.4	140.8	166.6	126.7	136.4	140.9
12. Madhya Pradesh	95.3	90.5	78.8	88.3	80.9	104.0	106.8	100.3
13. Uttar Pradesh	80.0	68.0	81.1	93.8	94.8	101.6	103.8	99.9
14. Bihar	86.7	74.1	67.8	96.8	93.5	107.6	113.9	106.6
Total 14 States:	**100.0**	**100.0**	**100.0**	**100.0**	**100.0**	**100.0**	**100.0**	**100.0**
Special Category States	**193.2**	**171.3**	**267.5**	**206.1**	**302.6**	**190.7**	**289.7**	**248.6**
All-States:	**103.3**	**102.6**	**106.2**	**34.6**	**110.5**	**104.8**	**110.1**	**107.9**

Though the transfers under the awards of the Finance Commissions have become favourable to backward States when they are taken as a group, elements of inequity are noticeable when each State is considered separately. In the award of the Seventh Finance Commission it is observed that the indices of per capita transfers in respect of middle income States, Tamil Nadu and Kerala are higher than those of Andhra Pradesh and Uttar Pradesh. Similarly, the per capita transfers recommended by the Eighth Finance Commission to West Bengal are higher than those of all backward States except Orissa. If we take the cumulative per capita transfers, the index in respect of West Bengal is higher than the indices of all backward States except Orissa. West Bengal's higher index is mainly due to the fact that it is getting larger grants-in-aid under Article 275 of the Constitution.

THREE

CENTRAL ASSISTANCE TO STATES

This chapter presents a brief history of Central assistance for State Plans, and analyses the criteria for distribution of Central assistance among the States. The per capita distribution of Central assistance to States since 1951 has also been analysed.

Transfer of resources from the Centre to the States has been taking place through Finance Commission (statutory) and Planning Commission and the Central Ministries (discretionary). Discretionary transfers amounted to more than two-thirds in the First Five-Year Plan Period and about 61 per cent during the Sixth Five-Year Plan. Transfers through the Planning Commission during the Sixth Plan period were about 39 per cent of the total transfers to States. A very high proportion of transfers through the Planning Commission is in the form of assistance for State Plans (as different from assistance for centrally sponsored schemes etc). Which amounts to about 70 per cent in the Sixth Plan Period.

The practice of giving Central assistance to States for financing development schemes was in vogue even before the advent of planning in 1951. On the termination of World War II, the Government of India and the Provincial Governments had embarked on certain development projects which received assistance in the form of post-war development grants. Some of these grants stopped by 1950-51, but some others for Grow More Food schemes, etc., continued in a different form.

First Five Year Plan

By the time the First Five Year Plan was launched in 1951, the exact distribution of the financial liabiliity of many schemes such as multipurpose river valley schemes, community development, special minor irrigation, local works, etc., was not decided upon. Accordingly they were included in the Central Sector for the First Plan, but were shifted to the state sector during the Second Plan.

No clear indication is available as to how the distribution of Central assistance to States was decided upon. Even though the amount of assistance for each State was arrived at after discussions regarding States' own resources and the nature of projects included in the plan, the position remained fluid throughout the five years for a variety of reasons such as (1) delay in finalisation of the plan (2) delay in availability of the recommendations of the Finance Commission, (3) delay in finalisation of patterns and magnitudes of assistance for schemes included in the Central sector for presentational purposes only but which were implemented by the States.

Second Five Year Plan

A majority of the schemes included in the Central sector but being implemented by the States, were transfered to the State Sector from 1956.

The plan outlays of individual States were first decided after discussions between the Planning Commission and the State Chief Ministers. The plan outlays were finalised on the basis of a number of criteria including population, spill over commitments, general levels of development, revenue position of the State, etc. Resources of all States together amounted to about 40 per cent of the total State plan outlays for the Second plan. However, the quantum of assistance for each State plan for the five year period was not indicated at the beginning. Central assistance to each State was decided as a result of Annual Plan discussions. Thus, there was an element of uncertainty regarding the amounts that could be expected by each State and there, consequently, were pressures in the whole procedure.

Third Five Year Plan

The outlays as well as the quantum of Central assistance for the Third Five Year Plan for each State were decided after discussions with State Chief Miniisters.

Plan outlays were determined on the basis of needs, problems, past progress and lags in development, likely contribution of resources which the State could make. Quantum of Central assistance followed from the plan outlay and the States' own resources. States which were able to make a larger effort in mobilising their own resources could have larger plan outlays. Intimation about Central assistance fixed for individual States was given out before the commencement of the plan. Central assistance for the Annual Plan was dicided after discussions with each State after examination of its resources and the requirements of plan programmes.

During the first three five year plans, stress was laid mainly on the principles which would determine the plan outlays rather than the quantum of Central assistance. The quantum of Central assistance was largely decided in the light of gap in resources of individual States in relation to the plan outlays decided upon.

Fourth Five Year Plan

The desirability of evolving objective principles for allocation of Central assistance was emphasized by several Chief Ministers during discussions on the preliminary Memorandum on the Fourth Five Year Plan held in June-July 1965. Views of the State Governments were invited on the subject, but as they were too divergent, the Planning Commission was asked to evolve a set of principles in the light of discussions at the National Development Council (NDC). Planning Commission finalised these guidelines and also the outlays and assistance. However, finalisation of the Fourth Plan was postponed due to the war with Pakistan and its aftermath.

Annual Plan for 1966-67 had to be finalised before the conclusion of discussions on the Fourth Five Year Plan. Therefore, assistance for the year was decided on an ad-hoc basis.

For 1967-68 also the assistance was given on an ad-hoc basis.

The ad-hoc distribution in 1966-67 and 1967-68 had deprived some of the States of their legitimate share in Central assistance. These affected States pressed for making up the entire shortfall in the year 1968-69 itself. The planning Commission while distributing the assistance for 1968-69, adjusted one third of the difference (shortfall or excess) between the assistance that was due to a State and the amount that was actually received by it during the two years 1966-68.

Formulation of a new Five Year Plan (Fourth Plan) was taken up in 1967-68. The National Development Council unanimously adopted a formula suggested by the NDC Committee under the Chairmanship of Dr. D.R. Gadgil, Dy. Chairman, Planning Commission. This formula, popularly known as the Gadgil Formula formed the basis for distribution of Central assistance for the Fourth Five Year Plan (1969-74).

The formula, briefly stated, is as under:

(1) The requirements of States of Assam, Jammu & Kashmir and Nagaland should first be met out of total pool of Central assistance.

(2) The balance of Central assistance should then be distributed among the remaining 14 States on the basis of the following criteria:

(a) 60 per cent on the basis of population (as on 1st October, 1966 supplied by the Registrar General).

(b) 10 per cent on the basis of per capita State income to be distributed only to those States whose per capita income is below the national average (averages of the comparable estimates of income presented by the Central Statistical Organisation (CSO) for the years 1962-63,1963-64 and 1964-65 were taken as the basis. Bihar, Kerala, Madhya Pradesh, Orissa, Rajasthan and Uttar Pradesh only became eligible under this head. "Deviation" method was to be applied).

(c) 10 per cent on the basis of tax effort of individual States (determined on the basis of States' per capita own tax receipts as percentage of States' per capita income).

(d) 10 per cent on the basis of spill over into the Fourth Plan of major continuing irrigation and power projects.

(e) 10 per cent for special problems of individual States (eg., border areas, desert areas, areas chronically affected by natural calamities, metropolitan areas etc.)

Adoption of the Gadgil Formula for distribution of Central assistance for State plans greatly reduced the area of discretion of the Planning Commission and brought about a considerable measure of objectivity into the process. Further, this formula did away with the then existing cumbersome schemewise patterns of grants and loans and introduced the system of block loans and grants. In many ways, the Gadgil Formula introduced such rational procedures which the Planning Commission have not been able to improve upon since the Fourth Five Year Plan.

As no review of the Gagdil Formula could be undertaken at the beginning of the Fifth Plan in 1974, for various reasons, it was continued for 1974-75, 1975-76 and 1976-77 also.

Together with the finalisation of the Fifth Plan, a review of the Gadgil Formula was undertaken in July-August, 1976. The NDC at its meeting held in September, 1976 approved an updated Gadgil formula as under:

Besides setting apart a certain amount for special category States, an amount of Rs. 100 crores was also set apart for providing extra assistance to States in respect of State plan schemes financed by IDA assistance. Balance amount was to be distributed as under the original Gadgil formula, but updating it by using 1971 population figures, per capita SDP figures for 1970-73, 1973-74 State tax receipts and Fifth Plan and revised spill over outlays.

In March 1977, the Government of India decided to terminate the Fifth Five Year Plan and commence a medium term plan for 5 years (with the "rolling" plan concept) from 1978-79.

The NDC at its meeting held in March 1979 resolved that a Committee should be formed to discuss fiscal arrangements in the light of Draft Five Year Plan 1978-83 which would, inter alia, review the Gadgil Formula and the scope of Centrally sponsored schemes.

Despite very detailed discussions in a number of sittings, the NDC Committee could not recommend any agreed formula. The Deputy Chairman, Planning Commission put forth a compromise formula under which the Gadgil Formula would apply to a certain amount and the amount of Rs. 2000 crores that would be available to States as a result of reduction in the outlays for Centrally sponsored schemes, would be distributed under Income Adjusted Total Population (IATP) method (i.e., inverse of per capita income multiplied by total population). As regards Gadgil Formula to be application, a slight modification was made in the 10 per cent to be allocated under special problems. This 10 per cent was decided to be allocated in the same proportion as the 90 per cent component. This modified formula was to be applicable for four years 1979-83.

The original Five Year Plan was to cover 1974-79. But it was terminated in 1977-78 and a revised Fifth plan was launched from 1978-79 upto 1982-83. There was a change of Government at the Centre in 1980 and the revised Fifth plan was terminated with effect from 1979-80, and the Sixth Five Year Plan was to come into effect for 1980-85.

The NDC at its meeting held in August 1980 decided, inter alia, to distribute Central assistance to States on the basis of a Modified Gadgil Formula, as under:

1. A lumpsum amount is to be set apart for meeting the requirements of eight 'Special Category States' viz., Assam, Himachal Pradesh, Jammu & Kashmir, Manipur, Meghalaya, Nagaland, Tripura and Sikkim, out of the total pool of Central assistance.

2. The balance of Central assistance is to be distributed among the remaining fourteen States on the basis of:

(a) 60 per cent - population - 1971 Census figures.

(b) 10 per cent - tax effort - per capita tax effort for 1978-79 and SDP average for 1973-76.

(c) 20 per cent - average per capita SDP for 1973-76-deviation method - to be allocated only to those States whose per capita income is below the national average.

(d) 10 per cent - special problems.

The Seventh Five Year Plan 1985-90 has commenced. The Modified Gadgil Formula is holding sway for the Seventh Plan also.

During the Fourth Plan period, out of the total assistance to be given to the States, a portion was set apart for the States of Assam, Jammu & Kashmir and Nagaland and the balance was distributed among the remaining 14 States.

During the Fifth Plan, the Special Category States increased from 3 to 8. It was also decided to allocate separate assistance (over and above Gadgil Formula) for IDA assisted projects. This was orginally limited to 15-25 per cent of World Bank disbursements but was increased later (i.e., to 70 per cent of the assistance received from the World Bank which roughly works out to about 35 per cent of the project outlay included in the plans). It was in the Fifth Plan that additional assistance out of the savings on Centrally Sponsored schemes was indicated, which was distributed on the basis of Income Adjusted Total Population.

For the Sixth and Seventh plans, the components of Central assistance are assistance under Gadgil Formula and assisttance for IDA assisted projects only.

An anlaysis of distribution of Central assistance among the States from the Fourth Plan onwards is briefly attempted here.

Distribution of Central assistance for State plans among the special category states and the remaining States is presented in the table below.

(*Rs. Crores*)

States	Fourth	Fifth*	Sixth	Seventh
1. **Special Category States**				
(a) Actuals	5.30	1,566	4,138	7,213
(b) % increase over previous plan		195.5	164.2	74.3
2. **Other States**				
(a) Actuals	3,004	6,514	13,444	20.171
(b) % increase over previous plan	-	116.8	106.4	50.0
3. **All States**				
(a) Actuals	3,534	8,080	17,582	27,384
(b) % increase over previous plan	-	128.6	117.6	55.7

* 1974-79 plus 1979-80 also

Compared to the Fourth plan, the assistance in the Fifth Plan for Special Category States was much higher than the assistance for other States. This was partly due to the fact that the number of special category states increased from 3 to 8 in the Fifth Plan. The high priority given for financing adequate outlays for the Special Category States is evident from the figures for 6th and 7th plans also. The share of Special Category states in the total Central assistance increased from 15 per cent in the Fourth Plan steadily to 26 per cent in the Seventh Plan. While not denying the necessity of according special treatment to these states, there does not seem to be sufficient reason for steeply stepping up the assistance plan after plan. Incidentally, the per capita income and outlays in some of the Special category States are higher than those in some of the backward States among the 14 States. This fact should have been considered while finalising the Seventh Plan allocations of assistance.

Indices of per capita Central assistance to States are indicated in Table 3.1. Since the per capita Central assistance to Special Category States is abnormally higher and is likely to distort the picture for 'other' States, indices have been worked out for the 14 'other States' only.

TABLE 3.1 : **Indices of Percapita Central Assistance**

States	First Plan	Second Plan	Third Plan	Annual Plans	Fourth Plan	Fifth Plan	Annual Plan	Sixth Plan	Seventh Plan	Cummultative 1951-90
Group-'A' States	**137.5**	**111.5**	**92.5**	**88.2**	**96.6**	**90.9**	**85.7**	**95.2**	**92.7**	**93.7**
1. Punjab	375.0	192.3	126.4	111.8	124.1	115.6	77.1	97.1	88.3	116.7
2. Haryana	-	-	-	147.1	131.0	115.6	125.7	120.5	96.5	101.0
3. Maharastra	58.3	76.9	73.6	70.6	81.0	77.9	82.9	89.5	90.2	85.8
4. Gujarat	79.2	100.0	94.3	91.2	100.0	92.2	85.7	95.2	98.1	94.6
Group 'B' States	**95.8**	**103.8**	**107.5**	**108.8**	**101.7**	**100.0**	**85.7**	**92.4**	**92.7**	**95.4**
5. West Bengal	166.7	84.6	77.4	79.4	82.8	80.5	80.0	76.2	70.9	76.9
6. Karnataka	95.8	115.4	118.9	117.6	98.3	101.3	80.0	82.9	75.0	85.5
7. Tamil Nadu	58.3	111.5	100.0	94.1	82.8	87.0	71.4	87.6	94.9	91.8
8. Kerala	70.8	92.3	128.3	132.3	137.9	135.1	97.1	101.4	141.8	125.7
9. Rajasthan	150.0	119.2	139.6	144.1	143.1	126.0	111.4	129.0	106.6	118.7
Group 'C' States	**83.3**	**88.5**	**100.0**	**97.1**	**101.7**	**102.6**	**111.4**	**107.1**	**107.3**	**105.4**
10. Andhra Pradesh	79.2	107.7	109.4	114.7	91.4	102.6	122.9	107.6	97.2	103.1
11. Orissa	208.3	150.0	139.6	117.6	122.4	127.3	168.6	148.1	138.3	142.2
12. Madhya Pradesh	91.7	123.1	120.8	108.8	105.2	92.2	100.0	111.4	114.9	110.1
13. Uttar Pradesh	54.2	65.4	86.8	88.2	100.0	103.9	108.6	99.0	103.2	99.6
14. Bihar	58.3	73.1	83.0	55.9	100.0	98.7	94.3	99.5	104.4	99.1
Non-Special Category States	**100.0**	**100.0**	**100.0**	**100.0**	**100.0**	**100.0**	**100.0**	**100.0**	**100.0**	**100.0**
Special Category States	**104.2**	**130.8**	**192.4**	**250.0**	**337.9**	**467.5**	**368.6**	**546.2**	**632.9**	**501.7**
All States	**100.0**	**100.0**	**103.8**	**105.9**	**112.1**	**118.2**	**114.3**	**123.8**	**128.2**	**121.4**

For Group-A States, the index of per capita Central assistance has come down from 137.5 in the First Plan to 92.7 in the Seventh Plan. For the Group-B States the decline is from 95.8 in the First Plan to 92.7 in the Seventh Plan. However, for the group-C (backward States) the index of per capita assistance has gone up from 83.3 in the First Plan to 107.3 in the Seventh Plan. Taking the entire period 1951-90 together also, there is progressivity, i.e., Group-A States have an index of 93.4, Group-B STates have an index of 95.5 and Croup-C States 105.4. This brings out the fact that the distribution of Central assistance has become favourable to less developed States over the plan periods. The tilt in favour of backward states occured from the Fourth plan onwards, only because of introduction of the Gadgil Formula with a concious effort to help the economically backward States.

Though the distribution of Central assistance for State plans has become favourable to the backward States when they are taken as a group the same does not hold good when individual States are considered. If the per capita allocations during the Sixth and Seventh Plans are taken into account, it will be noticed that Haryana of Group-A and Rajasthan and kerala of Group-B were getting higher allocations than Andhra Pradesh, Bihar and Uttar Pradesh of Group-C (backward States).

TABLE. 3.2 : **Per Capita Allocation of Central Assistance Under Tax Effort and Special Problems**

States	Tax Effort		Special Problems	
	Sixth Plan	Seventh Plan	Sixth Plan	Seventh Plan
Andhra Pradesh	10.9	26.5	7.8	14.0
Bihar	4.4	9.8	13.2	35.7
Gujarat	19.5	39.0	5.0	14.7
Haryana	50.8	10.1	9.3	-
Karnataka	16.1	38.5	4.6	16.1
Kerala	26.9	54.9	22.8	78.6
Madhya Pradesh	8.8	21.6	11.7	-
Maharashtra	11.0	23.6	-	8.0
Orissa	11.6	25.7	62.9	67.3
Punjab	41.4	73.0	11.0	-
Rajasthan	13.8	27.9	22.5	80.3
Tamil Nadu	13.7	35.0	10.3	56.8
Uttar Pradesh	4.0	8.2	12.2	11.9
West Bengal	8.7	16.2	3.7	11.9
Total 14 States	**12.0**	**25.8**	**12.0**	**25.2**

To locate the elements that are responsible for this inequitable distribution, one has to look at the components of the Central assistance under Gadgil Formula, especially for Sixth and Seventh Plans. The two components that are distorting the progressivity of the Gadgil Formula are - 10 per cent allocation for tax effort and 10 per cent allocation for special problems (Table 3.2).

Tax effort is calculated as per capita own tax revenues (for a particular period) as percentage of per capita SDP (for a specified period). After calculating these percentages direct proportion method is used for distributing the 10 per cent of Central assistance. This direct proportion method is responsible for the highly inequitable distribution. Under this method, if the tax effort is the same, say in Andhra Pradesh and Haryana , both the States would get the same allocation (in absolute terms). But as the population of Andhra Pradesh is more than four times that of Haryana, Andhra Pradesh would be getting about 1/4 of the per capita assistance for Haryana under this criterion. When the tax effort of both the States is the same, it is not reasonable that they should get such widely divergent per capita allocations of assistance. Further, with such a method, a bigger State with a higher tax effort would get lower per capita allocation than a smaller State with a lower tax effort. Thus the direct proportion method used for distributing assistance under tax effort is conferring unintended benefits on certain States. Hence, there is every reason for correcting this situation by introducing a weightage for population.

As regards the 10 per cent allocation for special problems, it it generally known that this amount is a sort of discretinary amount at the disposal of the Planning Commission. For sixth and Seventh Plan, against the 14 States' average of Rs. 37.2 per captia allocation under this criterion, the allocations were Rs. 101.4 for Kerala, Rs. 130.2 for Orissa, Rs. 102.8 for Rajasthan, and Rs. 67.1 for Tamil Nadu; but only Rs. 21.8 for Andhra Pradesh, and Rs. 24.1 for Uttar Predesh, which are admittedly backward States.

As will be seen from the above, it is a fact that the original Gadgil Formula as well as its revisions and modifications have brought to the question of Central assistance a definite objectivity and certainty. It has also ensured a better deal for the backward

States. However, to make this formula achieve its set goals, the 10 per cent for the tax effort should be allocated in a more rational manner and the dicretionary aspect of distrubuting the amount for special problems should be done away with.

FOUR

STATE PLAN OUTLAYS

In this chapter the growth and distribution of outlays in respect of State Plans have been analysed since the inception of Planning in India. The analysis of sectoral distribution and financing of State Plans outlays presented in this Chapter is confined to the periods covered by the Sixth and Seventh five Year Plans.

Preparations for planned economic development started in early 1950 and the First Five Year Plan commenced from April 1951. With the Seventh five Year Plan ending in 1889-90, we would be covering a total period of nearly four decades with our efforts for planned economic development.

A brief analysis of State Plan outlays and how they behaved over a period, may be in order. The outlays on State Plans increased from Rs. 1425 crores during 1951-56, to Rs. 78,o97 crores in the Seventh Plan period 1985-90. Over the period 1951-90, the total effort would amount to about Rs. 1,68,000 crores. In terms of per capita figures, the plan outlays have increased from Rs. 38 in 1951-56 to Rs. 1156 in 1985-90 and work out to Rs. 2486 over the entire 39 year period.

Sectoral distribution of State Plan outlays for the entire period 1951-90 is not included in this chapter. However, such distribution is readily available and included, for the Sixth and Seventh Five Year Plans. Out of the total State Plan outlay of about Rs. 1,68,000 crores for the period, the outlays for Sixth and Seventh Plans account for about Rs. 1,25,000 crores. Sectoral distribution of State Plan outlays for this

10 year period can generally be taken to indicate a representative picture for the entire period. These figures are given below:

(Rs. Crores)

Major Sectors	Sixth Plan outlays 1980-85	Seventh Plan outlays 1985-90	%age distribution 6th Plan	7th Plan	Total 1980-90
1. Agriculture, Rural Dev. and Cooperation	7,905	10,468	16.7	13.4	15.1
2. Irrigation & Power	23,422	38,736	49.6	49.6	49.6
3. Industry & Mines	2,186	3,776	4.6	4.8	4.7
4. Transport & Communications	3,707	5,781	7.9	7.4	7.6
5. Social & Community Services	9,495	17,940	20.1	23.0	21.5
6. Miscellaneous	489	1,396	1.1	1.8	1.5
Grand Total	47,204	78,097	100.0	100.0	100.0

The precentages given in the last column can generally be taken as representative of sectoral distribution of State Sector outlays. Nearly 50 per cent of the total outlay is being allocated to Irrigation and Power; about 15 per cent for Agricultural and Rural Development; and slightly more than one fifth for Social Services. The outlays on Irrigation and Power were much higher in the earlier Plans, but have come down, somewhat, in percentage terms though not in absolute terms. There has been a slight shift from Agricultur Sector to Social Services in the recent Plans. However, there can be sharper shifts and variations in sectoral priorities when iindiividual States are taken into consideration.

Tables 4.1 and 4.2 indicate per capita plan outlays in various plan periods and their indices respectively. For the purpose of a broad analysis of these statements, one may exclude the Special Category States, which would otherwise distort the picture with their very high per capita outlays.

Table 4.1 : Percapita Plan Outlays

(Rs.)

	First Plan 1951-56	Second Plan 56-61	Third Plan 61-66	Annual Plans 66-69	Fourth Plan 69-74	Fifth Plan 74-79	Annual Plans 79-80	Sixth Plan 80-85	Seventh Plan 85-90	Total 1951-90
I. Spl. Category States										
1. Assam	29	57	103	61	136	279	83	560	1035	2188
2. Himachal Pradesh	*	*	*	*	328	613	178	1308	2453	4978
3. Jammu & Kashmir	39	77	166	152	351	684	207	1503	2338	5183
4. Manipur	*	*	*	*	290	714	221	1689	3026	5998
5. Meghalaya	*	*	*	*	358	746	275	1759	3293	6241
6. Nagaland	*	*	280	400	747	1394	372	2710	5161	10129
7. Sikkim	*	*	*	*	*	1982	596	3861	7278	12959
8. Tripura	*	*	*	*	223	387	140	1193	2143	4166
Total - I:	**32**	**62**	**121**	**86**	**227**	**463**	**141**	**1006**	**1799**	**3694**
II. Other States										
1. Andhra Pradesh	33	52	91	58	98	277	82	579	971	2119
2. Bihar	25	40	67	40	85	206	53	461	730	1614
3. Gujarat	58	76	108	84	204	393	121	1079	1760	3665
4. Haryana	*	*	*	91	358	527	185	1395	2244	4621
5. Karnataka	46	62	100	70	128	302	84	610	942	2184
6. Kerala	31	49	101	73	156	244	69	607	825	2032
7. Madhya Pradesh	34	48	84	44	114	295	91	727	1342	2646
8. Maharastra	37	57	103	83	199	418	127	983	1672	3496
9. Orissa	56	54	120	60	114	243	75	568	1024	2179
10. Punjab	105	87	126	90	316	671	161	1164	1957	4547
11. Rajasthan	39	53	97	56	120	238	85	390	876	1994
12. Tamil Nadu	20	57	98	71	134	252	65	650	1188	2429
13. Uttar Pradesh	25	32	72	53	132	247	65	527	942	1985
14. West Bengal	54	48	80	39	82	252	86	641	756	1916
Total - II:	**39**	**51**	**91**	**60**	**137**	**278**	**81**	**682**	**1120**	**2418**
Grand Total	**38**	**51**	**91**	**61**	**142**	**309**	**90**	**715**	**1156**	**2486**
Population Used Year	**1953**	**1958**	**1963**	**1967**	**1971**	**1976**	**1979**	**1981**	**1981**	**1981**

Table 4.2 : Indices of Percapita Plan Outlays

	First Plan 1951-56	Second Plan 56-61	Third Plan 61-66	Annual Plans 66-69	Fourth Plan 69-74	Fifth Plan 74-79	Annual Plans 79-80	Sixth Plan 80-85	Seventh Plan 85-90	Total 1951-90
Group 'A' States	**151.4**	**135.2**	**120.7**	**141.8**	**169.3**	**164.0**	**167.5**	**157.7**	**160.0**	**157.0**
1. Punjab	269.2	170.6	138.5	150.0	230.7	241.4	198.8	170.7	174.7	188.0
2. Haryana	-	-	-	151.7	261.3	189.6	228.4	204.5	200.4	191.0
3. Maharastra	94.9	111.8	113.2	138.3	145.3	150.4	156.8	144.1	149.3	144.6
4. Gujarat	148.7	149.0	118.7	140.0	148.9	141.4	149.4	158.2	157.1	151.6
Group 'B' States	**92.7**	**105.6**	**102.9**	**99.7**	**87.1**	**92.9**	**96.7**	**91.6**	**82.5**	**87.6**
5. West Bengal	138.5	94.1	87.9	65.0	60.0	91.0	106.2	94.0	67.5	79.2
6. Karnataka	117.9	121.6	109.9	116.7	93.4	108.6	103.7	89.4	84.1	90.3
7. Tamil Nadu	51.3	111.8	107.7	118.3	97.8	90.6	80.2	95.3	106.1	100.5
8. Kerala	79.5	96.1	110.9	121.7	113.9	87.8	85.2	89.0	73.7	84.0
9. Rajasthan	100.0	103.9	106.6	93.3	87.6	85.6	104.9	86.5	78.2	82.5
Group 'C' States	**74.5**	**81.6**	**88.1**	**83.4**	**80.9**	**90.2**	**87.1**	**81.9**	**86.9**	**84.8**
10. Andhra Pradesh	84.6	101.9	100.0	96.7	71.5	99.6	101.2	84.9	86.7	87.6
11. Orissa	143.6	105.9	131.9	100.0	83.2	87.4	92.6	83.3	91.4	90.1
12. Madhya Pradesh	87.2	94.1	92.3	73.3	83.2	106.1	112.3	106.6	119.8	109.4
13. Uttar Pradesh	64.1	62.7	79.1	88.3	96.4	88.8	80.2	77.3	84.1	82.1
14. Bihar	64.1	78.4	73.6	66.7	62.0	74.1	65.4	67.6	65.2	666.7
Non-Special Category										
States	**100.0**	**100.0**	**100.0**	**100.0**	**100.0**	**100.0**	**100.0**	**100.0**	**100.0**	**100.0**
Spl. Category States	**82.1**	**121.6**	**133.0**	**143.3**	**165.7**	**166.5**	**174.1**	**147.5**	**160.6**	**152.8**
All States	**97.4**	**100.0**	**100.0**	**101.7**	**103.6**	**111.2**	**111.1**	**104.8**	**103.2**	**102.8**

Notes:
1. Group A: States with per capita income 10% or more above national average.
2. Group B: States with per capital income within +- 10 per cent of national average.
3. Group C: States with per capita income 10 per cent or more below the national average
4. For categories States, average for capita income for years 1977-78 to 1979-80 has been used.

The non-spcial category States have a total per capita outlays of Rs. 2418 for the period 1951-90. From the Fourth Five Year Plan onwards, per capita plan outlays were almost doubling every five years, for all States taken togehter. Table 4.2 gives indices for per capita outlays.

Group 'A' States started with an index of 151.4 in the First Plan and have increased it to 160.0 in the Seventh Plan, with some variations in between. It may be noted that the indices were consistently higher than 157.0, which is the index for the entire 39 year period.

Group 'B' States started with an index of 92.7 in the first plan, ending with 82.5 in the Seventh Plan. The index is 87.6 for the entire period 1951-90.

Group 'C' States have improved their position from 74.5 in 1951-56 to 86.9 in the Seventh Plan.

Thus, it would be seen that the Group-A (advanced States) have improved their position over a period and also maintained their preeminent position. Group-C States also improved their position but only to a small extent. However, it is interesting to note that Group-B States, as a whole, have lost their position.

Within these 3 groups, there are variations among individual States. Taking into account the entire 39 years period, Tamil Nadu ('B') and Madhya Pradesh ('C') have done better than the average. West Bengal, Kerala and Rajasthan of Group-B; and Andhra Pradesh, Uttar Pradesh and Bihar of Group-C are far below the average. Haryana and Punjab of Group-A have done much better than their Group average.

Even though the allocation of Central assistance based on Gadgil Formula introduced some progressivity since the Fourth Plan, Plan outlays are to a large extent dependent on own resources of the States. Advanced States were able to maintain large plan outlays with their own resources; and the backward States lagged behind, even with larger Central assistance. This may be seen from Table 4.3.

Table 4.3 : Own Resources and Central Assistance as % of Total Resources for State Plans

Sixth and Seventh Plans

(Percentages)

	Sixth Plan		Seventh Plan	
	Own resources	Central assistance	Own resources	Central assistance
Group 'A' States	82.3	17.7	83.8	16.2
1. Punjab	80.9	19.1	85.8	14.2
2. Haryana	79.2	20.8	86.6	13.4
3. Maharashtra	83.2	16.8	83.0	17.0
4. Gujarat	82.7	17.3	82.5	17.5
Group 'B' States	68.1	31.9	68.6	31.4
5. West Bengal	54.7	45.3	70.6	29.4
6. Karnataka	75.7	24.3	75.0	25.0
7. Tamil Nadu	78.2	21.8	75.0	25.0
8. Kerala	61.8	38.2	45.9	54.1
9. Rajasthan	53.6	46.4	62.0	38.0
Group 'C' States				
10. Andhra Pradesh	65.2	34.8	68.8	31.2
11. Orissa	46.0	54.0	57.6	42.4
12. Madhya Pradesh	69.7	30.3	73.1	26.9
13. Uttar Pradesh	59.3	40.7	65.1	34.5
14. Bihar	58.9	41.1	55.1	44.9
Non-special category States Total	69.1	30.9	72.0	38.0

As against the 'all-States' (non-special category) per centage of own resources to total resources in the Seventh Plan at 72.0, the Group-A States have an average of 83.8 per cent. Their plan outlays indices also are very high at 160.0 (Table 4.2). In Group-B, Karnataka and Tamil Nadu with own resources at 75 per cent each, have plan outlay indices of 84.1 and 106.1 respectively. In Group-C again, Madhya Pradesh, with a high percentage of own resources, has a higher plan outlay index.

Thus it can reasonably be established that, by and large, the magnitude (per capita) of plan outlays is directly dependent on State's own resources. Even with relatively larger Central assistance, the backward States are not in a position to even reach the per capita plan outlays of advanced States, let alone make up for past deficiencies.

FIVE

DISCRETIONARY TRANSFERS TO THE STATES

In this Chapter, the flow of discretionary transfers to the States is discussed. After presenting the flow of discretionary transfers under broad heads, the equity in the inter-state distribution has been analysed.

The term, 'discretionary' is used here to refer to the transfers other than those effected through the channels of Finance Commission and the Planning commission. These transfers are for non-plan purposes and effected by the Ministry of Finance, Government of India. The discretionary transfers consist of grants and loans. Non-plan grants are given to the States mainly for meeting natural calamities. Grants are also being given to the States for the development of handloom industries, improvement in the scales of pay of University and college teachers etc., Loans are given to the States against the net collections of small savings. Out of the net small savings collections in a State, two-thirds of the amount is being passed on to that state in the form of a loan. The other non-plan loans given to the States are mainly fertiliser loans, ways and means advances and loans to clear overdrafts. As the ways and means advances are recovered by adjustment against the share of Central taxes and Central assistance released to a State during a financial year, these have not been taken into account in the analysis of the flow of discretionary transfers to the States.

The analysis of discretionary transfers contained in this chapter is restricted to the period covered by the Fifth and Sixth Five Year Plans i.e., 1974-75 to 1984-85 because of the lack of readily available State-wise information for the earlier period. The information presented in this chapter is collected from the various issues of the Reserve Bank of India Bulletin presenting the finances of the State Governments. The RBI Bulletin presents the details of discretionary grants under two heads (1) national calamities and (2) others. Similarly, discretionary loans are presented under (1) loans against small savings and (2) others. Though the extent of'other grants' and 'other loans' is available from this information, elements constituting 'other grants' and 'other loans' cannot be had from this information. For the purpose of identifying the nature and extent of the 'other grants' and 'loans', composition of the discretionary grants and loans as available from the Explanatory Memoranda to the Central Budgets is presented in Appendix Table V-1. As may be seen from this statement, the discretionary transfers to the States have increased substantially from Rs. 1300 crores in 1980-81 to Rs. 4661 crores in the Budget Estimates for 1986-87. While grants constituted 28 per cent of the total discretionary transfers in 1980-81, their share has come down drastically to only 10 percent in the B.E. 1986-87. This is mainly because of the increase in the loans against small savings from a mere Rs. 715 crores in 1980-81 to Rs. 3200 crores in 1986-87. The conversion of outstanding overdrafts against a State into loans has also led to a substantial increase in the share of loans in certain years. The tilt in the composition of discretionary transfers towards loans has the effect of increasing the debt burden of the States.

While grants for natural calamities form a predominant proportion of the total discretionary grants, small savings loans form a predominant proportion in the total discretionary loans. The other important items under grants are grants towards handloom industry and grants for the improvement in the salary scales of college and University teachers. The important items among other loans are loans for fertilisers and loans to clear overdrafts.

The elements of discretion in respect of the grants for natural calamities is limited and that in respect of loans against small savings is non-existent. It is only in respect of 'other grants' and 'other loans' that there is an element of discretion. But as these elements do not constitute a significant proportion of total transfers other than those effected through the channels of planning Commission and the Finance Commission, the question arises as to how far one is justified in calling such transfers discretionary. Nevertheless, the term discretionary transfer is used in this Chapter to denote the transfers effected by the Finance Ministry and other Central Ministries to conform to the general usage.

INTER-STAFF VARIATIONS

The State-wise discretionary transfers are presented in Appendix Table V 2. These figures are not comparable with those in Appendix Table V-1 because of differences in coverage. Whereas the figures in Appendix Table V-1 are revised estimates, those in Appendix Table V-2 are actuals. For studying the inter-state variations in the flow of discretionary transfers, per capita discretionary transfers are presented in Appendix Table V-3. Indices of per capita discretionary transfers to the States are presented in Table 5.1.

The indices of per capita transfers to the States show that the flow of discretionary transfers to Group-A State was highly favourable both during the Fifth and Sixth Plan period. In fact, the index of per capita transfers in respect of Group-A States had increased from 107.5 during 1974-79 to 143.1 during the period 1980-85. The index in respect of Group-B and Group-C States was less than 100 during the Fifth as well as the Sixth Plan period indicating an unfavourable treatment meted out to these States in the flow of discretionary transfers. The index for Group-B States though less than 100 was slightly higher than the index for Group-C States. Thus the States at the bottom rung of the ladder in terms of per capita SDP received unfavourable treatment. Another matter of concern is that the index in respect of both Group-B and Group-C States has shown a decline from the level in 1974-79, while the index of Group-A States had shown a substantial increase. If we examine the composition of the discretionary transfers, Group-A States received a highly favourable treatment in the allocation of grants during the period 1974-79, with an index of 159.2. This position was reversed to some extent during 1980-85, with Group-C States recording a higher index in respect of grants. While the flow of discretionary loans was

Table 5.1 : Indices of Per Capita Discretionary Transfers to States

	1974-75 to 1978-79			1979-80			1980-81 to 1984-85		
	Grants	Loans	Total	Grants	Loans	Total	Grants	Loans	Total
Group 'A' States	**159.2**	**95.8**	**107.5**	**79.8**	**128.7**	**121.3**	**86.5**	**154.9**	**143.1**
1. Punjab	501.9	164.4	226.6	45.7	110.3	100.6	36.8	37.4	37.3
2. Haryana	352.9	76.5	127.4	26.2	92.8	82.8	54.0	143.9	128.4
3. Maharastra	77.2	84.9	83.5	95.4	142.2	135.1	66.3	182.8	162.7
4. Gujarat	67.6	89.0	85.1	87.9	126.4	120.6	160.3	165.4	164.5
Group 'B' States	**67.2**	**105.8**	**98.7**	**93.3**	**150.8**	**142.1**	**69.6**	**99.6**	**94.4**
5. West Bengal	84.8	211.8	188.4	55.0	132.2	120.6	75.4	177.8	160.2
6. Karnataka	25.4	61.6	54.9	24.1	54.3	49.8	37.2	81.1	73.5
7. Tamil Nadu	46.7	63.9	60.8	123.8	48.8	60.1	83.4	60.7	64.6
8. Kerala	29.3	67.3	60.3	31.6	23.4	24.6	40.6	50.0	48.4
9. Rajasthan	144.6	72.5	85.8	233.7	530.8	486.2	97.5	87.0	88.8
Group 'C' States	**97.3**	**98.0**	**97.8**	**112.8**	**55.8**	**64.4**	**125.0**	**78.1**	**86.1**
10. Andhra Pradesh	97.0	56.8	64.2	325.9	47.5	89.3	101.4	103.2	102.9
11. Orissa	370.1	68.0	123.7	67.4	41.8	45.6	507.2	60.9	137.9
12. Madhya Pradesh	40.4	77.4	70.6	31.9	44.5	42.6	59.7	54.4	55.3
13. Uttar Pradesh	86.6	121.9	115.4	103.5	64.8	70.6	122.6	72.2	80.9
14. Bihar	51.8	118.7	106.4	41.1	62.0	58.9	51.0	92.3	85.1
Total 14 States	**100.0**	**100.0**	**100.0**	**100.0**	**100.0**	**100.0**	**100.0**	**100.0**	**100.0**
Special Category States:	**408.0**	**128.1**	**179.7**	**318.4**	**62.5**	**100.9**	**340.6**	**123.7**	**161.1**
All States:	**115.9**	**101.5**	**104.1**	**111.7**	**98.0**	**100.1**	**112.9**	**101.3**	**103.3**

favourable to Group-B States during 1974-79, it became favourable to Group-A States during 1980-85. Though the Group-C States fared very badly in terms of total discretionary transfers, they fared relatively better in terms of discretionary grants during the period 1980-85.

Similar findings have emerged from a study of Centre State resource transfers by K.K.George and I.S. Gulati (Centre State Resource Transfers, 1951-84, Economic & Political Weekly, February 16, 1985). George and Gulati have covered a longer period from 1951-84. Another difference between the George and Gulati study and the analysis presented in this Chapter is that while the George's study has taken all the States' average as 100, 14 non-special category States' average has been taken as 100 in our study. The indices of per capita transfers in George's study are 118 in respect of Group-A States, 102 in respect of Group-B States and 87 in respect of Group-C States and these are in broad conformity with our study though the period of our study is limited to 1974-85. The results of George and Gulati study are presented in Appendix Table X-4.

SIX

INSTITUTIONAL FINANCE

The flow of institutional finance into a State is an important factor for speeding up the pace of economic development. The flow of two important elements of institutional finance, viz., bank credit and assistance sanctioned by all-India financial institutions has been analysed in this Chapter. Besides institutional finance, investments made by the Central Government in the public sector undertakings had been playing an important role in not only broadening the economic base of the States but also in creating conditions for further growth of the economy of the States. This Chapter also analyses the inter-state distribution of Central Government investments in the States from the point of view of balanced regional development.

Credit by Commercial Banks

The distribution of bank credit is a function of a number of variables, such as, the level of economic activity in the State, governmental investments in agriculture and industry and the network of banking institutions in a State. Government's policy right from the begining of the planning process has been addressed to the task of reducing the growing inequalities in the distribution of bank credit. In this context, a brief review of the evolution of banking policy is in order. One of the first steps that the Government took in the sphere of banking was the nationalisation of Imperial Bank of India in 1955. Extension of banking facilities in rural areas and semi-urban areas was one of the main objectives in nationalising the Imperial Bank. The State Bank of India Act required the bank to establish not less than 400 additional branches within a period of 5 years from July, 1955 particularly at the district and Sub-divisional centres. Another area that attracted the Government's attention was the decline in the ratio of paid up capital and reserves to deposits. The substantial increase in deposits in relation to owned capital enabled the industrialist share holder by contributig a small amount to banks' resources, to command the much larger resources available to the bank in the form of deposits collected from the public at large. In order to curb the control of the industry over bank credit, Credit Authorisation Scheme was introduced in November, 1965 in terms of which scheduled commercial banks were directed to secure prior approval of the Reserve Bank for granting any fresh credit limit of Rs. 1.00 crore or more to any single party, or any limit that would raise the total limit sanctioned to such a party by the entire banking system to Rs.1.00 crore or more. This ultimately led to the social control of the banking system in 1968 with the main objective of achieving a wider spread of bank credit, preventing its misuse, directing a larger volume of credit to flow to priority sectors and making it a more effective instrument of economic development. The National Credit Council (NCC) was set up in February, 1968 with a view to providing a forum for discussing and assessing credit priorities on an All-India basis. Although the Government had taken a number of steps, the progress made in achieving the social objectives was not adequate. This prompted the Government to take the major decision of nationalising 14 major commercial banks on July 19, 1969. It was expected that the nationalised banks would endeavour to ensure that the needs of productive efforts of diverse kinds, irrespective of size and social status of the borrowers and in particular those of farmers, small scale industries and self employed professional groups are met in an increasing manner, and to create fresh opportunities for backward areas in different parts of the country. Subsequently 6 more banks were nationalised.

Inter-State Distribution of Credit

As the nationalisation of major commercial banks was a landmark in the history of banking in India and was expected to bring about far reaching changes in the spread of banking facilities, the year 1969 has been taken as the starting point for analysis of inter-state distribution of bank advances. The position obtaining in

1969 has been compared with 1982 to assess as to how far the objective of balanced distribution of credit has been achieved, Appendix Tables V1.5 to V1.10 present the State-wise distribution of bank credit, bank advances, bank offices and credit-deposit ratios of commercial banks.

The indices of dustribution of commercial bank offices, and advances are presented in Table 6.1.

TABLE 6.1 : Indices of Bank Offices Per Lakh of Population, Per Capita Advances of Scheduled Commercial Banks and Per Capita Advances of Public Sector Banks.

	Scheduled Commercial Banks				Public Sector Banks	
STATES	Number of Bank Offices per lakh of population		Per Capita Advances		Per Capita Advances	
	1969	1982	1969	1981	1969	1984
Group 'A' States	**158.3**	**124.5**	**218.9**	**200.9**	**225.8**	**212.6**
1. Punjab	172.2	176.4	84.2	169.3	70.9	180.9
2. Haryana	115.2	119.7	45.3	120.1	44.4	114.9
3. Maharastra	147.7	109.8	336.6	264.2	347.2	288.6
4. Gujarat	188.1	127.5	130.3	130.4	140.0	125.2
Group 'B' States	**135.1**	**114.2**	**136.1**	**119.7**	**129.8**	**107.1**
5. West Bengal	75.5	80.0	242.3	135.5	227.7	113.9
6. Karnataka	172.2	142.0	94.9	121.1	93.7	125.2
7. Tamil Nadu	171.5	118.1	152.0	148.0	145.0	130.8
8. Kerala	188.1	168.8	73.9	121.3	69.3	93.8
9. Rajasthan	94.7	92.2	26.7	52.2	28.4	53.1
Group 'C' States	**53.6**	**81.0**	**29.2**	**46.6**	**30.9**	**49.9**
10. Andhra Pradesh	86.8	99.3	56.1	81.9	53.9	95.5
11. Orissa	30.5	82.4	12.2	34.3	12.8	40.7
12. Madhya Pradesh	54.3	85.3	25.3	42.1	29.0	45.0
13. Uttar Pradesh	56.3	75.9	32.2	46.6	33.4	45.8
14. Bihar	32.5	71.3	13.4	27.6	17.7	28.7
Total 14 States	**100.0**	**100.0**	**100.0**	**100.0**	**100.0**	**100.0**
Special Category States	**45.0**	**86.7**	**14.9**	**37.8**	**14.2**	**37.3**
All States	**97.4**	**99.3**	**95.7**	**96.7**	**95.7**	**96.6**

B_1 The distribution of commercial bank offices per lakh of population was highly favourable to Group-'A' States and least favourable to Group-'C' States in 1969. The indices in respect of all Group-'C' States were very much below 100. Only Andhra Pradesh had recorded an index of 86.8 which is somewhat closer to 100. The special category States fared worse even when compared to Group-'C' States. The distribution of bank

B_2 offices continued to be more favourable to advanced States in 1982. However, the redeeming feature is that the indices of concentration of bank offices have come down in respect of both Group-'A' and Group-'B' States, and have risen slightly in respect of Group-'C' States. But the index for Group-C continues to be below 100 even in 1982.

The per capita distribution of advacces of commercial banks show a high degree of concentration than the distribution of bank offices. While the index of per capita distribution of bank advances was 218.9 for Group-'A' States, it was only 29.2 in respect of Group-'C' States in 1969. Within Group-'A', the distribution of advances was highly favourable to Maharastra. The index of Group-'B' States though not as favourable as Group-'A' was very much above the average position. The relative position of different groups of States in the distribution of bank advances remained the same in 1981. The only difference is that while the indices of Group-A and 'B' States have come down marginally, the index of Group-'C' States has increased. Even at the improved level, the index of per capita distribution of advances in Group-'C' States is less than half the index in respect of Group-'B' and only a little over 1/4 of the index in respect of Group-'A' States. The Performance of special category States is worse than even Group-'C'. To examine whether the public sector banks have fared any better in the distribution of bank offices and advances, indices have been worked out taking only the public sector banks into account. The position revealed by these indices is no different from the aggregate picture. In fact, the advances of public sector banks to Group-A States in 1984 show a slightly higher degree of concentration than the advances of all commercial banks in 1982.

Credit-Deposit ratio is another important indicator which can be used to analyse the regional imbalances in the distribution of credit in relation to the deposits mobilised in a States. As may be seen from the Appendix Table V1.10 Credit Deposit ratio is found to be favourable to middle income States followed by high income States in the second position and backward States in the last. While the Credit-Deposit ratio in respect of Group-A and 'B' States has come down between 1969 and 1982, the ratio in respect of Group-C states has improved. But the relative position of States has remained the same.

To sum up, the per capita distribution of bank advances has continued to remain favourable to Group-'A' States. Even in terms of Credit-Deposits ratio, the low income States have not fared any better. Between 1969 and 1982, the differences in the distribution of advances have come down only marginally.

Assistance by All-India Financial Institutions

Assistance by term lending and promotional institutions is one of the means which can be effectively used to impinge on regional disparities in the distribution of investments and thereby generation of income. Location of industrial units is guided by consideration of locational advantage as well as the availability of infrastructural facilities, the latter exerting a greater pull thereby leading to the concentration of industrial units within the proximity of already developed industrial centres. This had in effect led to the channeling of institutional finance to those regions which are already developed. But with the greater emphasis of the Government on the dispersal of industries, it was expected that there would be greater flow of institutional finance to backward regions than hitherto, thus paving the way for balanced development of the country. For the purpose of analysing the inter-state variations in the flow of institutional finance, cumulative assistance rendered by some of the important all-India financial institutions viz., NABARD, LIC, IFCI, IDBI, ICICI and HUDCO has been taken into account. Out of these financial institutions, IFCI, IDBI and ICICI are solely engaged in financing industrial activity, while the investment pattern of the LIC is more varied. NABARD and HUDCO cater to agricultural refinancing and housing finance respectively. The indices of per capita cumulative investment by the financial institutions are presented in Table 6.2.

TABLE 6.2 : Indices of per Capita Investment by Financial Institutions

STATES	NABARD	LIC	IFCI	IDBI	ICICI	HUDCO	TOTAL
Group 'A' States	**169.9**	**172.8**	**179.9**	**214.7**	**235.6**	**159.9**	**187.7**
1. Punjab	405.6	156.1	169.2	155.0	107.7	161.0	185.0
2. Haryana	404.7	200.0	172.7	190.8	139.3	205.7	211.9
3. Maharastra	95.5	159.4	163.2	177.1	268.9	115.8	159.1
4. Gujarat	101.9	195.7	218.7	322.3	273.7	223.5	232.5
Group 'B' States	**68.0**	**108.4**	**102.9**	**84.4**	**90.0**	**116.4**	**99.9**
5. West Bengal	23.2	95.7	69.2	72.8	61.6	37.4	62.4
6. Karnataka	111.0	93.6	134.3	154.9	127.2	121.6	124.0
7. Tamil Nadu	71.2	119.2	121.0	17.2	124.0	128.8	127.4
8. Kerala	65.4	129.4	82.3	97.1	41.5	138.1	87.5
9. Rajasthan	91.0	113.5	112.5	111.9	82.8	203.0	104.1
Group 'C' States	**92.2**	**65.2**	**65.8**	**63.6**	**51.6**	**65.2**	**64.6**
10. Andhra Pradesh	147.7	73.5	124.4	120.6	91.1	118.0	108.3
11. Orissa	91.0	88.5	80.5	95.9	75.2	77.6	85.8
12. Madhya Pradesh	92.5	59.1	50.3	52.0	50.7	57.5	57.4
13. Uttar Pradesh	86.7	65.6	65.8	54.3	37.9	67.9	58.7
14. Bihar	58.7	54.0	26.7	31.0	34.7	21.7	37.8
Total 14 States	**100.0**	**100.0**	**100.0**	**100.0**	**100.0**	**100.0**	**100.0**
Special Category States	**28.7**	**57.1**	**48.1**	**66.9**	**80.4**	**39.4**	**54.9**
All - States:	**96.2**	**97.7**	**97.2**	**98.2**	**99.0**	**96.8**	**97.6**

This table reveals that the assistance rendered by almost all financial institutions has gone in favour of high income States (Group-'A') followed by the middle income States. The only exception is NABRAD in which case the assistance rendered to Group-'C' States is higher than Group-'B' States. Even here the assistance to Group-'A' States is nearly two times higher than the assistance Group-'C'. The variation in the indices of per capita assistance in respect of high income and low income States is so large that per capita assistance rendered by IDBI and ICICI to high income States is over three times higher than that given to low income States. While indices of Group-'A' States varied from 159.9 to 235.6, the indices in respect of Group-'C' States have not even reached 100 in the case of even a single financial institution. Group-'B' States though better placed than Group-C States, have fared very badly in comparison with Group-A States. The indices are found to be below 100 in respect of NABARD, IDBI, ICICI and are only marginally higher than 100 in respect of LIC, IFCI and HUDCO.

When we take the cumulative per capita assistance rendered by all financial institutions, the index of assistance to high income States is nearly double the assistance to Group-B States and is over 4 times the assistance to Group-C States. The low investments by the financial institutions in backward States may be due to the poor response of the industry to set up units in these States. Whatever may be the reasons for continuing imbalances, corrective action is urgently called for to ensure greater flow of institutional finance to backward States.

Central Government Investments in States

The investments in the Central Public Sector enterprises have witnessed a tremendous increase over the years. The investments had risen from a meagre Rs.29 crores at the commencement of the First Five Year Plan to a massive amount of Rs 36,390 crores at the end of 1984-85. At the end of 1984-85, the number of running public enterprises stood at 205. The investment of such an order would certainly have an impact of far-reaching importance on the economy of the States where these units are located. While it cannot be denied that the location of some of the units is guided by considerations of proximity to raw materials etc., the Centre has a lot of leeway in the location of some other units which are not location specific. This Section analyses whether this directionary power of the Centre has been used in favour of backward States or not.

The State-wise investments made in Central Government Public Sector undertakings are presented in Appendix Table V1.3 both in absolute and percapita terms. The indices of per capita investments are presented in Table 6.3.

The indices of per capita investments in Central Government undertakings are found to be favourable to backward States up to the end of the Fourth Plan. Though the index in respect of the middle income states was less than 100 during the three annual plans (1966-69) and the Fourth Plan, these States fared relatively better than the high income States. But the pattern of per capita investments considerably changed in favour of the high income States during the Fifth plan and the Sixth Plan. The larger investments made during Fifth and Sixth Plan periods in the high income States had not only more than offset the low investment made up to the end of the Fourth Plan but also taken these States to the top position in the cumulative investments made up to the end of March, 1984. While the index of per capita cumulative investment upto the end of March 1984 is 127.7 in respect of Group-A States, it is only 105.5 in respect of Group-C States. The position of Group-B States is more or less the same as Group-C. This clearly shows that the backward States with a favourable position up to the end of Fourth Plan had been discriminated to such an extent during the later plan periods that their position became worse in relation to high income States.

TABLE 6.3 : Indices of Percapita Investments in Central Government Public Sector Undertakings

STATES	First, second & Third Plans	Annual Plans 1966-67 1968-69	Fourth Plan 1969-74	Fifth Plan 1974-78	1978-79 to 1983-84	Cumulative as on 31-3-1984
Group 'A' States	**34.9**	**50.0**	**65.0**	**125.5**	**147.7**	**127.7**
1. Punjab	45.2(-)	22.7	17.0	122.8	53.3	62.1
2. Haryana	-	36.4	8.9	118.8	48.2	54.3
3. Maharastra	33.4	40.9	47.8	127.1	233.1	182.9
4. Gujarat	28.3	113.6	142.8	126.4	74.7	86.1
Group 'B' States	**102.5**	**86.4**	**84.2**	**66.1**	**71.3**	**73.8**
5. West Bengal	204.9	90.9	126.4	84.0	97.5	103.5
6. Karnataka	51.8	40.9	64.3	78.0	60.8	62.7
7. Tamil Nadu	116.8	104.5	58.4	45.0	92.9	85.3
8. Kerala	49.5	145.5	78.8	66.2	43.9	54.4
9. Rajasthan	4.4	45.5	80.0	54.9	30.7	36.4
Group 'C' States	**123.6**	**127.3**	**124.1**	**111.5**	**99.0**	**105.5**
10. Andhra Pradesh	28.1	45.5	62.4	60.2	139.7	112.0
11. Orissa	363.6	300.0	114.6	52.0	164.6	159.2
12. Madhya Pradesh	302.3	118.2	104.4	230.7	149.8	167.8
13. Uttar Pradesh	14.9	50.0	21.3	27.6	41.7	36.7
14. Bihar	153.0	254.5	351.1	217.2	96.2	143.1
Total 14 States	**100.0**	**100.0**	**100.0**	**100.0**	**100.0**	**100.0**
Special Category States	**38.7**	**68.2**	**84.7**	**97.1**	**133.0**	**114.7**
All - States	**97.73**	**109.1**	**99.2**	**99.8**	**101.8**	**100.8**

SEVEN

MARKET BORROWINGS

The evolution of market borrowings is traced in this Chapter. After presenting the evolution and growth of market borrowings, the vertical distribution of the market borrowings between the Centre and the States and the horizontal distribution among the States are analysed.

Market borrowings are in the form of subscriptions to the Government bonds/securities made by certain financial institutions under statutory obligations imposed upon them. These institutions are Commercial Banks, Life Insurance Corporation of India, General Insurance Corporation of India and Employees Provident Fund. The statutory obligation varies from 32 per cent of the net addition to the aggregate deposits of cooprative banks to 50 per cent of the net addition to Employees Provident Fund. The net market borrowing of the Centre and the States increased from Rs. Rs.16 crores in 1952-53 to Rs.147 crores in 1961-62 and to Rs. 342 crores in 1970-71. They are estimated at Rs. 7104.22 crores in 1986-87. The increase in the market borrowings between 1970-71 and 1986-87 has been quite phenomenal. While the market borrowings had increased by 133 per cent between 1961-62 and 1970-71, the increase between 1970-71 and 1986-87 is as much as 2000 per cent. Part of this increase has come about as a result of the increase in the total demand and time deposits of the commercial banks as well as a gradual increase in the Statutory Liquidity Ratio (SLR) of commercial banks. During 1985, SLR was raised from 36 per cent to 37 per cent in two phases to 36.5 percent effective from June 8, 1985 and to 37 per cent effective from July 10, 1985, with a view to providing resources within the framework of the Seventh Five Year Plan. Because of the substantial increase in their volume, market borrowings have come to occupy an important place in the scheme of financing plan outlays.

There are two aspects in the distribution of market borrowings: vertical distribution involving the Centre on the one hand and the States on the other hand and the horizontal distribution among the States. The vertical distribution of the market borrowings has been a bone of contention between the Centre and the States, the latter demanding an equal share and former not conceding this demand.

Distribution between the Centre and the States

The distribution of net market borrowings between the Centre and the States during various plan periods is presented in the Table Below.

Table 7.1 : Distribution of Net Market Borrowings

(Rs. Crores)

	Market borrowings			% share in Market Borrowings	
	Centre	States	Total	Centre	States
First Plan 1951-56	49	155	204	24.0	76.0
Second Plan 1956-61	400	356	756	52.9	47.1
Third Plan 1961-66	307	516	823	37.3	62.7
Annual Plans 1966-69	384	341	725	53.0	47.0
Fourth Plan 1969-74	1744	1044	2788	62.6	37.4
Fifth Plan 1974-79	3746	2133	5879	63.7	36.3
Annual Plan 1979-80	1850	521	2371	78.0	22.0
Sixth Plan 1980-85 (Latest Estimates)	17401	4719	22120	78.7	21.3
Seventh Plan 1985-90 (Estimates)	20620	9942	30562	67.5	32.5

It may be seen from the Table that the net market borrowings of the Centre which stood at Rs. 49 crores during the First Plan increased to Rs. 20,620 crores during the Seventh Plan, recording an increase of nearly 624 times. On the other hand, market borrowings of the States increased from Rs.155 crores in the First Plan to only Rs. 9942 crores in the Seventh Plan period, registering a relatively modest increase of 64 times. The Centre claimed only 24 per cent of the market borrowings during the First Plan but its share had been rising since then and stood at 78 per cent during the Sixth plan. Though the Centre's share has come down to 67 per cent during the Seventh Plan period, it has not alered the predominant position of the Centre in the distribution of market borrowings. In contrast, the share of the States declined from 76 per cent in the First Plan to 47 per cent in the Second Plan which further declined to 22 per cent in the Sixth Plan. Because of the 20 per cent step up allowed to the States, the States' share has increased to 33 per cent for the Seventh plan period. The above analysis clearly brings out how the States have been denied of their due share.

The predominant position of the Centre in terms of its share of market borrowings is also evident when we analyse the role of market borrowings in financing the Central and States' Plan outlays. In Table - 7.2, the share of net market borrowings in the plan outlays of the Centre and the States are presented.

Table 7.2 : Plan Outlays and Market Borrowings

(Rs. Crores)

	Plan outlay		Market Borrowings		% share of market borrowings in Plan Outlay	
	Centre incl.UTs	States	Centre	States	Centre	States
First Plan	535	1425	49	155	9.2	10.9
Second Plan	2690	2082	400	356	15.4	17.1
Third Plan	4412	4165	307	516	7.0	12.4
Annual Plans	3565	3060	384	341	10.8	11.1
Fourth Plan	8104	7675	1744	1044	21.5	13.6
Fifth Plan	19855	19571	3746	2133	18.9	10.9
Annual Plan	6042	6134	1850	521	30.6	8.5
Sixth Plan (Latest Estimates)	60689	50138	17401	4719	28.7	9.4
Seventh Plan (Estimates)	99302	80698	20620	9942	20.8	11.0

The contribution of market borrowings to the Central Plan Outlay which was 9.2 per cent during the First Plan increased to nearly 29 per cent during the Sixth Plan. Because of the step up allowed to the States, the share of market borrowings in the Central Plan Outlay has come down to about 21 per cent during the Seventh Plan. As against this, the share of market borrowings which was over 17 per cent of the States' Plan outlay in the Second Plan had come down to 9 per cent during the Sixth Plan. The percentage has improved slightly to 11 per cent for the Seventh Plan period. The Table clearly brings out that the Centre has been depending on market borrowings for financing its plan outlay to a greater extent than the States. Though the Centre is having more elastic sources of revenue as compared to the States, it has come to depend more on market borrowings for financing its plan.

The growing imbalance in the distribution of market borrowings between the Centre and the States is mainly because of the discretion exercised by the Centre. The shares are worked out for each Plan period by then Planning Commission in consultation with the Finance Ministry and the Reserve Bank of India.

Distribution Among the States

The distribution of market borrowings among the States was not based on any set procedure before 1969. The total amount which could be raised by flotation of bonds was determined by the Reserve Bank on the basis of the overall capacity of the Capital market for absorption of Government securities. Within this total, the share of each State was again determined by the RBI on the basis of accessibility of individual States to the Capital market and the response of the Capital market to the bond floatation by individual States. The result was that the industrially advanced States raised a larger share. With the nationalisation of commercial banks, gilt edged market became completely captive and the accessibility of the States to the capital market ceased to be an important factor. Higher market borrowings were being allocated to less developed states from 1971-72. The hilly and border States like Himachal Pradesh, Jammu and Kashmir, Manipur etc., which were hitherto not getting any share in market borrowings were being allocated market borrowings from 1972-73 onwards.

Because of the non-finalisation of the Fifth Plan till 1976, the market borrowings of the States were pegged at 1973-74 level in 1974-75 and 1975-76. In 1976-77 an increase of 10 per cent was allowed uniformly to all States over 1973-74 level, and the policy continued till the beginning of the Sixth Plan. As there was no unanimity among the States regarding the distribution, it was finally decided to allow a 10 per cent annual step up over 1979-80 level and to distribute for the first time additional market borrowings among the States having per capita incomes below the national average. In accordance with this formula, Rs. 3500 crores was allocated to all the States and additional market borrowings of Rs. 1000 crores was allocated among backward States for the plan period 1980-85. The annual step up was increased to 20 per cent during 1983-84 and 1984-85. The actual distribution of market borrowings came to Rs. 4725.14 crores during the Sixth Plan period consisting of Rs, 3720.69 crores of normal borrowings and Rs, 1004.45 crores of special borrowings. This amount is more or less the same as the one allocated at the beginning of the plan period.

During the Seventh Plan period (1985-90) an amount of Rs. 7011.95 crores has been allocated to all the States as normal market borrowings and special borrowings amounting to Rs. 2930.05 crores has been allowed to backward States. Within this overall amount, States have been allowed a 20 per cent step up during 1985-86 and a 10 per cent step up during 1986-87 over the preceding year's level.

Analysis of Inter-State Variations

The State-wise distribution of market borrowings from the Fourth Plan onwards both in absolute and per capita terms is presented in Appendix Table V11.1 - V11.6. The analysis of inter-state variations presented in this Chapter is confined to the period 1969-70 to 1989-90, mainly because of the fact that the Pre-1969 distribution of market borrowings was based on the accessibility of States to the Capital market as a result of which only industrially advanced States were able to corner the borrowings. As such, it was felt that no useful purpose would be served by analysing the Pre-1969 distribution. It was only in the post 1969 period that the distribution tended to become broad-based.

Table 7.3 presents the indices of per capita market borrowings of States for each plan period separately. These indices have been constructed taking the average per capita market borrowings of 14 major States as 100.

Table 7.3 : Indices of Per Capita Market Borrowings

States	Fourth Plan	Fifth Plan	Sixth Plan	Seventh Plan	Total* 1969-90
Group 'A' States	**112.6**	**133.2**	**96.4**	**85.5**	**97.8**
1. Punjab	111.5	133.1	90.5	80.4	93.4
2. Haryana	153.6	198.7	137.6	122.4	139.4
3. Maharastra	98.9	110.8	82.4	73.0	83.7
4. Gujarat	124.0	150.1	109.4	97.1	110.2
Group 'B' States	**86.0**	**136.4**	**106.3**	**108.4**	**111.1**
5. West Bengal	84.1	155.3	114.6	102.0	111.5
6. Karnataka	97.8	124.3	91.7	80.2	91.1
7. Tamil Nadu	78.6	108.2	82.0	107.0	100.9
8. Kerala	92.0	158.8	118.2	142.0	136.4
9. Rajasthan	81.9	143.4	134.6	126.2	127.6
Group 'C' States	**43.7**	**77.1**	**97.4**	**100.5**	**93.8**
10. Andhra Pradesh	54.8	82.9	91.3	96.7	91.9
11. Orissa	59.4	98.7	114.1	115.5	110.7
12. Madhya Pradesh	48.1	77.0	97.1	100.4	94.1
13. Uttar Pradesh	37.8	71.7	94.5	96.5	89.6
14. Bihar	35.1	72.9	100.6	104.1	95.3
Total 14 States	**100.0**	**100.0**	**100.0**	**100.0**	**100.0**
Special Category States	**71.8**	**174.7**	**142.4**	**130.0**	**133.9**
All - States	**70.5**	**110.3**	**109.4**	**101.6**	**101.8**

* Excludes Annual Plan 1979-80

Notes:

1. Group A: States with per capita income 10 per cent or more above national average.

   Group B: States with per capita income within ± 10 per cent of national average.

   Group C: States with per capita income 10 per cent of more below the national average.

2. For categorising States, average per capita income for the years 1977-78 to 1979-80 has been used. The All India average per capita income for this period is Rs. 1165.

3. States have been arranged in descending order of State Domestic Product.

During the Fourth plan period, the distribution was highly favourable to the higher income States (Group-'A') and least favourable to low income States (Group-'C'). While the index of per capita market borrowings was 112.6 in respect of Group-'A', it was only 43.7 for Group-'C' States. Within Group-'A', the distribution was highly favourable to Haryana (Index 153.6) followed by Gujarat (124.0). Within Group-'C' the distribution was highly unfavourable to Uttar Pradesh and Bihar, the last two States in the descending order of per capita State domestic product. During the Fifth Plan, though the position of Group-'B' and 'C' States had considerably improved, distribution becoming more favourable to Group 'B' as compared to all over States, Group-'A' States continued to get higher market borrowings which were only marginally lower than Group 'B' States.

During the Sixth and the Seventh Plan periods, Group-B States have maintained their favourable position of getting the highest per capita market borrowings, followed by Group-C amd Group-A States. If we take the per capita market borrowings for the entire period 1969-90, the index works out to more than 100 in respect of Group-B States and less than 100 in respect of both Group-A and 'C' States. However, Group-A states' index at 97.8 is higher than Group-C states' index of 93.8.

In sum, it can be stated that though the imbalances in the distribution of market borrwoings have been brought down to a great extent during the Sixth Plan and in the allocation for the Seventh Plan, the distribution continues to ramain favourable to the middle income States than the low-income States. The improvement in the position of Group-C States has been brought about mainly through the allocation of special market borrowings to them. Group-B States recording the highest per capita market borrowings may be due to the fact that two of the States in this Group, viz., Kerala and Rajasthan are also getting allocation under special market borrowings. With the distribution of market borrowings tending to become relatively more balanced over the plan periods, controversy in the area of Central State relations now centres round the respective shares of the Centre and the States in the market borrwings.

EIGHT

DEBT BURDEN OF STATES

The growth of public debt and debt servicing burden of the States are analysed in this chapter, at two points of time, viz, at the end of March 1974 and March 1984. As the loans from the Centre is an important element of the total public debt of the States, its servicing burden has been analysed separetely in this Chapter. For the purpose of comparison, an analysis of the growth of public debt of the Centre is also attempted.

There is a growing concern over the public debt of the States which is increasing from year to year. Table 8.1 reveals that the outstanding debt of the States which stood at Rs. 11,618 crores at the end of March 1974 increased to Rs. 37,184 crores by the end of March 1984. The outstanding debt of the States constituted 24.4 per cent of the States' domestic product at the end of 1973-74 and 26.4 per cent of the SDP at the end of 1983-84. Though there is no substantial increase in the outstanding public debt in terms of its percentage to States' domestic product, the per capita outstanding debt has more than doubled between 1973-74 and 1983-84 from Rs. 215 to Rs. 550.

In the context of the discussion of the outstanding debt of the States, it may be in order to compare the situation obtaining in the States with that of the Central Government. Table 8.2 presents the outstanding debt of the Centre.

TABLE 8.1 : Total Outstanding Debt of the States

States	Outstanding debt as on 31st March		Outstanding % of SDP	Debt as	Percapita Outstanding Date (Rs)	
	1974	1984	1974	1984	1974	1984
Group 'A' States	**2288**	**7805**	**18.47**	**19.05**	**227.21**	**61.51**
1. Punjab	364	1345	16.89	20.54	267.65	800.60
2. Haryana	308	985	23.62	22.80	308.00	763.57
3. Maharastra	1089	3508	18.91	17.56	216.07	558.60
4. Gujarat	527	1967	16.63	19.44	197.38	576.83
Group 'B' States	**3809**	**11053**	**25.66**	**26.75**	**235.27**	**552.93**
5. West Bengal	1017	3533	23.29	27.54	229.57	647.07
6. Karnataka	643	1639	22.84	21.16	219.45	441.78
7. Tamil Nadu	710	1937	20.69	21.17	172.33	400.21
8. Kerala	526	1531	28.85	32.72	246.95	600.39
9. Rajasthan	913	2413	37.97	34.88	353.88	703.50
Group 'C' States	**4391**	**14942**	**23.87**	**29.15**	**174.38**	**477.53**
10. Andhra Pradesh	896	2545	22.82	23.01	205.98	475.70
11. Orissa	653	1694	40.63	44.74	298.17	641.67
12. Madhya Pradesh	630	2538	19.42	28.33	151.08	486.21
13. Uttar Pradesh	1279	4935	20.56	26.49	144.85	445.00
14. Bihar	933	3230	27.44	36.60	165.43	462.09
Total 14 States	**10488**	**33800**	**22.90**	**25.31**	**203.89**	**528.62**
Special Category States	**1130**	**3384**	**56.29**	**47.98**	**416.97**	**937.40**
All - States	**11618**	**37184**	**24.39**	**26.45**	**214.55**	**550.47**

The outstanding debt of the Central Government had increased from Rs. 16931 crores at the end of 1974 to Rs. 65,356 crores at the end of 1984. The outstanding public debt of the Centre which constituted 33.5 per cent of the Net National Product in 1973-74 rose to 41.4 per cent in 1983-84. In per capita terms, the outstanding debt of the Centre had increased from Rs. 309 in 1973-74 to Rs. 953 in 1983-84. The outstanding debt of the Central Government referred to above does not include small savings and provident funds. All the net liabilities of the Centre (including small savings etc.) taken together which constituted 47 per cent of the NNP in 1973-74 increased to 60 per cent of NNP in 1983-84, The per capita net liabilities of the Centre increased from Rs. 437 in 1973-74 to Rs. 1384 in 1983-84. Even without taking into account small savings etc., there has been a substantial increase in the outstanding debt of the Centre as compared to the States.

TABLE 8.2 : Outstanding Debt and Net Liabilities of the Central Government

(Rs. Crores)

Items	Outstanding debt as at the end of March		Outstanding debt as % of NNP		Percapita outstanding debt (Rs.)	
	1974	1984(RE)	1973-74	1983-84	1973-74	1983-84
A. Internal Debt	11107	50045	22.0	31.7	203	730
B. External Debt	5824	15311	11.5	9.7	106	223
Total Debt (A+B)	**16931**	**65356**	**33.5**	**41.4**	**309**	**953**
C. Small Savings	3275	13298	6.5	8.4	60	194
D. Provident Funds	1135	3768	2.2	2.4	21	55
E. Other Accounts	188	7813	0.4	5.0	3	114
F. Reserve Funds and Deposits	2738	4875	5.5	3.1	50	71
Total Liabilities (A to F)	24267	95110	48.1	60.3	443	1388
Amount Due from Pakistan	(-)300	(-)300	0.6	(-)0.2	5	4
Net Liabilities of the Centre	**23967**	**94810**	**47.5**	**60.1**	**438**	**1385**

Source: Explanatory Memoranda to the Central Budgets.

The growth of Public debt by itself cannot be considered as an unhealthy development. Because of the paucity of internal recources, the States cannot sustain the large plan outlays without resource to public borrowings. It may be apt to quote here the views of the Eighth Finance commission.

> "We see nothing wrong in the growth of public debt. With the expanding public functions, no Government particularly in developing economy, can undertake large scale programmes of development without recourse to borrowing. We think, however, that it is but right that the borrowed funds should be used for investment purpose and not for consumption. While it is no doubt preferable that public debt is discharge though public savings, in

the event of such savings being inadequate or are required for achieving a better social or economic goal, there is no harm in discharging old debts by taking fresh loans".

Thus what is important is not the quantum of public debt but its effective utilisation for the creation of productive assets, which ultimately result in the generation of additional revenues to the Government. In the absence of its effctive utilisation the growing public debt will ultimately constrain the States into borrowing more and more just to meet the increasing debt servicing burden.

COMPOSITION OF OUTSTANDING DEBT

The outstanding debt of the States consists of internal debt, loans from the Centre, provident funds etc. The internal debt mainly consists of loans raised by the States from the market. The percentage compositions of outstanding debt of the State is presented in Table 8.2.

For all the States as well as the 14 major States loans from the Centre alone account for nearly three-fourths of the outstanding debt both in 1973-74 and in 1983-84, followed by internal debt accounting for over 16 per cent and the remaining accounted for by provident funds, etc. The predominance of loans from the Centre followed by internal debt holds goods in respect of all the three groups of States. Within this overall position, the relative importance of these elements only varied slightly among the three groups of States. At the end of 1974, the share of loans from the Centre is relatively higher in Group-'B' and Group-'C' States, while the share of internal debt was relatively higher in Group-'A' States. The position remained more or less the same at the end of 1984. The share of provident funds is found to be relatively higher in Group-'A' and Group-'C' states than in Group-'B' States.

As compared to 1974, the share of Central loans has declined by nearly 5 percentage points in Group-C States and marginally in Group-B States, while Group-A States have registered an increase. Another noticeable charge in 1984 as compared to 1974 is the fall in the share of internal debt and increase in the share of the Provident funds, etc., in all three groups of States.

TABLE 8.3 : Percentage Composition of Outstanding Debt

States	1974 March 31 (Accounts)				1984 March 31 (RE)			
	Internal Debt	Loans and Advances from Centre	Provident Funds	Total	Internal Debt	Loans and Advances from Centre	Provident Funds	Total
Group 'A' States	**25.1**	**66.0**	**8.9**	**100.0**	**18.2**	**68.8**	**13.0**	**100.0**
1. Punjab	24.2	66.7	9.1	100.0	33.2	54.7	12.1	100.0
2. Haryana	18.8	75.0	6.2	100.0	18.2	63.3	18.5	100.0
3. Maharastra	26.0	63.0	11.0	100.0	13.3	73.6	13.1	100.0
4. Gujarat	27.5	66.4	6.1	100.0	16.8	72.3	10.8	100.0
Group 'B' States	**19.8**	**74.0**	**6.2**	**100.0**	**17.0**	**73.0**	**10.0**	**100.0**
5. West Bengal	15.6	80.0	4.4	100.0	11.2	83.2	5.6	100.0
6. Karnataka	23.3	70.3	6.4	100.0	20.2	66.7	13.1	100.0
7. Tamil Nadu	31.8	60.0	8.2	100.0	22.9	68.9	8.2	100.0
8. Kerala	19.8	69.8	10.4	100.0	18.9	63.0	18.1	100.0
9. Rajasthan	12.7	83.4	3.9	100.0	17.5	71.9	10.6	100.0
Group 'C' States	**17.0**	**74.9**	**8.1**	**100.0**	**15.9**	**70.7**	**13.4**	**100.0**
10. Andhra Pradesh	18.5	77.2	4.3	100.0	19.7	72.6	7.7	100.0
11. Orissa	16.1	78.9	5.0	100.0	17.9	70.6	11.5	100.0
12. Madhya Pradesh	17.3	66.5	16.2	100.0	9.4	63.6	27.0	100.0
13. Uttar Pradesh	20.8	71.6	7.6	100.0	19.7	70.5	9.8	100.0
14. Bihar	10.6	80.3	9.1	100.0	11.1	75.0	13.9	100.0
Total 14 States	**10.8**	**72.6**	**7.6**	**100.0**	**16.8**	**71.0**	**12.2**	**100.0**
Special Category States	**6.6**	**87.7**	**5.7**	**100.0**	**8.4**	**80.6**	**11.0**	**100.0**
All States	**18.5**	**74.1**	**7.4**	**100.0**	**16.0**	**71.9**	**12.1**	**100.0**

INTER-STATE VARIATIONS IN OURSTANDING DEBT

For analysing the inter-State variations in outstanding public debt, two indicators have been used, viz., outstanding debt as percentage of SDP and Percapita outstanding debt (Table 8.1). While at the end of 1974, percentage of outstanding debt to SDP was the highest in Group-B States, Group-C States recorded the highest percentage at the end of 1984. In per capita terms, outstanding debt is found to be the lowest in Group-C as compared to other States both at the end of 1974 and 1984. While Group-B States recorded the highest per capita outstanding debt in 1974, it was the Group-A States which recorded the highest per capita outstanding debt in 1984. Though the percentage of outstanding debt to SDP in 1983-84 is found to be the highest in Group-C States, they fared relatively better in terms of per capita outstanding debt.

DEBT SERVICING BURDEN OF STATES

For analysing the debt servicing burden of the States, twc indicators have been worked out. In the first indicator, debt servicing has been expressed as a percentage of gross loans received during the year. This indicator has been worked out mainly to know whether debt servicing exceeds gross loans received during the year in any State. The second indicator expresses debt servicing as a percentage of the expenditure of the States. Debt servicing as percentage of gross loans is presented in Table 8.4.

For the year 1973-74 debt servicing burden for the 14 major States amounted to as much as 88.57 per cent of the gross loans. Among the three groups of States debt burden was the highest in Group-C States followed by Group-B States. Among the Group-C States, debt servicing exceeded the gross loans in three out of five States, viz., Andhra Pradesh, Madhya Pradesh and Bihar. By 1983-84 debt servicing is relatively lower in all the categories of States as compared to 1973-74. For all the 14 States, debt servicing worked out to 65.56 per cent of gross borrowings in 1983-84 as compared to 88.57 per cent in 1973-74. Among the three groups of States debt servicing is found to be relatively lower in low income States and higher in middle income States as compared to high income States in 1983-84.

TABLE 8.4 : Debt Burden of States

States	1973-74 Accounts					1983-84 Accounts				(Rs. Lakhs)
	Gross Loans	Interest payments	Repayment of Loans	Total Debt Servicing	Debt Servicing as percentage of	Gross Loans	Interest Payments	Repayment of Loans	Total Debt Servicing	Debt Servicing as percentage of Gross Loans
Group 'A' States	**36851**	**10667**	**17867**	**28534**	**77.43**	**163620**	**46388**	**60945**	**107333**	**65.60**
1. Punjab	2321	1782	1738	3520	151.66	47506	8961	24592	33553	70.63
2. Haryana	5051	1308	2221	3529	69.87	21769	5917	10533	16450	75.57
3. Maharastra	18652	5108	10067	15175	81.36	60800	19779	17194	36973	60.81
4. Gujarat	10827	2469	3841	6310	58.28	33545	11731	8626	20357	60.69
Group 'B' States	**60367**	**18524**	**35213**	**53737**	**89.02**	**177656**	**62759**	**61998**	**124757**	**70.22**
5. West Bengal	19397	4331	9748	14079	72.58	56915	18434	16164	34598	60.79
6. Karnataka	12425	3110	8696	11806	95.02	27489	9802	13816	23618	85.92
7. Tamil Nadu	6940	3769	5179	8948	128.93	37068	12723	15011	27734	74.82
8. Kerala	7241	2413	4393	6806	93.99	24623	9149	6655	15804	64.18
9. Rajasthan	14364	4901	7197	12098	84.22	31561	12651	10352	233003	72.88
Group 'C' States	**59674**	**20252**	**36435**	**56687**	**94.99**	**236284**	**70939**	**75618**	**146557**	**62.03**
10. Andhra Pradesh	9304	4524	7763	12287	132.06	35663	12302	11263	23565	66.08
11. Orissa	9683	2887	3981	6868	70.93	26985	9630	7376	17006	63.02
12. Madhya Pradesh	6598	3028	5706	8734	132.37	30377	8616	10415	19031	62.65
13. Uttar Pradesh	21703	5658	10308	15966	73.57	86644	25436	31622	57058	65.85
14. Bihar	12386	4155	8677	12832	103.60	56615	14955	14942	29897	52.81
Total 14 States	**156892**	**49443**	**89515**	**138958**	**885.57**	**577560**	**180086**	**198561**	**378647**	**65.56**
Special Category States	**20482**	**5724**	**7244**	**12968**	**63.31**	**23563**	**16268**	**13022**	**29290**	**124.31**
All States	**177374**	**55167**	**96759**	**151926**	**85.65**	**601123**	**196354**	**211583**	**407937**	**67.86**

TABLE 8.5 : Debt Servicing of Central Loans

(Rs. Lakhs)

States	1973-74 Accounts					1983-84 Accounts				
	Gross Loans from Centre	Payment of Interest on Loans from the Centre	Repayment of Loans to the Centre	Total Debt Servicing	Percentage of Total Debt servicing to Gross Loan from the Centre	Gross Loans from Centre	Interest Payments on Loans from the Centre	Repayment of Loans to Centre	Total Debt Servicing	Percentage of total Debt servicing to loans from the Centre
Group 'A' States	**29987**	**6696**	**17240**	**23936**	**79.82**	**134458**	**25304**	**54804**	**80108**	**59.58**
1. Punjab	1547	1134	1541	2675	172.92	30493	3657	23577	27234	89.31
2. Haryana	3885	994	2163	3157	81.26	18025	2718	9614	12332	68.42
3. Maharastra	15523	3095	9815	12910	83.17	56917	12488	14689	27177	47.75
4. Gujarat	9032	1473	3721	5194	57.51	29023	6441	6924	13365	46.05
Group 'B' States	**54524**	**13303**	**34224**	**47527**	**87.17**	**147577**	**37267**	**52914**	**90181**	**61.11**
5. West Bengal	18268	3325	9647	12972	71.01	49268	13080	14113	27193	55.19
6. Karnataka	11258	2149	8463	10612	94.26	22568	5637	12056	17693	78.40
7. Tamil Nadu	6025	2027	4935	6962	115.55	31391	6771	12142	18913	60.25
8. Kerala	6446	1803	4210	6013	93.28	19968	4515	5471	9986	50.01
9. Rajasthan	12527	3999	6969	10968	87.55	24382	7264	9132	16396	67.25
Group 'C' States	**51653**	**14947**	**34863**	**49810**	**96.43**	**192141**	**45858**	**67234**	**113092**	**58.86**
10. Andhra Pradesh	7750	3423	7570	10993	141.85	24642	8541	9191	17732	71.96
11. Orissa	8347	2167	3855	6022	72.15	21442	5524	6025	11549	53.86
12. Madhya Pradesh	5805	2036	5478	7514	129.44	26559	3286	8799	12085	45.80
13. Uttar Pradesh	18335	4052	9741	13793	75.23	68006	17337	29162	46499	68.37
14. Bihar	11416	3269	8219	11488	100.63	51492	11170	14057	25227	48.99
Total 14 States	**136164**	**34946**	**86327**	**121273**	**89.06**	**474176**	**108429**	**174952**	**283381**	**59.76**
Special Category States	**19127**	**5153**	**7061**	**12214**	**63.86**	**56081**	**11165**	**12176**	**23341**	**41.62**
All States	**155291**	**40099**	**93388**	**133487**	**85.96**	**530257**	**119594**	**187128**	**306722**	**57.84**

Since bulk of the loans received by the States is from the Centre, the debt servicing burden of the States in respect of Central loans has been analysed separately and presented in Table 8.5.

At 96.43 per cent of the gross loans from the Centre, debt servicing burden was found to be the highest in Group-C States (14 major States' average 89.06 per cent) in 1973-74. As in the case of total debt servicing, debt servicing burden of Central loans exceeded gross loans from the Centre in Andhra Pradesh, Madhya Pradesh and Bihar. By 1983-84, the debt servicing burden of Central loans has come down in all the three groups of States and stands around 60 per cent with only marginal variations among the three groups. Thus the pattern observed in respect of the servicing of the Central loans is the same as observed in case of total debt servicing.

The debt servicing burden of the States in relation to their expenditure is presented in Tables 8.6 and 8.7 for the years 1973-74 and 1983-84 respectively. In the year 1973-74, interest payments constituted 9.45 per cent of revenue expenditure and repayments 38.52 per cent of the capital expenditure of the 14 major States. Total debt servicing amounted to 18.27 per cent of the total revenue and capital expenditures of the 14 major States. Interest payments and repayments as percentage of revenue and capital expenditures respectively were relatively higher in Group-B States and 'C' states as compared to Group-A States. Between Group-B and Group-C States, the percentage was marginally higher in the former. The burden of interest payments as well as repayments had shown a significant fall by 1983-84. The overall debt servicing amounted to 12.28 per cent of the total expenditure as compared to 18.27 per cent in 1973-74. No major variations are noticed in the debt burden of the three groups of States with the percentage of debt servicing to total expenditure oscillating around 12 per cent in all the three groups.

The analysis of debt servicing burden of States reveals that the burden has come down significantly in all the three groups of States between 1973-74 and 1983-84 while in 1973-74, debt servicing in relation to gross loans was unfavourable to Group-C States, it has become favourable to them in 1983-84. Debt servicing in terms of the total expenditure, which was not favourable to Group-B and Group-C States, has come on par with Group-A States. The significant

TABLE 8.6 : Debt Burden as percentage of Total Expenditure During the Year 1973-74 (Accounts)

States	Interest payments	Revenue expenditure	Interest payments as % of Rev. Expr.	Repayment of Loans	Capital expenditure	Repayment of Loans as % capital Expdr.	Debt servicing (2+5)	Total expenditure (3+6)	Debt servicing as % Total Expdr.
1	2	3	4	5	6	7	8	9	10
Group 'A' States:	**10667**	**153790**	**6.94**	**17867**	**59643**	**29.96**	**28534**	**213433**	**13.37**
1. Punjab	1782	22470	7.93	1738	8419	20.64	3520	30889	11.40
2. Haryana	1308	12882	10.15	2221	10291	21.58	3529	23173	15.23
3. Maharastra	5108	84770	6.03	10067	27870	36.12	15175	112640	13.47
4. Gujarat	2469	33668	7.33	3841	13063	29.40	6310	46731	13.50
Group 'B' States:	**18524**	**175125**	**10.58**	**35213**	**77384**	**45.50**	**53737**	**252509**	**21.28**
5. West Bengal	4331	38253	11.32	9748	20636	47.24	14079	58889	23.91
6. Karnataka	3110	35983	8.64	3696	19572	44.43	6806	55555	12.25
7. Kerala	2413	23737	10.17	4393	9858	44.56	6806	33595	20.26
8. Tamil Nadu	3769	47263	7.97	5179	13289	38.97	8948	60552	14.78
9. Rajasthan	4901	29889	16.40	7197	14029	51.30	12098	43918	27.55
Group 'C' States	**20252**	**194522**	**10.41**	**36435**	**99994**	**36.44**	**56687**	**294516**	**19.25**
10. Andhra Pradesh	4524	41595	10.88	7763	14679	52.89	12287	56274	21.83
11. Orissa	2887	21247	13.59	3981	8623	46.17	6868	29870	22.99
12. Madhya Pradesh	3028	33439	9.05	5706	16049	35.55	8734	49488	17.65
13. Uttar Pradesh	5658	63635	8.89	10308	40161	25.67	15966	103796	15.38
14. Bihar	4155	34606	12.01	8677	20482	42.36	12832	55088	23.29
Total 14 States	**49443**	**523437**	**9.45**	**89515**	**237021**	**37.77**	**138958**	**760458**	**18.27**
Special Category States	**5724**	**43499**	**13.16**	**7244**	**18808**	**38.52**	**12968**	**62307**	**20.81**
All States	**55167**	**566936**	**9.73**	**96759**	**255829**	**37.82**	**151926**	**822765**	**18.47**

TABLE 8.7 : Debt Burden As Percentage Of Total Expenditure During The Year 1983-84 (Accounts)

(Rs. Lakhs)

States	Interest payments	Revenue expenditure	Interest payments as % of Rev. Expr.	Repayments of Loans	Capital expenditure	Repayment of Loans as % capital Expdr.	Debt servicing (2+5)	Total expenditure (3+6)	Debt servicing as % Total Expdtr.
1	2	3	4	5	6	7	8	9	10
Group 'A' States	**46388**	**604993**	**7.67**	**60945**	**276678**	**22.03**	**107333**	**881671**	**12.17**
1. Punjab	8961	81986	10.93	24592	61440	40.03	33553	143426	23.39
2. Haryana	5917	62274	9.50	10533	33754	31.21	16450	96028	17.13
3. Maharastra	19779	318122	6.22	17194	106275	16.18	36973	424397	8.71
4. Gujarat	11731	142611	8.23	8626	75209	11.47	20357	217820	9.35
Group 'B' States	**62759**	**715756**	**8.77**	**61998**	**268410**	**23.10**	**124757**	**984166**	**12.68**
5. West Bengal	18434	173930	10.60	16164	44125	36.63	34598	218055	15.87
6. Karnataka	9802	141655	6.92	13816	58556	23.59	23618	200211	11.80
7. Tamil Nadu	12723	191080	6.66	15011	84130	17.84	27734	275210	10.08
8. Kerala	9149	99244	9.22	6655	32939	20.20	15804	132183	11.96
9. Rajasthan	12651	109847	11.52	10352	48660	21.27	23003	158507	14.51
Group 'C' States	**70939**	**864175**	**8.21**	**75618**	**352631**	**21.44**	**146557**	**1216806**	**12.04**
10. Andhra Pradesh	12302	204193	6.02	11263	54560	20.64	23565	258753	9.11
11. Orissa	9630	78271	12.30	7376	21414	34.44	17006	99685	17.06
12. Madhya Pradesh	8616	162372	5.31	10415	70020	14.87	19031	232392	8.19
13. Uttar Pradesh	25436	276116	9.21	31622	135496	23.34	57058	411612	13.86
14. Bihar	14955	143223	10.44	14942	71141	21.00	29897	214364	13.95
Total 14 States	**180086**	**2184924**	**8.24**	**198561**	**897719**	**22.12**	**378647**	**3082643**	**12.28**
Special Category States	**16268**	**195405**	**8.33**	**13022**	**75978**	**17.14**	**29290**	**271383**	**10.79**
All States	**196354**	**2380329**	**8.25**	**211583**	**973697**	**21.73**	**407937**	**3354026**	**12.16**

point that emerges from this analysis is the decline in the debt servicing burden of the States in relation to their gross borrowing and total expenditure inspite of a substantial increase in the outstanding public debt.

DEBT SERVICING BURDEN OF THE CENTRE

The debt servicing burden of the Centre is presented in Table 8.8.

TABLE 8.8 : Debt Burden of the Central Government

	Debt Burden Interest Payments	Repay-ments	Total	Revenue Expen-diture *	Capital Expen-diture	Total Expen-diture	Debt burden as % of total Expdtr.
1977-78	1521.34	553.74	2075.08	9362.29	6397.56	15759.85	13.17
1978-79	1828.97	653.21	2482.18	10947.62	8083.09	19030.71	13.04
1979-80	2209.86	704.54	2914.40	12033.64	7159.62	19193.26	15.18
1980-81	2656.60	661.31	3317.91	14543.61	9633.25	24176.86	13.72
1981-82	3194.68	707.20	3901.88	15867.73	10546.89	26414.62	14.77
1982-83	3937.61	803.22	4740.83	13945.63	14627.64	33973.27	13.95
1983-84	4795.46	798.13	5593.59	22890.24	15280.57	38170.81	14.65
1984-85	5974.50	974.68	6949.18	27881.25	18018.61	45899.86	15.14
1985-86 (R.E)	7400.00	1280.85	8680.85	33616.52	25913.53	59530.05	14.58
1986-87 (BE)	8750.00	1821.23	10571.23	36849.84	24363.51	61213.35	17.27

* Net of States' share of Central Taxes.

Source: Explanatory Memoranda to the Central Budgets.

The debt servicing burden of the Centre has increased from 13.17 per cent of the total expenditure in 1973-74 to 17.27 per cent in 1986-87. This is in sharp contrast to the decline noticed in the debt servicing burden of the States from 18.27 per cent of the total expenditure in 1973.74 to 12.28 per cent in 1983-84. The other major difference in the debt servicing of the States and the Centre is the very high burden of interest payments of the latter. While the interest payments of the Centre amounted to 21 per cent of its revenue expenditure in 1983-84, they amounted to only 8.24 per cent in respect of the 14 major States. Quite a contrary position obtains in respect of loan repayments. While the loan repayments of the Centre amount to only 5.2 per cent of its capital expenditure, in respect of States, repayments constitute as much as 22 per cent of their capital expenditure (1983-84).

The fall in the debt servicing burden of the States in relation to their gross borrowings and their total expenditure is mainly on account of the debt relief recommended by the successive Finance Commissions. The Seventh Finance Commission categorised the Central loans outstanding at the end of 1978-79 into (1) non-productive (2) semi-productive and (3) Productive loans and recommended the consolidation. The Commission recommended their recovery of semi-productive loans in 30 annual instalments and recovery of productive loans in 15 annual instalments. The Commission recommended write-off of non-productible loans amounting to Rs. 942.82 crores. The commission also recommended that loans given against collection of small savings should be treated as 'loans in perpetuity', with States requiring to pay only interest. Though the Central Government did not accept this recommendation, in order not to disturb the order of debt relief recommended by the Commission for the years 1979-84, it was decided that the States would not be required to make any repayment during 1979-84 on account of such small savings loans as were outstanding at the end of 1978-79. The total debt relief to the States on account of the recommendations of the Seventh Finance Commission amounted to Rs. 3075.99 crores, for the period 1979-84.

The Eighth Finance Commission recommended the consolidation into a signle loan of Pre-1979 loans, (earlier consolidated by the seventh commission) and their repayment in 25 annual instalments by some States and in 30 annual instalments by other States. For the loans secured by the States during 1979-84, the Commission recommended their consolidation into a single loan and their repayments in varying periods of 15, 20, 25 and 30 years by different States. On the basis of these recommendations, the debt relief to the States worked out to Rs, 2285.39 crores for the period 1984-89.

To sum up, it may be stated that though the outstanding debt of the States has increased considerably, the debt servicing burden of the States is not alarming. As bulk of the debt burden of the States is on account of Central Loans, the present pattern of Central assistance to States, i.e., 70 per cent loan and 30 per cent grant may warrant a review. Any upward revision in the grant component will go a long way in reducing the debt burden of the States.

NINE

STRUCTURE OF STATE REVENUES

Statewise data regarding components of State revenues, yield from additional resource mobilisation, etc. have been presented in Appendix 1X for a period of 24 years from 1961-62 to 1985-86.

It will be seen from Appendix 1X - 17 that the revenues of States (16 major states) have increased enormously during this period of about two and a half decades, from Rs. 1,128 crores in 1961-62 to Rs. 29,972 crores in 1985-86. During this period, total transfers from the Centre (share of taxes and grants) increased at a rate higher than that of States' own revenues. Transfers from the centre which constituted 33.95 per cent of the total revenues of states in 1961-62 increased to 37.63 per cent in 1985-86. Further, within these transfers, share of Central taxes has risen at a faster rate than grants. This is a healthy trend (first initiated by the Seventh Finance Commission) in the sense that statutory transfers from the Finance Commission gained a significant edge over semi-discretionery and discretionery transfers for Plan and non-Plan purposes.

The share of tax and non-tax revenues in the total revenues of States have recorded a slight fall in 1985-86 compared to 1961-62. Table 9.1 indicates per centage share of Central transfers and State's own revenues in total revenues in 1961-62 and 1985-86 with States (excluding Assam and Jammu & Kashmir) arranged in three groups according to per capita SDP as explained in Chapter 1.

TABLE 9.1 : Percentage Shares in Total Revenues

	States	Transfers from the Centre 1961-62	1985-86	State's Own revenues 1961-62	1985-86
Group 'A' States					
1.	Punjab	22.48	24.97	77.52	75.03
2.	Haryana	41.76	17.98	58.24	82.02
3.	Maharastra	22.64	21.76	77.36	78.24
4.	Gujarat	39.85	23.80	60.15	76.20
Group 'B' States					
5.	West Bengal	34.78	43.43	65.22	56.57
6.	Karnataka	28.68	26.53	71.32	73.47
7.	Tamil Nadu	29.22	29.19	70.78	70.81
8.	Kerala	34.41	34.27	65.59	65.73
9.	Rajasthan	36.88	39.62	63.12	60.38
Group 'C' States					
10.	Andhra Pradesh	33.40	31.30	66.60	68.70
11.	Orissa	41.75	60.07	58.25	39.93
12.	Madhya Pradesh	36.10	40.28	63.90	59.72
13.	Uttar Pradesh	34.32	53.29	65.68	46.71
14.	Bihar	41.77	56.05	58.23	43.95
	Total 14 States	**32.88**	**36.00**	**67.12**	**64.00**

As regards Central transfers, in 1961-62, 10 out of 14 States had shares above the average and 5 of them are out of groups A and B. In 1985-86 only 6 states out of 14 had shares higher than the average and 2 of them only are from group B and group A States are below the average. This shows that there has been a trend towards relatively backward States getting larger shares of Central transfers.

Regarding States' own revenues, in 1985-86 all the group A States and the group B States also with the exception of West Bengal and Rajasthan, have a higher per centage of own revenues than the average for 14 states. In the case of group C States. contribution of their own revenues to total revenues is much below the average except for Andhra Pradesh.

By and large there appears to be a direct correlation between per capita income and ability to raise own resources. Of course, there are many other factors which encourage or inhibit the growth of SDP, but the determination and capacity to raise own resources contribute substantially to channel resources to develomental activities and thus increase the SDP.

In Table 9.2 per centage shares of share in taxes and grants from the Centre in the total revenues of States for the years 1961-62 and 1985-86 are indicated by groups of States.

TABLE 9.2 : Percentage Shares in Total Revenues

	1961-62			1985-86		
States	Total trans-fers	Share in taxes	Grants	Total trans-fers	Share in taxes	Grants
Group 'A' States						
1. Punjab	22.48	9.76	12.72	24.97	9.25	15.72
2. Haryana	41.76	13.67	28.09	17.98	8.37	9.61
3. Maharastra	22.64	12.19	10.45	21.76	11.94	9.82
4. Gujarat	39.85	28.72	11.13	23.80	13.35	10.45
Group 'B' States						
5. West Bengal	34.78	16.81	17.97	43.43	24.96	18.47
6. Karnataka	28.68	11.39	17.29	26.53	15.53	11.00
7. Tamil Nadu	29.22	17.62	11.60	29.19	18.10	11.09
8. Kerala	34.41	18.50	15.91	34.27	20.28	13.99
9. Rajasthan	35.88	15.49	21.39	39.62	20.35	19.27
Group 'C' States						
10. Andhra Pradesh	33.40	17.07	16.33	31.30	18.31	12.99
11. Orissa	41.75	17.69	24.06	60.07	29.17	30.90
12. Madhya Pradesh	36.10	14.88	21.22	40.28	22.30	17.98
13. Uttar Pradesh	34.32	19.47	14.85	53.29	32.84	20.45
14. Bihar	41.77	20.49	21.28	56.05	35.75	20.30
Total 14 States	**32.88**	**16.69**	**17.26**	**36.00**	**20.87**	**16.76**

In 1961-62 the per centage share of grants in total revenues was higher than shares of taxes for the 14 States taken together as well as for a majority of the States. This position changed drastically in 1985-86 in favour of share of Central taxes. In 1961-62, 8 out of 14 States had per centage shares of Central taxes higher than the 14 States average and 4 of them are from groups A and B. However, in

1985-86 only five States had per centage shares higher than the average and only one i.e. West Bengal is from groups A and B. All the backward States excepting Andhra Pradesh have per centage shares much higher than the average. This brings out two facts; firstly, there has been a marked shift away from discretionaly and semidiscretionary grants towards statutory transfers; and secondly, relatively backward States are getting larger chunks of share in Central taxes than before because of the distributive criteria being lately adopted by the Finance Commissions.

TABLE 9.3 : Percentage Shares in Own Resources

	States	Tax Revenues 1961-62	Tax Revenues 1985-86	Non-tax Revenues 1961-62	Non-tax Revenues 1985-86
Group 'A' States					
1.	Punjab	55.24	77.26	44.76	22.74
2.	Haryana	50.12	67.04	49.88	32.96
3.	Maharashtra	78.56	71.35	21.44	28.65
4.	Gujarat	76.53	76.19	23.47	23.81
Group 'B' States					
5.	West Bengal	80.68	85.26	19.32	14.74
6.	Karnataka	74.02	72.45	25.98	27.55
7.	Tamil Nadu	68.52	87.16	31.48	12.84
8.	Kerala	79.13	84.03	20.87	15.97
9.	Rajasthan	75.28	66.06	24.72	33.94
Group 'C' States					
10.	Andhra Pradesh	80.48	73.85	19.52	26.15
11.	Orissa	61.88	69.63	38.12	30.37
12.	Madhya Pradesh	79.14	59.04	20.86	40.96
13.	Uttar Pradesh	64.94	72.63	35.06	27.37
14.	Bihar	77.12	60.61	22.88	39.39
	Total 14 States	**72.97**	**73.47**	**27.03**	**26.53**

Table 9.3, 9.4 indicate per centage shares of different taxes in State's own tax revenues for 1961-62 and 1985-86, grouped under 3 categories based on per capita SDP.

The importance of different taxes in State's own tax revenues shifted significantly between 1961-62 and 1985-86. Land Revenue which constituted 17.53 per cent of the States' own tax revenues in 1961-62, declined to 2.57 per cent only in 1985-86. State Excise and

TABLE 9.4 : Percentage Shares of Different Taxes in States' Own Tax Revenues

States	Land Revenue		Stamps and Registration		State Excise	
	1961-62	1985-86	1961-62	1985-86	1961-62	1985-86
Group 'A' States						
1. Punjab	8.66	0.48	14.40	9.26	18.90	23.68
2. Haryana	15.06	0.84	12.71	9.88	13.88	20.19
3. Mahrashtra	8.56	1.20	7.77	3.33	1.75	8.43
4. Gujarat	16.08	1.30	7.38	4.48	1.07	0.57
Group 'B' States						
5. West Bengal	11.59	9.75	7.85	4.93	13.01	8.62
6. Karnataka	10.14	0.84	4.70	5.41	6.47	17.73
7. Tamil Nadu	9.91	1.45	11.68	5.64	0.74	15.20
8. Kerala	6.45	0.97	7.06	7.18	13.35	15.79
9. Rajasthan	39.53	3.38	8.70	4.63	20.13	14.97
Group 'C' States						
10. Andhra Pradesh	22.01	4.01	5.13	4.29	18.99	26.79
11. Orissa	18.07	2.52	5.53	5.01	12.47	7.50
12. Madhya Praaesh	22.17	2.19	4.39	5.20	14.42	15.00
13. Uttar Pradesh	32.16	3.03	6.38	10.35	12.82	15.47
14. Bihar	25.42	4.25	10.69	5.75	17.61	8.08
Total 14 States	**17.38**	**2.58**	**7.70**	**5.69**	**10.74**	**14.07**

TABLE 9.4 (Contd.)

States	Sales Tax		Motor Vehicles Taxes		Entertainment Tax	
	1961-62	1985-86	1961-62	1985-86	1961-62	1985-8
Group 'A' States						
1. Punjab	27.96	47.85	3.54	10.76	2.73	-
2. Haryana	31.06	45.67	3.29	15.74	2.59	1.92
3. Maharashtra	48.54	62.82	8.12	8.15	3.91	4.73
4. Gujarat	47.89	61.47	11.75	10.06	3.36	3.99
Group 'B' States						
5. West Bengal	40.09	57.56	4.39	9.19	3.48	3.32
6. Karnataka	21.24	51.53	10.32	11.68	1.84	3.76
7. Tamil Nadu	47.55	65.88	15.72	6.87	5.10	3.74
8. Kerala	43.10	60.29	10.94	8.07	0.49	0.05
9. Rajasthan	21.04	57.31	5.01	14.03	1.46	1.98
Group 'C' States						
10. Andhra Pradesh	32.21	51.47	6.00	7.80	2.58	3.12
11. Orissa	30.04	51.78	7.69	10.76	1.12	2.04
12. Madhya Pradesh	20.35	51.32	5.33	15.56	2.07	2.95
13. Uttar Pradesh	19.82	53.86	5.22	10.11	2.62	4.76
14. Bihar	31.64	69.55	0.39	7.34	3.10	2.01
Total 14 States	**33.78**	**57.30**	**7.20**	**9.80**	**2.88**	**3.26**

Sales Tax together amounted to 44.38 per cent of tax revenues in 1961-62, which increased to 71.30 per cent in 1985-86. The shifts in Stamps and Registration, Motor Vehicles Tax and Entertainment Tax are more modest. It should however be noted that the importance of different taxes in the tax structure of States is not and cannot be uniform. Receipts from Sales Tax in 1985-86 ranged from 36.87 per cent of State tax revenues in Jammu and Kashmir to 69.55 per cent in Bihar. In the case of State Excise , the range is from 0.57 per cent in Gujarat to 26.79 per cent in Andhra pradesh. Receipts from Land Revenue are not significant except in West Bengal. Receipts from Motor Vehicles Tax ranged from 5.75 per cent in Assam to 28.03 per cent in Jammu & Kashmir.

Contribution of State Excise to tax revenues has substantially gone up. There has been a marked increase in States like Maharashtra and Tamil Nadu where Prohibition has been removed in the recent past only. Now Gujarat is the only State which is still continuing this policy. In nine States, the contribution of receipts from State Excise as a percentage of State tax revenues in 1985-86 is higher than the 14 States average.

Contribution of Sales Tax to States' own tax revenues increased from 33.78 per cent in 1961-62 to 57.30 per cent in 1985-86. In 1961-62 only 5 States, all from groups A and B had per centage contributions higher than the average. In 1985-86, seven out of fourteen States had higher per centage contributions and only one States, i.e., Bihar is from group C. This shows that even though all States have improved their positions, it is the mainly the advanced States that fared better, because the level of development of the economy has a direct bearing on receipts from Sales Tax.

The position is more or less similar to Sales Tax, under Motor Vehicles Tax. However, the backward States of Orissa, Madhya Pradesh, Uttar Pradesh and Bihar have done rather well in 1985-86 as compared to 1961-62 and to other States.

TEN

CENTRE-STATE FINANCIAL TRANSFERS AN OVERALL ASSESSMENT

This chapter reviews the flow of aggregate budgetary and non-budgetary resources from the Centre and Centre-controlled institutions to the States. While each element constituting the total financial transfers is discussed in detail in the preceding chapters, this chapter is devoted to a presentation of an overview of total financial transfers both in terms of relative magnitude and equity in their distribution among the States.

The need for transfer of resources from the Centre to the States arose because of the imbalance in access to resources and responsibilities. While the States are saddled with more responsibilities, their financial powers are very limited. In recognition of this, the Constitution provides enabling provisions for transfer of resources from the Centre to the States in accordance with the awards of the Finance Commission to be appointed every five years. The Constitution also provides for transfer of resources to the States in the form of grants and loans for any public purpose. Over the years, other channels though not specifically provided for in the Constitution have become important in the transfer of resources to the States. With the initiation of planning process in India, Planning Commission has become an important channel regulating the flow of Central assistance for States' plans. Besides the Finance Commission and Planning Commission, sizeable transfers are being effected by the Central Ministries. Besides these budgetary transfers, there are a number of non-budgetary flows of resources effected by institutions which are directly under the control of the Central Government. These flows are in the form of assistance rendered by term-lending financial institutions, advances by commercial banks and Central Government investments in the States. Because of their magnitude, these non-budgetary flows have an important bearing on the economy of the States. Any review of Centre-State financial relations will not be complete, if the non-budgetary transfers are not taken into account.

MAGNITUDE OF TRANSFERS

As discussed in Chapter 6, budgetary transfers consist of transfers effected through Finance Commission, Planning Commission and the Ministry of Finance. The total transfers have increased from Rs. 1431 crore during the First Plan period to Rs. 59,631 crores during the period 1979-84. It is evident from Table 2.1 of Chapter 2 that over the years the transfers from the Planning Commission and Finance Commission have tended to become more or less equal. The share of discretionary transfers has increased from 7.3 per cent during 1951-56 to 20.5 per cent during 1979-84. The growth in the proportion of discretionary transfers has been a matter of concern to the States. The growth in the loans against small savings collections and loans to the States to cover their deficits have been two main contributory factors for the substantial increase in the share of discretionary transfers in the total transfers.

The magnitude of the budgetary transfers in absolute terms does not indicate a true picture unless the transfers are related to the budgetary resources of the Centre and the States. Such an analysis has been done by George and Gulati in their Study of Centre-State financial transfers covering the period 1951-84 (Centre-State Resource Transfers, 1951-84, Economic and Political Weekly, February 16, 1985). For the purpose of this Chapter, no fresh analysis has been attempted to study the financial flows in relation to the budgetary resources, instead the results of analysis presented in George and Gulati study have been made use of.

The George and Gulati study has clearly brought out the pre-eminent position of the Centre in the combined revenue and capital receipts of the Centre and the States. The table giving the per centage share of the States in the combined revenue and capital receipts is reproduced in this chapter as Table 10.1.

TABLE 10.1 : Share of States in the Combined Resources of the Centre and States 1951-84

Plan Periods (figure in percentage)

	I	II	III	Annual Plans	IV	V	VI
1. Own revenue account receipts of the States as percentage of the combined revenue accounts receipts of Centre and States	44	42	33	33	34	35	37
2. Own capital account receipts of the States as percentage of combined capital accounts receipts	22	21	19	17	21	21	20
3. States' total receipts as percentage of the aggregate resources (1+2)	38	34	28	30	30	31	32
4. States' total revenue account receipts (own plus transfers from the Centre) to the combined revenue account receipts of Centre and States	56	57	47	51	54	54	58
5. States' total capital account receipts as percentage of the combined capital account receipts of Centre and States	55	42	45	38	42	36	37
6. States' total revenue and capital account receipts as percentage of combined revenue and							

capital account receipts of Centre and States	56	51	47	46	50	47	52

Notes: 1. The figures in this and subsequent tables are given for periods starting from the First Plan including the three years of Annual Plans (1966-69). The time span covered by the Vth and VIth Plans are slightly different so as to conform to the periods covered by the Sixth and the Seventh Finance Commissions.

Fifth Plan 1974-75 to 1978-79
Sixth Plan 1979-80 to 1983-84

2. Figures in Rows 1 and 3 are exclusive of deficits of the States to Centre whereas those in Rows 4 to 6 are inclusive of deficits.

3. States' total revenue/capital account receipts referred to in Rows 4, 5 and 6 are taken to include gross Central Transfers. Source: George K.K., and Gulati, I.S., "Centre States Resource Transfers, 1951-84", *Economic and Political Weekly,* Vol. XX No. 7, February 16, 1985.

The own revenue receipts of the States which constituted 44 per cent of the combined revenue account receipts of the Centre and the States during the First Plan Period have come down to 37 per cent during the Sixth Plan period. The own capital receipts of the States as a percentage of combined capital receipts have come down from 22 to 20 per cent during the same period. If we take the States' own revenue and capital receipts, their share in the total combined revenue and capital receipts has come down from 38 per cent during the First Plan Period to 32 per cent during the Sixth Plan Period. The picture becomes balanced if we take into account the transfers from the Centre to the States. After accounting for the transfers from the Centre, the share of the States in the combined revenue and capital receipts works out to 52 per cent during the Sixth Plan period. While there was a marginal increase in the share of the States in the combined revenue receipts from 56 per cent during the First Plan to 58 per cent during the Sixth Plan, there was a substantial fall in the share of the States in the combined capital receipts from 55 per cent to 37 per cent.

This study has also brought out that the revenue account transfers to the States have increased from 23 per cent of the gross revenue receipts of the Centre during the First Plan to 35.9 per cent during the Sixth Plan. Loans to the States as percentage of Centre's capital receipts have shown a substantial decline from 61.5 per cent to 27.1 per cent during the same period. The total transfers to the States as a percentage of Centre's gross revenue and capital receipts have shown a decline from 36.4 per cent during the First Plan period to 32.6 per cent during the Sixth Plan. This clearly brings out that though there has been a substantial increase in the transfers to the States, the percentage of total transfers to the gross revenue and capital receipts of the Centre has registered a decline. The only redeeming feature for the States is that the decline in their share is confined to capital transfers.

Dependence of States on Central Transfers (1951-84)

	Plan Periods						
	I	II	III	Annual Plans	IV	V	VI
1. Revenue transfers as % of revenue expenditure of States	22.4	28.2	33.4	35.1	39.5	40.4	41.1
2. Loan Transfers as % of Capital Expenditure of States	71.9	58.7	64.5	63.2	63.2	83.1	74.6
3. Aggregate transfers as percentage of aggregate expenditure of States	37.8	39.8	45.7	45.2	47.4	42.1	41.6

Source: K.K. George and I.S. Gulati 'Centre-State Resource Transfers, 1951-84' **Economic and Political Weekly**, Vol. XX No. 7, February 16, 1985.

Another way of assessing the budgetary transfers from the Centre to the States is to relate them to the revenue and capital expenditures of the States. The dependence of the States on Central transfers is presented below:

The revenue transfers from the Centre as percentage of total revenue expenditure of the States has increased from 22.4 per cent during the First Plan to 41.1 per cent during the Sixth Plan. There is a marginal increase in the loan transfers from the Centre as percentage of capital expenditure of the States. Both these indicators reveal the increasing dependence of the States on the Centre for financing their expenditure.

EQUITY IN THE DISTRIBUTION OF CENTRAL TRANSFERS

The equity in the distribution of Finance Commission, Planning Commission and discretionary transfers for each plan period has already been discussed in detail in the relevant chapters. The distribution of per capita cumulative Central assistance for the period 1957-85, Finance Commission transfers for the period 1957-84 and discretionary transfers for the period 1974-85 is presented in Table 10.2.

As the State-wise transfers recommended by the First Finance Commission are not readily available, the analysis of per capita Finance Commission transfers is restricted to the period 1957-84. For lack of State-wise details, the analysis of discretionary transfers is restricted to the period 1974-85. While the distribution of per capita Central assistance for the period 1951-85 is found to be equitable, the distribution of per capita Finance Commission transfers for the period 1957-84 and per capita discretionary transfers for the period 1974-85 are found to be inequitable. In the case of per capita Finance Commission transfers, the index is marginally higher in respect of middle income States than the low-income States, but the distribution is unfavourable to high income States as compared to both middle income and low income States (Index 96.56). Thus the transfers under the recommendations of the Finance Commission can be treated as only marginally inequitable as between middle income (Group-B) and low income States (Group-C). The distribution of discretionary transfers is found to be highly inequitable with Group-C States managing to register an index of only 87.14 as against the Group-A States' index of 132.38. The Group-B States managed to remain a little below the average with an index of 99.63. The planning Commission and Finance Commission transfers taken together are found to be equitable.

George and Gulati have also analysed the equity in the distribution of Finance Commission, Planning Commission and discretionary transfers. The results of their study are presented in Appendix Table X.4. The results of George and Gulati study are not strictly comparable with our analysis because of the differences in the period covered as well as differences in the classification of States. The George and Gulati study shows unfavourable distribution of per capita cumulative Finance Commission and Planning Commission transfers to Group-C States. In respect of discretionary transfers, the results of George and Gulati are similar to our study.

TABLE 10.2 : Cumulative Budgetary Transfers to States

STATES	Percapita Transfers				Indices of Percapita			
	Central Assist-ance 1951-85 57-84	Finance Commn. trans-fers	Total trans-fers (2+3) 1974-75 to 1984-85	Discre-tionary trans-fers	Central Assist-ance 1951-85 1957-84	Finance Commn. trans-fers	Total trans-fers (6+7) 1974-75 to 1984-85	Discre-tionary trans-fers
1	2	3	4	5	6	7	8	9
Group 'A' States	**94.48**	**96.56**	**95.60**	**279.98**	**425.56**	**508.19**	**933.75**	**132.38**
1. Punjab	136.52	96.28	114.83	187.72	614.90	506.76	1121.66	88.76
2. Haryana	104.16	77.36	89.72	261.74	469.14	407.19	876.33	123.76
3. Maharastra	82.48	99.80	91.81	298.34	371.52	525.31	896.83	141.07
4. Gujarat	92.21	97.96	95.31	298.53	415.32	515.56	930.88	141.16
Group 'B' States	**97.31**	**108.74**	**103.47**	**210.70**	**438.29**	**572.30**	**1010.59**	**99.63**
5. West Bengal	80.92	110.81	97.03	346.60	364.48	583.22	947.70	163.88
6. Karnataka	92.82	98.39	95.82	141.33	418.08	517.84	935.92	66.83
7. Tamil Nadu	89.36	106.1	98.38	134.77	402.48	558.40	960.88	63.72
8. Kerala	114.18	126.9	121.00	104.84	514.29	667.89	1182.18	49.57
9. Rajasthan	126.92	106.85	116.10	255.25	571.67	562.36	1134.03	120.69
Group 'C' States	**103.95**	**107.96**	**106.11**	**184.29**	**468.20**	**568.20**	**1036.40**	**87.14**
10. Andhra Pradesh	107.38	108.81	108.15	195.48	483.66	572.70	1056.36	92.43
11. Orissa	144.63	153.86	149.61	268.87	651.45	809.77	1461.22	127.13
12. Madhya Pradesh	104.20	99.74	101.80	122.41	469.32	524.95	994.27	57.88
13. Uttar Pradesh	96.98	101.97	99.67	186.59	436.81	536.71	973.52	88.23
14. Bihar	95.24	105.60	100.82	186.32	428.96	555.78	984.74	88.10
Total 14 States	**100.00**	**100.00**	**100.00**	**211.49**	**450.41**	**526.32**	**976.73**	**100.00**
Special Category States	**408.77**	**222.09**	**308.17**	**336.09**	**1841.12**	**1168.89**	**3010.01**	**158.92**
All States	**116.50**	**112.15**	**114.16**	**218.15**	**524.73**	**590.27**	**1115.00**	**103.15**

EQUITY IN NON-BUDGETARY TRANSFERS

Three elements of the non-budgetary transfers, viz., advances by commercial banks, disbursements by all-India financial institutions, distribution of Central Government's investments in States have been considered for examining the question of equity. The distribution of advances by commercial banks and disbursements by financial institutions has all along remained favourable to Group-A States. Even in terms of Credit-Deposit ratio of commercial banks, the low income states have not fared any better. The cumulative assistance rendered by financial institutions to Group-A States is nearly 4 times that rendered to Group-C States in per capita terms. The distribution of cumulative investments by Central Government undertakings in the States which remained favourable to Group-C States till the end of the Fourth Plan period, became unfavourable to these States by the end of March, 1984.

DISTRIBUTION OF PLAN OUTLAYS

The distribution of per capita plan outlays has remained favourable to Group-A in every plan period. As between Group-B and Group-C States the distribution has remained favourable to Group-B in all the plan periods except in respect of the approved plan outlays for the Seventh Plan period. The analysis presented in Chapter 2 reveals that the inequity in the distribution of plan outlays is mainly on account of the capacity of the richer states in mobilising more resources of their own.

The broad reveiw of the Centre-State financial flows presented above reveals that these flows continue to remain inequitous. One welcome change in this trend is the gradual reduction in the degree of inequity over the various plan periods. While this development, however slow it may be, holds out some hope for the poorer states, some other developments have had the effect of containing the already truncated financial powers of the States. One such development is the gradual erosion in the share of the States in market borrowings. The Long Term Fiscal Policy of the Government of India aims at reducing the market borrowings from 2.1 per cent of GDP during 1980-85 to 1.6 per cent of GDP during the Seventh Plan. Any reduction in the market borrowings with reference to GDP will affect the States as they share the market borrowings with the Centre. While the Centre intends to make good this loss by allowing public undertakings to float bonds, this option is not available to the States. The new National Deposit Scheme with its attractive provisions may wean away the saving public from small savings, etc. As States get loans against the collection of small savings, any diversion from small savings will adversely affect them. Viewed in the context of the tardiness shown by the Centre in implementing the agreement reached with the States in respect of levy of additional excise duties in lieu of sales tax, the proposal to merge the additional duties with basic excise duties, cannot be viewed withour suspicion. The Long Term Fiscal Policy proposed to refer the merger of additional excise with basic rates of excise to the next Finance Commissions. The trends in the indirect taxes of the Centre, viz., reduction in the proportion of excise duties and increase in the proposition of customs have been to the disadvantage of the States. Such developments curtailing the powers of the States need to be contained in the interest of harmony in Centre-State relations.

PART TWO

INFORMATION BASE

TABLE-I.1 : POPULATION OF STATES 1981 CENSUS

	Total Population (lakhs)		Inter-Se-percentages		Ranking according to 1981 population	Decennial growth of population 1971-81(%)	Ranking according to population growth
	1971	1981	1971	1981			
1.Andhra Pradesh	435.03	535.50	7.94	7.82	5	23.10	19
2.Assam	146.25	198.97*	2.67	2.90	13	36.05	3
3.Bihar	563.53	699.15	10.28	10.20	2	24.06	14
4.Gujarat	266.98	340.86	4.87	4.97	10	27.67	10
5.Haryana	100.37	129.23	1.83	1.89	15	28.75	9
6.Himachal Pradesh	34.60	42.81	0.63	0.62	17	23.71	17
7.Jammu & Kashmir	46.17	59.87	0.84	0.87	16	29.69	8
8.Karnataka	292.99	371.36	5.34	5.42	8	26.75	11
9.Kerala	213.47	254.54	3.89	3.71	12	19.24	21
10.Madhya Pradesh	416.54	521.79	7.60	7.62	6	25.27	13
11.Maharashtra	504.12	627.84	9.20	9.16	3	24.54	15
12.Manipur	10.73	14.21	0.20	0.21	19	32.46	5
13.Meghalaya	10.12	13.36	0.18	0.19	20	32.04	6
14.Nagaland	5.16	7.75	0.09	0.11	21	50.05	2
15.Orissa	219.45	263.70	4.00	3.85	11	20.17	20
16.Punjab	135.51	167.89	2.47	2.45	14	23.89	16
17.Rajasthan	257.66	342.62	4.70	5.00	9	32.97	4
18.Sikkim	2.10	3.16	0.04	0.05	22	50.77	1
19.Tamil Nadu	411.99	484.08	7.52	7.06	7	17.50	22
20.Tripura	15.56	20.53	0.28	0.30	18	31.92	7
21.Uttar Pradesh	883.41	1108.62	16.12	16.18	1	25.49	12
22.West Bengal	443.12	545.81	8.08	7.97	4	23.17	18
TOTAL:	5414.86	6753.64	98.78	98.57		24.72	
Union Territories	66.74	98.21	1.22	1.43		47.15	
ALL-INDIA	5481.60	6851.85	100.00	100.00		25.00	

* Estimated as no census was conducted in Assam.

Source: 1. Census of India, 1981 Series 1, India paper 3 of 1981.

2. Census of India, 1981 Sereis 2, India paper 1 of 1982.

TABLE-I-2 : RURAL AND URBAN POPULATION (In Lakhs)

	1971 Census			1981 Census			Decennial growth of urban population 1971-81	Ranking of States on the basis of percentage of urban
	Rural population	Urban population total population	Urban population as % to	Rural population total population	Urban population	Urban population as % to population 1981		
1. Andhra Pradesh	351.00	84.03	19.32	410.62	124.88	23.32	48.61	8
2. Assam	132.98	13.27	9.98	178.50	20.47	10.29	54.26	21
3. Bihar	507.19	56.34	10.00	611.96	87.19	12.47	54.76	18
4. Gujarat	192.01	74.97	28.08	234.84	106.02	31.10	41.42	3
5. Haryana	82.64	17.73	17.66	100.96	28.27	21.88	59.45	9
6. Himachal Pradesh	32.18	2.42	6.99	39.55	3.26	7.62	34.71	22
7. Jammu & Kashmir	37.59	8.58	18.58	47.27	12.60	21.05	46.85	11
8. Karnataka	221.77	71.22	24.31	264.06	107.30	28.89	50.66	4
9. Kerala	178.81	34.66	16.24	206.83	47.71	18.74	37.65	13
10. Madhya Pradesh	348.69	67.85	16.29	415.93	105.86	20.29	56.02	10
11. Maharashtra	347.01	157.11	31.17	407.90	219.94	35.03	39.99	1
12. Manipur	9.31	1.41	13.23	10.46	3.75	26.39	165.96	7
13. Meghalaya	8.65	1.47	14.53	10.95	2.41	18.04	63.94	14
14. Nagaland	4.65	0.51	9.88	6.55	1.20	15.48	135.29	17
15. Orissa	200.99	18.45	8.41	232.60	31.10	11.79	68.56	19
16. Punjab	103.35	32.16	23.73	121.41	46.48	27.69	44.53	5
17. Rajasthan	212.22	45.44	17.64	270.51	72.11	21.05	58.69	12
18. Sikkim	1.90	0.20	9.52	2.65	0.51	16.14	155.00	16
19. Tamil Nadu	287.34	124.65	30.26	324.56	159.52	32.95	27.97	2
20. Tripura	13.94	1.62	10.41	18.27	2.26	11.01	39.51	20
21. Uttar Pradesh	759.53	123.89	14.02	909.63	198.99	17.95	60.62	15
22. West Bengal	333.45	109.67	24.75	401.34	144.47	26.47	31.73	6
TOTAL all States:	4367.78	1047.08	19.34	5227.35	1526.29	22.60	45.77	
Union Territories	22.88	43,86	65.72	27.23	70.98	72.27	61.83	
ALL - INDIA:	4390.66	1090.94	19.90	5254.58	1597.27	23.31	46.53	

TABLE-I.3 : AREA AND DENSITY OF POPULATION 1981

	Area in lakh sq. Km.	Density of population per Sq.Km.		Percentage to all India Area	Literates as % of total population	
	1981	1971	1981		1971	1981
1. Andhra Pradesh	2.77	157	195	8.42	24.57	29.72
2. Assam	0.79	150*	254	2.40	28.81	N.A
3. Bihar	1.74	324	402	5.29	19.94	26.01
4. Gujarat	1.96	136	174	5.96	35.79	43.75
5. Haryana	0.44	227	292	1.34	26.89	35.84
6. Himachal Pradesh	0.56	62	77	1.70	31.96	41.94
7. Jammu & Kashmir	2.22	N.A	59	6.75	-	N.A
8. Karnataka	1.92	153	194	5.84	31.52	38.41
9. Kerala	0.39	549	,55	..19	60.42	69.17
10. Madhya Pradesh	4.43	94	118	13.47	22.14	27.82
11. Maharashtra	3.08	164	204	9.37	39.18	47.02
12. Manipur	0.22	48	64	0.67	32.91	41.52
13. Meghalaya	0.22	45	60	0.67	29.49	33.35
14. Nagaland	0.17	31	47	0.52	27.40	41.99
15. Orissa	1.56	141	169	4.74	26.18	34.12
16. Punjab	0.50	269	333	1.52	33.67	40.74
17. Rajasthan	3.42	75	100	10.40	19.07	24.05
18. Sikkim	0.07	30	45	0.21	17.74	33.92
19. Tamil Nadu	1.30	317	372	3.95	39.46	45.78
20. Tripura	0.10	128	196	0.30	30.98	41.78
21. Uttar Pradesh	2.94	300	377	8.94	21.70	27.40
22. West Bengal	0.88	504	615	2.68	33.20	40.88
TOTAL:	31.68	171**	213	96.35		35.81
UNION TERRI·ORIES		1.20	56	82	3.65	56.93
ALL INDIA	32.88	177**	220	100.00		36.12

Source : Government of India, Ministry of Finance, 'Statistical Statements of Finances, and Plans of States and Union Territories - 1985' NEW DELHI

TABLE-I.4 : SCHEDULED CASTE AND SCHEDULED TRIBE POPULATION 1981 CENSUS

(In Lakhs)

	Scheduled Castes			Scheduled Tribes		
	Population	Percentage to total population of the States	Percentage to total SC population of the country	Population	Percentage to total population of the States	Percentage to total ST population of the country
1. Andhra Pradesh	79.6	14.9	7.6	31.8	5.9	6.2
2. Assam	-	-	-	-	-	-
3. Bihar	101.4	14.5	9.7	58.1	8.3	11.2
4. Gujarat	24.4	7.2	2.3	48.5	14.2	9.4
5. Haryana	24.6	19.1	2.4	-	-	-
6. Himachal Pradesh	10.5	24.6	1.0	2.0	4.6	0.4
7. Jammu & Kashmir	5.0	8.3	0.5	-	-	-
8. Karnataka	56.0	15.1	5.3	18.3	4.9	3.5
9. Kerala	25.5	10.0	2.4	2.6	1.0	0.5
10. Madhya Pradesh	73.6	14.1	7.0	119.9	23.0	23.2
11. Maharashtra	44.8	7.1	4.3	57.7	9.2	11.2
12. Manipur	0.2	1.2	Neg	3.9	27.3	0.8
13. Meghalaya	Neg	Neg	Neg	10.8	80.6	2.1
14. Nagaland	-	-	-	6.5	84.0	1.3
15. Orissa	38.7	14.7	3.7	59.2	22.4	11.4
16. Punjab	45.1	26.9	4.3	-	-	-
17. Rajasthan	58.4	17.0	5.6	41.8	12.2	8.1
18. Sikkim	0.2	5.8	Neg	0.7	23.3	0.1
19. Tamil Nadu	88.8	18.3	8.5	5.2	1.1	1.0
20. Tripura	3.1	15.1	0.3	5.8	28.4	1.1
21. Uttar Pradesh	234.5	21.2	22.4	2.3	0.2	0.5
22. West Bengal	120.0	22.0	11.5	30.7	5.6	5.9
Total States	1034.4	15.5	98.8	505.8	7.5	97.9
Union Territories	13.1	13.3	1.2	10.5	10.7	2.1
Grand Total+	1047.5	15.7	100.0	516.3	7.8	100.0

(+) Excluding Assam.

TABLE I.5 : ESTIMATED MID-YEAR POPULATION

(In Lakhs)

States	1971 Census	1972	1973	1974	1975	1976	1977	1978	1979	1980	1981 Census	1982	1983	1984
1. Andhra Pradesh	435	444	453	463	473	482	492	503	513	524	535	546	558	569
2. Assam	146	151	155	160	165	170	176	181	187	193	199	205	212	218
3. Bihar	564	576	589	602	615	628	642	655	670	684	699	714	730	746
4. Gujarat	267	274	280	287	294	302	309	317	325	333	341	349	358	367
5. Haryana	100	103	105	108	111	114	117	120	123	126	129	132	136	139
6. Himachal Pradesh	35	36	36	37	38	39	40	40	41	42	43	44	45	46
7. Jammu & Kashmir	46	47	49	50	51	53	54	55	57	58	60	62	63	65
8. Karnataka	293	300	307	315	322	330	338	346	354	362	371	380	389	398
9. Kerala	213	217	221	225	229	233	237	242	246	250	255	259	264	269
10. Madhya Pradesh	417	427	436	446	456	467	477	488	499	511	522	534	547	559
11. Maharashtra	504	515	527	538	550	562	575	588	601	614	628	642	656	671
12. Manipur	11	11	12	12	12	13	13	13	14	14	14	15	15	16
13. Meghalaya	10	10	11	11	11	12	12	12	12	13	13	14	14	14
14. Nagaland	5	5	5	6	6	6	6	7	7	7	8	8	8	8
15. Orissa	219	223	227	232	236	241	245	250	254	259	264	269	274	279
16. Punjab	136	139	142	145	148	151	154	158	161	164	168	172	175	179
17. Rajasthan	258	265	273	281	289	298	306	315	324	333	343	353	363	374
18. Sikkim	2	2	2	2	2	2	3	3	3	3	3	3	3	3
19. Tamil Nadu	412	419	425	432	439	446	454	461	469	476	484	492	500	508
20. Tripura	16	16	17	17	18	18	19	19	20	21	21	22	22	23
21. Uttar Pradesh	883	903	924	946	967	990	1,013	1,036	1,060	1,084	1,109	1,135	1,161	1,188
22. West Bengal	443	452	462	472	482	492	502	513	524	535	546	557	569	581
Total	**5,414**	**5,535**	**5,658**	**5,787**	**5,914**	**6,049**	**6,184**	**6,323**	**6,455**	**6,608**	**6,753**	**6,907**	**7,062**	**7,220**
Union Territories	*68*	*70*	*72*	*75*	*80*	*82*	*85*	*87*	*90*	*94*	*99*	*105*	*107*	*110*
Grand Total	**5,482**	**5,605**	**5,730**	**5,862**	**5,994**	**6,131**	**6,269**	**6,410**	**6,545**	**6,702**	**6,852**	**7,012**	**7,169**	**7,330**

Note : Projected on the basis of compund annual rate of growth between 1971-81 by the Centre for Monitoring Indian Economy (CMIE)

Source: 'Basic Statistics Relating to Indian Economy Vol.2-States September 1983' CMIE, Bombay.

TABLE I.6 : STATEWISE ESTIMATES OF TOTAL NET DOMESTIC PRODUCT

(At Current Prices) (Rs. Crores)

States	1960-61	1965-66	1970-71	1971-72	1972-73	1973-74	1974-75	1975-76
1. Andhra Pradesh	982.2	1,530.8	2,522.8	2,758.0	2,947.9	3,926.0	4,722.2	4,218.0
2. Assam	336.0	493.7	771.4	813.9	882.6	1,023.1	1,337.0	1,314.4
3. Bihar	993.0	1,676.0	2,245.4	2,362.6	2,783.7	3,400.1	4,139.5	4,062.2
4. Gujarat	738.2	1,152.4	2,189.2	2,242.0	2,108.6	3,169.1	3,017.5	3,693.1
5. Haryana	245.0	389.0	868.9	976.7	1,059.7	1,303.8	1,429.0	1,616.4
6. Himachal Pradesh	47.8	165.1	232.4	250.5	274.8	341.6	390.8	410.5
7. Jammu & Kashmir	94.8	127.1	249.6	274.9	292.5	352.0	418.5	480.0
8. Karnataka	691.6	1,163.7	1,984.5	2,066.1	2,151.8	3,002.0	3,390.4	3,225.4
9. Kerala	432.2	710.7	1,198.2	1,225.5	1,393.7	1,740.6	1,990.8	2,155.1
10. Madhya Pradesh	832.3	1,107.8	1,992.1	2,253.8	2,491.3	3,245.2	3,795.9	3,631.8
11. Maharashtra	1,597.4	2,354.5	3,875.5	4,094.4	4,342.2	5,757.9	7,359.3	7,676.8
12. Manipur	11.9	24.2	39.8	48.5	61.6	76.4	92.3	94.6
13. Orissa	374.1	640.1	1,046.7	1,066.0	1,306.9	1,617.7	1,664.1	1,735.9
14. Punjab	403.8	683.6	1,436.2	1,538.8	1,736.8	2,155.7	2,379.6	2,598.9
15. Rajasthan	559.4	825.3	1,578.8	1,464.1	1,605.4	2,285.1	2,413.3	2,506.0
16. Tamil Nadu	1,111.8	1,494.2	2,371.1	2,696.2	2,839.0	3,432.3	3,638.7	3,727.4
17. Tripura	28.4	46.4	77.9	88.6	85.8	110.3	138.2	146.4
18. Uttar Pradesh	1,843.1	2,985.7	4,256.5	4,434.1	5,490.6	6,220.3	7,154.2	7,005.1
19. West Bengal	1,339.5	2,070.2	3,168.1	3,490.0	3,571.7	4,366.3	5,150.6	5,395.3

TABLE I.6 : STATEWISE ESTIMATES OF NET DOMESTIC PRODUCT AT PRODUCT AT CURRENT PRICES (Contd.)

(At Current Prices) (Rs. Crores)

States	1976-77	1977-78	1978-79	1979-80	1980-81	1981-82	1982-83	1983-84(Q)
1. Andhra Pradesh	4275.6	4994.0	5511.1	6127.6	7209.3	8997.9	9463.0	11060.9
2. Assam	1514.2	1666.2	1856.1	2022.8	2358.6	2871.0	3342.0	3813.3
3. Bihar	4364.1	4730.6	5104.6	5398.9	6427.1	7126.0	7424.7	8824.8
4. Gujarat	4282.3	4756.7	4974.2	5689.7	6531.9	7720.2	8360.1	10118.7
5. Haryana	1902.2	2095.2	2300.6	2422.7	2981.8	3408.9	3834.4	4319.7
6. Himachal Pradesh	399.5	466.6	523.1	530.7	641.6	782.5	846.2	1006.5
7. Jammu & Kashmir	482.1	605.6	681.4	727.3	857.3	948.0	1057.6	1158.1
8. Karnataka	3282.9	3813.1	3995.1	4821.7	5341.5	6195.4	6489.1	7745.8
9. Kerala	2398.4	2520.5	2753.5	3155.6	3588.4	3711.4	4214.0	4679.4
10. Madhya Pradesh	3706.6	4509.9	4428.6	4352.3	5945.2	6542.5	7296.0	8959.6
11. Maharashtra	8573.6	9624.9	10658.1	12229.6	13895.0	15527.5	16974.8	19975.2
12. Manipur	95.3	110.9	114.0	141.1	182.2	206.0	223.2	255.8
13. Orissa	1674.2	2090.0	2198.6	2174.1	2818.2	3481.9	3630.3	-
14. Punjab	3061.8	3454.7	3718.8	4219.6	4592.5	5387.8	6081.8	6549.2
15. Rajasthan	3060.1	3400.8	3632.9	3881.5	4127.1	4964.0	5630.9	6918.9
16. Tamil Nadu	4303.9	4709.9	5023.0	6095.2	6435.8	7515.1	7799.0	9151.8
17. Tripura	164.2	174.7	196.8	217.1	245.1	-	-	-
18. Uttar Pradesh	8134.8	9463.9	9755.9	10320.3	13955.0	14597.0	16687.4	18632.5
19. West Bengal	5935.7	6423.2	6727.0	7361.9	8495.0	9070.4	9975.3	12823.8

Q : Quick Estimates

Source: Government of India, Ministry of Finance, 'Indian Economic Statistics', December, 1985.

TABLE I.7 : STATEWISE ESTIMATES OF PERCAPITA NET DOMESTIC PRODUCT AT CURRENT PRISES

(Rs.)

	1960-61	1965-66	1970-71	1971-72	1972-73	1973-74	1974-75
1. Andhra Pradesh	275	387	585	627	657	857	1,010
2. Assam	315	399	535	548	577	648	822
3. Bihar	215	332	402	415	480	575	683
4. Gujarat	362	498	829	827	761	1,116	1,037
5. Haryana	327	450	877	960	1,015	1,216	1,300
6. Himachal Pradesh	359	398	678	716	769	936	1,048
7. Jammu & Kashmir	269	317	548	588	610	716	830
8. Karnataka	296	448	641	698	664	907	1,000
9. Kerala	259	380	594	568	662	811	910
10. Madhya Pradesh	260	305	484	535	575	733	840
11. Maharashtra	409	534	783	808	838	1,087	1,360
12. Manipur	154	268	381	446	506	637	729
13. Orissa	216	329	478	480	575	699	715
14. Punjab	366	562	1,070	1,121	1,244	1,513	1,634
15. Rajasthan	284	373	651	560	618	869	895
16. Tamil Nadu	334	403	581	648	669	794	826
17. Tripura	249	333	502	563	534	649	789
18. Uttar Pradesh	252	373	486	497	603	668	752
19. West Bengal	390	532	722	779	781	935	1,081
ALL-INDIA	306	425	633	660	710	869	1,004

Source : Govt of India, Ministry of Finance, Indian Economic Statistics, December, 1985.

TABLE I.7 : STATEWISE ESTIMATES OF PER CAPITA NET DOMESTIC PRODUCT AT CURRENT PRICES (Contd.)

(Rs.)

	1975-76	76-77	1977-78	1978-79	1979-80	80-81	1981-82	82-83	1983 84(Q)
1. Andhra Pradesh	883	877	1003	1083	1179	1358	1659	1708	1955
2. Assam	783	875	933	1007	1063	1201	1416	1596	1762
3. Bihar	656	690	732	772	799	929	1007	1022	1174
4. Gujarat	1239	1398	1520	1554	1735	1944	2238	2368	2795
5. Haryana	1432	1642	1764	1889	1941	2331	2601	2858	3147
6. Himachal Pradesh	1078	1029	1178	1295	1289	1515	1806	1914	2230
7. Jammu & Kashmir	928	909	1113	1222	1266	1455	1568	1705	1820
8. Karnataka	951	986	1117	1142	1345	1453	1644	1679	1957
9. Kerala	954	1009	1043	1121	1271	1421	1445	1613	1761
10. Madhya Pradesh	784	789	929	892	858	1149	1240	1357	1636
11. Maharashtra	1388	1515	1666	1805	2026	2232	2446	2625	3032
12. Manipur	750	679	859	858	1032	1294	1423	1498	1673
13. Orissa	729	690	845	873	847	1101	1308	1339	-
14. Punjab	1749	2019	2231	2351	2610	2760	3169	3502	3691
15. Rajasthan	885	1015	1097	1139	1030	1222	1429	1575	1881
16. Tamil Nadu	832	944	1017	1069	1280	1336	1541	1578	1827
17. Tripura	813	896	928	1019	1095	1206		-	-
18. Uttar Pradesh	721	818	930	935	965	1272	1296	1443	1567
19. West Bengal	1109	1194	1266	1298	1392	1573	1645	1771	2231
ALL-INDIA	1026	1079	1194	1255	1339	1564	1741	1868	2201

Q : Qucik Estimates.
Source : Govt of India, Ministry of Finance, Indian Economic Statistics, December, 1985.

TABLE I.8 : SECTORAL DISTRIBUTION OF NET STATE DOMESTIC PRODUCT AT FACTOR COST AT CURRENT PRICES 1971-72 & 1981-82

(Rs. Crores)

	Primary		Secondary		Territory		Total	
	SDP	% to total	SDP	% to to total	SDP	% to total	SDP	% to total
1. Andhra Pradesh	1556	56.3	402	14.6	804	29.1	2762	100.0
2. Assam	498	59.9	118	14.2	216	25.9	832	100.0
3. Bihar	1459	58.6	410	16.5	619	24.9	2488	100.0
4. Gujarat	1085	46.8	564	24.2	668	28.8	2317	100.0
5. Haryana	612	59.9	199	19.5	211	20.6	1022	100.0
6. Himachal Pradesh	130	50.8	67	26.2	59	23.0	256	100.0
7. Jammu & Kashmir	150	56.6	41	15.5	74	27.9	265	100.0
8. Karnataka	1079	52.2	490	23.7	499	24.1	2068	100.0
9. Kerala	640	46.8	260	19.0	467	34.2	1367	100.0
10. Madhya Pradesh	1370	60.1	337	14.8	572	25.1	2279	100.0
11. Maharashtra	1114	25.4	1567	35.8	1701	38.8	4382	100.0
12. Manipur	22	44.9	9	18.4	18	36.7	49	100.0
13. Meghalaya	36	62.1	10	17.2	12	20.7	58	100.0
14. Nagaland	10	35.7	7	25.0	11	39.3	28	100.0
15. Orissa	777	66.4	149	12.7	245	20.9	1171	100.0
16. Punjab	912	60.4	251	16.6	347	23.0	1510	100.0
17. Rajasthan	890	59.4	244	16.3	364	24.3	1498	100.0
18. Tamil Nadu	1173	40.9	675	23.5	1022	35.6	2870	100.0
19. Tripura	61	67.0	7	7.7	23	25.3	91	100.0
20. Uttar Pradesh	2568	57.1	663	14.7	1266	28.2	4497	100.0
21. West Bengal	1527	43.8	795	22.8	1161	33.2	3483	100.0
TOTAL:	17669	50.1	7265	20.6	10359	29.3	35293	100.0

TABLE I.8 : SECTORAL DISTRIBUTION OF NET STATE DOMESTIC PRODUCT AT FACTOR COST AT CURRENT PRICES 1981-82 (Rs. Crores) (Contd.)

(Rs. Crores)

	Primary		Secondary		Territory		Total	
	SDP	% to total	SDP	% to total	SDP	% to total	SDP	% to total
1. Andhra Pradesh	4481	53.8	1383	16.6	2472	29.6	8336	100.0
2. Assam	1687	60.3	496	17.7	616	22.0	2799	100.0
3. Bihar	3853	54.7	1157	16.4	2031	28.9	7041	100.0
4. Gujarat	2684	35.6	2012	26.7	2846	37.7	7542	100.0
5. Haryana	1692	50.2	692	20.5	989	29.3	3373	100.0
6. Himachal Pradesh	414	54.0	140	18.2	213	27.8	767	100.0
7. Jammu & Kashmir	457	52.1	165	18.8	255	29.1	877	100.0
8. Karnataka	2691	46.4	1436	24.8	1667	28.8	5794	100.0
9. Kerala	1483	39.9	886	23.8	1348	36.3	3717	100.0
10. Madhya Pradesh	3575	54.6	1347	20.6	1628	24.8	6550	100.0
11. Maharastra	4561	29.0	5150	32.7	6030	38.3	15741	100.0
12. Manipur	93	61.6	8	5.3	50	33.1	151	100.0
13. Meghalaya*	43	65.1	5	7.6	18	27.3	66	100.0
14. Orissa	2225	63.9	469	13.5	788	22.6	3482	100.0
15. Punjab	2365	44.3	1168	21.9	1806	33.8	5339	100.0
16. Rajasthan	2692	53.8	896	17.9	1419	28.3	5007	100.0
17. Tamil Nadu	1948	29.1	1341	20.0	3403	50.9	6692	100.0
18. Tripura	128	59.0	19	8.8	70	32.2	217	100.0
19. Uttar Pradesh	6665	45.2	2953	20.0	5138	34.8	14756	100.0
20. West Bengal	3150	35.8	2379	27.1	3266	37.1	8795	100.0
TOTAL	46,887	43.8	24,102	22.5	36,053	33.7	1,07,042	100.0

* Relates to 1973-74

NOTE: Primary Sector includes agriculture, forestry and logging, fishing and mining and quarrying.
Secondary Sector includes manufacturing, construction, electricity gas and water supply.
Terrtiary Sector includes transport, communication, trade, finance and real estate and community and personal services.

Source: Govt of India, Central Statistical Organisation, 'Estimates of State Domestic Product 1960-61 to 1982-83' June, 1984.

TABLE-I.9 : COMPARABLE ESTIMATES OF PER CAPITA STATE DOMESTIC PRODUCT AT CURRENT PRICES

STATES	1960-61	1970-71	1971-72	1972-73	1973-74	74-75	1975-76	76-77	77-78	78-79	79-80	(Rs.) Average 1977-78 to 79-80
1. Andhra Pradesh	314	586	629	664	868	1020	897	900	1030	1087	1175	1097
2. Assam	349	570	559	632	676	849	848	896	994	990	1031	1005
3. Bihar	216	418	437	500	559	706	669	716	759	791	785	778
4. Gujarat	380	845	859	759	1116	1051	1236	1502	1626	1642	1877	1715
5. Haryana	359	932	1008	1091	1276	1408	1514	1761	1935	1990	2023	1983
6. Himachal Pradesh	-	676	731	813	953	1086	1165	1072	1259	1358	1287	1301
7. Jammu & Kashmir	267	557	566	602	720	887	825	939	1146	1215	1299	1220
8. Karnataka	292	675	699	740	992	1106	1038	1093	1259	1254	1438	1317
9. Kerala	278	636	633	709	876	969	1000	1101	1141	1243	1334	1239
10. Madhya Pradesh	274	489	539	585	714	825	790	807	951	927	901	926
11. Maharashtra	419	811	860	876	1115	1435	1455	1535	1677	1797	2058	1844
12. Manipur	-	408	449	533	792	914	904	799	888	889	1163	980
13. Meghalaya	-	644	568	648	729	921	899	926	1056	1156	1092	1101
14. Nagaland	-	508	527	586	683	829	949	948	1100	1252	1100	1151
15. Orissa	226	541	527	631	765	780	834	797	912	1046	966	975
16. Punjab	383	1067	1106	1208	1484	1585	1688	2050	2317	2382	2528	2409
17. Rajasthan	271	629	573	600	826	860	873	1041	1153	1188	1053	1131
18. Sikkim	-	-	-	-	-	-	-	-	-	-	-	-
19. Tamil Nadu	344	616	692	714	865	964	997	1066	1203	1225	1330	1253
20. Tripura	-	563	575	535	729	888	872	980	1149	1117	1202	1156
21. Uttar Pradesh	244	493	504	623	677	740	727	819	896	894	916	902
22. West Bengal	386	729	775	776	920	1080	1100	1177	1252	1312	1446	1337
All States		619	645	693	853	968	969	1051	1162	1203	1139	1168
ALL-INDIA	306	625	652	701	861	978	981	1074	1191	1230	1339	1253

Source : Fpr 1970-71 to 1978-79: Report of the Seventh and Eighth Finance Commission For 1970-80 'Basic Statistics Relating to Indian Economy, Vol.2 'States' September, 1985, CMIE Bombay.

TABLE I.10 : EMPLOYMENT AND OUTPUT IN THE FACTORY SECTOR 1980-81 (Including Electricity, gas, water, supply etc.)

	Factories		Employment		Value of output		Value Added		Percapita value added Rs.	Ranking on the basis of	
	Number	% to total	Lakh persons	% to total	Rs. Crores	% to total	Rs. Crores	% to total		Employ-ment added	Per-capita value
1. Andhra Pradesh	11,155	11.6	6.90	8.8	3,184	5.2	584	4.9	111	6	11
2. Assam	1,583	1.6	1.25	1.6	647	1.1	116	1.0	60	15	17
3. Bihar	4,250	4.4	3.84	4.9	3,107	5.1	501	4.2	73	8	15
4. Gujarat	11,208	11.6	7.15	9.1	7.160	11.7	1,139	9.5	342	5	2
5. Haryana	2,486	2.6	1.89	2.4	1,871	3.1	346	2.9	274	13	3
6. Himachal Pradesh	173	0.2	0.23	0.3	143	0.2	62	0.5	148	17	9
7. Jammu & Kashmir	327	0.3	0.28	0.4	109	0.2	18	0.2	31	16	18
8. Karnataka	5,381	5.6	4.02	5.1	2.592	4.2	603	5.1	167	7	7
9. Kerala	3,049	3.2	2.82	3.6	2,091	3.4	391	3.3	156	10	8
10. Madhya Pradesh	3,488	3.6	3.28	4.2	2,450	4.0	602	5.0	118	9	10
11. Maharashtra	15,576	16.1	13.56	17.3	14,405	23.6	2,986	25.0	486	1	1
12. Manipur	38	Neg	0.02	Neg 1	Neg	(a)	Neg	4	20	20	
13. Meghalaya	35	Neg	0.06	0.1	27	Neg	14	0.1	106	19	12
14. Nagaland											
15. Orissa	1,563	1.6	1.34	1.7	1,024	1.7	198	1.7	77	14	14
16. Punjab	5,688	5.9	2.45	3.1	2,491	4.1	386	3.2	235	11	6
17. Rajasthan	2,696	2.8	1.94	2.5	1,612	2.6	334	2.8	100	12	13
18. Sikkim											
19. Tamil Nadu	10,292	10.7	8.10	10.3	6,634	10.9	1,229	10.3	258	3	4
20. Tripura	222	0.2	0.12	0.2	13 Neg	3	Neg	11	18	19	
21. Uttar Pradesh	7,151	7.4	7.79	9.9	3,777	6.2	749	6.3	69	4	16
22. West Bengal	6,359	6.6	9.58	12.2	5,993	9.8	1,375	11.5	257	2	5
Union Territories	3,783	3.9	1.93	2.4	1,753	2.9	293	2.5	352		
ALL - INDIA :	96,503	100.0	78.54	100.0	61,084	100.0	11,929	100.0	178		

Source: Central Statistical Organisation (a) Rs. 58 Crores

Reproduced in 'Basic Statistics Relating to Indian Economy, Vol.2 States' CMIE, Bombay. 1985.

TABLE I.11 : NUMBER AND AREA OF OPERATIONAL HOLDINGS 1980-81

STATES	No. of Operational Holdings		Area of Operational Holdings		Average Size of holdings (hectrs.)
	No. in lakhs	% to All-India	Area in hectars	% to All-India	
1. Andhra Pradesh	76.6	8.57	143.3	8.80	1.87
2. Assam	23.0	2.57	31.2	1.92	1.36
3. Bihar	112.3	12.57	110.7	6.80	0.99
4. Gujarat	29.3	3.28	101.0	6.20	3.45
5. Haryana	10.1	1.13	35.6	2.19	3.52
6. Himachal Pradesh	6.4	0.72	9.8	0.60	1.54
7. Jammu & Kashmir	10.4	1.16	10.3	0.63	0.99
8. Karnataka	43.1	4.82	117.5	7.22	2.73
9. Kerala	41.8	4.68	18.1	1.11	0.43
10. Madhya Pradesh	64.1	7.17	219.3	13.47	3.42
11. Maharashtra	68.8	7.70	203.0	12.47	2.95
12. Manipur	1.4	0.16	1.7	0.10	1.24
13. Meghalaya	1.7	0.19	3.0	0.18	1.74
14. Nagaland	1.2	0.13	8.6	0.53	7.41
15. Orissa	33.3	3.73	53.0	3.26	1.59
16. Punjab	10.3	1.15	39.9	2.45	3.79
17. Rajasthan	44.9	5.02	199.3	12.24	4.44
18. Sikkim	0.6	0.07	1.1	0.07	1.94
19. Tamil Nadu	71.5	8.00	77.4	4.75	1.08
20. Tripura	3.1	0.35	3.3	0.20	1.08
21. Uttar Pradesh	178.2	19.94	179.4	11.02	1.01
22. West Bengal	58.8	6.58	55.5	3.41	0.94
Union Territories	0.9	0.10	1.5	0.09	1.79
ALL-INDIA	893.5	100.0	1627.9	100.0	1.82

Source: All-India Agricultural Census 1980-81 Reproduced in 'Basic Statistics Relating to Indian Economy Vol. 2 States 'September, 1985 CMIE, BOMBAY.

TABLE I.12 : STATE WISE PERCENTAGE OF NET IRIGATED AREA

States	1961-62		1981-82		1981-82	
	Net irrigated area 000 hect.	As % Net sown area	Net irrigated area 000 hect.	As % of Net sown area	Gross irrigated area 000 hect.	As % of Gross cropped area
1. Andhra Pradesh	3,029	26.8	3,692	36.2	4,680	35.9
2. Assam	612(b)	26.7	572	21.2	570	16.6
3. Bihar	1,942	23.3	3,001	38.2	3,580	33.7
4. Gujarat	750	7.8	2,155	22.3	2,520	23.1
5. Haryana	(a)	(a)	2,248	61.4	3,450	59.2
6. Himachal Pradesh	39	14.2	92	16.1	160	16.8
7. Jammu & Kashmir	287	41.7	307	42.9	400	40.8
8. Karnataka	920	9.0	1,471	14.2	1,680	15.8
9. Kerala	327	16.9	240	11.1	380	13.1
10. Madhya Pradesh	944	5.8	2,421	12.8	2,690	12.4
11. Maharashtra	1,081	6.0	1,927	10.5	2,510	12.3
12. Manipur	68	40.5	65	46.4	80	33.3
13. Meghalaya	(c)	(c)	50	25.9	50	25.0
14. Nagaland	12	25.5	62	40.5	70	43.8
15. Orissa	978	16.8	1,215	19.8	2,010	23.0
16. Punjab	3,210	42.6	3,408	81.0	5,970	86.1
17. Rajasthan	1,823	13.3	2,903	18.6	3,720	20.0
18. Sikkim	-	-	11	12.8	10	11.1
19. Tamil Nadu	2,503	41.6	2,709	47.2	3,430	49.6
20. Tripura	13	5.7	29	11.8	40	10.5
21. Uttar Pradesh	4,859	28.1	9,541	55.2	11,620	46.9
22. West Bengal	1,352	24.9	1,489	26.8	1,740	23.5
Union Territories	53	40.2	121	26.5	140	24.6
ALL-INDIA :	24,802	18.3	39,729	30.0	51.500	29.2

Notes: (a) Included in Punjab (b) Relates to 1953-54 (c) Included in Assam

Source: 'Basic Statistics Relating to the Indian Economy Vol. 2 States' September, 1985, CMIE, Bombay

TABLE I.13 : STATE-WISE NO. OF VILLAGES ELECTRIFIED

STATES	Total number of Villages (1971)	Villages electrified March end		Villages electrified as % of total number of villages	
		1972	1984	1972	1984
1. Andhra Pradesh	27,221	9,252	21,183(b)	34	78
2. Assam	21,995	670	8,555(b)	3	39
3. Bihar	67,566	8,313	32,794	12	49
4. Gujarat	18,275	4,706	14,930	26	82
5. Haryana	6,731	6,091	6,731	90	100
6. Himachal Pradesh	16,916	3,249	13,569(b)	19	80
7. Jammu & Kashmir	6,503	735	5,467	11	84
8. Karnataka	26,826	10,075	21,009(b)	38	78
9. Kerala	1,268	1,268	1,268	100	100
10. Madhya Pradesh	70,883	8,787	36,777	12	52
11. Maharashtra	35,778	13,661	31,357	38	88
12. Manipur	1,949	187	532	10	27
13. Meghalaya	4,583	71	1,138	2	25
14. Nagaland	960	77	563(b)	8	59
15. Orissa	46,992	3,610	22,073	8	47
16. Punjab	12,188	6,366	12,126(a)	52	100
17. Rajasthan	33,305	4,023	18,264	12	55
18. Sikkim	405*	-	141(b)	-	35
19. Tamil Nadu	15,735	12,837	15,654(b)	91	99
20. Tripura	4,727	85	1,705	2	36
21. Uttar Pradesh	1,12,561	23,755	56,862	21	51
22. West Bengal	38.074	3,328	18,211(b)	9	61
UNION TERRITORIES	4,685	948	2,036	2443	
ALL-INDIA	5,76,126	1,22,094	3,43,245	21	60

NOTES: (a) 62 Villages have been declared uninhabited

(b) as on 29 February, 1984.

* The revenue block has been reckoned as the smallest administrative unit by the Census authorities.

SOURCE: Central Electricity Authority Reproduced in 'Basic Amenities Relating to Indian Economy - States Sept, 1985 CMIE, Bombay.

TABLE-I.14 : TOTAL LENGTH OF ROADS 1974-75 and 1980-81

(Kms.)

	Total Road Length		of which surfaced (%)		Per lakh of population		Per 1000 Sq. Km. of area	
	1974-75	1980-81	1974-75	1980-81	1974-75	1980-81	1974-75	1980-81
1. Andhra Pradesh	95,968	1,25,768	54.4	50.5	221	235	349	457
2. Assam	24,206	59,790	20.9	15.1	166	300	306	757
3. Bihar	94,032	83,601	22.9	34.3	172	120	540	480
4. Gujarat	74,717	58,084	50.1	69.9	280	170	381	296
5. Haryana	25,071	22,980	60.8	86.2	251	178	570	522
6. Himachal Pradesh	11,191	19,678	25.7	21.7	319	458	200	351
7. Jammu and Kashmir	14,075	11,592	45.4	58.9	306	193	63	52
8. Karnataka	97,955	1,09,914	58.3	58.3	334	296	510	572
9. Kerala	78,113	1,04,253	24.8	22.4	367	409	2002	2673
10. Madhya Pradesh	88,786	1,04,725	45.1	50.6	213	201	200	236
11. Manipur	4,017	5,827	31.0	33.8	365	416	183	264
12. Maharashtra	1,10,650	1,17,345	41.1	69.2	220	187	359	381
13. Meghalaya	4,110	4,767	20.4	55.5	411	367	187	217
14. Nagaland	6,053	5,836	18.4	13.1	1211	730	356	243
15. Orissa	47,994	1,19,356	28.0	13.8	219	452	307	765
16. Punjab	27,100	45,919	71.9	76.9	155	273	422	918
17. Rajasthan	47,114	63,975	53.4	55.4	183	187	138	187
18. Sikkim	197	,061	48.7	95.4	99	354	28	152
19. Tamil Nadu	1,07,283	1,23,897	55.9	74.8	260	256	825	953
20. Tripura	5,838	7,830	21.9	16.3	365	373	531	712
21. Utar Pradesh	1,16,935	1,50,826	27.1	46.5	132	136	398	513
22. West Bengal	1,17,938	56,835	24.3	44.6	266	104	1325	639
UNION TERRITORIES	21,964	38,848	34.4	38.2	329	396	183	324
ALL - INDIA:	12,15,337	15,02,707	40.6	46.1	222	219	370	457

Source: CSO, Statistical Abstract, 1982.

TABLE: I.15 : RAILWAY ROUTE LENGTH : 1971-72 AND 1983-84

(Kms.)

STATES	1971-72	1983-84		
		Total route length	Per 000 sq. Km. area	Per lakh population
1. Andhra Pradesh	4,740	4,920	17.88	9.19
2. Assam	2,193	2,181	27.78	10.96
3. Bihar	5,163	5,362	30.84	7.67
4. Gujarat	5,638	5,635	28.74	16.53
5. Haryana	1,417	1,501	34.00	11.62
6. Himachal Pradesh	256	256	4.60	5.95
7. Jammu and Kashmir	6	77	0.34	1.28
8. Karnataka	2,806	3,024	15.76	8.14
9. Kerala	890	916	23.57	3.59
10. Madhya Pradesh	5,735	5,748	12.96	11.02
11. Maharastra	5,226	5,297	17.22	8.43
12. Manipur	-	-	-	-
13. Meghalaya	-	-	-	-
14. Nagaland	9	9	0.54	1.12
15. Orissa	1,876	1,982	12.73	7.50
16. Punjab	2,119	2,139	42.47	12.73
17. Rajasthan	5,587	5,614	16.40	16.36
18. Sikkim	-	-	-	-
19. Tamil Nadu	3,758	3,894	29.94	8.04
20. Tripura	12	12	1.14	0.57
21. Uttar Pradesh	8,632	8,882	30.17	8.00
22. West Bengal	3,696	3,726	41.98	6.82
UNION TERRITORIES	5,651	285	2.37	2.90
ALL INDIA	60,267	61,460	18.69	8.97

Source:'Basic Statistics Relating to the Indian Economy Vol.2 States - September 1985, CMIE, Bombay.

TABLE- I.16 : STATE WISE INSTALLED POWER GENERATING CAPACITY AS ON 31st March 1985

	Hydro (mw)	Thermal (mw)	Nuclear (mw)	Total (mw)	Power generation in 1984-85 (Million kwh)	Per capita power consum-ption in 1983-84(kwh)	Ranking on the basis of 1983-84 per capita consumption
1. Andhra Pradesh	1,825	1,952	-	3,777	14,365	142	7
2. Assam	-	349	-	349	848	42	19
3. Bihar	150	1,205	-	1,355	2,764	91	15
4. Gujarat	300	2,773	-	3,073	12,320	274	2
5 Haryana	-	415	-	415	1,263	245	4
6. Himachal Pradesh	306	-	-	306	1,121	89	16
7. Jammu & Kashmir	174	23	-	197	859	105	13
8. Karnataka	1,982	210	-	2,192	8,379	166	6
9. Kerala	1,012	-	-	1,012	4,887	113	12
10. Madhya Pradesh	115	3,243	-	3,358	13,139	137	8
11. Maharastra	1,315	4,703	420(a)	6,438	26,238	267	3
12. Manipur	105	-	-	105	811**	13	22
13. Meghalaya	175	-	-	175		69	17
14. Nagaland	27*	-	-	27		49	19
15. Orissa	630	470	-	1,100	3,598	135	9
16. Punjab	200	860	-	1,060	3,905	354	1
17. Rajasthan	271	220		931	3,033	126	10
18. Sikkim	-	-	-	-	16	52	18
19. Tamil Nadu	1,369	1,750	235	3,354	14,536	178	5
20. Tripura	-	-	-	-	-	21	21
21. Uttar Pradesh	1,422	3,743	-	5,165	16,671	103	13
22. West Bengal	41	2,196	-	2,237	6,728	123	11
UTs, DVC & BBMB	2,791	2,476	-	5,267	21,170		-
ALL INDIA	14,210	26,588	1,095	41,893	156,651	154	-

a = Distribution between Maharastra and Gujarat on 50:50 basis

* = Includes Tripura and Sikkim ** = Includes Meghalaya and Tripura

Source: Central Electricity Authority, Reproduced in ~Basic" statistics Relating to Indian Economy, Vol.2 States September 1985. CMIE. Bombay.

TABLE-I.17 : NO. OF REGISTERED MOTOR VEHICLES 1980-81

	STATES	Two Wheelers	Three Wheelers	Cars, Jeeps Taxies	Buses	Trucks	Tractors	Others including trailors	Total	Vehicles per lakh of population
1.	Andhra Pradesh	141,908	10,015	28,477	10,433	32,852	14,127	7,513	245,325	458
2.	Assam	10,415	346	16,807	1,855	18,256	4,234	5,765	57,678	290
3.	Bihar	74,928	3,672	44,139	8,961	26,607	15,283	8,104	181,694	260
4.	Gujarat	212,567	31,097	46,605	8,750	27,068	24,074	17,244	367,405	1,078
5.	Haryana	48,814	739	8,657	2,635	13,560	35,160	13,217	122,782	950
6.	Himachal Pradesh(a)	9,943	(b)	5,355	2,580	6,203	(b)	4,826	28,907	675
7.	Jammu & Kashmir(a)	16,449	(b)	7,751	2,560	5,106	(b)	3,539	33,405	591
8.	Karnataka	224,985	20,819	77,590	12,848	32,943	17,538	20,835	407,558	1,097
9.	Kerala	58,688	11,693	86,551	9,904	22,862	3,080	1,819	194,597	765
10.	Madhya Pradesh	175,363	(c)	47,712	11,459	35,080	26,123	11,660	307,397	589
11.	Maharastra	363,624	50,440	259,626	17,885	89,579	25,474	26,994	833,622	1,328
12.	Manipur	1,545	146	1,721	464	1,374	-	350	5,600	394
13.	Meghalaya									
14.	Nagaland	1,120	173	2,523	380	1,371	54	60	5,681	733
15.	Orissa	36,233	681	11,419	1,531	10,053	1,339	1,667	62,923	238
16.	Punjab	142,094	5,653	27,880	5,201	17,388	118,845	6,364	323.425	1.926
17.	Rajasthan	101,735	4,762	25,994	6,973	17,613	32,031	11,901	201,009	587
18.	Sikkim									
19.	Tamil Nadu	157,611	11,969	81,276	12,904	36,341	10,649	10,350	321,100	663
20.	Tripura	1,509	105	2,916	499	2,626	51	636	8,342	406
21.	Utter Pradesh	231,366	5,293	53,456	14,461	34,553	99,029	11,052	449,210	405
22.	West Bengal(a)	92,511	(b)	129,939	12,007	49,188	(b)	72,989	356,634	653
	Union Territories	424,956	22,665	150,307	9,467	45,985	1,020	2,334	656,719	6,687
	ALL-INDIA	25,28,364	180,268	11,16,701	153,757	526,608	428,111	239,204	51,73,013	755

a: Estimated
b: included in others
c: included in cars

Source: All-India Automobile & Auxillary Industries Association 'Automotive Industry of India, Facts and Figures 1984' Reproduced in 'Basic Statistics Relating to Indian Economy, Vol.2 States' CMIE, Bombay, September, 1985.

ᴀBLE I.18 : NUMBER OF HOSPITALS AND DISPENSARIES AS ON 1st JANUARY, 1984

STATES	Hospitals				Dispensaries				Total	Hospital
	Government	Local and Private	Total	% in Rural Areas	Government	Local and Private	Total	% in Rural Areas	Hospitals and dispensaries	per 1000 sq.km. of area
Andhra Pradesh	341	270	611	26.7	285	487	772	70.6	1383	5.0
Assam	81	30	111	34.2	436	-	436	93.1	547	7.0
Bihar (c)	100	126	226	8.4	701	301	1002	98.4	1228	7.1
Gujarat	119	795	914	8.3	223	1707	1930	59.5	2844	14.5
Haryana	69	18	87	9.2	234	8	242	50.6	329	7.5
Himachal Pradesh	52	13	65	40.0	231	4	235	91.1	300	5.4
Jammu & Kashmir(c)	30	5	35	5.7	-	-	648	95.8	683	3.1
Karnataka	161	72	233	20.2	1512	36	1548	82.1	1781	9.3
Kerala	152	606	758	78.5	652	98	750	94.7	1508	40.1
Madhya Pradesh	276	-	276	15.6	645	-	645	81.7	921	2.1
Maharastra	222	1052	1274	12.5	246	6010	6256	19.6	7530	24.5
Manipur	18	3	21	57.1	52	-	52	94.2	73	3.3
Meghalaya	7	4	11	9.1	58	-	58	98.3	69	3.1
Nagaland	33	2	35	82.9	76	-	76	100.0	111	6.5
Orissa	272	35	307	47.2	266	32	298	75.2	605	3.9
Punjab	217	39	256	43.4	1694	55	1749	87.8	2005	40.1
Rajasthan	190	40	230	10.0	1301	56	1357	68.1	1587	4.6
Sikkim	5	-	5	80.0	-	-	-	-	5	1.0
Tamil Nadu	307	69	376	25.8	419	247	666	46.9	1042	8.0
Tripura	16	-	16	25.0	149	-	149	92.6	165	16.5
Uttar Pradesh	522	193	715	10.4	1511	202	1713	74.6	2428	8.3
West Bengal	259	145	404	36.1	114	305	419	64.2	823	9.3
Union Territories	91	124	215	26.5	487	292	779	37.3	994	8.3
ALL-INDIA	3540	3641	7181	26.4	11292	9840	21780	59.4	28961	8.8

urce : Govt. of India, Directorate General of Health Services 'Health Statistics of India: 1984' New Delhi, February, 1985. Reproduced in 'Basic Statistics Relating to Indian Economy, Vol. 2 States" CMIE, Bombay, September, 1985.

TABLE I.19 : ENROLMENT RATIOS IN CLASSES I-V TO VI-VIII-1982-83

	Classes I-V (6-11 years)			Classes VI-VIII (11-14 years)		
	Boys	Girls	Total	Boys	Girls	Total
1. Andhra Pradesh	103.4	77.8	90.9	34.4	19.8	27.3
2. Assam	69.6	56.4	63.3	56.9	37.8	47.6
3. Bihar	105.3	48.7	77.9	43.3	13.5	28.8
4. Gujarat	127.2	92.9	110.6	64.4	39.9	52.6
5. Haryana	105.4	64.6	85.7	72.8	30.0	52.5
6. Himachal Pradesh	145.8	103.1	123.3	112.6	55.8	82.9
7. Jammu & Kashmir	110.1	58.4	83.2	60.8	27.4	43.8
8. Karnataka	89.3	76.6	83.2	56.2	38.1	47.5
9. Kerala	99.9	99.7	99.8	90.4	87.6	89.0
10. Madhya Pradesh	96.2	53.4	75.6	47.8	18.1	33.5
11. Maharastra	134.3	109.9	122.7	70.2	43.2	56.9
12. Manipur	125.9	99.8	112.7	64.6	38.4	50.9
13. Meghalaya	114.8	105.1	109.9	43.1	31.7	37.2
14. Nagaland	125.9	100.2	113.3	55.5	41.8	48.7
15. Orissa	98.4	68.4	83.9	42.7	22.4	32.8
16. Punjab	110.0	96.3	103.4	70.4	53.6	62.4
17. Rajasthan	100.1	37.4	69.8	53.6	14.1	34.4
18. Sikkim	182.2	134.5	158.6	66.8	38.9	52.9
19. Tamil Nadu	132.7	118.2	125.7	73.0	49.2	61.5
20. Tripura	127.4	95.3	111.2	53.7	31.7	41.9
21. Uttar Pradesh	100.9	48.5	75.4	60.2	21.6	41.5
22. West Bengal	101.9	70.4	86.6	43.2	26.6	35.0
ALL-INDIA	104.0	69.4	87.2	56.3	30.6	43.9

Source: Government of India, Department of Education 'Selected Education Statistics:1982-83' New Delhi, 1984. Reproduced in 'Basic Statistics relating to Indian Economy-Vol. 2 States CMIE, Bombay Sep. 1985.

TABLE-I.20 : NUMBER OF STATE GOVERNMENT EMPLOYEES, OF TEACHERS AND OTHER EMPLOYEES OF LOCAL BODIES AND AIDED INSTITUTIONS AS ON 31-3-1982.

States	State Govt. Employees	Employment of Local Bodies: Teachers	Others	Total (2+3+4)
(1)	(2)	(3)	(4)	(5)
1. Andhra Pradesh	4,20,189	1,76,058	38,864	6,35,111
2. Assam	2,19,296	5,971	14,275	2,39,542
3. Bihar	6,60,264	8,039	34,067	7,02,370
4. Gujarat	3,92,322	1,40,392	NS	5,32,714
5. Haryana (P)	1,97,183	4,395	11,692	2,13,270
6. Himachal Pradesh (P)	84,709	(o)	2,868	87,577
7. Jammu & Kashmir	1,56,804	3,088	8,469	1,68,361
8. Karnataka	3,89,540	(o)	81,228	4,70,768
9. Kerala	4,35,865	NA	NA	4,35,865
10. Madhya Pradesh (P)	5,42,825	(o)	43,554	5,86,379
11. Maharastra*	4,12,594	(o)	3,08,108	7,20,702
12. Manipur #	22,231	(o)	7,362	29,593
13. Meghalaya	22,426	9,320	-	31,746
14. Nagaland	45,270	-	153	45,423
15. Orissa	2,30,085	(o)	1,35,684	3,65,769
16. Punjab	2,65,573	NA	NA	2,65,573
17. Rajasthan	3,67,216	47,236	44,553	4,59,005
18. Sikkim	11,568 (NP)	(NS)	(NS)	12,725 +
19. Tamil Nadu	5,57,394	1,29,828	1,08,423	7,95,645
20. Tripura ##	85,150	(O)	6,336	91,486
21. Uttar Pradesh	7,65,782	4,22,881	2,10,693	13,99,356
22 West Bengal**	3,62,000	3,23,000	1,15,750	8,00,750

NA: Not available.
*: as on 1.7.1981.
**: as on 31.3.1981.
#: from the 7th Finance Commission's Report
##: as on 31.12.1981.
Source: Report of the Eight Finance Commission.

NP: Non-Plan (1982-83)
NS: Not Separately Specified by the State
P : Reported Provisional by the State
(o): Included under 'Others'
+: adjusted to Provide for plan employees.

TABLE-I.21 : PERCENTAGE OF POPULATION BELOW THE POVERTY LINE IN 1977-78.

State/UT	Rural	Urban	Combined
1. Andhra Pradesh	43.89	35.68	42.18
2. Assam	52.65	37.37	51.10
3. Bihar	58.91	46.07	57.49
4. Gujarat	43.20	29.02	39.04
5. Haryana	23.25	31.74	24.84
6. Himachal Pradesh	28.12	16.56	27.23
7. Jammu & Kashmir	32.75	39.33	34.06
8. Karnataka	49.88	43.97	48.34
9. Kerala	46.00	51.44	46.95
10. Madhya Pradesh	59.82	48.09	57.73
11. Maharashtra	55.85	31.62	47.71
12. Manipur	30.54	25.48	29.71
13. Meghalaya	53.87	18.16	48.03
14. Nagaland	NA	4.11	4.11
15. Orissa	68.97	42.19	66.40
16. Punjab	11.87	24.66	15.13
17. Rajasthan	33.75	33.80	33.76
18. Tamil Nadu	55.68	44.79	52.12
19. Tripura	64.28	26.34	59.73
20. Uttar Pradesh	50.23	49.24	50.09
21. West Bengal	58.94	34.71	52.54
22. All Union Territories	34.32	17.96	21.69
All India(Weighted)	50.82	38.19	48.13

Note 1. The above estimates are derived by using the all-India poverty line of Rs.65 per capita per month in 1977-78 prices corresponding to minimum daily calorie requirement of 2400 per person in rural areas and the poverty line of Rs.75 per capita per month corresponding to daily calorie requirement of 2100 in urban areas.

2. These results are based on the provisional and quick tabulation of the National Sample Survey (NSSO) on household consumer expenditure of 32nd round (July, 1977 to June, 1978).

3. The difference between the aggregate all India Private Consumption expenditure estimated by the Central Statistical Organisation in their National Accounts Statistics and that derived from the NSSO data has been adjusted prorata among the different States and Union Territories in the absence of any other information which could be used to allocate this difference among the States and Union Territories.

Source: Planning Commission, Sixth Five-Year Plan 1980-85.

TABLE-I.22 : STATE-WISE ASSESSMENT OF INCOME TAX (EXCLUDING TAX ON UNION EMOLUMENTS) FOR THE YEARS 1977-78 TO 1981-82

(Rs. in Crorres)

States	1977-78	1978-79	1979-80	1980-81	1981-82	Total 1977-78 to 1981-82
1. Andhra Pradesh	36.89	40.49	34.07	37.63	15.14	164.22
2. Assam	4.66	9.25	10.26	7.32	7.60	39.09
3. Bihar	12.91	15.83	10.90	16.07	15.61	71.32
4. Gujarat	80.21	93.17	86.47	87.95	100.79	448.59
5. Haryana	11.00	8.04	10.04	14.45	13.26	56.79
6. Himachal Pradesh	1.69	1.75	1.44	1.95	2.00	8.83
7. Jammu & Kashmir	3.76	4.24	4.16	5.56	6.42	24.14
8. Karnataka	15.60	27.40	31.70	31.95	40.02	146.67
9. Kerala	22.00	22.43	23.57	24.06	29.51	121.57
10. Madhya Pradesh	27.52	27.74	28.15	30.06	33.30	146.77
11. Maharastra	175.16	231.98	166.89	192.37	235.61	1,002.01
12. Manipur	0.37	0.35	0.35	1.76	0.36	3.19
13. Meghalaya	0.52	0.60	0.50	0.44	0.68	2.74
14. Nagaland	0.18	0.10	0.17	0.23	0.15	0.83
15. Orissa	4.30	4.33	3.98	5.46	6.45	24.52
16. Punjab	33.69	30.68	38.95	43.51	53.22	200.05
17. Rajasthan	20.71	18.10	23.14	26.27	26.69	114.91
18. Sikkim	-	-	-	-	-	-
19. Tamil Nadu	72.25	62.87	65.14	66.27	83.92	350.45
20. Tripura	0.43	0.47	0.45	0.39	0.55	2.29
21. Uttar Pradesh	40.97	45.81	50.74	53.52	67.16	258.20
22. West Bengal	88.35	73.41	74.67	71.03	84.71	392.17
All Sates	653.17	719.04	665.74	718.25	823.15	3,579.35
Union Territories	62.19	82.95	89.69	133.58	142.13	510.54
Total All-India	715.36	801.99	755.43	851.83	965.28	4,089.89

Source: Report of the Eighth Finance Commission, 1984.

TABLE-I.23 : NUMBER OF ASSESSMENTS, INCOME AND TAX DEMAND BY STATES FINANCIAL YEAR 1982-83 (Rs. in Crores)

STATES	No. of assess-ments	Gross Income	Gross Tax Demand	Tax Demand Less deductions and Rebates
1. Andhra Pradesh	78,008	214.84	26.93	25.24
2. Assam	22,585	49.20	5.71	5.33
3. Bihar	26,303	54.64	6.12	5.20
4. Gujarat	181,718	607.67	118.47	117.63
5. Haryana	8,632	24.38	2.70	2.63
6. Himachal Pradesh	3,863	9.04	0.90	0.85
7. Jammu & Kashmir	6,254	25.75	6.19	6.14
8. Karnataka	76,425	389.60	141.03	138.01
9. Kerala	36,247	145.64	35.38	33.45
10. Madhya Pradesh	28,604	70.82	8.12	7.59
11. Maharastra	274,506	1928.58	712.49	675.12
12. Manipur	467	1.10	0.04	0.04
13. Meghalaya	1,502	3.60	0.50	0.48
14. Nagaland	152	0.38	0.03	0.03
15. Orissa	19,651	47.84	4.40	3.94
16. Punjab	37,750	115.93	17.83	17.36
17. Rajasthan	28,935	75.61	9.47	9.29
18. Tamil Nadu	112,131	397.05	115.36	105.23
19. Tripura	2,057	3.71	0.43	0.42
20. Uttar Pradesh	89,379	228.30	28.44	26.41
21. West Bengal	216,951	977.56	387.68	371.40
22. Chandigarh	3,432	11.96	2.01	1.92
23. Delhi	94,279	215.41	30.30	28.37
24. Goa	2,419	4.24	0.32	0.26
TOTAL	13,52,250	5602.88	1661.00	1582.35

Source: Govt. of India, Ministry of Finance, Directorate of Inspection, 'State-Wise Income-Tax Statistical 1982-83.

TABLE I.24 : RANKING OF STATES ACCORDING TO SELECTED AGRICULTURAL INDICATORS

	Area under Foodgrains as % to Total cropped area 1980-81		Yield per hectare of Principal Crops 1979-80 to 1983-84 (Kgs. per Hectare								Percapita income from Agri. (including A.H) 1981-82	Rank
	%	Rank	Rice	Rank	Groundnut	Rank	Cotton	Rank	Sugarcane (Gur)	Rank		
1.	2.	3.	4.	5.	6.	7.	8.	9.	10.	11.	12.	13.
1. Andhra Pradesh	74.9	10	2010	3	860	4	265	4	8155	3	788	3
2. Assam	81.6	6	1040	10	-	-	-	-	4128	10	647	9
3. Bihar	92.5	1	847	14	-	-	-	-	3235	13	454	14
4. Gujarat	50.1	14	1214	9	839	5	189	7	6690	5	712	6
5. Haryana	79.3	7	2400	2	-	-	321	2	3865	11	1292	2
6. Karnataka	68.0	13	1980	5	722	7	100	8	7890	4	689	7
7. Kerala	39.3	15	1645	6	-	-	-	-	-	-	523	12
8. Maharashtra	72.6	11	1469	7	830	6	92	9	10205	2	676	8
9. Madhya Pradesh	87.9	2	739	15	620	9	79	10	2500	14	572	11
10. Orissa	85.01	3	915	12	1240	1	-	-	6310	6	767	4
11. Punjab	82.0	5	2910	1	950	3	235	3	5600	7	1400	1
12. Rajasthan	77.6	9	897	13	525	10	213	6	3720	12	750	5
13. Tamil Nadu	70.3	12	2000	3	1027	2	220	5	11065	1	382	15
14. Uttar Pradesh	78.2	8	1010	11	666	8	550	1	4415	[illegible]	575	10
15. West Bengal	84.7	4	1257	8	-	-	-	-	4885	8	501	13
16. Himachal Pradesh	95.6	-	1020	-	-	-	-	-	-	-	747	
17. Jammu & Kashmir	93.3	-	2020	-	-	-	-	-	-	-	713	
18. Manipur	95.4	-	1480	-	-	-	-	-	-	-	603	
19. Meghalaya	65.0	-	1200	-	-	-	-	-	-	-	582(a)	
20. Nagaland	92.9	-	895	-	-	-	-	-	-	-	445(a)	
21. Sikkim	-	-	-	-	-	-	-	-	-	-	-	
22. Tripura	75.8	-	1300	-	-	-	-	-	-	-	574(a)	
ALL-INDIA	77.3	-	1440	-	828	-	196	-	5905	-	611	

Source: Government of Andhra Pradesh, Finance and Planning (Planning Wing) Department, 'Seventh Five Year Plan 1985-90'.

TABLE I.25 : RANKING OF STATES OF ACCORDING TO SELECTED DEMOGRAPHIC INDICATORS

STATE	Population Density		Population Growth		Urban population		Growth of urban population		Workers engaged in Non Agricultural occupation		Literacy		Growth of Literacy	
	Persons per Sq. KM.	Rank	Increase during 1971-81	Rank	% to total Population	Rank	% Increase during	Rank	% to total workers	Rank	% of	Rank literage to total population	% increase of litercy rate 1971-81	Rank
1.	2.	3.	4.	5.	6.	7.	8.	9.	10.	11.	12.	13.	14.	15.
1. Andhra-Pradesh	195	10	23	11	23	7	48.61	9	30	10	30	10	21.86	10
2. Assam	254	8	36	1	•8.39	15	54.26	7	•34.24	•9	•28.81	•9	•4.83	15
3. Bihar	402	3	24	9	12	13	54.78	6	21	14	26	13	31.39	2
4. Gujarat	174	12	28	4	31	3	41.43	11	40	4	44	4	22.10	8
5. Haryana	292	7	29	3	22	8	59.45	3	39	6	36	8	34.40	1
6. Karnataka	194	11	27	5	29	4	39.99	12	35	8	38	7	22.02	9
7. Kerala	650	1	19	14	19	11	37.65	13	59	1	70	1	16.55	14
8. Maharashtra	204	9	25	8	35	1	39.59	12	38	7	47	2	20.42	12
9. Madhya-Pradesh	118	14	25	7	20	10	56.02	5	24	13	28	11	25.88	5
10. Orissa	169	13	20	13	12	14	68.47	1	25	12	34	9	30.75	3
11. Punjab	333	6	24	10	28	5	44.53	10	42	3	41	6	21.35	11
12. Rajasthan	100	15	33	2	21	9	58.69	4	31	9	24	14	27.84	4
13. Tamil Nadu	372	5	18	15	33	2	27.97	15	39	5	47	3	18.50	13

TABLE I.25 : RANKING OF STATES OF ACCORDING TO SELECTED DEMOGRAPHIC INDICATORS (Contd.)

14. Uttar-Pradesh	377	4	26	6	18	12	60.62	2	25	11	27	12	25.16	6
15. West-Bengal	615	2	23	12	26	6	31.73	14	45	2	41	5	23.31	7
16. Himachal-Pradesh	77	-	24	-	8	-	36.71	-	29	-	42	-	32.92	-
17. Jammu & -Kashmir	59	-	30	-	21	-	46.85	-	40	-	27	-	43.54	-
18. Manipur	64	-	32	-	26	-	164.08	-	31	-	41	-	25.65	-
19. Meghalaya	60	-	32	-	18	-	63.95	-	27	-	34	-	15.56	-
20. Nagaland	47	-	50	-	16	-	135.00	-	27	-	43	-	55.36	-
21. Sikkim	45	-	51	-	16	-	200.00	-	37	-	34	-	91.94	-
22. Tripura	196	-	32	-	32	-	39.50	-	33	-	42	-	35.96	-
ALL-INDIA	220	:	25	:	24	:	46.21	:	33	:	36	:	N.A.	

• Relates to 1971 Census data.

Source: Finance & Planning Department, Government of Andhra Pradesh
"Seventh Five Year Plan 1985-90, Draft Outline.

TABLE I.26 : RANKING OF STATES ACCORDING TO SELECTED SOCIAL SERVICE INDICATORS

Sl. No.	State	Enrolment of Children of the are group 6-11 years in Primary Classes(1982-83)		Enrolment of Children of the age group 11-14 years in Upper Primary Classes (1982-83)		Hospital Beds per lakh population (December, 1982)		Doctor Population ratio (1-1-82)	
		% to	Total Rank	% to	Rank Total	No.	Rank	Ratio	Rank
1	2	3	4	5	6	7	8	9	10
1.	Andhra Pradesh	90.9	6	27.3	15	70	8	2323	7
2.	Assam	63.3	15	47.6	7	53	11	2751	9
3.	Bihar	77.9	11	28.8	14	40	14	3803	11
4.	Gujarat	110.6	3	52.6	4	106	4	2326	8
5.	Haryana	85.7	8	52.5	5	67	9	14576	15
6.	Karnataka	83.2	10	47.5	8	93	7	1959	5
7.	Kerala	99.8	5	89.0	1	203	1	2176	6
8.	Maharashtra	122.7	2	56.9	6	146	2	1528	3
9.	Madhya Pradesh	75.6	12	33.5	12	36	15	12391	14
10.	Orissa	83.9	9	32.8	13	51	12	3261	10
11.	Punjab	103.4	4	62.4	2	124	3	782	1
12.	Rajasthan	69.8	14	34.4	11	62	10	3932	12
13.	Tamil Nadu	125.7	1	61.5	3	97	6	1523	2
14.	Uttar Pradesh	75.4	13	41.5	9	49	13	4641	13
15.	West Bengal	86.6	7	35.0	10	106	5	1663	4
16.	Himachal Pradesh	123.3	..	82.9	..	128	..	10935	..
17.	Jammu & Kashmir	83.2	..	43.8	..	96	..	2246	..
18.	Manipur	112.7	..	50.9	..	106	..	N.A	..
19.	Meghalaya	109.9	..	37.2	..	139	..	N.A.	..
20.	Nagaland	113.3	..	48.7	..	162	..	N.A.	..
21.	Sikkim	158.6	..	52.9	..	189	..	N.A.	..
22.	Tripura	112.2	..	41.9	..	71	..	N.A.	..
	ALL INDIA	87.2	..	30.6	-	84	..	..	..

Source: Government of Andhra Pradesh, Finance and Planning (Planning Wing) Department, 'Seventh Five Year Plan 1985-90'.

TABLE-I.27 RANKING OF STATES ACCORDING TO SELECTED INDUSTRIAL AND COMMERCIAL ACTIVITY INDICATORS

Sl. No.	State	Average Daily Employment of factory workers per '000 Population (1981-82)		Gross out put in Industry (Per-Capita) (1981-82)		Value added (per capita) (1981-82)		Consunption of Electricity (Per-Capita) (1983-84)	
		No.	Rank	Rs.	Rank	Rs.	Rank	KWH	Rank
(1)	(2)	(3)	(4)	(5)	(6)	(7)	(8)	(9)	(10)
1.	Andhra Pradesh	14	7	652	9	130	10	145	7
2.	Assam	6	10	360	14	70	15	41	15
3.	Bihar	5	14	639	12	132	13	92	14
4.	Gujarat	20	2	2,436	2	369	2	278	2
5.	Haryana	16	6	1,838	4	317	3	250	4
6.	Karnataka	10	9	813	8	182	7	170	6
7.	Kerala	12	8	952	7	172	8	115	12
8.	Maharashtra	21	1	2,701	1	539	1	274	3
9.	Madhva Pradesh	7	11	582	10	152	9	140	8
10.	Orissa	5	15	495	13	88	.2	137	9
11	Punjab	16	5	1,792	3	256	6	363	1
12.	Rajasthan	6	12	560	11	108	11	128	10
13.	Tamil Nadu	18	4	1,649	5	295	4	174	5
14.	Uttar Pradesh	7	13	502	15	132	14	102	13
15.	West Bengal	17	3	1239	6	264	5	126	11
16.	Himachal Pradesh	6	..	418	..	213	..	91	..
17.	Jammu & Kashmir	4	..	190	..	40	..	107	..
18.	Manipur	4	..	35	..	21	..	13	..
19.	Meghalaya	5	..	180	..	52	..	70	..
20.	Nagaland	..	..	..	..	..	..	50	..
21.	Sikkim	..	..	..	..	..	..	55	..
22.	Tripura	7	..	73	..	20	..	21	..
	ALL INDIA	12	..	1,075	..	212	..	156	..

(Contd.)

TABLE-I.27 RANKING OF STATES ACCORDING TO SELECTED INDUSTRIAL AND COMMERCIAL ACTIVITY INDICATORS (Contd.)

Industrial Consumption of Electricity (Per-Capita (1981-82)		No. of Banking Offices per lakh population		Bank Credit of Commercial (Per capita) (March, 1984) June, 1983		Motor Vehicals Banks Per lakh Population (1982-83)		Total Road Length per 100 Sq.Kms. of area (1980-81)	
(11)	(12)	(13)	(14)	(15)	(16)	(17)	(18)	(19)	(20)
KWH	Rank	No.	Rank	Rs.	Rank	No.	Rank	Kms.	Rank
68	11	6.0	8	385	9	735	11	45	12
24	15	3.2	15	124	15	406	13	76	4
47	12	4.2	14	142	14	307	14	48	11
155	1	7.4	4	547	7	1,510	3	30	13
107	5	7.2	5	512	8	1,209	5	52	9
126	4	8.5	3	561	5	1,358	4	57	8
76	9	9.5	2	549	6	876	6	267	1
137	3	6.5	7	1,344	1	1,728	2	58	7
70	10	5.5	11	199	12	358	10	24	14
89	7	5.0	12	195	13	296	15	76	4
140	2	10.3	1	699	2	2,616	1	92	3
42	13	5.6	10	262	10	775	8	19	15
97	6	7.0	6	666	3	844	7	95	2
36	14	5.8	9	238	11	539	12	51	10
73	8	4.6	13	608	4	768	9	65	6
23	..	10.6	..	329	..	883	..	35	..
20	..	9.6	..	360	..	748	..	52	..
1	..	3.2	..	67	..	742	..	26	..
20	..	6.8	..	121	..	21	..	21	..
4	..	6.8	..	188	..	379	..	34	..
8	..	5.7	..	67	..	403	..	15	..
3	..	3.9	..	191	..	455	..	72	..
77	..	5.8	..	517	..	980	..	49	..

(Contd.)

TABLE-I.27 RANKING OF STATES ACCORDING TO SELECTED INDUSTRIAL AND COMMERCIAL ACTIVITY INDICATORS (Contd.)

Sl. States	Total route length per '000 sq.Kms. ot Area (1982-83)		Total cropped area (lakh hect)	Area sown more than once (lakh hect)	Net area sown lakh hect (1980-81)
	(21)	(22)	(23)	(24)	(25)
1.Andhra Pradesh	18	10	122.8	15.4	107.4
2.Assam	28	8	34.5	7.9	26.6
3. Bihar	31	4	111.5	28.3	83.2
4.Gujarat	29	7	107.0	11.2	95.8
5.Haryana	34	3	54.6	18.6	36.0
6.Karnataka	16	13	106.6	7.6	989.9
7.Kerala	24	9	28.6	6.8	21.8
8.Maharashtra	17	11	214.0	27.0	187.0
9.Madhva Pradesh	13	14	202.7	19.7	183.0
10.Orissa	13	15	87.5	26.2	61.3
11.Punjab	43	1	67.3	25.7	41.9
12.Rajasthan	16	12	173.5	20.8	152.7
13.Tamil Nadu	30	6	64.7	11.1	53.6
14.Uttar Pradesh	30	5	245.7	73.5	172.2
15. West Bengal	42	2	76.2	20.6	55.6
16.Himachal Pradesh	5	..	9.5	3.7	5.7
17.Jammu & Kashmir	0.35	..	9.7	2.6	7.2
18.Manipur	..	..	2.2	0.8	1.4
19.Meghalaya	..	..	2.2	0.3	1.9
20.Nagaland	0.52	..	1.6	0.1	1.5
21.Sikkim	..	..	0.9	0.1	0.9
22.Tripura	1.1	..	3.8	1.3	2.5
Total	19	..	1,733.2	380.5	1,402.7

(Contd.)

TABLE-I.27 RANKING OF STATES ACCORDING TO SELECTED INDUSTRIAL AND COMMERCIAL ACTIVITY INDICATORS (Contd.)

Percent-age of Double cropped area	Rank	Net area irrigated lakh hect) (1980-81) sown (1980-81)	Percent age of net area irrigated to net area	Rank
(26)	(27)	(28)	(29)	(30)
14.3	11	34.6	32.2	6
29.7	8	5.7	21.4	8
34.0	6	29.5	35.5	5
11.7	13	20.0	20.0	9
51.7	2	21.3	59.2	2
7.7	15	13.6	13.7	12
31.2	7	2.4	11.0	14
14.4	10	23.3	12.5	13
10.8	14	19.3	10.6	15
42.7	4	12.2	19.9	10
61.3	1	33.8	80.7	1
13.6	12	29.8	19.5	11
20.7	9	25.7	48.0	4
42.7	3	94.5	54.9	3
37.0	5	14.9	26.8	7
64.9	..	0.9	15.8	..
36.1	..	3.0	41.7	..
57.1	..	0.7	50.0	..
15.8	..	0.5	26.3	..
6.7	..	0.6	40.0	..
11.1	..	0.1	11.1	..
52.0	..	0.3	12.0	..
Total 23.6	..	388.1	27.7	..

TABLE II.1 : PRINCIPLES AND CRITERIA FOR ALLOCATION OF CENTRAL TAXES AND DUTIES TO STATES OVER PERIODS COVERED BY EIGHT FINANCE COMMISSIONS.

Finance Commission	Income-Tax	Union Excise Duties (Basic)
(1)	(2)	(3)
First	55% of the net proceeds of Income-tax (other than on agricultural income and exclusive of proceeds attributable to Union Territories to be distributed among states 80% on the basis of population and 20% on the basis of collection.	40% of net proceeds of duties on tobacco matches and vegetable products to be distributed among states wholly on population basis.
Second	60% to be distributed among States 90% on population and 10% on collection basis.	25% of net proceeds of duties on tobacco matches, vegetables products, tea Coffee, sugar, paper and vegetable non-essential oils to be distributed, 90% on the population basis 10% to be used for adjustment.
Third	66-2/3% to be distributed among States, 80% on population and 20% on Collection basis. Since 1959, income-tax paid by companies was reclassified as corporation Tax and excluded from divisible pool.	The number of articles coverd for the purpose was raised from 7 to 36 but only 20% of net proceeds were to be distributed.
Fourth	75% to be distributed, 80% on population and 20% on collection basis.	20% net proceeds of duties on all articles (other than regulatory duties special excise and duties etc.) to be distributed, 80% on population, 20% on weightage on economic and social backwardness.
Fifth	75% to be distributed, 90% on population and 10% on the basis of assessment in a State. Advance tax collection was added to divisible pool with effect from 1967-68, net	20% of net proceeds, 80% on population basis, 2/3 of remaining 20% to be distributed to States with per capita income below average level its proportion to its shortfall from average and 1/3rd according to weightages index of backwardness

TABLE II.1 : (Contd.)

Finance Commission	Income-Tax	Union Excise Duties (Basic)
(1)	(2)	(3)
Sixth	80% to be distributed, 90% on population and 10% on basis of assessments.	20% of net proceeds (excluding auxilliary duties) 75% on population and 25% on basis of backwardness.
Seventh	85% to be distributed-90% on the basis of population and 10% on the basis of assessment.	100% of duty on generation of electricity on the basis of collection. 40% of the balance of the net proceeds (Excluding duty on generation of electricity) to be distrubuted to States-25% each on the basis of population, inverse of per capita SDP, population below the poverty line and on a formula of revenue equalisation.
Eighth	85% of the net proceeds to be distributed-10% on the basis of assessment, the remaining 90% by giving a weightage of 25% to population, 25% to the inverse per capita income multiplied by population and 50% to the distance of per capita income of a state from that of state which has the highest per capita income.	45% of the net proceeds to be distributed among the states. 40% of net proceeds to be distributed among all the states by giving a weightage of 25% to population, 25% to the inverse of per capita income multiplied by population and 50% to the distance of per capita income of a state from that of the state which has the highest per capita income. The Remaining 5% of the net proceeds are to be set aside and distributed only among those states which have deficits after taking into account their share of all taxes and duties including their share in the 40% of the net proceeds of excise duties. The distribution is in proportion to the deficits of the states.

TABLE II.1 : PRINCIPLES AND CRITERIA FOR ALLOCATION OF CENTRAL TAXES AND DUTIES TO STATE OVER PERIODS COVERED BY EIGHTH FINANCE COMMISSIONS - (Contd.)

Finance Commission	Additional Union Excise Duties (replacing state's Sale Tax on Mill-Made textiles, sugar and tobacco)	Estate duty on property (other than on agricultural land)
(1)	(2)	(3)
First	Nil	Nil
Second	These duties levied in 1957 and net proceeds assigned to States were to be distributed on the basis guranteed level of States income from this source in 1956-57, plus on population basis.	Net proceeds assigned to to be classified between attributable to "immovable" property and "other" property and determined according to ratio of gross values of such properties. That Attributable to "immovable" property to be distributed in proporation to value of such property in a State. That of "Other" property to be distributed on population basis.
Third	The amount guaranteed was slightly raised by taking into account of inclusion of silk cloth under this duty. Basis of distribution of remainder was changed to percentage increase in collection of sales tax in State since 1957-58	Same 1961 Census adopted for distribution of duty on "Other" (movable) property on population basis.
Fourth	Greater weightage was given to collection commpared to population for determining share of a State out of the "remaining" divisible pool.	Same.
Fifth	"Remaining" divisible pool (above same level of guranteed amount) to be distributed on the basis of 50% in proportion to population and 50% in proportion to sales tax Collection.	Net proceeds assigned to States attributable be distributed in proportion to "immovable" property to gross value of such property located in a State and brought under assessment in a particular year. That attributable to "other" property to be distributed in proportion to population.

TABLE II.1 : (Contd.)

Sixth	System of guranteed amount abolished. Total net proceeds to be distributed 70% on population, 20% State Product and 10% on collection.	After deducting 2.5% of net proceeds for Union Territoriwes rest to be distributed as per principle laid laid down earlier by Vth Commission.
Finance Commission	Additional Union Excise Duties (replacing State's sales Tax on Mill-made textiles, sugar and tobacco)	Estate Duty on Property (other than on agricultural land.)
Seventh	Total net proceeds to be distributed among the States SUGAR based on average of dispatches to each state for 1974-77.TEXTILES TOBACCO. On the basis of the product of the population and per capita SDP.	Net proceeds to be distributed in proposition to the gross value of the immovable property and property other than immovable property taken together located in each State and brought into assessment.
Eighth	Net proceeds of Additional Excise duties on Sugar, Textiles and Tobacco to be distributed on the basis of a uniform formula by giving equal weightage to State Domestic product and population.	Same.

TABLE II.1 : PRINCIPLES AND CRITERIA FOR ALLOCATION OF CENTREAL TAXES AND DUTIES TO STATE OVER PERIODS COVERED BY EIGHT FINANCE COMMISSIONS (Contd.)

Finance Commission	Ad-hoc grants in lieu of Railway passenger fares tax.	Grant-in-aid under Article 275.
(1)	(2)	(3)
First	Nil	Generally criteria of "budgetary adequacy" was followed with a view to help cover non-plan revenue deficits even after devolution of of taxes under other heads from centre to States.
Second	A fixed sum of Rs. 12.5 crores representing annual collection from this source during 1958 to 1959, 1959-60 was decided to be distributed among states in proportion toshare of State in net proceeds of actual railway passenger travel in a State. The tax imposed in 1957 was later merged in the railway fare.	Same.
Third	Same	Same
Fourth	Finance Commission was not referred this matter, hence no recommendation on this point. Railway Convention Commiitee raised the amount under this to Rs. 16.25 Crores for distribution among States.	Same
Fifth	Commission rejected States 'plea for reintroduction of railway passenger tax. It estimated that a large amount of Rs. 25 crores should be paid but not made recommendation on this account.	Same
Sixth	The Commission worked out percentage share of States on basis of railway mileage actual passenger earnings of each State from non-suburban traffic for 4 year ending 1971-72.	The Commission recommended grants to fill gross in resources in order to maintain or upgrade essential administrative and social services like primary education, health, welfare etc.

TABLE II.1 : (Contd.)

Seventh	Percentage shares have been worked out on the basis of average non-suburban passenger earnings.	Devolution of taxes is the main channel of Transfer of of resources. Grants-in-aid are recommended for a few States only. Upgradation grants under non-developmental heads have been recommended.
Eighth	Percentage shares have been worked out on the basis of average non-suburban passenger earnings	Grant-in-aid are recommended to 11 States to cover the revenue gaps after taking into account devolution of taxes and duties. Up-gradation grants under non-developmental heads have been recommended to 16 States which have had a deficit before devolution. Grants to meet special problems have been recommended to 10 States.

SOURCE: REPORTS OF FINANCE COMMISSIONS.

TABLE II.2 : STATES' SHARES IN CENTRAL TAXES

INCOME TAX

(Percentage)

State	Fifth Commi-ssion	Sixth Commi-ssion	Seventh Commi-ssion	Seventh Commi-ssion	Eighth Commi-ssion
1	2	3	4 *	5	6
1. Andhra Pradesh	8.01	7.76	8.023	8.021	8.187
2. Assam	2.67	2.54	2.522	2.521	2.789
3. Bihar	9.99	9.61	9.540	9.536	12.080
4. Gujarat	5.13	5.55	5.959	5.957	4.409
5. Haryana	1.73	1.77	1.819	1.819	1.074
6. Himachal Pradesh	-	0.60	0.595	0.595	0.555
7. Jammu & Kashmir	0.79	0.81	0.818	0.818	0.838
8. Karnataka	5.40	5.33	5.442	5.440	4.979
9. Kerala	3.83	3.92	3.950	3.948	3.760
10. Madhya Pradesh	7.09	7.30	7.356	7.354	8.378
11. Maharashtra	11.34	11.05	10.953	10.949	8.392
12. Manipur	-	0.18	0.188	0.188	0.220
13. Meghalaya	-	0.18	0.178	0.178	0.184
14. Nagaland	0.08	0.09	0.085	0.085	0.088
15. Orissa	3.75	3.73	3.739	3.738	4.202
16. Punjab	2.55	2.75	2.714	2.713	1.744
17. Rajasthan	4.34	4.50	4.364	4.362	4.545
18. Sikkim	-	-	-	0.035	0.035
19. Tamil Nadu	8.18	7.94	8.050	8.048	7.565
20. Tripura	-	0.27	0.258	0.258	0.269
21. Uttar Pradesh	16.01	15.23	15.429	15.422	17.907
22. West Bengal	9.11	8.89	8.018	8.015	7.800
Total	100.00	100.00	100.00	100.00	100.00

* Excluding Sikkim

TABLE II.2 (Contd.)STATES' SHARES IN CENTRAL TAXES

UNION EXCISE DUTIES (BASIC)

(Percentage)

State	Fifth Commission	Sixth Commission	Seventh Commission (Excluding Sikkim)	Seventh Commission (Including Sikkim)	Eighth Commission
1. Andhra Pradesh	7.15	8.16	7.698	7.691	8.587
2. Assam	2.51	2.71	2.793	2.793	2.977
3. Bihar	13.81	11.47	13.025	13.021	13.202
4. Gujarat	4.17	4.57	4.103	4.101	3.506
5. Haryana	1.49	1.53	1.177	1.177	1.017
6. Himachal Pradesh	-	0.63	0.521	0.521	0.589
7. Jammu & Kashmir	1.12	0.90	0.839	0.83	0.856
8. Karnataka	4.65	5.45	4.877	4.876	5.077
9. Kerala	4.28	3.86	4.036	4.035	3.800
10. Madhya Pradesh	8.48	8.15	8.727	8.725	8.852
11. Maharashtra	7.93	8.58	6.633	6.632	6.216
12. Manipur	-	0.21	0.218	0.21	0.233
13. Meghalaya	-	0.19	0.200	0.200	0.194
14. Nagaland	0.08	0.11	0.097	0.097	0.096
15. Orissa	4.72	4.06	4.682	4.682	4.592
16. Punjab	2.17	1.87	1.226	1.226	1.317
17. Rajasthan	5.28	5.00	4.813	4.813	4.695
18. Sikkim	-	-	-	0.028	0.039
19. Tamil Nadu	6.50	7.43	7.641	7.637	7.317
20. Tripura	-	0.30	0.373	0.373	0.292
21. Uttar Pradesh	18.82	17.03	18.293	18.290	19.097
22. West Bengal	6.84	7.79	8.028	8.025	7.449
Total	100.00	100.00	100.00	100.00	100.00

TABLE-II.2(CONTD.) : STATES' SHARES IN CENTRAL TAXES

UNION EXCISE DUTIES (ADDITIONAL)
(Percentage)

State	Fifth Commission	Sixth Commission	Seventh Commission			Eighth Commission (Sugar Textile & Tobacco)
			Sugar	Textile	Tobacco	
1. Andhra Pradesh	8.13	8.39	5.247	8.020	8.018	7.504
2. Assam	2.47	2.47	2.408	2.298	2.297	2.566
3. Bihar	8.40	9.36	5.933	7.221	7.219	8.627
4. Gujarat	6.33	5.91	8.742	6.015	6.013	5.941
5. Haryana	1.70	1.94	2.666	2.790	2.789	2.488
6. Himachal Pradesh	-	0.59	0.860	0.734	0.734	0.663
7. Jammu & Kashmir	-	0.73	0.831	0.744	0.744	0.853
8. Karnataka	6.00	5.62	4.901	6.083	6.081	5.561
9. Kerala	4.84	3.58	3.783	4.020	4.019	3.963
10. Madhya Pradesh	6.34	6.98	6.019	6.422	6.419	6.942
11. Maharastra	13.89	11.65	17.082	13.510	13.506	11.461
12. Manipur	-	0.17	0.143	0.185	0.185	0.178
13. Meghalaya	-	0.17	0.029	0.171	0.171	0.183
14. Nagaland	-	0.08	0.115	0.084	0.084	0.098
15. Orissa	3.13	3.59	2.178	3.457	3.456	3.653
16. Punjab	2.98	2.68	6.220	4.270	4.268	3.675
17. Rajasthan	4.42	4.17	4.729	4.366	4.365	4.827
18. Sikkim	-	-	0.057	-	0.034	0.039
19. Tamil Nadu	9.63	7.27	6.449	7.710	7.707	7.549
20. Tripura	-	0.25	0.172	0.257	0.256	0.287
21. Uttar Pradesh	12.99	16.10	13.184	12.549	12.544	14.318
22. West Bengal	8.75	8.30	8.254	9.094	9.091	8.624
Total	100.00*	100.00	100.00	100.00#	100.00	100.00

* After providing the guaranteed amounts.

\# Excluding Sikkim. When Government of Sikkim gives up its sales tax on textiles, it would be entitled to a share in the additional duties of excise on textiles and the percentage distribution then would be as indicated in the last column.

TABLE-II-2 (CONTD.) : STATES' SHARES IN CENTRAL TAXES

(Percentage)

GRANT IN LIEU OF TAX ON RAILWAY PASSENGER FARES

State	Fifth Commi-ssion	Sixth Commi ssion	Seventh Commi ssion	Eight Commission ssion
1. Andhra Pradesh	8.56	8.01	6.99	7.68
2. Assam	2.88	2.70	2.46	2.03
3. Bihar	10.86	10.58	9.50	9.51
4. Gujarat	6.91	7.47	5.28	6.67
5. Haryana	2.46	2.57	1.97	1.84
6. Himachal Pradesh	-	0.17	0.13	0.14
7. Jammu & Kashmir	0.01	0.02	0.74	0.95
8. Karnataka	3.83	3.47	3.21	3.43
9. Kerala	1.78	1.61	2.61	3.18
10. Madhya Pradesh	9.92	9.89	5.84	5.85
11. Maharastra	9.12	8.87	15.87	15.70
12. Manipur	-	-	-	0.02
13. Meghalaya	-	-	-	0.05
14. Nagaland	0.01	0.01	0.26	0.16
15. Orissa	2.36	2.24	1.73	1.58
16. Punjab	4.76	5.06	3.81	3.88
17. Rajasthan	6.43	6.59	5.48	4.87
18. Sikkim	-	-	-	0.01
19. Tamil Nadu	5.54	5.14	6.85	6.61
20. Tripura	-	0.02	0.04	0.04
21. Uttar Pradesh	19.06	19.85	18.58	17.85
22. West Bengal	5.51	5.73	8.65	7.95
Total	100.00	100.00	100.00	100.00

TABLE-II-2 (CONTD.) : STATES' SHARES IN CENTRAL TAXES

(Percentage)

State	ESTATE DUTY			
	Fifth Commission	Sixth Commission	Seventh Commission	Eight Commission
1. Andhra Pradesh	8.37	8.04		
2. Assam	2.76	2.70		
3. Bihar	10.80	10.41		
4. Gujarat	4.80	4.93		
5. Haryana	1.76	1.86		
6. Himachal Pradesh	-	0.64		
7. Jammu & Kashmir	0.83	0.85		
8. Karnataka	5.48	5.41		
9. Kerala	3.93	3.94		
10. Madhya Pradesh	7.53	7.70		
11. Maharaṣtra	9.20	9.31		
12. Manipur	-	0.20		
13. Meghalaya	-	0.19		
14. Nagaland	0.09	0.10		
15. Orissa	4.08	4.05		
16. Punjab	2.59	2.50		
17. Rajasthan	4.68	4.76		
18. Tamil Nadu	7.83	7.61		
19. Tripura	-	0.29		
20. Uattar Pradesh	17.15	16.32		
21. West Bengal	8.12	8.19		
Total	100.00	100.00	*	*

* Percentage distribution not indicated. Estate Duty abolished with effect from 1985-86.

Source: Finance Commission Reports.

TABLE: II-3: COMPOSITION OF SHARED TAXES IN SELECTED YEARS

(Rs. Crores)

Year (1)	Income Tax (2)	Union Excise Duties (3)	Estate Duty (4)	Total (5)
1950-51	48	-	-	48
1955-56	55	17	2	74
1960-61	87	75	3	165
1965-66	123	146	7	276
1969-70	293	322	7	622
1970-71	359	390	6	755
1971-72	462	475	7	944
1972-73	492	567	8	1,067
1973-74	532	631	11	1,174
1974-75	512	702	10	1,224
1975-76	734	857	8	1,599
1976-77	652	1,028	10	1,690
1977-78	675	1,113	10	1,798
1978-79	707	1,239	11	1,957
1979-80	865	2,530	11	3,406
1980-81	1,002	2,777	12	3,791
1981-82	1,017	3,240	17	4,274
1982-83	1,132	3,491	16	4,639
1983-84	1,172	4,057	17	5,246
1984-85 (RE)	1,232	4,525	20	5,777
1985-86 (RE)	1,846	5,625	19	7,490
1986-87 (BE)	2,016	6,189	12	8,217

Source: Central Budgets.

TABLE-II-4: TRANSFERS TO THE STATES ON THE BASIS OF THE RECOMMENDATIONS OF THE FINANCE COMMISSION DURING 1951-52 - 1983-84

Rs. Crores

	Share in Divisible Taxes & Duties					Statutory and other grants				
	Income Tax	Union duties of excise Basic	Additional	Estate Duty	Total	Article 275 grants	In lieu of Tax on Railway Fares	Other grants	Total	Grand Total
(1)	(2)	(3)	(4)	(5)	(6)	(7)	(8)	(9)	(10)	(11)
1st Five-Year Plan										
1951-52	53	..	..	..	53	1	..	16	17	70
1952-53	57	17	..	..	74	5	..	14	19	93
1953-54	57	15	..	..	72	7	..	14	21	93
1954-55	56	15	..	..	71	7	..	15	22	93
1955-56	55	17	..	2	74	7	..	17	24	98
Total	278	64	..	2	344	27	..	76	103	447
2nd Five-Year Plan										
1956-57	59	18	..	2	79 *	8	..	12	20	99
1957-58	74	29	11	2	116 *	36	5	7	48	164
1958-59	76	33	40	2	151 *	36	11	10	57	208
1959-60	79	36	39	3	157 *	36	13	13	62	219
1960-61	87	37	38	3	165 *	37	14	12	63	228
Total	375	153	128	12	668	153	43	54	250	918
3rd Five-Year Plan										
1961-62	94	41	40	4	179	40	12	4	56	235
1962-63	95	79	46	4	224	61	12	7	80	304
1963-64	119	92	44	4	259	62	13	7	82	341
1964-65	124	86	41	7	258	65	13	10	88	346
1965-66	123	100	46	7	276	64	13	11	88	364
Total	555	398	217	26	1196	292	63	39	394	1590
Three Annual Plans										
1966-67	137	184	47	5	373	141	16	12	169	542
1967-68	175	203	32	7	417	141	16	8	165	582
1968-69	195	241	50	6	492	141	16	9	166	658
Total	507	628	129	18	1282	423	48	29	500	1782

TABLE II.4 (Contd.)

4th Five-Year Plan										
1969-70	293	266	56	7	622	153	16	10	179	801
1970-71	359	318	72	6	755	142	16	13	171	926
1971-72	462	369	106	7	944	141	16	11	168	1112
1972-73	492	432	135	8	1067	146	16	15	177	1244
1973-74	532	465	166	11	1174	131	16	17	164	1338
Total	2138	1850	535	39	4562	713	80	66	859	5421
5th Five-Year Plan										
1974-75	512	524	178	10	1224	482	16	8	506	1730
1975-76	734	646	211	8	1599	503	16	..	519	2118
1976-77	652	774	254	10	1690	500	16	..	516	2206
1977-78	676	817	303	10	1806	583	16	1	600	2406
1978-79	700	944	301	11	1956	615	16	1	632	2588
Total	3274	3705	1247	49	8275	2683	80	10	2773	11048
6th Five-Year Plan										
1979-80	862	2201	330	11	3404	256	17	1	274	3678
1980-81	1003	2378	396	12	3789	281	16	1	298	4087
1981-82	1019	2759	462	17	4257	292	16	1	309	4566
1982-83(RE)	1132	2999	492	16	4639	399	16	Neg.	415	5054
1983-84(BE)	1175	3293	604	16	5088	399	16	Neg.	415	5503
Total	5191	13630	2284	72	21177	1627	81	3	1711	22888

* Does not take into account State 'share' in tax on railway passenger fares. These transfers are shown under 'Other grants'.

Source: Report of Seventh Finance Comission [Appendix IV.1(ii)] for data upto the year 1976-77 and State Budgets/Finance Accounts for later years.

TABLE-II.5 : ESTIMATED TRANSFER OF RESOURCES RECOMMENDED BY THE SEVENTH & EIGHTH FINANCE COMMISSIONS

STATE	Estimated transfer during 1979-84 as recommended by Seventh Finance Commission					Estimated transfer during 1984-89 as recommended by Eighth Finance Commission					
	Taxes and Duties*	Art.275 Grant			Percentage to total in Column.5	Taxes and Duties**	Article 275 Grant				Percentage to total in Column11
		Revenue Gap	Upgradation	Total			Revenue Gap#	Upgradation Grant	Margin Money Grant	Total	
1	2	3	4	5	6	7	8	9	10	11	12
1. Andhra Pradesh	1502.89	..	19.60	1522.49	7.31	2754.78	..	80.49	61.25	2896.52	7.34
2. Assam	496.94	..	21.71	518.65	2.49	1251.67	274.33	63.35	18.13	1607.48	4.07
3. Bihar	2149.85	..	63.02	2212.87	10.62	4005.82	..	130.27	84.38	4220.47	10.70
4. Gujarat	963.87	..	..	963.87	4.63	1417.18	..	..	71.87	1489.05	3.77
5. Haryana	308.57	..	..	308.57	.48	427.97	..	..	11.25	439.22	1.11
6. Himachal Pradesh	110.26	207.07	7.74	325.07	1.56	530.69	223.04	16.26	4.38	774.37	1.96
7. Jammu & Kashmir	159.05	199.56	18.28	376.89	1.81	738.21	329.18	48.55	3.75	1119.69	2.84
8. Karnataka	1005.00	..	..	1005.00	4.82	1712.97		..	15.00	1727.97	4.38

TABLE II.5 (Contd.)

State											
9. Kerala	766.16	..	4.18	770.34	3.70	1258.94	..	16.81	12.50	1288.25	3.27
10. Madhya Pradesh	1533.88	..	63.58	1597.46	7.67	2788.11	..	157.69	11.88	2957.68	7.50
11. Maharashtra	1714.06	..	..	1714.06	8.22	2617.30	..	..	18.12	2635.42	6.68
12. Manipur	37.76	146.32	9.95	194.03	0.93	299.18	146.95	22.30	0.62	469.05	1.19
13. Meghalaya	36.68	92.61	4.86	134.15	0.64	242.88	119.15	19.20	0.63	381.86	0.97
14. Nagaland	17.91	218.35	4.33	240.59	1.15	325.47	190.52	10.81	0.62	527.42	1.34
15. Orissa	815.27	136.92	32.26	984.45	4.72	1561.60	207.60	74.84	65.62	1909.66	4.84
16. Punjab	419.53	..	..	419.53	2.01	611.15	..	20.00	15.00	646.15	1.64
17. Rajasthan	883.52	..	19.29	902.81	4.33	1538.18	42.63	53.48	41.88	1676.17	4.25
18. Sikkim	0.48	35.72	0.65	36.85	0.18	63.52	36.16	4.14	0.63	104.45	0.27
19. Tamil Nadu	1476.39	..	27.21	1503.60	7.21	2443.07	..	..	21.87	2464.94	6.25
20. Tripura	59.66	136.57	3.61	199.84	0.96	357.67	187.05	14.59	1.87	561.18	1.42
21. Uttar Pradesh	3202.72	..	112.02	3314.74	15.90	5915.60	..	108.18	81.25	6105.03	15.47
22. West Bengal	1572.60	..	24.51	1597.11	7.66	2820.62	443.61	126.37	59.38	3449.98	8.74
TOTAL	19233.05	1173.12	436.80	20842.97	100.00	35682.58	2200.22	967.33	601.88	39452.01	100.00

* Includes share of Grants in lieu of Railway Passenger Fares Tax amounting to Rs.81.25 crores but excluded Rs. 64 crores in respect of Share in Estate Duty and receipt on account of Wealth Tax on Agri. Property.

** Includes Share of Grants in lieu of Railway Passenger Fares Tax amounting to Rs. 475 crores but excluded Rs. 103 crores in respect of Share in Estate Duty and receipt on account of Wealth Tax on Agri. Property.

Revenue Gap Grants in Table 3 and Table 7.

Source: Report of the Eigth Finance Commission.

TABLE · SE TRANSFER OF RESOURCES UNDER THE FINANCE COMMISSION'S AWARDS

Rs. Crores

STATES	Second Commn. 1957-58 TO 1961-62	Third Commn. 1962-63 TO 1965-66	Fourth Commn. 1966-67 TO 1968-69	Fifth Commn. 1969-70 TC 1973-74	Sixth Commn. 1974-75 TO 1978-79	Seventh Commn. 1979-80 TO 1983-84	Eigth Commn. 1984-85 TO 1988-89	Total transfer II to VIII Commn.
GROUP 'A' STATES	197.56	263.69	290.50	906.08	1369.80	3406.03	5209.84	11643.50
1. Punjab	51.92	58.99	38.77	113.77	168.97	419.53	646.15	1497.50
2. Haryana	-	-	20.77	75.27	120.66	308.57	439.22	964.49
3. Maharastra	109.85	119.52	157.19	486.82	711.53	1714.06	2635.42	5934.39
4. Gujarat	35.79	85.18	73.77	230.82	368.64	963.87	1489.05	3247.12
GROUP 'B' STATES	335.63	405.36	566.54	1564.81	2789.03	5778.86	10607.31	22047.54
5. West Bengal	103.36	93.72	118.33	448.92	822.93	1597.11	3449.98	6634.35
6. Karnataka	73.46	81.23	130.56	247.28	383.64	1005.00	1727.97	3649.14
7. Tamil Nadu	72.88	91.75	125.10	370.78	538.57	1503.60	2464.94	5167.62
8. Kerala	37.91	68.45	113.67	232.78	979.97	770.34	1288.25	2991.37
9. Rajashtan	48.02	70.21	78.88	265.05	563.92	902.81	1676.17	3605.06
GROUP 'C' STATES	445.85	560.71	725.31	2324.46	4090.67	9632.01	18089.36	35868.37
10. Andhra Pradesh	90.05	122.12	140.49	412.79	776.01	1522.49	2896.52	5960.47
11. Orissa	47.25	101.20	140.21	287.37	577.32	984.45	1909.66	4047.46
12. Madhya Pradesh	71.54	86.81	97.77	343.10	543.57	1597.46	2957.68	5697.93
13. Uttar Pradesh	141.69	147.95	226.23	772.47	1349.05	3314.74	6105.03	12057.10
14. Bihar	95.32	102.63	120.61	508.73	844.72	2212.87	4220.47	8105.35
TOTAL 14 STATES	979.04	1229.76	1582.35	4795.35	8249.50	18816.90	33906.51	69559.41
SPL.CATEGORY STATES	69.93	81.00	162.67	520.64	1359.35	2026.07	5545.50	9765.16
15. Himachal Pradesh	-	-	-	50.22	204.06	325.07	774.37	1353.72
16. Jammu & Kashmir	24.57	21.75	39.66	115.34	232.28	376.89	1119.69	1930.18
17. Nagaland	-	0.68	35.13	81.61	135.67	240.59	527.42	1021.10
18. Sikkim	-	-	-	-		36.85	104.45	141.30
19. Tripura	-	-	-	33.74	132.19	199.84	561.18	926.95
20. Meghalaya	-	-	-	18.84	87.52	134.15	381.86	622.37
21. Assam	45.36	58.57	87.88	194.09	439.62	518.65	1607.48	2951.65
22. Manipur	-	-	-	26.80	128.01	194.03	469.05	817.89
ALL STATES	1048.97	1310.76	1745.02	5315.99	9608.85	2084.97	39452.01	79324.57

TABLE II.7 : PER CAPITA TRANSFERS OF RESOURCES UNDER THE FINANCE COMMISSSION AWARDS

STATES	Second Commn. 1957-58 TO 1961-62	Third Commn. 62-63 TO 65-66	Fourth Commn. 66-67 TO 68-69	Fifth Commn. 69-70 TO 73-74	Sixth Commn. 74-75 TO 78-79	Seventh Commn. 79-80 TO 83-84	Eigth Commn. 84-85 TO 88-89	Rs. Crores Total transfer II to VIII Commn.
GROUP 'A' STATES	26.60	31.29	30.79	89.98	121.33	269.04	411.52	919.72
1. Punjab	29.83	29.23	28.64	83.21	111.90	249.72	384.61	891.37
2. Haryana	-	-	22.34	75.27	105.84	239.20	340.48	747.67
3. Maharashtra	29.26	28.39	33.60	96.59	126.61	272.94	419.65	944.97
4. Gujarat	18.52	38.70	29.82	86.45	122.07	282.66	436.67	952.23
GROUP 'B' STATES	27.41	29.53	37.63	96.65	155.03	289.09	530.63	1102.93
5. West Bengal	31.84	24.95	28.58	101.34	167.26	292.51	631.86	1215.08
6. Karnataka	32.83	32.40	47.56	84.40	115.25	270.89	465.76	983.60
7. Tamil Nadu	22.31	26.27	33.39	90.00	120.76	310.66	509.28	1067.69
8. Kerala	23.51	38.07	57.33	109.29	206.00	302.09	505.20	1173.09
9. Rajasthan	25.49	32.32	32.34	102.73	189.23	263.21	488.68	1051.04
GROUP 'C' STATES	22.62	25.70	30.41	92.31	145.68	307.83	578.12	1146.32
10. Andhra Pradesh	25.92	32.23	34.58	94.89	161.00	284.58	541.41	1114.11
11. Orissa	28.55	54.20	68.54	131.22	239.55	372.00	723.35	1533.13
12. Madhya Pradesh	23.68	25.29	25.79	82.28	116.42	306.03	566.61	1091.56
13. Uttar Pradesh	19.86	19.01	26.56	87.48	136.27	298.89	550.50	1087.21
14. Bihar	21.56	20.73	22.19	90.20	134.51	316.58	603.79	1159.56
TOTAL 14 STATES	24.86	27.96	32.73	83.22	143.82	294.29	530.29	1087.89
SPECIAL GATEGORY STATES	48.02	47.89	87.54	192.11	434.30	561.24	1536.15	2705.03
ALL STATES	25.69	28.70	34.76	32.23	158.85	308.56	584.04	1174.31
POPULATION	1958	1963	1967	1971	1976	1981	1981	1981

TABLE II.8 : REVENUE SURPLUS/DEFICIT BEFORE AND AFTER DEVOLUTION: 1984-89 (Rs. in Crores)

	STATES		Non-Plan revenue position without devolution of taxes		Revenue surplus after devolution taxes #		Revenue deficit after devolution taxes @
1.	Andhra Pradesh	(-)	845.98	(+)	1,908.80		-
2.	Assam	(-)	1,444.46		-	(-)	192.79
3.	Bihar	(-)	3,152.50	(+)	853.32		-
4.	Gujarat	(+)	1,034.13	(+)	2,451.31		-
5.	Haryana	(+)	965.95	(+)	1,393.92		-
6.	Himachal Pradesh	(-)	713.77		-	(-)	183.08
7.	Jammu & Kashmir	(-)	995.39		-	(-)	257.18
8.	Karnataka	(+)	351.71	(+)	2,064.68		-
9.	Kerala	(-)	635.43	(+)	623.51		-
10.	Nadhya Pradesh	(-)	801.77	(+)	1,986.34		-
11.	Maharashtra	(+)	3,790.48	(+)	6,407.78		-
12.	Manipur	(-)	422.73		-	(-)	123.55
13.	Meghalaya	(-)	341.30		-	(-)	98.42
14.	Nagaland	(-)	484.04		-	(-)	158.57
15.	Orissa	(-)	1,663.80		-	(-)	102.20
16.	Punjab	(+)	1,147.55	(+)	1,758.70		-
17.	Rajasthan	(-)	1,240.63	(+)	307.25**	(-)	9.70*
18.	Sikkim	(-)	92.65		-	(-)	29.13
19.	Tamil Nadu	(+)	774.12	(+)	3,217.19		-
20.	Tripura	(-)	502.46		-	(-)	144.79
21.	Uttar Pradesh	(-)	2,113.59	(+)	3,802.01		-
22.	West Bengal	(-)	3,034.33		-	(-)	213.71
Total All States		(-)	18,484.83				
		(+)	8,063.94	(+)	26,774.81	(-)	1,513.12

....

* For 1984-85 ** For 1985-89

Excluding Estate Duty and Wealth Tax on Agricultural Property.

Source : Report of the Eighth Finance Commission, 1984.

TABLE II.9 : REVENUE DEFICITS OF THE STATES AS REASSESSED

(Rs. Crores)

STATES (1)	Total 1984-89 (2)	1984-85 (3)	1985-86 (4)	1986-87 (5)	1987-88 (6)	1988-89 (7)
Assam	192.79	63.63	50.14	37.66	29.67	11.69
Himachal Pradesh	183.08	51.70	45.95	38.25	31.17	16.01
Jammu & Kashmir	257.18	77.27	66.41	52.78	41.04	19.68
Manipur	123.55	34.85	30.87	25.83	21.10	10.90
Meghalaya	98.42	27.87	24.64	20.56	16.74	8.61
Nagaland	158.57	44.19	39.64	33.30	27.36	14.08
Orissa	102.20	46.07	32.51	16.17	6.87	0.58
Rajasthan	9.70	9.70	-	-	-	-
Sikkim	29.13	8.29	7.31	6.08	4.93	2.52
Tripura	144.79	40.99	36.29	30.24	24.68	12.59
West Bengal	213.71	95.40	64.88	35.35	17.55	0.53
Total	1,513.12	499.96	398.64	296.22	221.11	97.19

Source : Report of the Eighth Finance Commission, 1984.

TABLE II.10 : REVENUE GAP GRANTS-IN-AID TO STATES

(Rs. Crores)

STATES (1)	Total 1984-89 (2)	1984-85 (3)	1985-86 (4)	1986-87 (5)	1987-88 (6)	1988-89 (7)
Assam	215.48	66.81	55.15	43.31	35.60	14.61
Himachal Pradesh	206.24	54.29	50.55	43.99	37.40	20.01
Jammu & Kashmir	288.73	81.13	73.05	60.70	49.25	24.60
Manipur	139.20	36.59	33.96	29.70	25.32	13.63
Meghalaya	110.85	29.26	27.10	23.64	20.09	10.76
Nagaland	178.72	46.40	43.60	38.29	32.83	17.60
Orissa	111.70	48.37	35.76	18.60	8.24	0.73
Rajasthan	10.19	10.19	-	-	-	-
Sikkim	32.81	8.71	8.04	6.99	5.92	3.15
Tripura	163.10	43.04	39.92	34.78	29.62	15.74
West Bengal	233.91	100.17	71.37	40.65	21.06	0.66
TOTAL	1,690.93	524.96	438.50	340.65	265.33	121.49

Source : Report of the Eighth Finance Commission, 1984

TABLE II.11 : GRANTS-IN-AID FOR SPECIAL PROBLEMS

(Rs. Crores)

STATES	Total 1984-89	1984-85	1985-86	1986-87	1987-88	1988-89
1. Assam	5.00	1.00	1.00	1.00	1.00	1.00
2. HimachalPradesh	0.50	0.10	0.10	0.10	0.10	0.10
3. Jammu & Kashmir	2.48	0.49	0.50	0.50	0.50	0.49
4. Madhya Pradesh	10.00	2.00	2.00	2.00	2.00	2.00
5. Manipur	2.00	0.40	0.40	0.40	0.40	0.40
6. Meghalaya	1.00	0.20	0.20	0.20	0.20	0.20
7. Punjab	20.00	4.00	4.00	4.00	4.00	4.00
8. Rajasthan	10.00	2.00	2.00	2.00	2.00	2.00
9. Sikkim	1.00	0.20	0.20	0.20	0.20	0.20
10. Tripura	0.80	0.16	0.16	0.16	0.16	0.16
Total	52.78	10.55	10.56	10.56	10.56	10.55

Source: Report of the Eighth Financ Commission, 1984.

TABLE II.12 : MARGIN MONEYS RECOMMENDED BY THE EIGHTH AND SEVENTH FINANCE COMMISSIONS FOR FINANCING RELIEF EXPENDITURE (Rs. in Crores)

STATES	Margin Money recommended by Eighth Finance Commission	Margin Money recommended by Seventh Finance Commission
1. Andhra Pradesh	24.50	8.58
2. Assam	7.25	3.46
3. Bihar	33.75	13.08
4. Gujarat	28.75	9.56
5. Haryana	4.50	1.47
6. Himachal Pradesh	1.75	0.51
7. Jammu & Kashmir	1.50	1.30
8. Karnataka	6.00	2.00
9. Kerala	5.00	1.59
10. Madhya Pradesh	4.75	1.83
11. Maharashtra	7.25	4.57
12. Manipur	0.25	0.08
13. Meghalaya	0.25	0.07
14. Nagaland	0.25	0.14
15. Orissa	26.25	8.71
16. Punjab	6.00	2.68
17. Rajasthan	16.75	7.74
18. Sikkim	0.25	0.01
19. Tamil Nadu	8.75	8.59
20. Tripura	0.75	0.18
21. Uttar Pradesh	32.50	10.80
22. West Bengal	23.75	13.60
TOTAL	240.75	100.55

Source: Report of the Eighth Finance Commission, 1984.

TABLE II.13 : CENTRE'S CONTRIBUTION TO MARGIN MONEY

(Rs. Crores)

	STATES	1984-85	Total 1984-89
1.	Andhra Pradesh	12.250	61.250
2.	Assam	3.625	18.125
3.	Bihar	16.875	84.375
4.	Gujarat	14.375	71.875
5.	Haryana	2.250	11.250
6.	Himachal Pradesh	0.875	4.375
7.	Jammu & Kashmir	0.750	3.750
8.	Karnataka	3.000	15.000
9.	Kerala	2.500	12.500
10.	Madhya Pradesh	2.375	11.875
11.	Maharashtra	3.625	18.125
12.	Manipur	0.125	0.625
13.	Meghalaya	0.125	0.625
14.	Nagaland	0.125	0.625
15.	Orissa	13.125	65.625
16.	Punjab	3.000	15.000
17.	Rajasthan	8.375	41.875
18.	Sikkim	0.125	0.625
19.	Tamil Nadu	4.375	21.875
20.	Tripura	0.375	1.875
21.	Uttar Pradesh	16.250	81.250
22.	West Bengal	11.875	59.375
	Total	120.375	601.875

Source: Report of the Eighth Finance Commission, 1984.

TABLE II.14 : GRANTS-IN-AID FROM 1984-85 TO 1988-89 FOR UPGRADATION OF SERVICES

Rs. Crores

STATES	Total 1984-89	1984-85	1985-86	1986-87	1987-88	1988-89
1. Andhra Pradesh	80.49	13.09	28.50	16.74	16.72	5.44
2. Assam	58.35	9.49	20.66	12.14	12.12	3.94
3. Bihar	130.27	21.18	46.13	27.10	27.06	8.80
4. Himachal Pradesh	15.76	2.56	5.58	3.28	3.27	1.07
5. Jammu & Kashmir	46.07	7.49	16.31	9.58	9.57	3.12
6. Kerala	16.81	2.73	5.95	3.50	3.49	1.14
7. Madhya Pradesh	147.69	24.01	52.30	30.72	30.68	9.98
8. Manipur	20.30	3.30	7.19	4.22	4.22	1.37
9. Meghalaya	18.20	2.96	6.44	3.79	3.78	1.23
10. Nagaland	10.81	1.76	3.83	2.25	2.24	0.73
11. Orissa	74.84	12.17	26.50	15.57	15.54	5.06
12. Rajasthan	43.48	7.07	15.40	9.04	9.03	2.94
13. Sikkim	3.14	0.51	1.11	0.66	0.65	0.21
14. Tripura	13.79	2.24	4.88	2.87	2.87	0.93
15. Uttar Pradesh	108.18	17.59	38.31	22.50	22.47	7.31
16. West Bengal	126.37	20.55	44.75	26.28	26.25	8.54
Total	914.55	148.70	323.84	190.24	189.96	61.81

Source: Report of the Eighth Finance Commission, 1984.

TABLE II.15 : STATE-WISE AND SECTOR-WISE PROVISIONS MADE FOR UPGRADATION

(Rs. Crores)

STATES	Police Administration			Education			Jail Admn.	Tribal Administration			Health			Judicial Administration		
	Revenue	Capital	Total	Revenue	Capital	Total	Capital	Revenue	Capital	Total	Revenue	Capital	Total	Revenue	Capital	Total
1. Andhra Pradesh	4.07	7.62	11.69	22.08	12.60	34.68	7.21	1.04	6.23	7.27	2.82	4.66	7.48	-	6.19	6.19
2. Assam	0.62	12.50	13.12	-	24.26	24.26	6.92	1.57	3.49	5.06	1.05	2.31	3.36	0.54	2.81	3.35
3. Bihar	4.44	26.53	30.97	-	40.79	40.79	10.72	3.76	14.85	18.61	4.09	6.74	10.83	2.60	7.54	10.14
4. Gujarat	1.39	-	1.39	6.90	-	6.90	2.12	3.86	4.49	8.35	1.62	2.13	3.75	0.10	2.47	2.57
5. Haryana	0.76	0.11	0.87	-	-	-	3.76	-	-	-	0.57	0.77	1.34	0.04	0.72	0.76
6. Himachal Pradesh	0.49	2.00	2.49	1.14	7.38	8.52	0.29	0.23	0.50	0.73	0.51	0.99	1.50	-	0.66	0.66
7. Jammu & Kashmir	0.44	18.86	19.30	7.70	7.33	15.03	6.14	-	-	-	0.61	1.41	2.02	-	1.50	1.50
8. Karnataka	3.48	13.43	16.91	28.91	-	28.91	13.34	0.20	2.42	2.62	1.95	2.51	4.46	-	3.46	3.46
9. Kerala	1.34	5.74	7.08	-	-	-	0.94	0.36	0.25	0.61	1.11	1.32	2.43	-	3.24	3.24
10. Madhya Pradesh	3.12	35.38	38.50	15.45	-	15.45	54.02	7.11	20.34	27.45	2.72	1.54	4.26	0.28	1.99	2.27
11. Maharashtra	3.42	44.12	47.54	16.83	-	16.83	14.99	1.57	4.60	6.17	3.12	4.59	7.71	1.26	4.44	5.70
12. Manipur	0.44	3.45	3.89	-	8.78	8.78	3.71	0.60	1.43	2.03	0.22	0.54	0.76	0.14	0.22	0.36
13. Meghalaya	0.45	1.94	2.39	2.54	7.08	9.62	4.93	-	-	-	0.17	0.38	0.55	-	0.13	0.13
14. Nagaland	0.29	0.02	0.31	-	2.58	2.58	6.57	-	-	-	0.13	0.31	0.44	-	0.21	0.21
15. Orissa	1.50	11.62	13.12	9.06	16.77	25.83	3.27	3.46	17.46	20.92	1.95	2.08	4.03	0.56	1.36	1.92
16. Punjab	1.14	15.19	16.33	-	-	-	7.59	-	-	-	0.87	1.38	2.25	-	0.71	0.71
17. Rajasthan	2.03	5.80	7.83	11.27	-	11.27	4.39	2.90	3.96	6.86	1.56	2.48	4.04	0.86	2.28	3.14
18. Sikkim	0.40	1.97	2.37	-	-	-	0.03	-	0.08	0.08	0.10	0.24	0.34	-	0.04	0.04
19. Tamil Nadu	3.23	22.27	25.50	-	-	-	6.89	0.27	0.27	0.54	2.62	3.68	6.30	-	5.10	5.10
20. Tripura	0.46	5.06	5.52	0.13	4.15	4.28	0.17	1.61	0.49	2.10	0.21	0.50	0.71	-	0.14	0.14
21. Uttar Pradesh	5.72	52.34	58.06	-	-	-	19.18	0.11	0.07	0.18	6.16	9.78	15.94	-	3.42	3.42
22. West Bengal	1.93	54.47	56.40	-	32.67	32.67	14.21	1.35	3.95	5.30	2.19	3.19	5.38	2.99	3.07	6.06
Total	41.16	340.42	381.58	122.01	164.39	286.40	191.39	30.00	84.88	114.88	36.35	53.53	89.88	9.37	51.70	(X)

Source: Report of the Eighth Finance Commission, 1984. (x) Total (17) 61.07

TABLE II.15 : STATE-WISE AND SECTOR-WISE PROVISIONS MADE FOR UPGRADATION (Rs. in Crores) (Contd.)

STATES	Distt & Rev. Admn.	Training Admn.	Treasuries & Accounts Admn.			Special Problems			Grand Total			Grants Recommended		
	Capital	Capital	Revenue	Capital	Total	Revenue	Capital	To-tal	Revenue	Capital	Total	Reve-nue	Capi tal	Total
1. Andhra Pradesh	3.81	1.47	-	0.69	0.69	-	-	-	30.01	50.48	80.49	30.01	50.48	80.49
2. Assam	0.39	0.77	0.85	0.27	1.12	5.00	-	5.00	9.63	53.72	63.35	9.63	53.72	63.35
3. Bihar	1.39	2.31	4.07	0.44	4.51	-	-	-	18.96	111.31	130.27	18.96	111.31	130.27
4. Gujarat	1.74	1.48	-	0.60	0.60	-	-	-	13.87	15.03	28.90	-	-	-
5. Haryana	0.71	0.69	-	0.36	0.36	-	-	-	1.37	7.12	8.49	-	-	-
6. Himachal Pradesh	0.87	0.39	-	0.31	0.31	-	0.50	0.50	2.37	13.89	16.26	2.37	13.89	16.26
7. Jammu & Kashmir	1.05	0.71	-	0.32	0.32	-	2.48	2.48	8.75	39.80	48.55	8.75	39.80	48.55
8. Karnataka	2.21	1.36	-	0.60	0.60	-	-	-	34.54	39.33	73.87	-	-	-
9. Kerala	0.54	1.53	-	0.44	0.44	-	-	-	2.81	14.00	16.81	2.81	14.00	16.81
10. Madhya Pradesh	3.09	1.90	0.10	0.65	0.75	-	10.00	10.00	28.78	128.91	157.69	28.78	128.91	157.69
11. Maharashtra	3.81	1.44	-	0.69	0.69	-	-	-	26.20	78.68	104.88	-	-	-
12. Manipur	0.26	0.13	0.22	0.16	0.38	-	2.00	2.00	1.62	20.68	22.30	1.62	20.68	22.30
13. Meghalaya	0.09	0.10	0.23	0.16	0.39	1.00	-	1.00	4.39	14.81	19.20	4.39	14.81	19.20
14. Nagaland	0.30	0.21	-	0.19	0.19	-	-	-	0.42	10.39	10.81	0.42	10.39	10.81
15. Orissa	3.31	0.81	1.24	0.39	1.63	-	-	-	17.77	57.07	74.84	17.77	57.07	74.84
16. Punjab	1.11	0.93	-	0.36	0.36	10.00	10.00	20.00	12.01	37.27	49.28	10.00	10.00	20.00
17. Rajasthan	2.63	1.28	1.77	0.27	2.04	-	10.00	10.00	20.39	33.09	53.48	20.39	33.09	53.48
18. Sikkim	0.03	0.10	-	0.15	0.15	0.50	0.50	1.00	1.00	3.14	4.14	1.00	3.14	4.14
19. Tamil Nadu	3.16	1.95	0.78	0.52	1.30	-	-	-	6.90	43.84	50.74	-	-	-
20. Tripura	0.18	0.39	0.15	0.15	0.30	-	0.80	0.80	2.56	12.03	14.59	2.56	12.03	14.59
21. Uttar Pradesh	5.32	2.68	2.57	0.83	3.40	-	-	-	14.56	93.62	108.18	14.56	93.62	108.18
22. West Bengal	1.72	1.27	3.05	0.31	3.36	-	-	-	11.51	114.86	126.37	11.51	114.86	126.37
Total	37.72	23.90	15.03	8.86	23.89	16.50	36.28	52.78	270.42	993.07	1,263.49	185.53	781.80	967.33

Source: Report of the Eighth Finance Commission, 1984.

TABLE II.16 : TOTAL GRANTS-IN-AID UNDER ARTICLE 275: 1984-89 RECOMMENDED BY EIGHTH FIN. COMMN.

(Rs. Crores)*

State	Total 1984-98	1984-85	1985-86	1986-87	1987-88	1988-89
(1)	(2)	(3)	(4)	(5)	(6)	(7)
1. Andhra Pradesh	141.74	25.34	40.75	28.99	28.97	17.69
2. Assam	355.81	92.70	92.21	71.85	64.11	34.94
3. Bihar	214.65	38.06	63.01	43.98	43.93	25.67
4. Gujarat	71.87	14.37	14.37	14.37	14.38	14.38
5. Haryana	11.25	2.25	2.25	2.25	2.25	2.25
6. Himachal Pradesh	243.68	61.19	60.47	51.61	45.00	25.41
7. Jammu & Kashmir	381.48	97.95	98.70	79.62	68.16	37.05
8. Karnataka	15.00	3.00	3.00	3.00	3.00	3.00
9. Kerala	29.31	5.23	8.45	6.00	5.99	3.64
10. Madhya Pradesh	169.57	28.39	56.68	35.10	35.05	14.35
11. Maharashtra	18.12	3.62	3.62	3.62	3.63	3.63
12. Manipur	169.87	41.96	43.22	35.99	31.62	17.08
13. Meghalaya	138.98	34.20	35.52	29.42	25.86	13.98
14. Nagaland	201.95	50.64	49.91	43.02	37.56	20.82
15. Orissa	348.06	92.85	94.57	66.47	56.08	38.09
16. Punjab	35.00	7.00	7.00	7.00	7.00	7.00
17. Rajasthan	137.99	51.70	34.16	19.42	19.40	13.31
18. Sikkim	40.93	10.21	10.14	8.65	7.57	4.36
19. Tamil Nadu	21.87	4.38	4.38	4.37	4.37	4.37
20. Tripura	203.51	50.60	50.12	42.97	37.82	22.00
21. Uttar Pradesh	189.43	33.84	54.56	38.75	38.72	23.56
22. West Bengal	629.36	174.54	169.94	120.75	101.12	63.01
Total	3769.43	924.02	997.03	757.20	681.59	409.59

* Rounded off to nearest lakh.
Source: Report of the VIII Finance Commission

TABLE II.17 : REPHASING OF OUTLAYS RECOMMENDED BY THE 8 TH FINANCE COMMISSION FOR UPGRADATION OF STANDARDS OF ADMINISTRATION AND SPECIAL PROBLEMS

(Rs. Lakhs)

STATES	Grant recommended for 1984-89	Adopted for 1984-85	Net for 1985-89	REPHASING FOR 1985-89			
				1985-86	1986-87	1987-88	1988-89
(1)	(2)	(3)	(4)	(5)	(6)	(7)	(8)
1. Andhra Pradesh	8049.27	525.77	7523.50	2188.00	1848.39	2021.83	1465.28
2. Assam	6333.77	447.81	5885.96	2051.48	1528.74	1542.83	762.91
3. Bihar	13027.92	816.33	12211.59	4195.01	3146.39	3215.19	1655.00
4. Himachal Pradesh	1624.95	110.54	1514.41	514.87	389.94	389.72	210.88
5. J & K	4855.82	315.57	4540.25	1471.83	1152.11	1201.06	715.25
6. Kerala	1679.92	129.90	1550.02	521.95	394.06	405.67	228.34
7. Madhya Pradesh	15768.52	1145.22	14623.30	4803.97	3727.51	3856.95	2234.87
8. Manipur	2229.41	158.29	2071.12	715.40	543.99	544.32	267.41
9. Meghalaya	1920.04	120.90	1799.14	568.40	483.86	467.34	279.54
10. Nagaland	1079.73	60.16	1019.57	366.92	265.33	266.77	120.55
11. Orissa	7484.62	485.88	6998.74	2273.97	1770.83	1856.37	1097.57
12. Punjab	1600.00	-	1600.00	400.00	400.00	400.00	400.00
13. Rajasthan	5348.30	527.81	4820.49	1295.47	1181.57	1282.92	1060.53
14. Sikkim	413.54	39.39	374.15	11.69	98.28	96.87	63.31
15. Tripura	1158.96	119.59	1339.37	449.26	348.81	349.48	191.82
16. Uttar Pradesh	10817.92	680.44	10137.48	3507.76	2613.30	2662.57	1353.85
17. West Bengal	12637.11	714.55	11922.56	4201.35	3089.58	3141.55	1490.08
Total:	96329.80	6398.15	89931.65	29641.33	22982.69	23710.44	13597.19

Note:The rephasing has been done consequent on the Govt of India's decision to implement the recommendations of the VIII Finance Commission from 1985-86 instead of 1984-85

Source: Government of India, Ministry of Finance, 'Statistical Statements on Finances and Plans of States and Union Territories 1985'.

TABLE III.1 : COMPOSITION OF CENTRAL ASSISTANCE TO THE STATES OR THE PLAN

(Rs. Crores)

		Assistance for State Plans			Assistance for Central/Centrally Sponsored Schemes			Grand Total	Assistance for State Plans as % of Total
		Grants	Loans	Total	Grants	Lcans	Total		
1.	First Plan	-	-	350	-	-	530	880	39.8
2.	Second Plan	254	804	1058	-	-	-	-	-
3.	Third Plan	-	-	2515	175	48	223	2738	91.8
4.	Three Annual Plans	-	-	1767	-	-	150	1917	92.2
5.	Fourth Plan								
	1969-70	189	446	635	69	1	70	705	90.1
	1970-71	200	456	656	66	13	79	735	89.2
	1971-72	227	498	725	144	18	162	887	81.7
	1972-73	236	529	765	352	170	522	1287	59.4
	1973-74	225	529	754	338	25	363	1117	67.5
	Total	1077	2458	3535	969	227	1196	4731	74.7
6.	Fifth Plan								
	1974-75	269	569	838	197	77	274	1112	75.4
	1975-76	371	720	1091	252	85	337	1428	76.4
	1976-77	530	783	1313	340	103	443	1756	74.8
	1977-78(RE)	730	1191	1921	484	171	655	2576	74.6
	Total	1900	3263	5163	1273	436	1709	6872	75.1

TABLE III.1 (Contd.)

7.	Annual Plan								
	1978-79 (R.E.)	1029	1759	2788	730	175	905	3785	75.5
	1979-80(RE)	956	1554	2510	854	109	963	5411	72.3
8.	Sixth Plan								
	1980-81(RE)	1102	1805	2907	1053	115	1168	4075	71.3
	1981-82(RE)	1221	1821	3042	925	110	1035	4077	74.6
	1982-83(RE)	1496	2231	3727	1158	120	1278	5005	74.5
	1983-84 (R.E)	1726	2399	4125	1689	123	1812	5937	69.5
	1984-85 (R.E)	1832	2553	4385	2254	173	2427	6812	64.4
	Total	7377	10809	18186	7079	641	7720	25906	70.2
9.	Seventh Plan								
	1985-86(RE)	2537	3748	6285	2646	173	2819	9104	69.0
	1986-87(BE)	2556	3600	6156	2997	170	3167	9323	66.0

Source: Report of the Seventh Finance Commission and Central Budgets.*

TABLE III.2 : CENTRAL ASSISTANCE FOR STATE PLANS

Rs. Crores

	First Plan 1951-56 (Actuals)	Second Plan 1956-61 (Actuals)	Third Plan 1961-66 (Actuals)	Annual Plan 1966-69 (Actuals)	Fourth Plan 1969-74 (Actuals)	Fifth Plan 1974-79 (Actuals)	Annual Plan 1979-80 (Actuals)	Sixth Plan 1980-85 (Actuals)	Seventh Plan 1985-90 (Allocation)
I.SPL.CATEGORY STATES:									
1. Assam	22.00	30.59	99.87	84.22	173.47	242.16	123.97	1343.68	2065.08
2. Himachal Pradesh	-	-	-	-	98.44	126.68	74.51	498.37	866.93
3. Jammu & Kashmir	10.00	19.46	61.24	58.18	138.64	477.02	111.39	1057.88	1838.68
4. Manipur	-	-	-	-	26.13	55.97	30.20	286.83	545.00
5. Meghalaya	-	-	-	-	30.49	63.81	26.82	248.89	441.28
6. Nagaland	-	-	10.79	15.98	33.48	71.42	27.90	296.35	666.88
7. Sikkim	-	-	-	-	-	39.49	18.03	136.99	247.62
8. Tripura	-	-	-	-	29.83	50.66	25.69	268.91	541.58
TOTAL - I	32.00	50.05	171.90	158.38	530.48	1127.21	438.90	4137.90	7213.05
II.OTHER STATES:									
1. Andhra Pradesh	61.00	96.17	220.49	161.55	232.23	382.64	222.07	1211.44	1641.47
2. Bihar	55.00	83.84	215.91	155.20	327.19	475.09	221.82	1464.40	2304.74
3. Gujarat	32.00	49.67	111.56	76.40	153.56	214.15	96.32	682.57	1055.63
4. Haryana	-	-	-	46.41	76.32	101.52	54.38	326.56	394.46
5. Karnataka	47.00	67.53	156.52	109.15	167.04	257.62	99.32	646.88	881.72
6. Kerala	24.00	37.88	121.75	89.70	170.10	241.26	84.77	541.98	1140.51
7. Madhya Pradesh	61.00	96.58	219.55	141.90	253.59	332.45	174.52	1220.27	1896.35
8. Maharashtra	48.00	74.30	166.82	111.05	238.88	338.15	173.26	1182.69	1789.82
9. Orissa	77.00	65.69	136.74	80.72	155.43	235.08	149.83	819.34	1152.43
10. Rajasthan	60.00	59.44	161.36	119.46	212.69	290.50	127.50	929.87	1154.49
11. Punjab	141.00	88.29	134.39	51.77	97.46	134.44	43.72	341.96	467.73
12. Tamil Nadu	42.00	95.29	186.79	120.95	196.55	298.11	117.91	890.42	1454.46
13. Uttar Pradesh	87.00	120.60	356.24	259.42	510.40	796.37	403.12	2311.09	3614.85
14. West Bengal	113.00	72.95	155.15	112.70	212.78	303.96	144.46	875.04	1222.65
TOTAL - II	848.00	1008.23	2343.27	1636.38	3004.22	4401.34	2113.00	13444.51	20171.31
GRAND TOTAL:	880.00	1058.28	2515.17	1794.76	3534.70	5528.55	2551.51	17582.41	27384.36

Source: Annual Plan 1979-80, Reserve Bank of India Bulletin
All other periods Govt. of India, Ministry of Finance, 'Statistical Statements on Finances and Plans of States and Union Territories.

TABLE III.3 : PERCAPITA CENTRAL ASSISTANCE

Rs. in crore

	First Plan	Second Plan	Third Plan	Three Annual Plans	Fourth Plan	Fifth Plan	Annual Plan	Sixth Plan	Seventh Plan 1990	Total 1951 to
I.SPL.CATEGORY STATES.										
1. Assam 23	28	78	58	119	142	66	675	1038	2103	
2. Himachal Pradesh	-	-	-	-	285	325	182	1164	2025	3889
3. Jammu & Kashmir	30	56	166	149	300	900	195	1767	3071	6301
4. Manipur	-	-	-	-	244	431	216	2019	3835	6644
5. Meghalaya	-	-	-	-	301	532	223	1863	3303	6073
6. Nagaland	-	-	280	400	649	1190	399	3824	8605	14487
7. Sikkim -	-	-	-	-	1974	601	4335	7836	13991	
8. Tripura	-	-	-	-	192	281	128	1310	2638	4465
TOTAL- 1.	25	34	102	85	196	360	129	1147	2000	3843
II. OTHER STATES										
1. Andhra Pradesh	19	28	58	39	53	79	43	226	307	790
2. Bihar 14	19	44	19	58	76	33	209	330	759	
3. Gujarat	19	26	50	31	58	71	30	200	310	725
4. Haryana	-	-	-	50	76	89	44	253	305	774
5. Karnataka	23	30	63	40	57	78	28	174	237	655
6. Kerala 17	24	68	45	80	104	34	213	448	963	
7. Madhya Pradesh	22	32	64	37	61	71	35	234	363	843
8. Maharastra	14	20	39	24	47	60	29	188	285	657
9. Orissa 50	39	74	40	71	98	59	311	437	1089	
10. Punjab 90	50	67	38	72	89	27	204	279	894	
11. Rajasthan	36	31	74	49	83	97	39	271	337	909
12. Tamil Nadu	14	29	53	32	48	67	25	184	300	703
13. Uttar Pradesh	13	17	46	30	58	80	36	208	326	763
14. West Bengal	40	22	41	27	48	62	28	160	224	589
TOTAL-II	24	26	53	34	58	77	35	210	316	766
GRAND TOTAL	24	26	55	36	65	91	40	260	405	930
Pop. Estimates Used	1953	1958	1963	1967	1971	1976	1979	1981	1981	1981.

TABLE III.4 : CENTRAL ASSISTANCE TO STATES UNDER THE FIRST FIVE-YEAR PLAN

(Rs Crores)

	STATES	Central Assistance for State Plans		Assistance for Centrally sponsored schems	Total (3+4)
		Original allocation	Actual payment		
	(1)	(2)	(3)	(4)	(5)
1.	Andhra Pradesh	10.0	35.0	26.0	61.0
2.	Assam	11.0	14.0	7.0	21.0
3.	Bihar	15.0	25.0	30.0	55.0
4.	Bombay*	22.0	42.0	38.0	80.0
5.	Jammu & Kashmir	10.0	8.0	2.0	10.0
6.	Kerala	7.0	13.0	11.0	24.0
7.	Madhya Pradesh	16.0	27.0	34.0	61.0
8.	Madras	20.0	36.0	6.0	42.0
9.	Mysore	8.0	25.0	22.0	47.0
10.	Orrisa	10.0	11.0	66.0	77.0
11.	Punjab	13.5	20.0	121.0	141.0
12.	Rajasthan	9.0	15.0	45.0	60.0
13.	Uttar Pradesh	15.0	27.0	61.0	88.0
14.	West Bengal	26.5	34.0	79.0	113.0
	Total	193.0	332.0	548.0	880.0
	Gujrat*				32.0
	Maharashtra	-	-	-	48.0

Note: During the First Plan, outlays on schemes such as multipurpose river valley schemes, community development projects projects, for special minor irrigation, local works, scarcity affected areas, basic and social education, industrial housing etc. were included in the Central sector because the exact distribution of their financial liability had not been decided upon in the begining. On a basis comparable with the subsequent State Plan outlays, they should have been in the States' sector.col. 4 represents these. outlays and assistantce.

SOURSE: Planning Commission.

TABLE III.5 : CENTRAL ASSISTANCE TO STATES: SECOND FIVE YEAR-PLAN

	States	1956-57	1957-58	1958-59	1959-60	1960-61	Total 1956-61	(Rs. Lakhs) Original allocation of Central assistance (Rs.crores)
1.	Andhra Pradesh	1,730	2,064	1,869	1,764	2,190	9,617	100.9
2.	Assam	545	629	407	578	900	3,059	33.8
3.	Bihar	1,070	1,596	1,755	1,672	2,291	8,384	92.3
4.	Gujarat*	624	989	1,009	1,095	1,250	4,967	*
5.	Haryana	#	#	#	#	#	#	#
6	Jammu & Kashmir	408	306	278	408	546	1,946	24.4
7	Kerala	294	874	784	726	1,110	3,788	38.0
8.	Madhya Pradesh	1,160	2,139	2,007	2,071	2,281	9,658	104.7
9.	Maharshtra*	943	1,495	1,524	1,656	1,812	8,430	139.3*
10.	Mysore	647	1,587	1,303	1,366	1,850	6,753	73.9
11	Nagaland	+	+	+	+	+	+	..
12.	Orrisa	1,351	1,664	1,275	1,092	1,187	6,569	68.9
13.	Punjab	1,646	1,933	1,636	1,788	1,826	8,829	97.1
14.	Rajasthan	823	1,179	1,185	1,205	1,552	5,944	57.5
15.	Madras	1,337	1,867	2,077	2,348	1,900	9,529	95.5
16.	Uttar Pradesh	2,132	2,303	2,233	2,490	2,902	12,060	138.5
17.	West Bengal	1,210	1,625	1,583	1,321	1,556	7,295	82.6
	Total	15,920	22,250	20,925	21,580	25,153	1,05,828	1,147.4

\# Included under Punjab.
\+ Nagaland was a Union Territory.
* Figures are for composite State of Bombay-Break-up estimated for 1956-57 to 1959-60.]

Source: Planning Commission.

TABLE III.6 : CENTRAL ASSISTANCE TO STATES (THIRD FIVE-YEAR PLAN)

(Rs. Crores)

	States	1961-62	1962-63	1963-64	1964-65	1965-66	Total 1961-66
	(1)	(2)	(3)	(4)	(5)	(6)	(7)
1.	Andhra Pradesh	31.00	32.93	41.00	50.56	65.00	220.49
2.	Assam	12.27	17.44	21.71	24.45	24.00	99.87
3.	Bihar	31.50	36.00	36.33	54.48	57.50	215.91
4.	Gujarat	20.61	24.50	16.17	22.43	27.85	111.56
5.	Jammu & Kashmir	8.35	10.39	10.36	13.95	18.50	61.55
6.	Kerala	15.76	21.10	21.64	28.45	34.80	121.75
7.	Madhya Pradesh	27.35	36.45	51.08	52.57	52.10	219.55
8.	Maharshtra	24.47	26.14	28.66	37.25	50.30	166.82
9.	Mysore	27.50	28.64	27.31	36.67	36.40	156.52
10.	Nagaland	N.A.	N.A.	N.A.	N.A.	N.A.	10.80
11.	Orissa	17.27	21.80	21.98	40.74	34.95	136.74
12.	Punjab	18.25	21.80	22.70	33.89	37.75	134.39
13.	Rajsthan	21.23	26.50	30.50	40.83	42.30	161.36
14.	Madras	27.50	31.40	36.95	44.74	46.20	186.79
15.	Uttar Pradesh	48.01	56.30	57.88	85.95	108.10	356.24
16.	West Bengal	23.00	20.99	32.36	38.80	40.00	155.15
	Total	354.07	412.38	456.63	605.86	675.75	2,515.49

* Figures for 1961-62, 1962-63 and 1963-64 are based on final payments.
Figures for 1964-65 and 1965-66 are based on revised allocations.

Source: Planning Commission.

TABLE III.7 : CENTRAL ASSISTANCE TO STATES FOURTH PLAN 1969-74

Rs. Lakhs

States		Fourth Plan Allocation (1969-74)	CENTRAL ASSISTANCE ALLOCATIONS 1969-70	1970-71	1971-72	1972-73	1973-74 Original	Revisedafter 11.69%cut
Andhra Pradesh		24,000	4,290	4,356	4,800	5,033	5,521	4,875
Assam		18,280	2,768	3,284	3,656	3,296	4,534	4,004
+Mizoram					+413	+329	+329	
Meghalaya	3,720	542	710	744	722	1,002	885	
Total: Assam Mizoram & Meghalaya		22,000	3,310	3,994	4,400	4,431	5,865	5.218
Bihar		33,800	6,040	6,134	6,760	7,088	7,778	6,868
Gujarat		15,800	2,820	2,864	3,160	3,313	3,643	3,217
Haryana		7,850	1,400	1,423	1,570	1,646	1,811	1,599
Jammu & Kashmir		14,500	2,350	2,629	2,900	3,200	3,421	3,021
Karnataka	17,300	3,060	3,137	3,460	3,628	4,015	3,546	
Kerala	17,500	3,110	3,175	3,500	3,670	4,045	3,572	
Madhya Pradesh		26,200	4,670	4,756	5,240	5,495	6,039	5,332
Maharashtra	24,550	4,380	4,451	4,910	5,149	5,660	4,998	
Nagaland		3,500	600	635	700	759	806	712
Orissa	16,000	2,840	2,902	3,200	3,355	3,703	3,270	
Punjab	10,100	1,790	1,835	2,020	2,118	2,337	2,064	
Rajastan		22,000	3,890	3,994	4,400	4,614	5,102	4,506
Tamil Nadu	20,200	3,600	3,664	4,040	4,236	4,660	4,115	
Uttar Pradesh		52,600	9,400	9,544	10,520	11,031	12,105	10,689
West Bengal	22,100	3,950	4,007	4,420	4,634	5,089	4,494	
Total		3,50,000	61,500	63,500	70,000	72,987 +413	81.271 +329	71,767 +329
Himachal Pradesh		10,140	1,550	1,705	1,950	2.200	2,531	2.235
Manipur		3,025	472	519	572	750	851	752
Tripura		3,466	500	817	799	800	862	761
Grand Total	3,66,631	64,022	66,541	73,321	76.737	85.515	75.515	

Share out of Rs. 3500 crores only.

\+ Mizoram, which is carved out of Assam and is now a Union Territory, has been shown in the Statement since its share was earlier included in Assam.

Source: Planning Commission.

TABLE-III-8: CENTRAL ASSISTANCE TO STATES: FOURTH PLAN 1969-74.

Rs. Lakhs

States	Central assistance (Disbursements).					Total Fourth Plan
	1969-70	1970-71	1971-72	1972-73	1973-74	
(1)	(2)	(3)	(4)	(5)	(6)	(7)
Andhra Pradesh	4,137	4,356	4,782	5,033	4,875	23,223
Assam,Mizoram	3,275	3,128	3,644	3,296	4,004	17,347
Meghalaya	-	710	744	722	873	3,049
Total: Assam, Mizoram & Meghalaya	3,275	3,838	4,388	4,018	4,877	20,396
Bihar	6,029	6,006	6,728	7,088	6,868	32,719
Gujarat	2,820	2,857	3,149	3,313	3,217	15,356
Haryana	1,396	1,423	1,568	1,646	1,599	7,632
Jammu & Kashmir	2,266	2,561	2,846	3,170	3,021	13,864
Karnataka	3,011	3,137	3,460	3,550	3,546	16,704
Kerala	3,093	3,175	3,500	3,670	3,572	17,010
Madhya Pradesh	4,589	4,756	5,187	5,495	5,332	25,359
Maharashtra	4,380	4,451	4,910	5,149	4,998	23,888
Nagaland	591	600	689	756	712	3,348
Orissa	2,816	2,902	3,200	3,355	3,270	15,543
Punjab	1,712	1,836	2,020	2,114	2,064	9,746
Rajasthan	3,789	3,971	4,389	4,614	4,506	21,269
Tamil Nadu	3,600	3,664	4,040	4,236	4,115	19,655
Uttar Pradesh	9,379	9,544	10,520	10,908	10,689	51,040
West Bengal	3,865	3,867	4,418	4,634	4,494	21,278
Total	60,788	62,944	69,794	72,749	71,755	3,38,030
Himachal Pradesh	1,736	1,730	1,943	2,200	2,235	9,844
Manipur	401	449	317	750	696	2,613
Tripura	527	478	417	800	761	2,983
Grand Total	63,452	65,601	72,471	76,499	75,447	3,53,470

Source: Planning Commission.

TABLE-III.9: CENTRAL ASSISTANCE TO STATES REVISED ALLOCATION FOR 1974-79

(Rs. Crores)

States	Total alloction	Population 60%	Per Capita income 10%	Per Capita tax effort 10%	I & P Projects 10%	Special problems 10%
(1)	(2)	(3)	(4)	(5)	(6)	(7)
Andhra Pradesh	421.38	250.19	60.26	37.70	73.23	-
Assam	289.36	-	-	-	-	-
Bihar	542.04	324.13	110.91	25.20	33.63	48.17
Gujarat	240.80	153.57	-	37.65	46.14	3.44
Haryana	113.88	57.76	-	40.86	14.11	1.15
Himachal Pradesh	156.07	-	-	-	-	-
Jammu & Kashmir	494.64	-	-	-	-	-
Karnataka	266.63	168.57	-	38.54	59.52	-
Kerala	272.77	122.80	29.58	36.83	14.75	68.81
Madhya Pradesh	374.19	239.58	71.14	30.13	33.34	-
Maharashtra	383.56	289.98	-	49.82	43.76	-
Manipur	67.08	-	-	-	-	-
Meghalaya	70.95	-	-	-	-	-
Nagaland	76.58	-	-	-	-	-
Orissa	262.81	126.23	35.39	14.66	7.40	79.13
Punjab	151.84	77.94	-	43.52	30.38	-
Rajsthan	313.58	148.20	39.81	30.97	37.24	57.36
Sikkim	40.06	-	-	-	-	-
Tamilnadu	340.11	236.98	-	53.26	51.14	44.73
Tripura	58.29	-	-	-	-	-
UttarPradesh	902.42	508.15	146.07	25.16	80.83	142.21
West Bengal	345.57	254.86	-	28.86	13.69	48.16
Total	6,184.61*	2,958.94	493.16	493.16	493.16	493.16

Source: Planning Commission (Vide their note dt. 10-8-1978 circulated for the NDC Committee Meeting) *Excluding assistance for IDA financed Projects.

Source: Planning Commission.

TABLE-III.10 : FIFTH FIVE-YEAR PLAN - ASSISTANCE FOR IDA PROJECTS

(Rs. Crores)

States	1974-75 ?	1975-76 ?	1976-77 ?	1977-78 Estimates	1978-79 Estimates	Total 1974-79
(1)	(2)	(3)	(4)	(5)	(6)	(7)
Andhra Pradesh	-	4.15	2.75	3.75	4.55	15.20
Assam	0.06	0.70	0.06	0.06	0.88	
Bihar	-	0.65	0.75	0.50	0.56	2.46
Gujarat	-	1.39	-	1.30	1.48	4.17
Haryana	-	0.41	1.00	0.40	0.42	2.23
Himachal Pradesh	-	0.22	-	0.20	0.24	0.66
Jammu & Kashmir	-	-	2.00	-	-	2.00
Karnataka -	0.72	2.00	W19.50	2.94	25.16	
Kerala -	1.14	-	1.10	1.18	3.42	
Madhya Pradesh	-	1.73	1.00	1.60	1.86	6.19
Maharashtra -	0.87	1.12	0.74	1.00	3.73	
Manipur	-	-	-	-	-	-
Meghalaya -	-	-	-	-	-	
Nagaland	-	-	-	-	-	-
Orissa -	1.31	2.00	1.25	1.37	5.39	
Punjab -	0.60	0.25	0.55	0.65	2.05	
Rajsthan	2.00	4.28	2.25	3.75	4.81	17.09
Sikkim -	-	-	-	-	-	
Tamilnadu -	0.36	0.50	0.35	0.37	1.58	
Tripura	-	-	-	-	-	-
Uttar Pradesh	-	2.76	1.25	2.50	3.02	9.53
West Bengal -	0.70	0.50	0.70	0.70	2.60	
Total	2.00	21.35	18.07	38.25	25.21	104.88

?. Releases.

W. Including Rs. 7 crores saving from 1976-77

Note. - final figures for 77-78 and 78-79 are not readily abailable.

Source. - Planning Commission.

TABLE-III-11: CENTRAL ASSISTANCE FOR STATE PLANS - 1974-75

(Rs.Crores)

States	Normal Assistance for plan	IDA Assistance	Advance assistance for: Natural calamities	Advance assistance for: Meeting resource gap	Advance assistance for: Total	Total Assistance.
*(1)	(2)	(3)	(4)	(5)	(6)	(7)
Andhra Pradesh	48.75	-	-	-	-	48.75
Assam	40.04	-	1.84	-	1.84	41.88
Bihar	68.68	-	4.00	-	4.00	72.68
Gujarat	32.17	-	9.89	-	9.89	42.06
Haryana	15.99	-	2.00	-	2.00	17.99
Himachal Pradesh	22.35	-	-	-	-	22.35
Jammu & Kashmir	30.21	-	-	29.00	29.00	59.21
Karnataka	35.46	-	-	-	-	35.46
Kerala	35.72	-	-	-	-	35.72
Madhya Pradesh	53.32	-	6.50	-	6.50	59.82
Maharshtra	49.98	-	-	-	-	49.98
Manipur	7.52	-	-	-	-	7.52
Meghalaya	8.85	-	-	-	-	8.85
Nagaland	7.12	-	-	-	-	7.12
Orissa	32.70	-	7.91	-	7.91	40.61
Punjab	20.64	-	-	-	-	20.64
Rajasthan	45.06	2.00	10.24	-	10.24	57.30
Sikkim	-	-	-	-	-	-
Tamil Nadu	41.15	-	7.50	-	7.50	48.65
Tripura	7.61	-	-	-	-	7.61
Uttar Pradesh	106.89	-	-	-	-	106.89
West Bengal	44.94	-	-	-	-	44.94
Total755.15	2.00	49.88	29.00	78.88	836.03	

* Allocations for normal assistance and actual releases under others.

Source Planning Commission.

TABLE-III.12 : CENTRAL ASSISTANCE FOR STATE PLANS 1975-76.

(Rs. Crores)

State	Normal assistance for plan	I.D.A. assistance	Advance Assistance for Natural Calamities	Irr. and Power Projects	Meeting resource gaps.	Total	Total Assistance
(1)	(2)	(3)	(4)	(5)	(6)	(7)	(8)
Andhra Pradesh	48.75	4.15		5.00	..	5.00	57.90
Assam	40.04	0.06	-	-	-	40.10	
Bihar	68.68	0.65	9.75	7.00	24.35	41.10	110.43
Gujarat	32.17	1.39	9.15	7.30	-	16.45	50.01
Haryana	15.99	0.41	-	5.00	7.08	12.08	28.48
Himachal Pradesh	22.35	0.22	-	-	0.80	0.80	23.37
Jammu& Kashmir	30.21	-	-	0.75	55.25	56.00	86.21
Karnataka	35.46	0.72	-	12.15	-	12.15	48.33
Kerala	35.72	1.14	-	4.60	2.24	6.84	43.70
Madhya Pradesh	53.32	1.73	-	4.50	-	4.50	59.55
Maharashtra	49.98	0.87	-	5.50	-	5.50	56.35
Manipur	7.52	-	-	-	1.74	1.74	9.26
Meghalaya	8.85	-	-	-	-	-	8.85
Nagaland	7.12	-	-	-	1.66	1.66	8.78
Orissa	32.70	1.31	7.55	1.00	7.92	16.47	50.48
Punjab	20.64	0.60	-	-	4.40	4.40	25.64
Rajasthan	45.06	4.28	2.50	6.00	-	8.50	57.84
Sikkim	(6.06)	-	(0.73)	-	-	(0.73)	(6.79)
Tamil Nadu	41.15	0.36	-	1.00	14.64	15.64	57.15
Tripura	7.61	-	-	-	-	-	7.61
Uttar Pradesh	106.89	2.76	5.65	23.25	28.85	57.75	167.40
West Bengal	44.94	0.70	-	1.00	-	1.00	46.64
Total	755.15	21.35	34.60	84.05	148.93	267.58	1,044.08

* Allocations under normal assistance and releases under others.

Note Figures for Sikkim are excluded from totals.

Source Planning Commission.

TABLE-III.13: CENTRAL ASSISTANCE FOR STATE PLANS 1976-77.

(Rs. Crores)

State	Normal assistance for plan	I.D.A. assistance	Advance Assistance for Natural Calamities	Irr. and Power Projects	Meeting resource gaps.	Total	Total Assistance
(1)	(2)	(3)	(4)	(5)	(6)	(7)	(8)
1. Andhra Pradesh	53.63	2.75	3.53	0.75	12.25	16.53	72.91
2. Assam	44.04	0.70	2.00	-	-	2.00	46.74
3. Bihar	75.55	0.75	10.70	3.00	-	13.70	90.00
4. Gujarat	35.39	-	4.25	3.00	10.00	17.25	52.64
5. Haryana	17.59	1.00	-	6.50	-	6.50	25.09
6. Himachal Pradesh	24.59	-	0.48	-	-	0.48	25.07
7. Jammu & Kashmir	33.23	2.00	-	-	72.81	72.81	108.04
8. Karnataka	39.01	2.00	7.00	3.55	7.90	18.45	59.46
9. Kerala	39.29	-	1.50	2.50	2.71	6.71	46.00
10. Madhya Pradesh	58.65	1.00	5.00	17.5	-	6.75	66.40
11. Maharashtra	54.98	1.12	-	3.85	-	3.85	59.95
13. Manipur	8.27	.	0.44	-	2,37	2.81	11.08
13. Meghalaya	9.74	-	-	-	5.27	5.27	15.01
14. Nagaland	7.83	-	-	-	5.43	5.43	13.26
15. Orissa	35.97	2.00	5.10	2.00	17.04	24.14	62.11
16. Punjab	22.70	0.25	-	1.50	4.75	6.25	29.20
17. Rajasthan	49.57	2.25	2.44	3.00	0.81	6.25	58.07
18. Sikkim	12.15	-	-	-	-	-	12.15
19. Tamil Nadu	45.27	0.50	18.70	-	26.50	45.20	90.97
20. Tripura	8.37	-	0.51	-	3,74	4.25	12.62
21. Uttar Pradesh	117.58	1.25	11.25*	8.00	45.09	64.34	183.17
22. West Bengal	49.43	0,53	-	0.50	4.50	5.00	54.93
Total	842.83	18.07	72.90	39.90	221.17	333.97	1.194.87

* Note-Releaser.

Source Plan Finance Division.

Source Planning Commission

TABLE - III.14 : CENTRAL ASSISTANCE FOR STATE PLANS 1977-78

(Rs. Crores)

	States	Central Assistance		
		On Gadgil Formula	For I.D.A. financed projects.	Total
1.	Andhra Pradesh	94.49	3.75	98.24
2.	Assam	56.51	0.06	56.57
3.	Bihar	95.99	0.50	96.49
4.	Gujarat	31.94	1.30	40.24[1]
5.	Haryana	11.06	0.40	11.46
6.	Himachal Pradesh	28.05	0.20	28.25
7.	Jammu and Kashmir	112.37	-	112.37
8.	Karnataka	37.29	19.50	56.79
9.	Kerala	53.17	1.10	54.27
10.	Madhya Pradesh	70.81	1.60	72.41
11.	Maharashtra	81.33	0.74	82.07
12.	Manipur	14.09	-	14.09
13.	Meghalaya	15.59	-	15.59
14.	Nagaland	21.19	-	21.19
15.	Orissa	38.25	1.25	39.50
16.	Punjab	26.15	0.55	26.70
17.	Rajasthan	51.77	3.75	55.52
18.	Sikkim	12.17	-	12.17
19.	Tamil Nadu	49.30	0.35	49.65
20.	Tripura	11.07	-	11.07
21.	Uttar Pradesh	159.07	2.50	161.57
22.	West Bengal	72.272	0.70	72.97
	Total	1,143.93	38.25	1,189.18

1. Anticipated additional devolution of Central taxes of Rs. 7.00 crores in respect of Gujarat State is also included.

2. After reduction of Rss. 4.50 crores on account of advance Plan assistance agreed to be released for 1976-77.

Source Planning Commission.

TABLE - III.15 : CENTRAL ASSISTANCE FOR STATE PLANS 1978-79

(Rs. Crores)

State	Under	For IDA Gadgil Formula	Total financed projects
Andhra Pradesh	154.32	32.00	186.23
Assam	104.89	0.15	105.04
Bihar	174.34	1.00	175.34
Gujarat	65.54	2.50	68.04
Haryana	32.67	5.50	38.17
Himachal Pradesh	57.45	0.60	58.05
Jammu & Kashmir	130.81	-	130.81
Karnataka	88.81	19.50	108.31
Kerala	95.32	2.50	97.82
Madhya Pradesh	120.34	4.00	124.34
Maharashtra	137.94	5.00	142.94
Manipur	24.68	-	24.68
Meghalaya	23.65	-	23.65
Nagaland	26.89	-	26.89
Orissa	74.67	5.00	79.67
Punjab	51.06	1.00	52.06
Rajasthan	97.13	8.00	105.13
Sikkim	15.74	-	15.74
Tamilnadu	94.90	1.00	95.90
Tripura	18.82	0.10	18.92
Uttar Pradesh	285.06	4.00	289.06
West Bengal	127.99	2.50	130.49
Total	2,002.93	94.35	2,097.28

Source - Planning Commission.

TABLE - III.16 : COMPONENTS OF CENTRAL ASSISTANCE FOR THE FIVE YEAR PLAN - (1980-85)

(Rs. Crores)

States	Normal	I.A.T.P. @	Special Problems	Externally Aided	Total 1980-85
(1)	(2)	(3)	(4)	(5)	(6)
I. ALL. CATEGORY STATES:					
1. Assam					827.02
2. Himachal Pradesh		Break-up			437.35
3. Jammu & Kashmir					1009.00
4. Manipur		not			240.50
5. Meghalaya				196.00	
6. Nagaland		Available			209.50
7. Sikkim					119.50
8. Tripura					204.13
TOTAL -I				3243.00	
II. OTHER STATES					
1. Andhra Pradesh	635.73	128.62	42.00	99.35	905.70
2. Bihar	896.22	239.71	92.00	32.57	1260.50
3. Gujarat	306.15	64.59	17.00	211.94	599.68
4. Haryana	155.74	19.68	12.00	47.43	234.85
5. Karnataka	322.90	76.92	17.00	122.38	539.20
6. Kerala	260.26	61.78	58.00	50.12	430.16
7. Madhya Pradesh	652.79	147.27	61.00	152.33	1013.39
8. Maharashtra	521.91	102.53	-	251.47	875.91
9. Orissa	344.73	75.93	166.00	72.87	659.53
10. Punjab	191.22	23.44	18.48	68.86	300.00
11. Rajasthan	407.41	82.87	77.00	59.03	626.31
12. Tamil Nadu	436.32	119.99	50.00	58.49	664.80
13. Uttar Pradesh	1353.14	338.98	135.00	101.92	1929.04
14. West Bengal	445.48	117.69	20.00	97.09	680.26
TOTAL - II	6930.00	1600.00	765.48	1423.85	10719.33
ALL STATES (I + II)	6930.00	1600.00	765.48	1423.85	13962.33

@ Effective from 1979-80, on account of transfer of Central and Centrally Sponsored schemes to States.
Central Assistance to 8 Special category States was granted outside I.A.T.P. formula.

Source: Govt.of India, Min. of Finance.
Unallocated Rs. 32.07 crores.

TABLE III.17 : CENTRAL ASSISTANCE TO NON-SPECIAL CATEGORY STATES ON THE BASIS OF THE ORIGINAL GADGIL FORMULA AND UNDER THE REVISED FORMULA DURING THE SIXTH PLAN 1980-85

(Rs. Crores)

	States	On the basis of the original formula	On the basis of the revised formula
1.	Andhra Pradesh	696.86	677.73
2.	Bihar	873.18	988.22
3.	Gujarat	387.61	323.15
4.	Haryana	197.86	167.74
5.	Karnataka	409.89	339.90
6.	Kerala	300.78	318.26
7.	Madhya Pradesh	673.11	713.79
8.	Maharashtra	738.66	521.91
9.	Orissa	344.95	510.73
10.	Punjab	235.15	209.70
11.	Rajasthan	441.14	484.41
12.	Tamil Nadu	511.80	486.32
13.	Uttar Pradesh	1323.92	1488.14
14.	West Bengal	555.57	465.48
15.	Unallocated	4.52	4.52
	Total	7700.00	7700.00

FORMULA FOR DISTRIBUTION

	Original Formula	Revised Formula
1. Population	60%	60%
2. Tax Effort	10%	10%
3. Per Capita income below national average	10%	20%
4. Continuing Major Power & Irrigation Projects	10%*	-
5. Special Problems	Balance on prorata basis of the above 90%	10%
Total	100	100

It has been assumed for the purpose of this exercise that the proporation of Central assistance for continuing Irrigation & Power Projects during 1980-85 could remain more or less the same as during 1979-83.

Source: Govt. of India, Ministry of Finance.

TABLE III.18 : CENTRAL ASSISTANCE ACTUALLY RELEASED IN 1980-81

(Rs.Lakh)

STATES	Normal Central assistance	For externally aided Projects	For Hill Areas/Western Ghats Development	Total
(1)	(2)	(3)	(4)	(5)
1. Andhra Pradesh	16240.00	2814.30	-	19034.30
2. Assam	13376.00	79.60	960.00	14415.60
3. Bihar	23935.00	262.55	-	24197.55
4. Gujarat	7726.00	1739.78	-	9465.78
5. Haryana	3860.00	1480.75	-	5340.75
6. Himachal Pradesh	7565.92	60.35	-	7626.27
7. Jammu & Kashmir	16944.50	1.59	-	16946.09
8. Karnataka	8749.00	1120.62	191.00	10060.62
9. Kerala	7775.00	13.58	212.30	8000.38
10. Madhya Pradesh	17575.00	172.03	-	177747.03
11. Maharashtra	13381.00	4486.98	309.30	18177.28
12. Manipur	3675.00	-	-	3675.00
13. Meghalaya	3460.00	-	-	3460.00
14. Nagaland	3514.00	-	-	3514.00
15. Orissa	13541.00	1234.26	-	14775.26
16. Punjab	4994.00	1194.57	-	6188.57
17. Rajasthan	12770.00	270.10	-	13040.10
18. Sikkim	2014.10	-	-	2014.10
19. Tamil Nadu	13011.00	563.94	470.00	14044.94
20. Tripura	3213.00	-	-	3213.00
21. Uttar Pradesh	31791.00	895.90	4120.00	36806.90
22. West Bengal	11929.00	1671.74	545.00	14145.74
TOTAL	241039.52	18062.64	6807.60*	265909.76
Less releases to REC	645.00			645.00
TOTAL ALL STATES	240394.52			265264.76

* This does not include Rs.2.40 lakhs released for Techno Economic Survey of Western Ghats.

(Contd.)

TABLE III.18: CENTRAL ASSISTANCE ACTUALLY RELEASED IN 1980-81

(Rs. Lakhs)

STATES	Non-Plan medium term loan	Non-Plan grant for natural	A.P.A. for drought relief calamities	GRAND TOTAL
	(6)	(7)	(8)	(9)
1. Andhra Pradesh		204.41	3923.68	23182.39
2. Assam	4000.00	559.28		18974.88
3. Bihar	1689.75	1500.00	27390.30	
4. Gujarat		829.80	268.40	10563.98
5. Haryana		274.17	572.37#	6187.29
6. Himachal Pradesh		27.14*	679.09	8332.50
7. Jammu & Kashmir				16946.09
8. Karnataka		100.87	400.00	10561.49
9. Kerala		400	??????	8400.88
10. Madhya Pradesh			3876.00	21623.03
11. Maharashtra			1167.53	19344.81
12. Manipur	1306.00			4981.00
13. Meghalaya				3460.00
14. Nagaland	774.00			4288.00
15. Orissa		2820.39	1056.00	18651.65
16. Punjab				6188.57
17. Rajasthan			2440.59	15480.69
18. Sikkim				2014.10
19. Tamil Nadu				14044.94
20. Tripura	1465.00			4678.00
21. Uttar Pradesh		5224.50	3191.74%	45223.14
22. West Bengal		984.14		15129.88
TOTAL	7545.00	13114.45	19078.40	305647.61
Less Release to REC:				645.00
TOTAL ALL STATES :				305002.61&

* Arrear payment to Himachal Pradesh on account of 1979-80 calamities.

% Includes Advance Plan assistance of Rs. 5.50 crores for flood relief in 1980-81.

Also includes Rs. 2.00 crores of arrearsof APA to Haryana on account of 1979-80 drought.

& This does not include Rs. 2.40 lakhs releasedfor Techno Economic survey of Western Ghats.

Source: Govt. of India, Ministry of Finance 'Statistical Statements on Finances and Plans of State and: Union Territories, 1985"

TABLE III.19 : CENTRAL ASSISTANCE ACTUALLY RELEASED IN 1981-82

(Rs. Lakhs)

STATES	Normal including MHA/ R.E.C.	I.D.A	Special assistance for Devep. of Hill Areas/ Western ghat	TOTAL
(1)	(2)	(3)	(4)	(5)
1. Andhra Pradesh	15679.00	1703.08	-	17382.08
2. Assam	15303.00	43.40	981.20	16327.60
3. Bihar	24096.00	389.45	-	24485.45
4. Gujarat	7672.00	2841.17	-	10513.17
5. Haryana	3217.49	990.87	-	4208.36
6. Himachal Pradesh	7779.00	188.59	21.60	7989.19
7. Jammu & Kashmir	19479.00*	13.20	-	19492.20
8. Karnataka	8550.00	1024.93	233.48	9808.41
9. Kerala	10402.03	1.63	321.18	10724.84
10. Madhya Pradesh	17850.00	413.33		18263.33
11. Maharashtra	12093.00	5405.69	380.56	17879.25
12. Manipur	4207.00	-	8.00	4215.00
13. Meghalaya	3755.54	-	20.19	3775.73
14. Nagaland	4020.00	-	-	4020.00
15. Orissa	11890.00	1564.70	-	13454.70
16. Punjab	4850.50	1503.76	-	6354.26
17. Rajasthan	10768.00	1014.54	-	11782.54
18. Sikkim	2392.00	-	-	2392.00
19. Tamil Nadu	11097.00	1116.04	635.06	12848.10
20. Tripura	3931.00	-	-	3931.00
21. Uttar Pradesh	38115.00e	1111.51	5524.75	44751.26
22. West Bengal	11359.16	1746.30	619.85	13725.31
TOTAL	243505.72	21072.19	8745.87	278323.78
Amount less paid to R.E.C.	(-) 355.00			(-)355.00
TOTAL	248150.72	21072.19	8745.87	277963.78

h. Includes arrears of 1980-81 drought Rs. 196.20 lakhs.

c. Includes arrears of 1980-81 floods Rs. 124.34 lakhs.

d. Arrears of 1979-80 and 1980-81 drought.

e. Includes arrears of 1980-81 Rs. 19.02 crores.

*. Includes of APA of Rs. 3.14 crores and Rs. 14.15 crores on account of interest liability adjustable during 1932-83.

(Contd.)

TABLE III.19 : CENTRAL ASSISTANCE ACTUALLY RELEASED IN 1981-82

(Rs. Lakhs)

STATES	Natural calamities		GRAND TOTAL
	Advance Plan assistance	Non-Plan Grants	
	(6)	(7)	(8)
1. Andhra Pradesh	1493.82	-	18875.90
2. Assam	-	-	16327.60
3. Bihar	-	200.00	24685.45
4. Gujarat	-	500.00	11013.17
5. Haryana	694.20	-	4902.56
6. Himachal Pradesh	348.00	80.05	8417.24
7. Jammu & Kashmir	-	-	19492.20
8. Karnataka	1461.28b	117.46	11387.15
9. Kerala	-	637.13c	11361.97
10. Madhya Pradesh	2500.00d	-	20763.33
11. Maharashtra	-	-	17879.25
12. Manipur	-	100.00	4315.00
13. Meghalaya	-	-	3775.73
14. Nagaland	-	-	4020.00
15. Orissa	-	156.00	13610.70
16. Punjab	-	-	6354.26
17. Rajasthan	6504.04	3101.39	21387.97
18. Sikkim	-	116.13	2508.13
19. Tamil Nadu	2989.79	-	15837.89
20. Tripura	-	-	3931.00
21. Uttar Pradesh	-	2599.25	47350.51
22. West Bengal	200.00	500.00	14425.31
<u>TOTAL</u>	<u>16191.13</u>	<u>8107.41</u>	<u>302622.32</u>
Amount less paid to R.E.C.	(-)355.00		
<u>TOTAL</u>	<u>16191.13</u>	<u>8107.41</u>	<u>302267.32</u>

b Includes arrears of 1980-81 drought Rs. 196.20 lakhs.

c. Includes arrears of 1980-81 floods Rs. 124.34 lakhs.

d. Arrears of 1979-80 and 1980-81 drought.

e. Includes arrears of 1980-81 Rs. 19.02 crores.

*. Includes APA of Rs. 3.14 crores and Rs. 14.15 crores on account of interest liability adjustable during 1982-83.

Source: Govt. of India, Ministry of Finance, 'Statistical Statements on Finances and Plans of States and Union Teritories, 1985'.

TABLE III.20 : RELEASES DURING 1982-83

(Rs.in Lakhs)

	STATES	Normal including M.H.A./ R.E.C.	I.D.A.	Special assistance for develp. of Hill areas Western Ghats	Total
	(1)	(2)	(3)	(4)	(5)
1.	Andhra Pradesh	16704.00	1891.23	-	18595.23
2.	Assam	23843.00	151.20	1370.00	25364.20
3.	Bihar	26696.00	894.18	-	27590.18
4.	Gujarat	8424.00	4530.90	-	12954.90
5.	Haryana	4057.51	1261.97	-	5319.48
6.	Himachal Pradesh	8643.60	-	-	8643.60
7.	Jammu & Kashmir	19739.00@	33.38	19.50*	19791.88
8.	Karnataka	8307.00	1337.99	265.17	9910.16
9.	Kerala	8654.00	983.30	346.00	9983.30
10.	Madhya Pradesh	17571.15	2218.68	-	19789.83
11.	Maharashtra	13190.00	6042.95	454.00	19686.95
12.	Manipur	6029.00	-	-	6029.00
13.	Meghalaya	4910.00	-	-	4910.00
14.	Nagaland	5706.00	-	-	5706.00
15.	Orissa	13047.36	1488.55	-	14535.91
16.	Punjab	4953.50	1254.65	-	6208.15
17.	Rajasthan	13430.00	1882.65	-	15312.65
18.	Sikkim	2835.00#	-	9.62*	2844.62
19.	Tamil Nadu	12603.78	1262.10	641.08	14506.96
20.	Tripura	5209.56	-	-	5209.56
21.	Uttar Pradesh	40562.00	2907.06	7000.00	50469.06
22.	West Bengal	27017.00	2091.95	600.00	29708.95
	TOTAL ALL STATES	292132.46	30232.74	10705.37	333070.57

* Represents arrears of Central assistance reco. development and ecological restoration studies under the Hill area development programme -1981-82.

\# Includes Rs. 7 crore to J 7 K and Rs. 3 crore to Sikkim to be adjusted in 1983-84.

(Contd.)
TABLE III.20 : RELEASE DURING 1982-83 contd.

(Rs. Lakhs)

STATES	Advance Plan Assistance	Non-Plan Grants	Term loan covering opening	GRAND TOTAL (5+6+7+8) deficits
	(6)	(7)	(8)	(9)
1. Andhra Pradesh	6586.00	-	1895.00	27076.23
2. Assam	-	451.00	12743.00	38558.20
3. Bihar	1472.50	1403.32**	19739.00	50205.00
4. Gujarat	3387.00@	2546.70	7460.00	26348.60
5. Haryana	1035.00	-	7579.00	13933.48
6. Himachal Pradesh	1250.00	301.43	3691.00	13886.03
7. Jammu & Kashmir	-	-	-	19791.88
8. Karnataka	1500.00b	-	-	11410.16
9. Kerala	200.00	-	9393.00	19576.30
10. Madhya Pradesh	3942.94	-	15488.00	39220.77
11. Maharashtra	4294.20	-	8140.00	32121.15
12. Manipur	-	7.67b	6629.00	12665.67
13. Meghalaya	-	19.00	1641.00	6570.00
14. Nagaland	-	-	2196.00	7902.00
15. Orissa	2210.54@	12158.15	2443.00	31347.60
16. Punjab	-	-	9735.00	15943.15
17. Rajasthan	9712.45+	899.57d	28346.00	54270.67
18. Sikkim	16.00	-	-	2860.62
19. Tamil Nadu	1737.00c	-	-	16243.96
20. Tripura	186.00	29.00	3072.00	8496.56
21. Uttar Pradesh	300.00@	3901.00	85.00	54755.06
22. West Bengal	6366.00#	61.97	34071.00	70207.92
TOTAL ALL STATES	44195.63	21778.81	174346.00	573391.01

\# Includes Rs. 5 crore for Gujarat, Rs. 7.62 crore for Orissa, Rs. 3 crore for West Bengal and the Rs. 3 crore of Uttar Pradesh as advance Plan assistance for flood/cyclone.

b Includes some advance release for 1983-84.

c Includes some advance release for 1983-84 and Rs. 2.37 crore as arrears.

\+ Includes Rs. 11 crore as ad-hoc advance release for 1983-84 and Rs. 21.02 crore arrears.

** Includes Rs. 3 crore as arrears.

d Arrears.

Source:Govt. of India Ministry of Finance. 'Statistical Statements on Finances and Plans of States and Union Teritories, 1985'.

TABLE III.21 : CENTRAL ASSISTANCE RELEASED IN 1983-84

(Rs. Lakhs)

States	Normal including MHA Grant and R.E.C. loan Total	Externally aided project assitance Total	Hill Area Total	Total (1+2+3) Loan	Total (1+2+3) Grant	Total
(1)	(2)	(3)	(4)	(5)	(6)	(7)
1. Andhra Pradesh	19313.00	2169.59	-	15037.813	6444.777	21482.59
2. Assam	36690.26*	470.70	1721.22	24929.294	13952.886	38882.18
3. Bihar	30276.00	839.30	-	21780.710	9334.590	31115.30
4. Gujarat	8879.00	5618.87	-	9384.472	5113.398	14497.87
5. Haryana	4604.45	2256.00	-	4806.062	2054.388	6860.45
6. Himachal Pradesh	9992.00	356.23	15.00	1034.823	9328.407	10363.23
7. Jammu & Kashmir	23350.00	131.70	15.00	15771.190	7725.510	23496.70
8. Karnataka	9830.32	2222.87	367.00	8187.324	4232.866	12420.19
9. Kerala	8535.00	2125.59	444.00	7506.813	3597.777	11104.59
10. Madhya Pradesh	20412.00	3913.90	-	16656.520	7669.380	24325.90
11. Maharashtra	16575.08	8611.80	582.00	16983.887	8784.993	25768.88
12. Manipur	7078.00	-	15.00	839.200	6253.800	7093.00
13. Meghalaya	6728.90	-	15.00	672.890	6071.010	6743.90
14. Nagaland	7489.54	-	15.00	748.954	6755.586	7504.54
15. Orissa	13942.00	2330.25	-	11390.575	4881.675	16272.25
16. Punjab	5715.66	1163.40	3.00	4815.342	2066.718	6882.06
17. Rajasthan	13698.30	1844.58	-	10949.156	4588.724	15537.88
18. Sikkim	3246.00**	-	10.00	371.300	2884.700	3256.00
19. Tamil Nadu	14460.22	2648.11	868.42	12006.923	5969.827	17976.75
20. Tripura	6094.00	-	10.00	609.400	5494.600	6104.00
21. Uttar Pradesh	46133.00	3435.86	8670.27	34625.045	23614.085	58239.13
22. West Bengal	14831.64#	2249.80	638.01	11801.187	5918.263	17719.45
Total All States	327869.37	42388.55	13388.92##	230908.880	152737.960	383646.84

* Includes Rs. 4471.26 lakhs for relief and rehabilitation of the victims of February 1983 riots.

** Includes Rs. 28 lakhs grants-in-aid in lieu of exicise duties.

\# Includes Rs. 90.64 lakhs for relief expenditure on Assam refugees after February 1983 riots in Assam.

\## Excludes Rs. 10 lakhs released to TCPO for surveys and studies of Western Ghats and Rs. 0.94 lakhs for Expenditure of Western Ghats Sectt. by Planning Commission.

(Contd.)

TABLE-III-21 : CENTRAL ASSISTANCE RELEASED IN 1983-84

(Rs. Lakhs)

	States	Spl.Medium term loan	Advance Plan assistance			Non-Plan Grant	Grand TOTAL		
			Loan	grant	Total		Loan	Grant	Total
		(8)	(9)	(10)	(11)	(12)	(13)	(14)	(15)
1.	Andhra Pradesh	-	2113.461	905.769	3019.23	5587.75	17151.274	12938.296	30089.57
2.	Assam	-	-	-	-	-	24929.294	13952.886	38882.18
3.	Bihar	16929.00	-	-	-	-	38709.710	9334.590	48044.30
4.	Gujarat	-	-	-	-	2426.47	9384.472	7539.868	16924.34
5.	Haryana	1993.00	298.186	127.794	425.93	946.23	7097.248	3128.412	10225.66
6.	Himachal Pradesh	-	50.000	450.000	500.00	583.49	1084.823	10361.897	11446.72
7.	Jammu & Kashmir	-	-	-	-	-	15771.190	7725.510	23496.70
8.	Karnataka	484.00	280.00	120.000	400.00	13.00	8951.324	4365.866	13317.19
9.	Kerala	6226.00+	2237.685	1597.685	3835.37	-	15970.498	5195.462	21165.96
10.	Madhya Pradesh	2027.00	1505.966	645.414	2151.38	334.67	20139.486	8649.464	28838.95
11.	Maharastra	-	350.000	150.000	500.00	1695.89	17333.887	10630.883	27964.77
12.	Manipur	-	-	-	-	-	839.200	6253.800	7093.00
13.	Meghalaya	-	-	-	-	28.10	672.890	6099.110	6772.00
14.	Nagaland	-	-	-	-	-	748.954	6755.586	7504.54
15.	Orissa	4100.00	1555.785	803.765	2359.55	1525.16	17046.360	7210.600	24256.96
16.	Punjab	2132.00	280.000	120.000	400.00	-	7227.342	2186.718	9414.06
17.	Rajasthan	4371.00	1385.447	593.763	1979.21	662.05	17205.603	5844.537	23050.14
18.	Sikkim	-	-	-	-	138.87	371.300	3023.570	3394.87
19.	Tamil Nadu	5578.00	3294.605	1604.605	4899.21	2297.20	20879.528	9871.632	30751.16
20.	Tripura	-	-	-	-	225.00	609.400	5719.600	6329.00
21.	Uttar Pradesh	200.00	319.900	137.100	457.00	3322.25	35144.945	27073.435	62218.38
22.	West Bengal	7372.00	1177.862	504.798	1682.66	-	20351.049	6423.061	26774.11
	TOTAL	51912.00	14848.897	7760.693	22609.59	19786.13	297669.777	180284.783	477954.56

\+ Includes Rs. 20.00 crores given for acquisition land for the Naval Academy.

Source : Govt. of India, Ministry of Finance 'Statistical Statements on Finances and Plans of States and Union Territories, 1985'.

TABLE III.22 : CENTRAL ASSISTANCE RELEASED IN 1984-85

(Rs. in lakhs)

	STATES (1)	Normal Central assistance including MHA Grants & REC loans (2)	Central assistance for externally aided projects (3)	Hill Area/ Western development programme (4)	TOTAL Loan (5)	Grant (6)	Total (7)
I. SPECIAL CATEGORY STATES							
1.	Assam	36902.820	177.800	2297.830	24650.474	14727.976	39378.450
2.	Himachal Pradesh	10908.000	584.250	-	1149.225	10343.025	11492.250
3.	Jammu & Kashmir	25864.000	196.900	-	17372.630	8688.270	26060.900
4.	Manipur	7671.000	-	-	767.100	6903.900	7671.000
5.	Meghalaya	5998.960	-	-	600.800	5398.160	5998.860
6.	Nagaland	8390.000	-	-	839.000	7551.000	8390.000
7.	Sikkim	3176.000#	-	-	380.600	2795.400	3176.000
8.	Tripura	8247.000	-	-	824.700	7422.300	8247.000
Total (I)		107157.780	958.950	2297.830	46584.529	63830.031	110414.560
II. NON-SPECIAL CATEGORY STATES							
1.	Andhra Pradesh	21870.000	2368.050	-	16966.635	7271.415	24238.050
2.	Bihar	35013.000	1063.300	-	25253.410	10822.890	36076.300
3.	Gujarat	11052.000	6117.610	-	12018.727	5150.883	17169.610
4.	Haryana	5280.000	2146.200	-	5198.040	2227.860	7426.200
5.	Karnataka	11475.000	3809.220	457.000	10744.654	4996.566	15741.220
6.	Kerala	8507.000	1299.840	542.000	6918.988	3429.852	10348.840
7.	Madhya Pradesh	23064.000	5252.280	-	19821.396	8494.884	28316.280
8.	Maharastra	19598.000	7512.630	693.000	19046.741	8756.889	27803.630
9.	Orissa	13882.080	2938.150	-	11739.161	5031.069	16770.230
10.	Punjab	6731.000	1432.200	-	5714.240	2448.960	8163.200
11.	Rajasthan	15435.000	1242.170	-	11674.019	5003.151	16677.170
12.	Tamil Nadu	16154.000	2319.880	1025.000	13333.568	6665.312	19998.880
13.	Uttar Pradesh	52782.000	3006.180	10432.000	38699.254	27520.926	66220.180
14.	West Bengal	1976.350*	1341.790	637.910	2356.439	1599.561	3956.050
TOTAL(II)		242769.430	42349.500	13786.910	199485.622	994202.18	298905.840
GRAND TOTAL (I+II)		349927.210	43308.450	16084.740**	246070.151	163250.249	409320.400

#. Includes Rs.70.00 lakhs in lieu of market borrowing. *. Includes Rs. 30.35 lakhs for relief of Assam refugees. **Does not include Rs.2.00 lakhs released to TCPO.

(Contd.)

TABLE-III-22: CENTRAL ASSISTANCE RELEASED IN 1984-85

(Rs. in lakhs)

	STATES	Special Medium turn non-plan	Advance Plan assistance			Non-Plan Grant	Grand Total
			Loan	Grant loan	Total		
		(8)	(9)	(10)	(11)	(12)	(13)
I. SPECIAL CATEGORY STATES							
1.	Assam	-	-	-	-	2650.000C	42028.450
2.	Himachal Pradesh	-	136.660	809.340	946.000	204.810	12643.060A
3.	Jammu & Kashmir	1000.000	-	-	-	186.042	27246.942
4.	Manipur	-	-	-	-	2.753	7673.753
5.	Meghalaya	-	-	-	-	216.335	6215.295
6.	Nagaland	-	-	-	-		8390.000
7.	Sikkim	-	-	-	-	382.000	3558.000
8.	Tripura	-	-	-	-	500.000	8747.000
TOTAL (I)		1000.000	136.660	809.340	946.000	4141.940	116502.500
II. NON-SPECIAL CATEGORY STATES							
1.	Andhra Pradesh	-	3602.810	1766.190	5369.000	1803.690	31410.740
2.	Bihar	-	-	-	-	1509.630	37585.930
3.	Gujarat	-	-	-	-	-	17169.610
4.	Haryana	-	541.744	232.176	773.920	-	8200.120
5.	Karnataka	-	2090.200	895.800	2986.000	86.700D	18813.920
6.	Kerala	-	-	-	-	1480.450	11829.290
7.	Madhya Pradesh	-	780.500	334.500	1115.000	322.970	29754.250
8.	Mahareastra	-	2128.602	912.258	3040.860	-	30844.490
9.	Orissa	-	350.000	150.000	500.000	1111.430	18381.660
10.	Punjab	29025.000	-	-	-	-	21895.170
11.	Rajasthan	5218.000	-	-	-	-	21895.170
12.	Tamil Nadu	-	28.000	12.000	40.000	1636.510	21725.890B
13.	Uttar Pradesh	-	471.800	202.200	674.000	3206.840	70101.020
14.	West Bengal	-	-	-	-	2500.000	6456.050
TOTAL (II)		34243.000	9993.656	4505.124	14498.780	13708.220	361355.840
GRAND TOTAL (I+II)		35243.000	10130.316	5314.464	15444.780	17850.160	477858.340

A. Does not includes Rs.200 lakhs relealsed as non-plan grant for transport arrangements to remote areas of H.P.

B. Does not includes Rs. 1350 lakhs of non-plan for Newsprint paper project in Tamil Nadu.

C. Indludes arrears of Rs.300 lakhs.

D. Arrears. Source : Government of India Ministry of Finance, 'Statistical Statements on Finance.

TABLE-III-23: ALLOCATION OF CENTRAL ASSISTANCE UNDER MODIFIED GADGIL FORMULA FOR STATE PLANS (1985-90)

(Rs. in Crores)

	STATES	Population %age	(60% Amount	Tax Effort %age	(10%) Amount	Per Capita %age	income (20%) Amount
I. SPECIAL CATEGORY STATES							
1.	Assam	-	-	-	-	-	-
2.	Himachal Pradesh	-	-	-	-	-	-
3.	Jammu & Kashmir	-	-	-	-	-	-
4.	Manipur	-	-	-	-	-	-
5.	Meghalaya	-	-	-	-	-	-
6.	Nagaland	-	-	-	-	-	-
7.	Sikkim	-	-	-	-	-	-
8.	Tripura	-	-	-	-	-	-
TOTAL : (I) :		:	:	:	:	:	
II. NON-SPL. CATEGORY STATES :							
1.	Andhra Pradesh	8.456	838.41	8.577	141.73	12.960	428.33
2.	Bihar	10.955	1086.19	4.160	68.74	22.082	729.81
3.	Gujarat	5.190	514.59	8.051	133.04	-	-
4.	Haryana	1.951	193.44	7.868	130.02	-	-
5.	Karnataka	5.696	564.76	8.651	142.96	-	-
6.	Kerala	4.150	411.47	8.457	139.75	5.213	172.29
7.	Madhya Pradesh	8.097	802.82	6.833	112.92	14.663	484.61
8.	Maharashtra	9.800	971.67	8.965	148.15	-	-
9.	Orissa	4.266	422.98	4.108	67.83	7.326	242.12
10.	Punjab	2.634	261.16	7.417	122.57	-	-
11.	Rajasthan	5.009	496.64	5.782	95.55	6.937	229.27
12.	Tamil Nadu	8.009	794.09	10.251	169.40	-	-
13.	Uttar Pradesh	17.173	1702.70	5.520	91.22	30.819	1018.57
14.	West Bengal	8.614	854.08	5.360	88.57	-	-
TOTAL (II) :		100.000	9915.00	100.00	1652.50	100.00	3305.00
GRAND TOTAL(I+II):		100.000	9915.00	100.000	1652.50	100.00	3305.00

(Contd.)

TABLE-III-23 ALLOCATION OF CENTRAL ASSISTANCE UNDER MODIFIED GADGIL FORMULA (1985-90)

(Rs. Crores)

	STATES	Total(90%) Amount	Special Problems (10%)	Total	Externally Aided	Grand Total
	(1)	(8)	(9)	(10)	(11)	(12)
I. SEPECIAL CATEGORY STATES:						
1.	Assam	-	-	2057.08	8.00	2065.08
2.	Himachal Pradesh	-	-	781.93	85.00	866.93
3.	Jammu & Kashmir	-	-	1820.68	18.00	1838.68
4.	Manipur	-	-	545.00	-	545.00
5.	Meeghalaya	-	-	441.28	-	441.28
6.	Nagaland	-	-	666.88	-	666.88
7.	Sikkim	-	-	247.62	-	247.62
8.	Tripura	-	-	541.58	-	541.58
TOTAL(I) :		-	-	7102.05	111.00	7213.05
II. NON-SPL.CATEGORY STATES						
1.	Andhra Pradesh	1408.47	75.00	1483.47	158.00	1641.47
2.	Bihar	1884.74	250.00	2134.74	170.00	2304.74
3.	Gujarat	647.63	50.00	697.63	358.00	1055.63
4.	Haryana	323.46	-	323.46	71.00	394.46
5.	Karnataka	707.72	60.00	767.72	114.00	881.72
6.	Kerala	723.51	200.00	923.51	217.00	1140.51
7.	Madhya Pradesh	1400.35	-	1400.35	496.00	1896.35
8.	Maharashtra	1119.82	50.00	1169.82	620.00	1789.82
9.	Orissa	732.98	177.45	910.43	242.00	1152.43
10.	Punjab	383.73	-	383.73	84.00	467.73
11.	Rajasthan	821.46	275.00	1096.46	58.00	1154.46
12.	Tamil Nadu	963.49	275.00	1238.49	216.00	1454.49
13.	Uttar Pradesh	2812.49	132.36	2944.85	670.00	3614.85
14.	West Bengal	942.65	65.00	1007.65	215.00	1222.65
TOTAL(II) :		14872.50	1609.81	16482.31	3689.00	20171.31
GRAND TOTAL (I+II) :		14872.50	1609.81	23584.36	3800.00	27384.36

Source: Government Of India, Ministry of Finance, 'Statistical Statements on Finances and Plans of States and Union territories, 1985'.

TABLE-IV-1 : EVOLUTION OF STATE PLAN OUTLAYS SINCE FIRST FIVE YEAR PLAN

(Rs. Crores)

	First Plan 1951-56	Second Plan 1956-61	Third Plan 1961-66	Annual Plans 1966-69	Fourth Plan 1969-74	Fifth Plan 1974-79	Annual Plan 1979-80	Sixth Plan 1980-85	Seventh Plan 1985-90	Cumulative 1951-90
I. SPL. CATEGORY STATES:										
1. Assam	28.00	63.15	132.24	87.12	198.41	473.84	155.00	1115.00	2100.00	4352.76
2. Himachal Pradesh	*	*	*	*	113.43	238.95	73.00	560.00	1050.00	2035.38
3. Jammu & Kashmir	13.00	26,82	61,24	59,28	162.22	362.64	118.00	900.00	1400.00	3103.20
4. Manipur	*	*	*	*	31,15	92.88	31.00	240.00	430.00	825.03
5. Meghalaya	*	*	*	*	36.24	89.53	33.00	235.00	440.00	833.77
6. Nagaland	*	*	10,79	15.98	38.52	83.63	26.05	210.00	400.00	784.97
7. Sikkim	*	*	*	*	*	39.64	17.88	122.00	230.00	409.52
8. Tripura	*	*	*	*	*34.66	69.68	28.00	245.00	440.00	817.34
TOTAL: I	41.00	89.97	204.27	162.33	614.63	1450.77	481.93	3627.00	6490.00	13161.90
II. OTHER STATES:										
1. Andhra Pradesh	107.00	180.64	344.78	235.62	425.51	1333.58	421.50	3100.00	5200.00	11348.63
2. Bihar	102.00	176.87	331.74	217.37	479.21	1296.06	356.85	3225.00	5100.00	11285.10
3. Gujarat	99.00	146.83	237.68	207.80	545.03	1185.76	392.00	3680.00	6000.00	12494.10
4. Haryana	*	*	*	84.62	358.26	601.34	227.00	1800.00	2900.00	5971.22
5. Karnataka	94.00	138.72	250.69	192.15	374.14	997.67	299.00	2265.00	3500.00	8111.37
6. Kerala	44.00	79.00	181.59	144.74	333.35	568.96	170.00	1550.00	2100.00	5171.64
7. Madhya Pradesh	94.00	145.50	288.35	166.82	475.51	1379.71	455.00	3800.00	7000.00	13804.39
8. Maharastra	125.00	214.03	433.60	388.83	1004.51	2347.61	762.50	6175.00	10500.00	21951.08
9. Orissa	85.00	89.36	224.06	122.75	249.34	585.02	191.00	1500.00	2700.00	5700.53
10. Punjab	163.00	151.43	254.23	121.85	428.48	1013.49	260.00	1957.00	3285.00	7639.48
11. Rajasthan	66.00	99.86	210.69	136.60	308.81	709.24	275.00	2025.00	3000.00	6831.20
12. Tamil Nadu	85.00	186.19	342.33	265.99	551.69	1122.32	307.00	3150.00	5750.00	11760.52
13. Uttar Pradesh	166.00	228.32	560.25	451.40	1162.58	2445.86	690.00	5850.00	10447.00	22001.41
14. West Bengal	154.00	155.84	300.49	161.47	363.55	1246.83	450.00	3500.00	4125.00	10457.18
Total - II	1384.00	1992.59	3960.48	2898.01	7059.96	16833.45	5256.85	43577.00	71607.00	154569.37
GRAND TOTAL:	1425.00	2082.56	4164.75	3060.39	7674.59	18284.22	5738.78	47204.00	78097.00	167731.29

* : was not a state diuring the period.

Note : Outlay dentoes actual expenditure upto fourth Plan

Source: State Plans Division, Planning Commission.

TABLE-IV-2 : PER CAPITA PLAN OUTLAYS

(Rs.)

	First Plan 51-56	Second Plan 56-61	Third Plan 61-66	Annual Plans 66-69	Fourth Plan 69-74	Fifth Plan 74-79	Annual Plan 79-80	Sixth Plan 80-85	Seventh Plan 85-90	Total 1951-90
I. SPL. CATEGORY STATES:										
1. Assam	29	57	103	61	136	279	83	560	1035	2188
2. Himachal Pradesh	*	*	*	*	328	613	178	1302	2453	4978
3. Jammu $ Kashmir	39	77	166	152	351	684	207	1500	2338	5183
4. Manipur	*	*	*	*	290	714	221	1689	3026	5998
5. Meghalaya	*	*	*	*	358	746	275	1759	3293	6241
6. Nagaland	*	*	280	400	747	1394	372	2710	5161	10129
7. Sikkim	*	*	*	*	*	1982	596	3861	7278	12959
8. Tripura	*	*	*	*	223	287	140	1193	2143	4166
Total-I	32	62	121	86	227	463	141	1006	1799	3694
II. OTHER STATES:										
1. Andhra Pradesh	33	52	91	58	98	277	82	579	971	2119
2. Bihar	25	40	67	40	85	206	53	461	730	1614
3. Gujarat	58	76	108	84	204	393	121	1079	1760	3665
4. Haryana	*	*	*	91	358	527	185	1395	2244	4621
5. Karnataka	46	62	100	70	128	302	84	610	942	2184
6. Kerala	31	49	101	73	156	244	69	607	825	2032
7. Madhya Pradesh	34	48	84	44	114	295	91	727	1342	2646
8. Maharastra	37	57	103	83	199	418	127	983	1672	3496
9. Orissa	56	54	120	60	114	243	75	568	1024	2179
10. Punjab	105	87	126	90	316	671	161	1164	1957	4547
11. Rajasthan	39	53	97	56	120	238	85	590	876	1994
12. Tamil Nadu	20	57	98	71	134	252	65	650	1188	2429
13. Uttar Pradesh	25	32	72	53	132	247	65	527	942	1985
14. West Bengal	54	48	80	39	82	253	86	641	756	1916
Total - II :	39	51	91	60	137	278	81	682	1120	2418
III. GRAND TOTAL:	38	51	91	61	142	309	90	715	1156	2486
Population Used	1953	1958	1963	1967	1971	1976	1979	1981	1981	1981

* Was not a state during the period.

Source: State Plans Division, Planning Commission, upto IVth Plan.
For other plans Percapita figures have been worked out on the basis of the outlays indicated in Table.II.1.

TABLE-IV-3 : PLAN OUTLAYS - UNION TERRITORIES

(Rs. Crores)

	Territory	First Plan 51-56	Second Plan 56-61	Third Plan 61-66	Annual Plans 66-69	Fourth Plan 69-74	Fifth Plan 74-79	Annual Plan 79-80	Sixth Plan 80-85	Seventh Plan 85-90
1.	A & N Islands	0.83	3.62	6.17	5.29	14.70	33.72	16.03	96.60	285.00
2.	Arunachal Pradesh	2.31	3.74	7.32	7.79	21.12	63.30	23.41	212.00	400.00
3.	Chandigarh	#	#	9.56	2.72	17.37	39.76	14.00	100.75	203.09
4.	Dadra and Nagar Haveli	#	#	0.25	0.71	2.33	9.41	3.31	23.09	46.29
5.	Delhi	5.85	11.42	93.09	63.88	155.10	316.01	108.00	800.00	2000.00
6.	Goa, Damen and Diu	#	#	15.27	19.82	41.93	85.00	30.00	192.00	360.00
7.	Lakshdweep	#	0.42	0.99	0.95	1.90	5.23	3.00	20.35	43.90
8.	Mizoram	#	#	#	#	9.30	46.59	17.72	130.00	260.00
9.	Pondicherry	0.50	3.66	6.01	5.26	14.37	34.04	11.57	71.54	170.00
	TOTAL:	9.49	22.86	138.66	106.42	278.12	634.06	227.04	1646.33	3768.28

\# was not a Union Territory during this period.

Note: Outlay denotes actual expenditure upto Fourth Plan.

Source: 1. State Plans Division, planning Commission.
2. Govt of India, Ministry of Finance, 'Statistical Statements on Finances and Plans of States and Union Territories' 1985.

TABLE-IV-4: PER CAPITA PLAN OUTLAYS - UNION TERRITORIES

(in Rupees)

Territory	First Plan 1951-56	Second Plan 1956-61	Third Plan 1961-66	Annual Plans 1966-69	Fourth Plan 1969-74	Fifth Plan 1974-79	Annual Plans 1979-80	Sixth Plan 1980-85	Seventh Plan 1985-90
1. A & N Islands	218	670	1,143	637	1,278	3,372	1,603	4,830	14,250
2. Arunachal Pradesh	75	114	224	207	452	1,055	390	3,029	5,715
3. Chandigarh	#	#	853	185	676	994	280	2,015	4,062
4. Dadra $ Nagar Haveli	#	#	46	104	315	1,176	368	2,309	4,629
5. Delhi	30	47	387	173	381	632	189	1,290	3,225
6. Goa, Daman,& Diu	#	#	246	296	489	850	273	1,745	3,273
7. Lakshdweep	#	183	430	352	594	1,557	750	5,088	10,975
8. Mizoram	#	#	#	#	280	1,165	443	2,600	5,200
9. Pondicherry	15	102	169	124	304	567	193	1,192	2,833
TOTAL	28	57	295	103	417	771	249	1,676	3,837
POPULATION USED	1953	1958	1963	1967	1971	1976	1979	1981	1981

\# Was not a Union Territory during this period.

N.B:- Outlay denotes actual expenditure upto the Fourth Plan

Soure: Planning commission,
State Plan's Division upto IVth Plan. For other plans Percapita Figures have been worked out on the basis of the outlays indicated in Table-II.2.

TABLE-IV-5 : APPROVED PLAN OUTLAYS - STATES 1974-75 TO 1984-85

(Rs. Crores)

		1974-75	1975-76	1976-77	1977-78	1978-79	1979-80
1.	Andhra Pradesh	127.39	157.80	262.35	268.75	449.00	421.50
2.	Assam	53.66	58.62	72.66	119.39	155.00	155.00
3.	Bihar	168.98	189.10	242.04	306.94	384.14	356.85
4.	Gujarat	143.32	172.65	193.25	291.58	335.00	392.00
5.	Haryana	81.60	92.25	110.53	154.40	210.00	227.00
6.	Himachal Pradesh	31.16	32.08	37.36	56.85	73.00	73.00
7.	Jammu & Kashmir	48.00	53.75	79.24	89.68	108.00	118.00
8.	Karnataka	110.75	139.00	200.18	243.50	309.00	299.00
9.	Kerala	73.89	90.00	111.50	142.52	176.00	170.00
10.	Madhya Pradesh	152.25	215.36	272.00	357.77	413.00	455.00
11.	Maharastra	275.84	350.00	459.50	663.80	735.00	762.50
12.	Manipur	12.06	14.00	16.59	23.19	28.26	31.00
13.	Meghalaya	13.63	14.60	20.22	24.46	29.11	33.00
14.	Nagaland	14.00	15.24	17.70	19.27	24.53	26.05
15.	Orissa	71.24	89.25	124.67	155.50	191.00	191.00
16.	Punjab	107.87	163.30	219.00	265.50	260.00	260.00
17.	Rajasthan	79.80	105.50	135.00	175.30	235.00	275.00
18	Sikkim	@	6.31	12.20	12.47	15.80	17.88
19	Tamil Nadu	112.00	142.59	201.00	260.12	305.00	307.00
20.	Tripura	11.00	12.08	14.56	15.78	22.70	28.00
21.	Uttar Pradesh	255.19	388.00	518.00	654.75	755.00	690.00
22.	West Bengal	147.87	170.00	232.00	316.42	371.40	450.00
Total All States		2091.50	2671.48	3651.55	4717.94	5584.94	5738.78
Union Territories		88.30	96.10	117.46	168.40	214.25	227.04
Total States and U. Ts.		2179.80	2767.58	3669.01	4886.34	5799.19	5965.82

@ Was not a State during this year.

* Tentative

Source: State Plans Division, Planning Commission.

TABLE-IV-6 : APPROVED PLAN OUTLAYS - STATES 1974-75 TO 1986-87

(Rs. Crores)

	STATES	1980-81	1981-82	1982-83	1983-84	1984-85	1985-86	1986-87
1.	Andhra Pradesh	501.00	531.31	605.00	826.00	918.31	810.00	1000.00
2.	Assam	198.00	210.00	238.00	291.00	360.00	410.00	500.00
3.	Bihar	476.61	560.00	670.00	681.00	751.00	851.00	1150.00
4.	Gujarat	524.03	632.00	760.00	900.00	935.00	804.00	950.00
5.	Haryana	250.12	290.00	320.00	407.00	430.00	480.00	525.00
6.	Himachal Pradesh	90.00	100.00	120.00	140.00	168.17	177.00	205.00
7.	Jammu & Kashmir	147.48	160.00	168.00	185.00	235.00	260.00	315.00
8.	Karnataka	384.55	419.00	475.00	575.00	650.00	651.00	765.00
9.	Kerala	273.00	275.00	275.00	320.00	355.00	355.00	390.00
10.	Madhya Pradesh	541.00	640.43	725.00	855.00	1060.00	1170.00	1381.00
11.	Maharastra	882.90	1080.10	1322.00	1500.00	1650.00	1700.00	2100.00
12.	Manipur	41.85	43.00	48.00	52.80	61.00	70.00	87.00
13.	Meghalaya	43.31	46.55	51.20	56.32	65.00	75.00	91.00
14.	Nagaland	36.13	38.00	42.58	51.00	56.10	65.00	78.00
15.	Orissa	250.16	275.00	300.00	345.00	400.00	450.00	600.00
16.	Punjab	300.00	340.34	385.00	440.00	440.00	500.00	575.00
17.	Rajasthan	333.80	340.00	340.00	401.00	387.00	430.00	525.00
18.	Sikkim	21.02	23.13	25.41	30.50	35.08	41.00	50.00
19.	Tamil Nadu	411.23	514.00	711.00	845.00	927.00	960.00	1153.00
20.	Tripura	39.81	45.00	50.00	58.00	68.00	86.00	105.00
21.	Uttar Pradesh	933.83	1023.00	1132.00	1290.00	1502.45	1642.00	2030.00
22.	West Bengal	575.10	638.00	490.00	540.00	411.00	675.00	776.00
	TOTAL All States	7255.59	8223.86	9253.19	10789.62	11865.11	12662.00	15351.00
UNION TERRITORIES		254.50	327.72	393.46	480.53	557.57	641.56	871.53
TOTAL ALL STATES 7s UTs.		7510.09	8551.58	9646.65	11270.15	12422.68	13303.56	16222.53

Source: State Plans Division, Planning Commission.

TABLE-IV-7 : ACTUAL PLAN EXPENDITURE DURING THE SIXTH PLAN 1980-85

(Rs. Crores)

	1980-81 Actuals	1981-82 Actuals	1982-83 Actuals	1983-84 Actuals	1984-85 Actuals	Total 1980-85	Approved Plan outlays 1980-85
I. SPL. CATEGORY STATES:							
1. Assam	192.61	208.10	225.85	289.02	356.40	1271.98	1115.00
2. Himachal Pradesh	96.51	118.07	129.31	143.00	181.81	668.70	560.00
3. Jammu & Kashmir	147.48	165.00	175.00	195.77	233.43	916.98	900.00
4. Manipur	40.17	43.57	47.18	54.93	61.20	247.05	240.00
5. Meghalaya	42.55	44.00	50.99	58.98	63.12	259.64	235.00
6. Nagaland	35.52	37.46	42.73	54.80	59.88	230.39	210.00
7. Sikkim	20.32	24.20	23.59	29.04	36.65	133.80	122.00
8. Tripura	39.87	47.78	55.03	62.22	76.07	280.97	245.00
TOTAL I	615.03	688.18	748.68	887.76	1068.56	4008.21	3627.00
II. OTHER STATES							
1. Andhra Pradesh	487.59	517.85	484.54	781.71	909.16	3180.85	3100.00
2. Bihar	465.47	574.67	593.37	588.17	709.94	2931.62	3225.00
3. Gujarat	575.65	717.82	807.59	864.56	960.23	3925.85	3680.00
4. Haryana	240.29	275.69	319.27	330.63	372.09	1537.97	1800.00
5. Karnataka	394.38	411.46	496.03	613.69	682.58	2598.14	2265.00
6. Kerala	305.26	324.22	277.00	393.52	404.26	1704.26	1550.00
7. Madhya Pradesh	617.70	640.09	715.35	905.47	990.57	3869.18	3800.00
8. Maharastra	917.30	1155.90	1329.07	1427.12	1641.41	6470.80	6175.00
9. Orissa	248.21	281.71	300.84	326.66	406.48	1563.90	1500.00
10. Punjab	299.37	341.00	432.60	460.36	430.32	1963.65	1957.00
11. Rajasthan	310.71	383.34	337.85	449.07	434.13	1915.10	2025.00
12. Tamil Nadu	451.76	667.30	735.64	842.09	916.94	3613.73	3150.00
13. Uttar Pradesh	971.61	1159.06	1234.95	1173.92	1814.77	6354.31	5850.00
14. West Bengal	420.35	447.90	449.21	479.32	550.53	2347.31	3500.00
Total:II	6705.72	7898.01	8513.33	9636.29	11223.41	43976.76	43577.00
GRAND TOTAL	7320.75	8586.19	9263.01	10524.05	12291.97	47984.97	47204.00

Source: Govt. of India, Ministry of Finance, 'Statistical Statements on Finances and Plans of States and Union Territories' 1985 and State Plans Division, Planning Commission.

TABLE-IV-8: PLAN EXPENDITURE AS PERCENTAGE OF TOTAL EXPENDITURE

STATES (1)	1980-81 (2)	1981-82 (3)	1982-83 (4)	1983-84 (5)	1984-85 (6)	Total 1980-85 (7)
I. Spl. CATEGORY STATES:						
1. Assam	21.29	26.20	17.88	27.39	20.18	21.99
2. Himachal Pradesh	28.55	27.85	23.03	33.28	29.76	23.18
3. Jammu & Kashmir	36.62	37.98	34.73	31.58	34.56	34.77
4. Manipur	18.35	16.36	27.17	29.60	28.01	23.24
5. Meghalaya	41.74	32.70	40.89	40.01	35.19	37.72
6. Nagaland	19.13	25.19	19.19	17.60	26.68	21.04
7. Sikkim	47.25	54.07	50.57	45.39	50.30	49.31
8. Tripura	26.77	34.76	34.62	33.89	32.55	32.57
TOTAL - (I)	26.24	28.86	24.54	29.64	26.74	27.14
II. NON - SPL. STATES						
1. Andhra Pradesh	28.25	24.92	20.16	27.18	22.24	24.14
2. Bihar	26.00	28.58	22.29	17.64	19.09	21.65
3. Gujarat	38.39	42.54	39.63	35.50	35.73	37.95
4. Haryana	29.56	28.61	25.20	24.55	27.47	26.80
5. Karnataka	23.03	21.55	23.17	23.03	18.38	21.42
6. Kerala	37.26	33.55	19.52	31.72	26.29	28.53
7. Madhya Pradesh	28.75	27.82	30.96	34.17	29.68	30.35
8. Mahaashtra	29.65	28.82	28.89	26.48	27.26	27.99
9. Orissa	27.60	26.63	20.06	17.90	23.85	22.38
10. Punjab	22.34	15.73	23.02	20.65	14.38	18.47
11. Rajasthan	20.57	20.54	16.61	22.00	17.80	19.25
12. Tamil Nadu	26.51	31.30	28.37	22.72	25.24	26.24
13. Uttar Pradesh	34.08	32.78	28.39	23.60	23.64	27.38
14. West Bengal	19.72	18.05	13.69	14.96	11.96	15.06
Total - II	27.89	27.08	24.69	24.14	22.76	24.87
GRAND TOTAL	27.74	27.21	24.68	24.52	23.06	25.05

Source: Government of India, Ministry of Finance, 'Statistical Statements on Finances and Plans of States and Union Territories' 1985.

TABLE-IV-9 : SIXTH FIVE YEAR PLAN 1980-85 - OUTLAYS - STATES

(Rs. Lakhs)

HEAD OF DEVELOPMENT	Andhra Pradesh	Assam	Bihar	Gujarat	Haryana	Himachal Pradesh
1	2	3	4	5	6	7
Research & Education	460	900	500	1000	1000	
Crop Husbandry	1700	5000	4200	3100	5500	3014
Land Reforms	300	850	3850	1000	75	600
Minor Irrigation	7900	7450	16870	8800	2371	2100
Soil & Water Conservtion	360	800	2000	2900	1000	1577
Command Area Development	3500	160	3200	1880	6905[1]	-
Food	-	-	-	-	-	625
Amimal Husbandry	1400	1650	1900	1770	1100	675
Dairy Development	600	4400	760	200	223	425
Fisheries	1400	600	696	2000	195	180
Forests	1050	2520	1800	8900	1450	2900
Investment in Agri. Financial Institutions	2275	125	765	350	1250	-
Marketing	20	250	1000		35	-
Storage & Warehousing	90	100	20	170	130	-
C.D. and Panchayats	5950	800	2235	630	1650[2]	300
Special Programme for Rural Development	8725	4225	19000	14400	2893	1690
Development of Backward Areas including Hill Areas	-	-	-	250	-	-
I. AGRICULTURE & ALLIED SERVICES	35730	25830	58796	47350	25777	14086
II. CO-OPERATION	2951	2560	2725	3200	2680	675
Irrigation	79129	6250	85000	98000	36225	1045
Flood Control Projects	2000	2240	15800	2000	11400	335
Power	78970	37030	80000	94150	54500	13973

III. IRRIGATION FLOOD CONTROL & POWER	160099	45520	180800	194150	102125	15353
Village & Small Industries	3000	3000	4700	6150	1946	905
Medium & Large Industries	5566	2200	4515	8810	1100	800
Mining	2000	275	650	1150	40	100
IV. INDUSTRY AND MINERALS	10566	5475	9865	16110	3086	1805
Ports, Light Houses & Shipping	300	-	-	2500	-	-
Civil Aviation	-	-	40	-	200	190
Roads and Bridges	5500	8400	22735	22000	11000	10000
Road Transport	17500	1250	2000	9000	5200	950
Water Transport	200	550	50	-	-	10
Tourism	100	250	150	260	550	700
Telecommunications	-	-	-	-	-	15
V. TRANSPORT & COMMUNICATIONS	23600	10450	24975	33760	16950	11865
General Education	6500	7620	14300	5260	6012[5]	
Art and Culture	300	330	150	300		
Technical Education	500	800	950	600	325	1775
Sub-Total:	7300	8750	15400	6160	6337	1775
Scientific Services and Research	-	-	-	-	-	-
Medical & Public Health	6500	3200	8240	7000	4800	1618
Severage & Water Supply	20300	4655	10014	15075	10750	5000
Housing		10500	2000	4625	8530	2600
Police Housing					550	1148
Urban Development	3500	260	1100	2450	700	375
State Capital Projects		-	-	2900	-	-

Information and Publicity	200	75	55	85	150	50
Labour & Labour Welfare	300	290	315	2050	275	70
Employment Schemes	-	-	-	-	-	-
Welfare of S.C., S.T. and Other Backward Classes	20074	1100	3200	8000	825	450
Social Welfare	2850	200	260	450	360	198
Nutrition	1100	270	1000	1650	400	242
Others	-	-	-	500	-	-
VI. SOCIAL AND COMMUNITY SERVICES	72624	20800	44209	54850	27747	10926
Secretariat-Economic Services	2640	95	90	5	50	25
Economic Advice and Statistics	170	85	190	250	34	20
Others	20	60	-	325	6	-
VII. ECONOMIC SERVICES	2830	240	280	580	90	45
Stationary and Printing	100	150	25	-	245	170
Public Works	1500	475	750	-	1300[11]	900
others	-	-	75[13]	18000[14]	-	175
VIII. GENERAL SERVICES	1600	625	850	18000	1545	1245
GRAND TOTAL:	310000	111500	322500	368000	180000	56000

TABLE -IV-9 (Contd.)

(Rs. Lakh)

HEAD OF DEVELOPMENT	Jammu & Kashmir	Karnataka	Kerala	Madhya Pradesh	Mahara-shtra	Manipur
1	8	9	10	11	12	13
Research & Education	377	850	1400	400	1600	120
Crop Husbandry	2145	3854	8594	5685	6782	900
Land Reforms	400	2020	3070	1500	300	40
Minor Irrigation	4350	10000	4000	26775	16465	850
Soil & Water Conservation	500	2080	1029	3800	1588	550
Command Area Development	800	1300	725	9475	2670	50
Food	-	-	500	-	-	-
Animal Husbandry	1800	1334	1517	2475	1832	300
Dairy Development	100	845	721	370	3287	250
Fisheries	230	1303	2000	700	1207	475
Forests	1028	3075	1862	3800	4875	20
Investment in Agri. Financial Institutions	50	650	1100	900	1400	5
Marketing	370	160	125	30	178	40
Storage & Warehousing	400	275	70	160	51	200
C.D. & Panchayats	600	250	4140	1500	8100	700
Special Programme for Rural Development	2410	4915	2510	15500		
Development of Backward Areas including Hill Areas	4500[3]	-	250	-	-	-
I. AGRICULTURE AND ALLIED SERVICES	20060	32911	33613	73070	50335	4500
II. COOPERATION	500	5000	2200	4790	5744	180
Irrigation	6794	44050	25605	78000	113866	4000
Flood Control Projects	3100	180	2500	480	60	550
Power	17000	60140	31273	150000	215700	1865

III. IRRIGATION FLOOD CONTROL & POWER	26894	104370	59378	228480	329626	6415
Village & Small Industries	3470	7400	4980	3340	6026	1250
Medium & large Industries	3307	8660	10820	2980	12940	700
Mining	500	208	150	575	250	50
IV. INDUSTRY & MINERALS	7277	16268	15950	6895	19216	2000
Ports, Light House and Shipping	-	660	825	-	600	-
Civil Aviation	-	-	-	-	30	-
Roads and Bridges	6400	6600	6600	13000	25000	3200
Road Transport	1640	6800	2000	2750	18000	300
Water Transport	-	51	575	-	100[4]	-
Tourism	2400	410	675	500	330	50
Telecommunications	-	-	-	-	-	-
V. TRANSPORT & COMMUNICATIONS	10440	14521	10675	16250	44060	3550
General Education	3500	5060	4120		11210	1620
Art and Culture	120	150	200	10450	220	80
Technical Education	150	550	700		1850	100
Sub-Total:	3770	5760	5020	10450	13280	1800
Scientific Services and Research	-	80	1200	-	-	-
Medical and Public Health	4800	6553	3655	19400	8946	970
Severage & Water Supply	9800[6]	13200	9050	14650	65400	2735
Housing	1080	10510	4800	5810	12500	420
Police Housing	1000					
Urban Development	1600	3000	1900	1500	7000	160
State Capital Project	-	-		1000		-

Information & Publicity	60	520	90	120	66	50
Labour & Labour Welfare	400[7]	809	297	290	3793	40
Employment Schemes	-	5590[19]	-	-	45000	-
Welfare of S.C., S.T. and Other Backward Classess	279	4209	2500	4000	6000	250
Social Welfare	200	600	467	500	410	135
Nutrition	120	2258	1700	2000	2600	110
Others	-	-	-	340	-	-
VI. <u>SOCIAL AND COMMUNITY SERVICES</u>	<u>23109</u>	<u>53080</u>	<u>30679</u>	<u>50060</u>	<u>164995</u>	<u>6670</u>
Secretariat-Economic Services	75	120	300	200	100	15
Economic Advice and Statistics	-	35	275	125	219	40
Others	20	95[8]	50	30	5[9]	110[10]
VII. <u>ECCONOMIC SERVICES</u>	<u>95</u>	<u>250</u>	<u>625</u>	<u>355</u>	<u>324</u>	<u>165</u>
Stationary and Printing	125	100	400	100	-	20
Public Works	1500	-	1480	-	3200[12]	500
Others	-	-	-	-	-	
VIII. <u>GENERAL SERVICES</u>	<u>1625</u>	<u>100</u>	<u>1880</u>	<u>100</u>	<u>3200</u>	<u>520</u>
<u>GRAND TOTAL</u>:	<u>90000</u>	<u>226500</u>	<u>155000</u>	<u>380000</u>	<u>6175000</u>	<u>24000</u>

TABLE-IV-9 (Contd.)

HEAD OF DEVELOPMENT	Meghalaya	Nagaland	Orissa	Punjab	Rajasthan	Sikkim
1	14	15	16	17	18	19
Research & Education	27		300	1000	300	1187[15]
Crop Husbandry	803	850	4250	7237	2800	
Land Reforms	150	100	2500	-	133	119
Minor Irrigation	600	1000	8500	943	3400	400
Soil & Water Conservation	700	600	600	2060	565	662
Command Area Development	-	-	1000	3881	9426	-
Food	-	-	-	17	-	48
Animal Husbandry	520	525	1000	1349	995	
Dairy Development	70	-	-	236	1064	500
Fisheries	90	70	1000	175	225	100
Forests	500	680	1250	1290	1500	570
Investment in Agri. Financial Institutions	5	-	500	1723	800	90
Marketing	40	-	80	30	2	-
Storage and Warehousing	20	-	35	120	25	-
C.D. and Panchayats	240	700	525	1815	33	25
Special Programme for Rural Development	300	650	10500	3600	10575	-
Development of Backward Areas including Hill Areas	1000	500	-	-	-	-
I. AGRICULTURE AND ALLIED SERVICES	5065	5675	32040	25476	31843	3701
II. COOPERATION	328	150	3000	4150	2438	160
Irrigation	100	-	36000	32729	37500	-
Flood Control Projects	100	-	1500	2100	1775[16]	50
Power	4500	1525	41000	73294	67500	1200

III. <u>IRRIGATION FLOOD CONTROL & POWER</u>	<u>4700</u>	<u>1525</u>	<u>78500</u>	<u>108123</u>	<u>106775</u>	<u>1250</u>
Village & Small Industries	400	500	2700	2061	1950	360
Medium & Large Industries	450	440	3200	6087	4509	174
Mining	100	260	600	20	1900	120
IV. <u>INDUSTRY & MINERALS</u>	<u>950</u>	<u>1200</u>	<u>6500</u>	<u>8168</u>	<u>8359</u>	<u>654</u>
Ports, Light House & Shipping	-	-	600	-	-	-
Civil Aviation	-	-	-	70	-	-
Roads and Bridges	4000	5000	8900	7000	10000	2420
Road Transport	800	550	1000 17	4000	3000	480
Water Transport	-	-		-	-	-
Tourism	200	55	325	255	650	175
Telecommunications	-	-	-	-	-	-
V. <u>TRANSPORT & COMMUNICATIONS</u>	5000	5605	10825	11325	13650	3075
General Education			4925		9545	
Art and Culture	1102	1165	235	5600	350	930
Technical Education			300		230	
<u>Sub-Total</u>	<u>1102</u>	<u>1165</u>	<u>5460</u>	<u>5600</u>	<u>10125</u>	<u>930</u>
Scientific Services & Research	-	-	-	-	-	-
Medical and Public Health	710	800	2960	4900	4098	435
Severage & Water Supply	4439	1675	4500	13794	19829	950
Housing	300	1150	2100	5735	2485	302
Police Housing			-			
Urban Development	160	415	450 18	2660	550	120
State Capital Projects	-	-		-	-	-

Information & Publicity	15	50	100	180	100	40
Labour & Labour Welfare	49	60	185	245	287	40
Employment Programme	-	-	-	-	-	-
Welfare of SC, ST and other Backward Classes	2	-	1400	3200	550	90
Social Welfare	65	100	200	507	162	33
Nutrition	125	130	650	80	327	130
Others	-	-	-	-	-	-
VI. SOCIAL & COMMUNITY SERVICES	6967	5545	18905	36901	38513	3070
Secretariat Economic Services	20	20	60	50	50	
Economic advice and Statistics	30	50	150	85	72	44
Others	10	30	-	15	-	
VII. Economic Services	60	100	210	150	122	44
Stationery and Printing	30	60	150	60	100	18
Public Works	250	1080	770[20]	1247	700	228
Others	150	60[21]	-	100[22]	-	-
VIII. GENERAL SERVICES	430	1200	920	1407	800	246
GRAND TOTAL:	23500	21000	150000	195700	202500	12200

Table-IV-9 (Contd.)

(Rs. Lakhs)

HEAD OF DEVELOPMENT	Tamil Nadu	Tripura	Uttar Pradesh	West Bengal	Total
1	20	21	22	23	24.
Research and Education	1800	41	2100	1544	19920
Crop Husbandry	11703	1086	5420	9041	90650
Land Reforms	181	283	4791	5000	27262
Minor Irrigation	3940	1310	27996	15050	171970
Soil & Water Conservation	1800	697	4448	2000	32316
Command Area Development	800	-	8500	1320[24]	55592
Food	100	125	-	320	1735
Animal Husbandry	3353	730	1549	2650	30924
Dairy Development	580	142	1419	690	12132
Fisheries	2400	333	659	2700	18513
Forests	5900	1239	7090	2200	55954
Investment in Agri. Fin. Institutions	550	15	2500	600	15668
Marketing	500	200	700	920	4815
Storage & Warehousing	-	58	200	335	2078
C.D. & Panchayats	7800	448	1837	1800	33529
Special Programme for Rural Dev.	12000	655	14796	12600	150744
Development of Backward Areas including Hill Areas	-	-	-	4500	11000
I. AGRICULTURE AND ALLIED SERVICES	53407	7362	84005	63270	733902
II. COOPERATION	2533	500	5536	4600	56600
Irrigation	14979	1900	104974	24000	830146
Flood Control Projects	2800	500	13270	20000	82740
Power	102280	2211	212590	88655	1429356

III. IRRIFATION FLOOD CONTROL & POWER	120059 -	4611	330834	132655	2342242
Village & Small Industries	8000	850[23]	12523	6000	81511
Medium & Large Industries	8992	536	18002	21134	125922
Mining	185	10	1810	200	11153
IV. INDUSTRY AND MINERALS	17177	1396	32335	27334	218586
Ports. Light House and Shipping	900	-	-	-	6385
Civil Aviation	-	-	-	100	630
Roads & Bridges	13900	2800	31932	13500	1239887
Road Transport	7550	370	12000	14000	111140
Water Transport	300	-	-	600	2436
Tourism	800	60	1054	307	10256
Telecommunications	-	- -	-	-	15
V. TRANSPORT & COMMUNICATIONS	23450	3230	44986	28507	370749
General Education	8000	1442		25300	149309
Art and Culture	200	50	13873	500	3185
Technical Education	1100	58		1700	9913
Sub-total	9300	1550	13873	27500	162407
Scientific Services & Research	-	-	275	150	1705
Medical & Public Health	6780	856	13498	8400	109119
Severage & Water Supply	49575	1727	2494	10300	312365
Housing	10642	850	11058	5500	104645
Police Housing				400	1950
Urban Development	8200	395	5982	7000	49477
State Capital Projects	-	-	-	24700	28600

Information and Publicity	150	90	200	400	2846
Labour and Labour Welfare	397	35	465	500	11192
Employment Programme	-	-	10000	475	61065
Welfare of S.C., S.T. & Backward Classes	8030	841	3229	2680	70900
Social Welfare	1350	160	846	925	10978
Nutrition	2600	580	883	2500	21455
Others	-	-	-	-	840
VI. SOCIAL & COMMUNITY SERVICES	97024	7084	85256	91430	949544
Seretariat Economic Services	50	10	1200	20	5239
Economic Advice & Statistics	250	22	300	54	2456
Others	-	10		100	886
VII. ECONOMIC SERVICES	300	42	1500	174	8581
Stationery and Printing	50	25	548	130	2606
Public Works	1000	250	-	1900	19030
Others	-	-	-	-	18560
VIII. GENERAL SERVICES	1050	275	548	2030	40196
GRAND TOTAL:	315000	24500	585000 (*)	350000	4720400

REFERENCES

1 Includes Rs. 500 lakhs for Mewat Area Development.
2 Includes Rs. 1000 lakhs for 'Food for Work'.
3 Includes Rs. 4000 lakhs for Ladakh.
4 For Kokan Railways (Land Acquisition).
5 Includes Rs. 286 lakhs for sports.
6 Includes outlays for Drainage and Severage Schemes for Srinagar & Jammu .

7 Includes Rs. 200 lakhs for 'Self Employment Scheme'.
8 Includes Rs. 80 lakhs for Computer Centre & 15 lakhs for Weights.
9 For Studies in Rural Development & Regional Planning.
10 Includes Rs. 100 lakhs for District Council & Rs. 10 lakhs for Weights & Measures
11 For General Administration.
12 Includes Rs. 200 lakhs for Judicial Buildings.
13 For Autonomous Development Authority.
14 For Decentralised District Planning.
15 Agriculture Programmes (Rs. 1187 lakhs) - Crop Husbandry= Rs. 1034 lakhs; I.R.D. = Rs. 65 lakhs; Storage = 48 lakhs; Marketing = Rs. 40 lakhs.
16 Includes Rs. 275 lakhs for Colonisation.
17 Included under Ports and Shipping.
18 Included under 'Housing'.
19 Includes Rs. 1350 lakhs for Stipendiary Employment Scheme and Rs. 4240 lakhs for Employment Affirmation Scheme.
20 Includes Police Hosing.
21 For Administrative Training Institute.
22 Includes Rs. 50 lakhs each for Administrative Institute and PUNSUP.
23 Includes Rs. 50 lakhs for Employment Promotion Schemes.
24 Includes Rs. 500 lakhs for 'Area Development.

* Sectoral break-up is tentative and excludes Hill Area Plan.

N.B. The above outlays do not include special Central Assistance for Hill and Tribal Areas as also Special Componant Plans for Scheduled Castes.

Source Govt. of India, Ministry of Finance 'Statistical Statements on Finances and Plans of States and Union Territories. 1985.

TABLE - IV-10 : SIXTH FIVE YEAR PLAN - PUBLIC SECTOR OUTLAYS

(Rs. Crores)

	HEAD OF DEVELOPMENT	Centre	States	Union Territories	Total
	1	2	3	4	5.
I.	AGRICULTURE	2450.13	3119.02	125.92	5695.07
	Agricultural Research & Education	340.00	197.67	*	537.67
	Crop Husbandry	293.00	906.50	34.48	1233.98
	Soil and Water Conservation	90.00	323.16	20.41	433.57
	Animal Husbandry and Dairying	393.00	430.56	22.82	851.38
	Fisheries	174.00	186.13	12.29	371.42
	Forestry	103.00	559.34	28.10	692.64
	Land Reforms	30.10	272.62	1.91	304.63
	Management of Natural Disasters	15.00	-	-	15.00
	Agricultural Marketing	46.63	48.55	0.91	96.11
	Food,Storage and Warehousing	294.00	33.61	5.00	337.61
	Investment in Agricultural Financial Institutions	664.38	156.68	-	821.06
II.	RURAL DEVELOPMENT	2314.87	3020.03	28.83	5363.73
	Integrated Rural Development and related Programmes	997.55	1508.09	1.00	3496.64
	National Rural Employment Programme	9.80			
	Community Development and Panchayat Institutions	7.17	335.29	9.74	352.20
	Cooperation	330.15	565.00	18.09	914.24
	Special Emoployment Programme	-	610.65	-	610.65
III.	SPECIAL AREA PROGRAMMES	-	1480.00	-	1480.00
	Hills Areas	-	560.00	-	560.00
	Tribal Areas	-	470.00	-	470.00
	North Eastern Council	-	340.00	-	340.00
	Development of Backward Areas	-	110.00	-	110.00
IV.	IRRIGATION AND FLOOD CONTROL	635.00	11396.48	129.55	?13160.03?
	Major and Medium	90.00	8302.46	56.90	8448.36
	Minor	70.00	1710.70	29.60	1310.30
	Command Area Development	300.00	555.92	0.35	866.27
	Flood Control including Anti-Sea Erosion	175.00	827.40	42.70	1045.10

V.	ENERGY	11995.00	14293.56	246.88	26535.44
	Power	4725.00	14293.56	246.88	19265.44
	New and Renewable sources of Energy	100.00	-	-	100.00
	Petroleum	4300.00	-	-	4300.00
	Coal	2870.00	-	-	2870.00
VI.	INDUSTRY AND MINERALS	12771.47	2185.86	60.24	15017.57
	Village and Small scale	923.40	815.11	41.94	1780.45
	Large and Medium	11843.07	1370.75	18.30	13237.12
*	Included under Crop Husbandry.				
VII.	TRANSPORT	8418.64	3707.34	285.99	12411.97
	Railways	5100.00	-	-	5100.00
	Roads	830.00	2398.87	210.09	3438.96
	Road Transport	70.00	1111.40	14.15	1195.55
	Ports	575.00			
	Light Houses	12.00	63.85	43.75	1414.60
	Shipping	720.00			
	Inland Water Transport	45.00	24.36	2.30	71.66
	Civil Aviation	850.00	6.30	2.80	859.10
	Meteorology	43.00	-	-	43.00
	Tourism	72.00	102.56	12.90	187.46
	Farakha Barrage	50.00	-	-	50.00
	INSAT - Space Segment	51.64	-	-	51.64
VIII.	COMMUNICATIONS AND INFORMATION AND BROADCASTING	3101.98	28.61	3.67	3134.26
	Communication	2810.00	0.15	0.12	2810.27
	INSAT - Space Segment	51.65	-	-	51.65
	Broadcasting and Television	210.33	-	-	210.33
	Information & Publicity	30.00	28.46	3.55	62.01
IX.	SCIENCE AND TECHNOLOGY	848.15	17.05	-	865.20
	Atomic Energy	248.98	-	-	248.98
	Space	245.80	-	-	245.80
	Scientific Research	304.87	17.05	-	321.92
	Ecology and Environment	40.00	-	-	40.00
	National Test Ho[illegible]	8.50	-	-	8.50

X.	SOCIAL SERVICES	4453.42	8830.88	750.96	14035.26
	Education				
	(a) General Education	515.75	1493.09	153.39	2162.23
	(b) Art and Culture	51.00	31.85	1.05	83.90
	(c) Technical Education	168.00	99.13	10.48	277.61
	Health including medical	601.00	1091.19	128.86	1821.05
	Family Planning	1010.00	-	-	1010.00
	Housing	300.00	1065.95	124.92	1490.87
	Urban Development	110.00	780.77	106.76	997.53
	Water Supply and Sanitation	614.22	3123.65	184.15	3922.02
	Welfare of Scheduled Castes, Scheduled Tribes and other-backward Classes	240.00	709.00	11.30	960.30
	Special Central Additive for Scheduled caste Component Plans	600.00	-	-	600.00
	Social Welfare	150.00	109.78	12.19	271.97
	Nutrition	14.95	214.55	8.64	238.14
	Labour and Labour Welfare	78.50	111.92	9.22	199.64
XI.	OTHERS	261.34	522.17	17.96	801.47
	Statistics	68.87	24.56	2.01	95.44
	Rehabilitation of displaced persons	154.12	-	-	154.12
	Planning Machinery	20.07	-	-	20.07
	Stationery and Printing	12.00	26.06	1.49	39.55
	Public Works	-	190.30	4.87	195.17
	Training for Development	2.28	-	-	2.28
	Other unclassified services	4.00	281.25	9.59	294.84
	TOTAL (I TO XI)	47250.00	48600.00	1650.00	97500.00

Source: Govt. of India, Ministry of Finance "Statistical Statements on Finances and Plans of States and Union Territories"

TABLE-IV-11 : SEVENTH FIVE YEAR PLAN (1985-90)- STATES' OUTLAYS

(Rs. Lakhs)

	Head/Sub Head of Development	Andhra Pradesh	Assam	Bihar	Gujarat	Haryana	Himachal Pradesh
	1	2	3	4	5	6	7
I.	Agriculture and Allied Services.						
	Research & Education	740[4]	2800[18]	2000	3033	2400	843
	Crop Husbandry *	8340	11675	9565	7720	7500	5994
	Soil & Water Conservation	810	1200	2000	5763	1725	1928
	Animal Husbandry	1680	1950	2400	1820	2500	976
	Dairy Development	1700	800	1250	182	450	425
	Fisheries	2140	1000	950	2426	750	430
	Forests	6570	7000	4500	12964	6700	11684
	Investment in Agri. Fin.-Institutions	2360	150	800	971	1500	75
	Marketing	220	350	1100	100	-	107
	Storage & Warehousing	220	150	50	21	283	-
	Total (I)	24780	27075	24615	35000	23808	22462
II.	Rural Development						
	Integrated Rural Development-Programme (IRDP)	9200	5200	14800	5284	1298	724
	National Rural Employment-Programme (NREP)	11350	3000	20000	3700	980	690
	Drought Prone Area-Programme (DPAP)	2470	-	1850	1575[51]	337	-
	Other Programmes	-	-	-	220	-	-
	Community Development and -Panchayats	1110	3600	3375	485	1884	475
	Land Reforms	440	1000	5580	910	135	1365
	Integrated Rural Energy-Programme (IREP)	60	50	200	250	100	400
	Special Programme for Area Development (State Programmes)						
	(i) Development of Backward Areas	-	63 500[19]	450[1]	-	1510[6]	-
	(ii)Others	-	510	-	-	-	-
	Total (II)	24620	13860	46255	12424	6244	3654
III.	Cooperation	3100	3500	3200	3640	3926	700

IV.	Irrigation & Flood Control						
	(a) Major & Medium Irrigation Irrigation	118230	13700	128500	146909	41850	1350
	(b) Minor Irrigation	14740	16000	26000	13455	1417	5400
	(c) Command Area Dev.	11050	1000	3500	6067	8625	300
	(d) Flood Control Projects (including Anti-Sea Erosion)	4790	2700	14400	1200	7569	400
	Total (IV)	148810	33400	172400	167631	59461	7450
V.	Power						
	(i) Power	110490	48500	106500	143700	101025	26011
	(ii)New & Renewable Sources of Energy	100	150	1800	1050	250	350
	Total (V)	110590	48650	108300	144750	101275	26361
VI.	Industry & Minerals						
	Village & Small Industries	9360	5000	7000	13023	3600	1030
	Medium & Large Industries	16210	4800	9000	10895	1945	1461
	Mining 5670	425	5600	1867	70	150	
	Total (VI)	31240	10225	21600	25785	5615	2641
VII.	Transport						
	Minor Ports & Light House	600	-	-	2386	-	-
	Shipping	-	-	-	-	-	800
	Civil Aviation	-	-	65	-	332	13200
	Roads & Bridges	8920	13500	37000	25785	10700	2325
	Road Transport	17410	1720	2500	8494	8000	50
	Inlands Water Transport	120	1000	45	650	-	808
	Tourism	220	400	700	425 52	1100	75
	Others	-	-	-	849	-	
	Total (VII)	27270	16620	40310	38589	20132	17250
VIII.	Scientific Services & Research						
	S & T Programmes	610	300	300	450	165	100
	Environmental Programme	290	150	25	100	1569	-
	Water Pollution Control	130	50	135	250	-	25
	Total (VIII)	1030	500	460	800	1734	125

IX.	Social & Community Services Education						
	General Education	18100	15900	30575	8071	13779	5220
	Art and Culture	1580	600	200	403	312	300
	Technical Education	1190	1600	800	1820	1500	550
	Sports & Youth Services	-	500	500	202	550	400
	Sub-Total (Education)	20870	18600	32075	10496	16141	6470
	Medical & Public Health	16420	7500	14640	10314	7877	2625
	Sewerage & Water Supply	27800	13125	18000	16866	16944	8500
	Housing	25000	4000	5500	15137	3950	1420
	Police Housing	740	1090 20	3360	1305	800	80
	Urban Development	9000	1200	1900	9768	2000	925
	State Capital Projects	-	-	-	3337	-	-
	Information & Publicity	1260	250	200	758	480	100
	Labour & Labour Welfare	1470	600	500	3786	387	100
	Special Employment Schemes-(State Programmes)	2580	-	-	1125 55	18	9
	Welfare of SC, ST & O.B.C.s	28960	1500	6300	11649 54	3400	722 10
	Social Welfare	2970	300	410	1031	678	240
	Nutrition	5360	2000	3500	59550	2794	282
	Total (IX)	142430	50075	85385	145122	55469	21464
X.	Economic Services						
	Sectt. Economic Services	480	21 140	2 500	304	116	81
	Economic Advice and Statistics	350	100	185	789	55	28
	Weights & Measures	50	85	60	182 55	40	16
	District Planning	-	-	1000	24405	9900	500
	Other General Economic Services	-	-	-	-	-	-
	Total (X)	880	325	1745	25680	10111	625
XI.	General Services						
	Stationary and Printing	220	150	80		225	400
	Public Works	5030	5550 22	4600	-	1800	1500
	Civil Supplies	-	60		366		295
	Training	-	10 25	50 3	213 58	200 7	73
	Other General Services		-	-		-	-
	Total (XI)	5250 5	5770	4730	579	2225	2268
GRAND TOTAL 520000		210000	510000	600000	290000	105000	

Table-IV-11 (Contd.)

(Rs. Lakhs)

1		Jammu & Kashmir 8	Karnataka 9	Kerala 10	Madhya Pradesh 11	Maharashtra 12	Manipur 13.
I.	Agriculture and Allied Services						
	Researcj & Education	1450	680	1390	500	3745	251
	Crop Husbandry *	4730	8750	10470	15200	16500	1448
	Soil & Water Conservation	1250	2100	705	5150	11866	1060
	Animal Husbandry	2500	1200	1450	3373	3775	530
	Dairy Development	371	1500	750	627	4300	80
	Fisheries	450	2000	4000	1048	1600	465
	Forests	3392	6200	7000	7877	10600	1441
	Investment in Agri. Fin.- Institutions	32	1240	800	85	776	20
	Marketing	400	30	2650	100	200	10
	Storage & Warehousing	400	300	100	-	200	55
	Total (I)	14975	24000	29315	33960	53561	5360
II.	Rural Development						
	Integrated Rural Development-Programme (IRDP)	1125	8130	4700	9867	11400	700
	National Rural Employment-Programme (NREP)	850	5400	5300	12925	9130	250
	Drought Prone Area - Programme (DPAP)	487	2700	-	2250	2525 44	-
	Other Programmes	-	-	-	-	49	-
	Community Development and - Panchayats	900	170	1400	2530	70	300
	Land Reforms	500	600	900	2439	325	150
	Integrated Rural Energy-Programme (IREP)	50	100	150	300	300	35
	Special Programmes for Area Development (State Programmes)	13				45	-
	(i) Development of Backward Areas	9590	-	450 17		49 49	-
	(ii)Others	-	-	100		32000	-
	Total (II)	13502	17100	13000	30311	55848	1435
III.	Cooperation	650	6000	2360	9483	12000	300

IV.	Irrigation & Flood Control						
	(a) Major & Medium Irrigation	5286	52300	28000	137592	132000	6000
	(b) Minor Irrigation	4200	15100	5000	43360	25000	1000
	(c) Command Area Dev.	550	4700	2900	16196	31991	300
	(d) Flood Control Projects (including Anti-Sea Erosion)	2000	400	2500	500	70	500
	Total (IV)	12036	72500	38400	197648	189061	7800
V.	Power						
	(i) Power	27822	80000	39680	264600	304837	3597
	(ii)New & Renewable Sources of Energy	110	100	200	1400	417	45
	Total (V)	27932	80100	39880	266000	305304	3642
VI.	Industry & Minerals						
	Village & Small Industries	3400	15200	7700	10869	6300	1400
	Medium & Large Industries	3500	9000	12600	4615	29890	950
	Mining	350	500	400	998	310	60
	Total (VI)	7250	24700	20700	16432	36500	2410
VII.	Transport						
	Mionor Ports & light Houses	-	2800	1300	-	745	-
	Shipping	-	-	-	-	-	-
	Civil Aviation	-	-	-	375	150	-
	Roads & Bridges	8450	12940	12200	28139	27382	6400
	Road Transport	2220	8500	2900	5725	49067	600
	Inland Water Transport	2350 14	60	950	-	150	-
	Tourism	3050	700	900	1099	450 48	100 35
	Others	-	-	-	-	25	150
	Total (VII)	16070	25000	18250	35338	77969	7250
VIII.	Scinetific Seryices & Research						
	S & T Programmes	100	200	1700	650	200	200
	Environmental Programme	50	100	90	1684	70	-
	Water Pollution Control	50	100	350	-	130	50
	Total (VIII)	200	400	2140	2334	400	250

IX.	Social & Community Services Education						
	General Education	7162	11200	4300	17435	21645	3082
	Art & Culture	200	750	850	1163	800	100
	Technical Education	500	600	1500	2233	8908	130
	Sports & Youth Services	400	650	650	420	1085	400
	Sub-Total (Education)	8262	13200	7300	21251	32438	3712
	Medical & Publick Health	6306	11800	5200	15733	37400	1300
	Sewerage & Water Supply	21830	25200	11900	30293	134500	4590
	Housing	1900	11400	6300	10337	22495	620
	Police Housing	800	700	200	412	1932	220
	Urban Development	3907	3000	2500	4429	16000	255
	State Capital Projects	-	-	-	3331	-	500
	Information & Publicity	203	700	450	324	760	100
	Labour & Lablur Welfare	300	1500	575	592	5682	100
	Special Employment Schemes (State Programmes)	300	1300	-	276	44250	500
	Welfare of SC, ST & O.B.Cs.	594	4800	2200	16395	9000	400
	Social Welfare	253	2600	500	899^{35}	1200	170^{29}
	Nutrition	755	11000	4000	3389	5000	220
	Total (IX)	45410	87200	41125	107661	310657	12687
X.	Economic Services						
	Sectt. Economic Services	100	490	505	534^{34}	340^{48}	50
	Economic Advice and Statistics	-	160	500	65	308	60
	Weights & Measures	25		100	22		20
	District Planning	-	1550^{16}	-	-	1700^{49}	606
	Other General Economic	-	-	-	-	-	-
	Total(X)	125	2200	1105	621	2348	736
XI.	General Services						
	Stationery & Printing	150	275	650	162	-	50
	Public Works	1625	10525	3000	-	6300	1000
	Civil Supplies		-	75	-		80
	Training	75^{15}	-	-	-	52^{50}	-
	Others (General Services)	-	-	-	-	-	-
	Total (XI)	1850	10800	3725	162	6352	1130
	GRAND TOTAL :	140000	350000	210000	700000	1050000	43000

Table-IV-11 (Contd.)

(Rs. Lakhs.)

	1	Meghalaya 14	Nagaland 15	Orissa 16	Punjab 17	Rajasthan 18	Sikkim 19
I.	Agriculture & Allied Services						
	Research & Education	100 38	200 18	600 18	1400	504	65
	Crop Husbandry *	1600	2390	9225	10925	3284	1404
	Soil & Water Conservation	1250	1000	1300	3500	1008	1000
	Animal Husbandry	650	1200	1400	3300	1679	931
	Dairy Development	100	100	100	440	735	75
	Fisheries	180	300	1260	598	400	120
	Forests	2900	1800	4500	3200	4985	950
	Investment in Agri. Fin. Institutions	5	-	400	2500	798	-
	Marketing	140	25	110	25	10	60
	Storage & Warehousing	25	35	60	125	63	45
	Total (I)	6950	7050	18955	26013	13466	4650
II.	Rural Devalopment						
	Integrated Rural Dev. Programme (IRDO)	298	430	6200	1057	6161	62
	National Rural Employment Programme (NREP)	240	120 38	5000	1580	3160	90
	Drought Prone Area Programme (DPAP)	39	5 59	1460 24	-	1500 31	-
	Other Programmes	50	30	3000	-	1867	-
	Community6 Development & Panchayats	300	1000	955	3872	1371	75
	Land Reforms	195	200	3500	-	498	120
	Intagrated Rural Energy Programme (IREP)	125	20	150	90	120	50
	Special Programmes for Area Development (State Programes)						
	(1) Development of Backward Areas	40	500 80	-	36	-	-
	(2) Other	1000	300	-	2110	-	-
	Total (II)	2208	2605	20265	8709	14677	397
III.	Cooperation	545	250	5000	6385	4620	200

IV.	Irrication $ Flood Central						
	(a) Major & Meduim Irrigation	55	-	55000	27078	63546	500
	(b) Minor Irrigation	970	1500	11000	4622	4788	1000
	(c) Command Area Dev.	-	-	1900	1600	9912	-
	(d) Flood Centrol Projects (including Anti-Sea Erosion)	135	-	1700	3700	1469	105
	Total (IV)	1160	1500	69600	37000	79715	1605
V.	Power						
	(i) Power	7000	3350	78000	163800	87420	3394
	(ii) New & Renewable Sources of Energy	150	30	850	160	552	100
	Total (V)	7150	3380	78850	163960	87972	3494
VI.	Industry and Minetals						
	Village & Small Industries	625	800	4000	3460	4605	330
	Medium and Large Industries	1100	1100	8000	8831	6607	370
	Mining	180	870	2000	30	7840	150
	Total	1905	2770	14000	12321	19052	850
VII.	Transport						
	Minor Ports & Light Houses	-	-	1600	-	-	-
	Shipping	-	-	-	-	-	-
	Civil Aviation	-	-	250	120	-	-
	Roads and Bridges	6800	8890	12400	9800	3452	3740
	Road Transport	1200	960	4400	8300	4240	728
	Inland Water Transport	-	-75	-	-	-	
	Tourism	350	400	625	200	1292	200
	Others	-	-	-	-	-	-
	Total(VII)	170	85	400	500	840	80
VIII.	Scientific Services and Reserch						
	S & T. Programmes	150	80	216	400	344	22
	Environmental Programme	20	5	84	100	496	58
	Water Pollution	-	-	100	-	-	-
	Total (VIII)	170	85	400	500	840	80

IX.	Social and Community services Education						
	General Education	2815	1960	15000	7962	18830	2640
	Art & Culture	100	200	300	458	840	160
	Technical Education	112	240	1000	2504	1550	-
	Sports & Youth Services	275	200	1250	283	420	-
	Sub-Total (Education)	3302	2600	17550	11207	21640	2800
	Medical & Public Health	1600	1500	5450	10350	8257	581
	Sewerage and Water Supply	5000	2600	7000	13050	22008	1800
	Housing	400	850	3780	5174	4636	560
	Police Housing	640 41	800	300	2000	210	-
	Urban Development	500	800	650	4075	1531	150
	State Capital Projects	-	-	-	-	840	-
	Information & Publicity	60	350	300	325	160	47
	Labour & Labour Welfare	65	260	650	350	975	40
	Special Employment Schemes (State Programmes)	-	175	-	-	-	-
	Welfare of SC, ST & Other Backware Classes	5	-	1500	3500	1074	125
	Social Welfare	200	160	200	700	239	70
	Nutrition	500	450	1600	1650	1596	270
	Total (IX)	12272	10545	38980	32381	63166	6343
X.	Economic Services						
	Sectt. Economic Services	30	140	130	75 37	630 32	76
	Economic Advice and Statistics	35	80	185	91	84	45
	Weights & Measures	30 42	50	35	10	17	22
	District Planning	300	-	2400	-	-	-
	Other General Economic Services	-	-	-	-	-	-
	Total (X)	395	270	2750	176	731	143
XI.	General Services						
	Stationery & Printing	250 43	150	440	300	151	27
	Public Works	2605	875	1160	2000	1626	488
	Civil Supplies	40	150 61	250	10	-	-
	Training	-	100 62	-	125	-	-
	Others	-	20	-	-	-	-
	Total (XI)	2895	1295	1850	2435	1777	570
	GRAND TOTAL :	44000	40000	270000	328500	300000	23000

Table-IV-11 (Contd.)

(Rs. Lakhs)

	1	Tamil Nadu 20	Tripura 21	Uttar Pradesh 22	West Bengal 23	Total all States 24	
I.	Agriculture & Allied Services						
	Research & Education	1300	100	1906	1710	27717	
	Crop Husbandry *	20000	2205 18	28614	8415	195954	
	Soil & Water Conservation	3000	700	10250	1165	59730	
	Animal Hisbandry	3000	1000	2550	3630	43494	
	Dairy Development	500	200	2240	1845	18770	
	Fisheries		2400	600	1250	6175	30542
	Forests		7000	1500	16200	5045	134008
	Investment in Agri. Fin.		-	64			
	Institutions	510	75	2660	100	15856	
	Marketing	750	300	887	1070	8644	
	Storage & Watehousing	250	100	280	345	3107	
	Total (I)	38710	6780	66837	29500	537822	
II.	Rural Development						
	Integrated Rural Dev.Programme (IRDP)	12875	650	17250	14000	131411	
	National Rural Employment Programme (NREP)	10250	401	19250	10000	123666	
	Drought Prone Area Programms (DPAP)	1275	27	3800	1300	23534	
	Other programmes	-	800	-	-	6016	
	Community Development & Panchayats	3800	733	10025	1200	39630	
	Land Reforms	120	411	9500	6500	35388	
	Integrated Rural Energy Programme (IREP)	500	-	600	75	3715	
	Special Programmes for Area Development (State Programmes)						
	(i) Development of Backward Areas	-	-	2600 57	5500 25	21149	
	(ii) Others	-	-		1400	37420	
	Total (ii)	28820	2995	63025	39975	421929	
III.	Cooperation	3500	600	11859	5000	87018	

IV.	Irrication & Flood Control						
	(a) Major & Medium Irrigation	21200	2700	142000	20800	114496	
	(b) Minor Irrigation	6500	1500	51200	7800	261552	
	(c) Command Area Development	4000	-	10700	900	116191	
	(d) Flood Control Projects (including Anti-Sea Erosion)	1300	600	16100	10500	72638	
	Total (IV)	33000	4800	220000	40000	1594977	
V.	Power						
	(i) Power		200000	4600	339500	124800	2268676
	(ii) New & Renewable Source of Energy	1000	200	800	125	9939	
	Total (V)	201000	4800	340300	124925	2278615	
VI.	Industry & Minerals						
	Village & Small Industries	13000	1000	17150	9000	137852	
	Medium and Large Industries	14500	600	39963	21700	207737	
	Mining		1000	10	2860	800	32140
	Total (VI)	28500	1610	59973	31500	377629	
VII.	Transport						
	Minor Ports & Light Houses	300	-	-	-	9731	
	Shipping		700	-	-	-	700
	Civil Aviation	-	-	190	190	2472	
	Roads and Bridges	13000	4500	86000	8500	366698	
	Road Transport	13200	700	19059	12000	174248	
	Inland Water Transport	500	-	100	670	6720	
	Tourism		500	100	2450	370	16431
	Others	-	-	-	-	1099	
	Total (VII)	28200	5300	107799	21730	578099	
VIII.	Scientific Services & Research						
	S & T Programmes	450	200	1000	320	8157	
	Environmental Programmes	250	50	500	90	5781	
	Water Pollution Control	170	-	-	250	1790	
	Total (VIII)	870	250	1500	660	15728	

IX.	Social and Community Services Education						
	General Education	27000	2547	23095	28000	286318	
	Art & Culture	640	60	880	590	11486	
	Technical Education	2125	70	7600	2280	38812	
	Sports & Youth Services	1000	290	1650	1130	12255	
	Sub-Total (Education)	30765	2967	33225	32000	348871	
	Medical & Public Wealth	15000	1300	30080	12800	224033	
	Sewerage and Water Supply	60000	3000	33800	7000	484806	
	Housing		15000	1000	21118	4875	165352
	Police Housing	1500	300	5040	5200 28	27539	
	Urban Development	16000	700	24700	8120	112110	
	State Capital Projects	-	-	-	15100	23108	
	Information & Fublicity	300	127	1250	580	9084	
	Labour and Labour Welfare	1500	198	1995	350	21975	
	Special Employment Schemes (State Programmes)						
	Welfare of SC, ST & Other	-	28	-	400	50924	
	Backward Classes	10500	4432 29	11405	3460	121921	
	Social Welfare	3000	307	2000	1160	19187	
	Nutrition		54000	2000	4470	5000	169386
	Total (IX)	207565	16231	169083	96045	1773296	
X.	Economic Services						
	Sectt. Economic Services	100	47	1279	307	6454	
	Economic Advice & Statistics	300	32	1272	100	4824	
	Weights and Measures	-	15	80	100	959	
	District Planning	-	-	30	19870	62231	
	Other General Economic Services	-	-	80	-	80	
	Total (X)	400	94	2711	20377	74548	
XI.	Gerneral Services						
	Stationery & Printing	85	90	1053	100	5008	
	Public Wors	2350	350	-	2608	54992	
	Civil Supplies	2000	100	560	80	4121	
	Training		-	-	-	-	898
	Others		-	-	-	-	20
	Total (X)	4435	540	1613	2788	65039	
	GRAND TOTAL	575000	44000	1044700	412500	7809700	

REFERENCES

Seventh Five Year Plan (1985-90) Agreed Outlays (Stetes)

- * Including Dry land/Rainfed Farming and Land Stock Improvement.
- 1 For 'Autonomous Development Authority'.
- 2 Includes Rs. 50 lakhs for 'Evaivation and Rs.150 lakhs for 'Monitoring of 20-point programme'.
- 3 For 'Manpower Training'.
- 4 Includes provision for 'Failed Wall Subsidy (Rs.740 lakhs)' 'Disaster Management' (Rs.1110 lakhs) and 'Dry Land Farming Rs. 2950 lakhs)'.
- 5 Excluding Tamil Nadu's contribution for 'Telegu-Genga'.
- 6 For 'Mewat Area Development'.
- 7 For 'Haryana Institute Public Administration'.
- 8 For 'Inter Model Transport Study'.
- 9 Includes Rs.175 lakhs for 'Nucleus Budget for Tribal Areas' and Rs. 15 lakhs 'Tribal Development Machinery'.
- 10 Includes Rs. 70 lakhs for 'Ex-servicemet's Corporation'.
- 11 Includes Rs. 31 lakhs for 'Institutional Finance and Public Enterprises Organisation'.
- 12 For 'Himachal Institute of Public Administration'.
- 13 For 'Ladakh Sub-Plan'.
- 14 Includes provision for 'Parks and Gardens'.
- 15 For 'Institute of Management for Public Administration'.
- 16 For 'Districl Level Sub-Flan'.
- 17 For 'Training Programme and Social Input in Area Development'.
- 18 Includes 'Assistance for SF/MF also.
- 19 Includes Rs. 500 lakhs for (Border Area Development Programme' and Rs. 10 lakhs for 'grant-in-aid to voluntary organisations in Hill Areas'.
- 20 Includes Rs. 200 lakhs for 'Fire Protection Scheme'.
- 21 Includes Rs. 40 lakhs for 'Public Enterprises Organisation'.
- 22 Includes Rs.450 lakhs for 'Development Programme under jail Deptt. and Rs. 4400 lakhs for upgradation of Administration.
- 23 For 'Administration Staff College'.
- 24 For 'Economic Rehabilitation of Rural Poor'.
- 25 For 'West Bengal Comprehensive Development Corporation Project'.
- 26 Includes Rs.120 lakhs for 'Zoo and Public Latrines'.
- 27 For 'State Rural Employment Programme (SREP)'.
- 28 Includes Rs. 3000 lakhs for 'Tripura Tribal Councils'.
- 29 Includes Rs. 10 lakhs for 'legal Aid & Advice'.
- 30 For National Savings
- 31 For DWCRA, SIAD/Massive Programme.
- 32 Includes Rs.252 lakhs for computerisation & Modernisation.
- 33 Includes Rs.191 lakhs for Legal Aid to Poor and Sanjay Gandhi Institute for youth leadership.
- 34 Includes Rs. 202 lakhs for 'Computer Centre'.
- 35 For City Bus Terminal and Parking.
- 36 For Interest Subsidy (State Programme)

37 Rs. 10 lakhs for 'Economic Coordination' and 20-Point Programme.
38 Includes Rs. 200 lakhs for SF/MF.
39 For Pilot Project for Village Development
40 For Border Arcas Development Programme
41 Includes Rs. 100 lakhs for aid to municipalities.
42 For District Councial.
43 Includes Rs.1405 lakhs for upgradation of standard of Admn.
44 For 'Share Capital to Regional Rural'. Development Bank.
45 For 'Area Development in Ratnagiri'.
46 For 'Konkon Railway'.
47 Includes Rs. 100 lakhs for 'Svavlamban Yojana' and Rs.150 lakhs for 'payment of honourarium to educated unemployed for part-time employment'.
48 Includes Rs. 52 lakhs for 'Assistance for Studies in Rural Development and Regional Planning'.
49 For 'Felt Needs programme of Districts'.
50 For 'Maharashtra Institute of Development Administration'.
51 Includes provision for 'Strengthaning and supporting Special programme organigation (Rs.80 lakhs), Strengthening of Training Facilities for Rural Development (Rs.10 lakhs), Project Linkage (Rs. 35 lakhs), Loans to Antyodaya Families (Rs.40 lakhs), Regional Rural Banks (Rs. 11 lakhs) and Integrated Village Environmental Improvement Programme (Rs. 44 lakhs).
52 For 'Modernisation of wireless equipments'.
53 Includes Rs. 122 lakhs for 'Admn. Machinery for T.A.S.P.'
54 Includes Rs. 303 lakhs for 'Social Inputs'.
55 For Decentralised District Planning'.
56 For 'Training/of Development Personnel'.
57 For 'Special Programme for area development'.
58 For 'Special Watershed Management Programme'.
59 For 'promotion of voluntary schemes and Social Action Programme'.
60 For 'Special Development Schomesw'.
61 For 'Admn. Training Institute'.
62 For 'Parlimentary Affairs'.
63 For 'Char Areas'.
64 Includes Rs. 210 lakhs for 'Development of Financial Institutions'.

Source: Government of Inida, Ministry of Finance, 'Statistical Statements on Finance and Plans of States and Union Territories' 1985.

TABLE-IV-12 : PATTERN OF PLAN OUTLAY IN THE PUBLIC SECTOR

Rs. Crores)

	HEAD	First Plan 1951-56 Actuals	Second Plan 1956-61 Actuals	Third Plan 1961-66 Actuals	Annual Plans 1966-69 Actuals	Fourth Plan 1969-74 Actuals	Fifth Plan 1974-79 Actuals
1.	Agriculture and Community Development	290	549	1,089	1,107	2,320	4,865
2.	Major and Medium Irrigation	583 @	882 @	664	471	1,354	3,877
3.	Power		-	1,252 #	1,213	2,931	7,400
4.	Village and small Industries	42	1,125	241	126	243	592
5.	Organised Industry and Minerals	55	-	1,726	1,510	2,864	8,989
6.	Transport and Communications	518	1,261	2,112	1,222	3,080	6,870
7.	Social services and miscelianeous	472	855	1,493	976	2,987	6,833
	Total	1,960	4,672	8,577	6,625	15,779	39,426

@ Includes power

Includes organised industry and minerals.

Source: Ministry of Finance, "Indian Economic@ Statistics' , December, 1982.

TABLE-IV-13 : DISTRIBUTION OF PUBLIC SECTOR PLAN OUTLAY

(Rs. Crores)

Plan Period	Centre*	States	Total	States's share in the total outlay (%)
First Plan 1951-56 (Actuals)	535	1425	1960	72.7
Second plan 1956-61 (Actuals)	2590	2082	4672	44.5
Third Plan 1961-66 (Actuals)	4412	4165	8577	48.6
Annual Plans 1966-69 (Actuals)	3565	3060	6625	46.2
Fourth Plan 1969-74	8104	7675	15779	48.6
Fifth Plan 1974-79 (Actuals)	19855	19571	39426	49.6
Annual Plan 1979-80 (Acutals)	6042	6134	12176	50.4
Sixth Plan 1980-85 (Revised Estimates)	60689	50132	110821	45.2
Seventh Plan 1985-90 (Estimates)	99302	80698	180000	44.8

* Includes outlay in respect of Union Territories

Source: 1. Government of India, Ministry of Finance 'Indian Economic Statistics' (I to VI Plan)

2. Government of India, Planning Commission. 'Seventh Five Year Plan 1985-90'

TABLE-IV-14 : OUTLAY AND INVESTMENT

(Rs. crores)

	First Plan (1951-56)	Second Plan (1956-61)	Total (1951-61)	Third Plan (1961-66)	Annual Plans (1966-69)	Fourth Plan (1969-74)	Fifth Plan@ (1974-79)	Annual Plan (1979-80)	Sixth Plan (1980-85)	Seventh Plan (1985-90)
1. Public Sector Outlay	1,960	4,672	6,632	8,577	6,625	15779	39,426	12,177	97,500	180,000
2. Public Sector Invostment	1,560	3,731	5,291	6,300 +	N.A.	13,655 +	36,703 +	N.A.	84,000	154,218
3. Private Sector Investment*	1800	3,100	4,900	4,100 +	N.A.	8,980 +	27,048 +	N.A.	74,710	168,148
4. Total investment (2+3)	3.360	6.831	10.191+	10.400+	N.A.	22.635+	63.751+	N.A.	158.710	322.366
Investment: Percentage Distribution										
Public Sector	46.4	54.6	51.9	60.6	N.A.	60.3	57.6	N.A.	52.9	47.8
Private Sector	53.6	45.4	40.1	39.4	N.A.	39,7	42.4	N.A.	47.1	52.2
Total	100.0	100.0	100.00	100.0	100.0	100.0	100.0	100.0	100.0	100.0

* Excludes transfors from public to private sector.

\+ Plan provision.

@ For the time period originelly onvisaged for the Fifth Plan.

Source Planning Commission. Government of India, Ministry of Finance, Indian Economics Statistics 1985'

TABLE-IV-15 : FINANCING OF PLAN OUTLAY IN THE PUBLIC SECTOR - FIRST PLAN

(Rs. Crores)

	Plan Provision	Actuals
1. Surplus from current revenue at 1950-51 of taxation (including additional taxation)	570	637
2. Public loans (net)	115	204
3. Small Savings (net)	225	243
4. Contribution of Railway	170	115
5. Unfunded debtion miscellaneous capital receipts	178	239
6. External Assistance	521	189
7. Deficit financing	290	333
8. Total	2069*	1960

* Later revised to Rs. 2378 crores.

Source Planning Commission.

Source: Government of India, Ministry of Finance, 'Indian Economics Statistics 1985'

TABLE-IV-16 : FINANCING OF PLAN OUTLAY IN THE PUBLIC SECTOR SECOND AND THIRD PLANS

		Second Plan		Third Plan	
		Plan Provision	Actuals	Plan Provision	Actuals
1.	Balance from current revenues (excluding additional taxation)	350	11	550	(-)419
2.	Contribution of railways	150	157*	100	62
3.	Surpluses of other public enterprises	@@	@@	450	373
4.	Loans from the public (net)	700	772**	800	823
5.	Small savings (net)	500	406	600	565
6.	Compulsory deposits and annuity deposits (net)	-	-	-	117
7.	Provident funds (net)	250	175	265	336
8.	Steel equilisation funds (net)	40	105	34	
9.	Balance of Miscellaneous Capital receipts over non-plan disbursements	46	170	238	
10.	Additional taxation including measures to increase the surplus of public enterprises	850 @	1052	1710	2892
11.	Budgetary receipts dorreswponding to external assistance	800	1049***	2200	2423
12.	Deficit Financing	1200	954	550	1133
	Total	4800	4672	7500	8577

* Inclusive of increased fares and/freights.
** Includes investments by the State Bank out of PL 480 funds.
*** Includes investment of PL 480 Funds by the Reserve Bank in special securities in 1960-61
@ Includes Rs. 400 crores, which was left as a gap in the plan to be covered by additional domestic efforts.
@@ Included in item 1 and 8.

Source Planning Commission. Government of India, Ministry of Finence, 'Indian Economics Statistics 1985'.

TABLE-IV-17 : FINANCING OF THE ANNUAL PLAN OUTLAYS IN THE PUBLIC SECTOR (1966-1969)

(Rs. Crores)

	Original Estimates	Actuals
1. Balance from current revenue 1965-66 rate of taxation	866	346
2. Contribution of railways	-64	-115
3. Surpluses of other public enterprises	65	513
4. Additional taxation	1060	908
5. Loans from public (net)	571	725
6. Small savings	391	355
7. Gold bonds, prize bonds, compulsory deposits and annuity deposite	41	64
8. State provident funds.	253	303
9. Miscellaneous capital receipts (net)	126	443
10. Deficit finsancing	335	676
11. Budgetary resources corresponding to external assistance	2435	2410
Aggregate resources	6665	6628

Source: Planning Commission.
Source: Government of India, Ministry of Finance, 'Indian Economics Statistics 1985;.

TABLE- IV-18 : FINANCING OF PLAN OUTLAY IN THE PUBLIC SECTOR-FOURTH PLAN

(Rs. Crores)

		Original Scheme of Financing			Latest Estimates*		
		Centre	State	Total	Centre	State	Total
I.	Domestic budgetary resources other than negotiated loans from LIC and States enterprises market borrowings.	7332	1502	8734	5354 **	1546	6900
1.	Banance from current revenues at 1968-69 rates, of taxation	1625	48	1673	111	-347	-236
2.	Contribution of public enterprises at 1968-69 fares, freights and tariffs	1534	495	2029	815	320	1135
	a) Railways	265	-	265	-165	-	-165
	b) Post & Telegraphs	225	-	225	318	-	318
	c) IDC,ARC, REC, DVC and atomic power generation units	259	-	259	181	-	181
	d) Others	785	495	1280	481	320	801
3.	Retained profits of Reserve Bank	165	37	202	219	77	296
4.	Market borrowings of Central and State Governments(net)	900	515	1415	1567	568	2135
5.	Borrowings by FCI and financial institutions	405	-	405	177	-	177
	a) Food Corporation of India	155	-	155	-	-	-
	b) Financial institutions	250	-	250	177	-	177
6.	Small Savings	274	495	769	438	724	1162
7.	Annuity deposits, compulsory deposits, prize bonds and gold bonds	-104	-	-104	-98	-	-98
8.	State provident funds	343	317	660	495	379	874

9.	Miscellaneous capital receipts(Net)	2090	-405	1685	1630	-175	1455
10.	Additional resources mobilisation	2100	1098	3198	3222	1058	4280
III.	Loans from LIC and State enterprises market borrowings (gross)	-	506	506	-	833	833
1.	LIC Loans to state Governments for housing and water supply	-	100	100	-	111	111
2.	Market borrowings of State enterprises	-	258	258	-	476	476
3.	L.I.C Loan from State Enterprises	-	148	148	-	246	246
IV.	Total domestic budgetary resources	9332	3106	12438	8576	3437	12013
V.	Budgetary receipts corresponding to external assistance (net)	2614	-	2614	2087	-	2087
	a) Other than PL 480	2234	-	2234	1661	-	1661
	b) PL 480 as assistance	380	-	380	426	-	426
VI.	Deficit financing	850	-	850	1705	355	2060 *
VII.	Aggregate resources	12796	3106	15902	12368	3792	16160
VIII.	Assistance for State Plans	-3500	3500	-	-3575 + +	3575 + +	-
IX.	Resources for the plan	9296	6606	15902	8796	7364	16160 @

* Actuals for the first three years, anticipated for 1972-73 and annual plan estimates for 1973-74.

** Inclusive of States's hare in fresh taxation by the Centre since 1969-70

\+ Net of States's hare.

\+ + Inclusive of Central assistance for Himachal Pradesh, which became a state in 1971, for 1971-74 and for Manipur and Tripura, which became states in 1972 for 1972-74. Their own resources for the periods just mentioned are also included in the total of States' resources.

@ Actual expenditure in the public sector during the fourth plan period amounted to Rs. 15,779 crores.

Source Government of India, Ministry of Finance, 'Indian Economics Statistics 1985'.

TABLE-IV-19 : ESTIMATED RESOURCES FOR THE PUBLIC SECTOR IN FIFTH PLAN

(Rs. crores)

		Fifth Plan (1974-79)	First 3 years (1974-77)
I.	Domestic Budgetary Resources	32115	15208
1.	Balance from current revenues at 1973-74 rates of taxation	4901	3338
2.	Gross surplus of public enterprises at 1973-74 fares, freights and tariffs	849	624
	(a) Railways	-1818	-1005
	(b) Posts and Telegraphs	380	818
	(c)Others	2287	1448
3.	Market Borrowings of Government, Public enterprises and local bodies	5879	3030
4.	Small savings	2022	1092
5.	State provident funds	1987	1050
6.	Terms-loans from financial institutions(net)	628	340
7.	Miscellaneous capital receipts(net)	556	-556
8.	Additional resource mobilisation	14693	6290
	(a) Centre	8694	3772
	(b) States	6199	2517
9.	Borrowings against utilisations of foreign exchange reserves	600	-
II.	External assistance (net)	5834	3434
	(a) Other than oil and special credits	5834	2526
	(b) Oil and special credits	-	908
III.	Deficit Financing	1354	754
IV.	Aggregate resources	39303	19396

Source: Government of India, Ministry of Finance, 'Indian Economics Statistics 1985'.

TABLE-IV-20 : PATTERN OF FINANCING THE PUBLIC SECTOR PLAN - SIXTH PLAN 1980-85

(Rs. Crores)

		Sixth Plan (Original)	1980-81 Actuals	1981-82 Actuals	1982-83 Actuals	1983-84 Actuals	1984-85 Revised Estimates	1980-85 Revised Estimates
Plan Outlay		97500	15023	18373	21725	25314	30386	110821
1.	Balance from current revenues at 1979-80 rates	14478	2662	2561	923	(-)932	(-)3321	1893
2.	Additional Resource Mobilisation (Tax and Non-Tax)	12524	785	2451	4045	6961	6904	20146
	Total (1+2)	27002	3447	5012	4968	5029	3583	2203
3.	Contribution of Public Enterprises	9395	1231	836	1235	1063	1445	5810
4.	Additional Resource Mobilisation	8778	141	1703	2777	3762	4441	12824
	Total (3+4)	18173	1372	2539	4012	4825	5886	18634
5.	Market Borrowings	19500	3160	3700	4683	5148	5429	22120
6.	Small Savings	6463	1121	1361	1721	2409	3300	9912
7.	Provident Funds	3702	618	605	1005	781	947	3956
8.	Term Loans from Financial Institutions	2722	438	446	495	549	654	2582
9.	Miscellaneous Capital Receipts	4009	(-)303	839	839	2779	3211	7365
10.	Inflow of Foreign Resources	9929	1719	1352	1652	1660	2146	8529
11.	Drawing of Foreign Resources Reserves	1000	-	-	-	-	-	-
12.	Daficit Financing uncovered gap	5000	3451	2519	2350	2134	5230	15684
13.	Resource for the Plan.	97500	15023	18373	21725	25314	30386	110821

Source: Government of India, Ministry of Financings Statistics 1951,

TABLE-IV-21 : ESTIMATES OF RESOURCES FOR THE PUBLIC SECTOR PLAN 1980-85 - CENTRE

(Rs. Crores)

Item	Sixth plan Estimates	1980-81 Actuals	1981-82 Actuals	1982-83 Actuals	1983-84 Actuals	1984-85 Revised Estimate	1985-90 Latest Estimate
Plan Outlay	48900	7305	9545	11695	14093	18051	60689
1. Balance from current revennes at 1979-80 rates of taxes	1178	691	528	-590	-2103	-2953 -4427	
2. ARM(Tax & Non-Tax measures)	8390	550	1748	2727	3901	4207	13133
Total (1+2)	9563	1241	2275	2137	1798	1254	8706
3. Contribution of Public Enterprises	9911	1411	1549	2645	2941	3872	12413
4. ARM (By Public Enterprises)	3900	-49	849	1311	1697	1892	5700
Total (3+4)	13811	1362	2398	3956	4638	5764	18118
5. Market Borrowings (Excluding Market Borrowings of Financial Institutions	15000	2579	2913	3771	4038	4100	17401
6. Small Savings	2112	409	1517	619	1010	1300	3855
7. Provident Funds	1660	274	298	525	355	353	1805
8. Term Loan from Financial Institutions.	-	-	-	-	-	-	-
9. Miscellaneous Capital Receipts (net)	6170	118	1498	1325	3533	3616	10090
10. Inflow of Foreign Resources	9929	1719	1352	1652	1660	2146	8529
11. Drawing down of Foreign Exchange Reserved	1000	-	-	-	-	-	-
12. Uncovered Gap/Deficit Financing	5000	2577	1392	1656 [1]	1317 [2]	3985	10927
13. Total Resources	64250	10279	12644	15641	18349	22518	79431
14. Central Assistance for States Plan including natural clamities.	-15350	-2974	-3099	-3946	-4256	-4467-18742	
15. Resources Available for the Plan (13-14).	48900	7305	9545	11695	14093	18051	60689

1 Exclusive of Rs.1743 crores of loans given by the Centre to the States to cover the the deficit with Reserve Bank of India as on March 31, 1982.

2 Exclusive of Rs. 500 crores of loans given by the Centre in 1983-84 to States to cover a part of the deficit with Reserve Bank of India.

Source: Government of India, Ministry of Finance, 'Indian Economics and Statistics 1985'

TABLE-IV-22 : ESTIMATES OF RESOURCES FOR THE PUBLIC SECTOR DURING SIXTH FIVE YEAR PLAN 1980-85 - STATES

Rs. Crores

	Item	Sixth Plan Estimates	1980-81 Actuals	1981-82 Actuals	1982-83 Actuals	1983-84 Actuals	1984-85 Revised Estimates	1980-85 Latest Estimates
Plan Outlay		48600	7718	8828	10030	11221	12335	50132
1.	Balance from current revenues at 1979-80 rates of taxes.	13300	1971	2033	1513	1171	-368	6320
2.	Additional Resource Mobilisation (Tax & non-tax Measures)	4134	235	703	1318	2060	2697	7013
3.	Total (1+2)	17434	2206	2736	2831	3231	2329	13333
4.	Contribution of Public Enterprises	-516	-180	-713	-1410	-1878	-2427	-6608
5.	Additional Resource Mobilisation by Public Enterprises	4878	190	854	1466	2065	2449	7124
6.	Total (4+5)	4362	10	141	56	187	122	516
7.	Market Borrowings (excluding market borrowings of Financial Institutions).	4500	581	787	912	1110	1329	4719
8.	Small Savings	4351	712	844	1102	1399	2000	6057
9.	Provident Fund	2042	344	307	480	426	594	2151
10.	Term loans from Financial Institutions.	2722	438	446	495	549	654	2582
11.	Miscellaneous Capital Receipts (net)	-2161-421	-659	-486	-754	-405	-2725	
12.	Inflow of Foreign Resources	-	-	-	-	-	-	-
13.	Drawing down of foreign exchange reserves.	-	-	-	-	-	-	-
14.	Budgetary Deficit	-	874[1]	1127	694[2]	817	1245	4757
15.	Total Resources	33250	4744	572[illegible]	6084	6965	7868	31390
16.	Central Assistance for State Plans	15350	2783	29[illegible]	[illegible]04	4030	4313	17567
17.	Assistance to States for relief on account of natural calamities	-	191		442	226	154	1175
18.	Resources available for the Plan (12+13+14)	48600	7718	[illegible]	10030	11221	12335	50132

1 Out of this Rs. 316 crores is withdrawal from Reserves.

2 Excludes Rs. 1743 crores of loans given by Centre to the States to clear their deficits with the R.B.I. as on 31-3-1982.

Source: Government of India, Ministry of Finance, 'Indian Economi[illegible] atistics 1985'.

TABLE-IV-23: ESTIMATES OF RESOURCES FOR PUBLIC SECTOR PLAN 1985-90

(Rs. Crores)

		1985-86 Annual Plan (Estimates)			1985-90 Seventh Plan (Estimates)		
		Centre	States	Total	Centre	States	Total
	PLAN OUTLAY	19142	13097	32239	99302	80698	180000
1.	Balance from Current Revenues at 1984-85 rates of taxes	-738	1260	522	-12011	6762	-5249
2.	Contribution of Public Enterprises	5157	-88	5069	37454	-1969	35485
3.	Market Borrowings (Net)	5100	1600	6700	20620	9942	30562
4.	Small Savings	1525	2375	3900	6377	11539	17916
5.	Provident Funds	370	858	1228	2300	5027	7327
6.	Term loans from financial institutions	-	802[1]	802	-	4639[1]	4639
7.	Miscellaneous Capital Receipts (Net)	6011	-1837[2]	4174	19809	-7191	12618
8.	Additional Resource Mobilisation	1075	2128	3203	22490	22212	44702
9.	Net Capital inflow from Abroad	3375[3]	-	3375	18000	-	18000
10.	Uncovered gap/deficit financing	3316	-	3316	14000	-	14000
11.	Total Resources	25191	7098	32289	129039	50961	18000
12.	Central Assistance for State Plans	-6049	5999[4]	-50	-29737	29737	-
13.	Resources available for the Plan	19142	13097	32239	99302	80698	18000

1 Includes loan from life Insurance Corporation of Rs. 10 crores for North Eastern Council for Annual Plan 1985-86 and of Rs.100 crores for the Seventh Plan 1985-90.
2 Includes part adjustment of overdrafts at the end of 1984-85.
3 Includes Rs. 865 crores on account of commercial borrowings/equity participation from abroad by Public Sector Enterprises.
4 Excludes Rs. 50 crores provided in the Central Budget for assistance to States for relief against natural calamities.
* At 1984-85 prices.

Source: Government of India, Ministry of Finance, 'Indian Economic Statistics 1985'.

TABLE-IV-24 : STATES' FINANCIAL RESOURCES - SIXTH FIVE YEAR PLAN 1980-85 (SUMMARY) (Rs. in Crores)

	States' Budgetary Resources and Contribution of Public Enterprises		Market Borrowings and Negotiated Loans	
	Original	L.E.	Original	L.E.
1	2	3	4	5
I. SPECIAL CATEGORY STATES:				
1. Assam	92.02	-460.87	195.96	198.64
2. Himachal Pradesh	47.60	37.80	75.05	83.62
3. Jammu & Kashmir	-233.38	-309.84	124.38	117.19
4. Manipur	-25.29	-132.03 ?	24.79	22.07
5. Meghalaya	-23.44	-68.17	62.44	57.06
6. Negaland	-32.94	-128.84 ?	33.44	30.13
7. Sikkim	-0.55	-29.24	3.05	1.88
8. Tripura	4.52	-75.76	36.35	61.15
TOTAL (I)	-171.46	-201.95	555.46	571.74
II. NON-SPECIAL CATEGORY STATES				
1. Andhra Pradesh	1699.27	1372.38	495.03	516.02
2. Bihar	1388.16	363.50	576.34	603.22
3. Gujarat	2643.87	2660.15	436.45	425.80
4. Haryana	1345.00	878.61	220.15	231.79
5. Karnataka	1372.86	1384.08	352.94	373.43
6. Kerala	803.64	487.61	316.20	292.88
7. Madhya Pradesh	2265.38	1966.62	521.23	528.38
8. Maharashtra	4753.53	4735.27	545.56	543.72
9. Orissa	510.41	318.51	330.06	327.80
10. Punjab	1429.28	1160.64	227.72	273.43
11. Rajasthan	933.75	297.79	464.94	536.29
12. Tamil Nadu	2035.91	2274.42	449.29	452.97
13. Uttar Pradesh	2845.51	2146.40	1075.45	1076.94
14. West Bengal	2177.99	301.96	641.75	614.87
TOTAL (II)	26204.56	20347.94	6653.11	6797.54
GRAND TOTAL (I+II)	26033.10	20145.99	7208.57	7369.28

(Contd.) TABLE-IV-24 : STATES' FINANCIAL RESOURCES - SIXTH FIVE YEAR PLAN 1980-85 (SUMMARY)

(Rs. Crores)

	Central Assistance	Surplus(+)/Deficit	Plan Outlay - with R B.I.			
	Original Ests.	L.E.	Original Ests.	L.E.	Original Ests.	L.E.
	6	7	8	9	10	11
I. SPECIAL CATEGORY STATES						
1. Assam	827.02	1225.67	-	-312.14	1115.00	1275.58
2. Himachal Pradesh	437.35	460.78	-	-72.86	560.00	655.06
3. Jammu & Kashmir	1009.00	1057.53	-	-53.37	900.00	918.25
4. Manipur	240.50	286.60	-	-85.21	240.00	246.85
5. Meghalaya	196.00	248.54	-	-24.09	235.00	261.52
6. Nagaland	209.50	291.19	-	-54.88	210.00	227.36
7. Sikkim	119.50	136.35	-	-23.16	122.00	132.15
8. Tripura	204.13	266.95	-	-20.56	245.00	272.90
TOTAL (I)	3243.00	3973.61	:	-646.27	3627.00	3989.67
I. NON-SPECIAL CATEGORY STATES:						
1. Andhra Pradesh	905.70	1007.51	-	-294.09	3100.00	3190.00
2. Bihar	1260.50	1434.64	-	-571.32	3225.00	2972.68
3. Gujarat	599.68	646.02	-	-168.65	3680.00	3900.62
4. Haryana	234.85	291.55	-	-193.93	1800.00	1595.88
5. Karnataka	539.20	564.27	-	-262.13	2265.00	2583.91
6. Kerala	430.16	482.97	-	-406.39	1550.00	1669.85
7. Madhya Pradesh	1013.39	1084.42	-	-324.19	3800.00	3903.61
8. Maharashtra	875.91	1068.98	-	-133.31	6175.00	6481.28
9. Orissa	659.53	758.08	-	-153.03	1500.00	1557.42
10. Punjab	300.00	337.93	-	-201.33	1957.00	1973.33
11. Rajasthan	626.31	723.51	-	-310.38	2025.00	1867.97
12. Tamil Nadu	664.80	757.36	-	-139.04	3150.00	3623.79
13. Uttar Pradesh	1929.04	2207.39	-	-611.26	5850.00	6041.99
14. West Bengal	680.26	760.94	-	-599.01	3500.00	2276.78
TOTAL (II) 10719.33	12125.57	:	-4368.06	43577.00	43639.11	
GRAND TOTAL (I+II)	13962.33	16099.18	:	-5014.33	47204.00	47628.78

Source: Government of India, Ministry of Finance, 'Statistical Statements on Finance and Plans of States and Union Territories, 1985'.

TABLE-IV-25 : STATES' FINANCIAL RESOURCES - SIXTH FIVE YEAR PLAN 1980 - 85

RS.CRORES

		ASSAM			HIMACHAL PRADESH		
		Originally approved	Total of Annual Plans	L.E.	Originally approver	Total of Annual Plans	L.E.
	1	2	3	4	5	6	7
I.	Plan Outlay	1115.00	1297.00	1275.58	560.00	618.67	655.06
II.	State Govt.'s Budgetary Resources at 1979-80 rates						
	1) Balance from Current Revenues	-231.58	-337.69	-513.43	-53.64	-58.50	5.79
	ii) Share of Small Savings	127.98	133.04	152.05	43.85	59.20	76.17
	iii) State Provident Fund	18.00	25.48	34.36	34.85	49.00	54.58
	iv) Misc. Capital Receipts	-139.78	-179.42	-90.28	-17.54	-12.21	-66.52
	v) Others	50.21	48.00	-119.28	3.71	5.52	-58.80
	TOTAL - II	175.17	-310.59	-536.58	11.23	43.01	11.16
III.	Contribution of State Enterprises at 1979-80 rates						
	i) State Elec. Boards	-84.18	-71.96	72.79	-6.59	-15.60	-31.28
	ii) Road Transport Corpns.	3.37	-11.19	-18.28	-10.17	-28.75	
	TOTAL - III	-80.81	-83.15	-91.07	-16.7[illegible]	-40.55	-60.03
IV.	Additional Resource Mobilisation	348.00	247.61	166.78	53.13	82.68	86.67

V. States' Budgetary Resources and contribution of Public Enterprises at Current rates (II + III + IV)	92.02	-146.13	-460.87	47.60	85.14	37.80
VI. Market Borrowings (Net)	142.00	147.47	148.62	39.53	41.08	41.90
VII. Negotiated Loans						
i) Loans from LIC	27.56	26.22	22.93	14.28	12.55	11.79
ii) Loans from RBI	8.54	8.53	7.17	2.43	1.42	0.09
iii) Loans from REC	17.86	17.86	17.86	18.81	81.82	28.98
iv) Other Loans	-	-	2.06	-	-	0.86
Total - VII	53.96	52.61	50.02	35.52	32.79	41.72
VIII. Market T Borrowings and Negotiated Loans (VI+VII)	195.96	200.08	198.64	75.05	73.87	83.62
IX. States' total Resources (V + VIII)	287.98	53.95	-262.23	122.65	159.01	121.42
X. Central assistance						
i) Normal	823.00	1209.51	1216.44	435.20	457.23	456.55
ii) For Externally aided Projects	4.02	5.54	9.23	2.15	8.69	11.89
iii) Adjt. of A.P.A.	-	-	-	-	-6.76	-7.66
iv)						
TOTAL - X	827.82	1215.05	1225.67	437.35	459.16	460.78
XI. Aggregate Resources (IX + X)	1113.00	1269.00	963.44	560.00	618.17	582.20
XII. Surplus (+)/Deficit- with R.B.I.	-	-28.00	-312.14	-	-	-72.86

(Contd.) TABLE-IV-25 : STATES' FINANCIAL RESOURCES - SIXTH FIVE YEAR PLAN 1980-85

		JAMMU & KASHMIR			MANIPUR		
		Originally approved	Total of Annual Plans	L.E.	Originally apporved	Total of Annual Plans	L.E.
	1	8	9	10	11	12	13
I.	Plan Outlay	900.00	895.48	918.25	240.00	246.65	246.85
II.	State Govt.'s Budqetary Resources at 1979-80 rates						
	i) Balance from Current Revenues	-233.59	-295.68	-294.58	-40.28	-63.76	-88.91
	ii) Share of Small Savings	38.14	49.74	44.28	0.50	0.89	0.91
	iii) State Provident Fund	53.45	47.92	41.62	4.80	4.61	5.55
	iv) Misc. Capital Receipts	-190.29	-153.17	-199.15	-5.85	-15.06	10.98
	v) Others	8.50	-	42.59	-	-	-82.14
	TOTAL - II	-323.79	-351.19	-365.24	-40.83	-73.32	-150.61
III.	Contribution of State Enterprises at 1979-80 rates						
	i) State Elec. Boards	-28.21	-33.91	-64.35	-	0.04	-
	ii) Road Transport Corpns.	-18.85	-8.95	-26.93	0.51	-2.20	-3.55
	TOTAL - III	-47.06	-42.86	-91.28	0.51	-2.16	-3.55
IV.	Additional Resource Mobilisation	137.47	140.79	146.68	15.03	20.85	10.13
V.	States' Budetare Resources and contribution of Public Enterprises at current rates (II + III + IV)	-233.38	-253.26	-309.84	-25.29	-54.63	-147.03

VI. Market Borrowings (Net)	70.57	73.84	73.65	16.11	17.11	17.47
VII. Negotiated Loans						
i) Loans from LIC	30.11	24.06	22.66	7.58	5.36	2.10
ii) Loans from RBI	1.55	1.55	1.10	0.40	0.40	0.41
iii) Loans from REC	22.15	22.25	5.41	0.70	0.72	2.09
iv) Other Loans	-	-	14.37	-	0.88	-
TOTAL - VII	53.81	47.86	43.54	8.68	7.36	4.60
VIII. Market Borrowings and Negotiated Loans(VI+VII)	124.38	121.70	117.19	24.79	24.47	22.07
IX. States' Total Resources (V + VIII)	-109.00	-131.56	-192.65	-0.50	-30.16	-124.96
X. Central Assistance						
i) Normal	1009.00	1025.45	1053.76	240.50	285.26	286.60
ii) For Externally aided projects	-	3.76	3.77	-	-	-
iii) Adjt. of A.P.A.	-	-	-	-		-
TOTAL - X	1009.00	1029.21	1057.53	240.50	285.26	286.60
XI. Aggregate Resources (IX + X)	900.00	897.65	864.88	240.00	255.10	161.64
XII. Surplus (+) Deficit - with R.B.I.	-	+2.17	-53.37	-	+8.45	-75.21

(Contd.) TABLE-IV-25 : STATES' FINANCIAL RESOURCES - SIXTH FIVE YEAR PLAN 1980-85

	MEGHALAYA			NAGALAND		
	Originally approved	Total of Annual Plans	L.E.	Originally approved	Total of Annual Plans	L.E.
1	14	15	16	17	18	19
I. Plan Outlay	235.00	262.38	261.52	210.00	223.81	227.36
II. State Govt.'s Budgetary Resources at 1979-80 rates						
i) Balance from current Revenues	-35.38	-51.95	-47.06	-75.74	-107.57	-102.67
ii) Share of Small Savings	3.40	4.98	8.39	0.92	1.02	0.96
iii) State Provident Fund	2.73	3.51	4.96	12.51	11.73	13.38
iv) Misc. Capital Receipts	-5.41	9-48	-45.67	2.40	-5.99	-48.58
v) Others	6.31	0.14	+6.97	23.00	6.71	-25.16
TOTAL - II	-2835	-52.80	-72.41	-36.91	-94.10	-168.07
III. Contribution of State Enterprises at 1979-80 rates						
i) State Elec. Boards	-6.71	-18.58	-21.19	-	-	-
ii) Road Transport Corpns.	-2.23	-4.72	-4.79	-	-	-
TOTAL - III	-8.94	-23.30	-25.98	-	-	-
IV. Additional Resource Mobilisation	13.85	29.30	30.22	3.97	9.16	14.23

V.	States' Budgetary Resources and contribution of Public Enterprises at current rates (II + III + IV)	-23.44	-47.80	-68.17	-32.94	-84.94	-148.84
VI.	Market Borrowings (Net)	22.77	23.74	25.46	21.14	22.09	23.59
VII	Negotioted Loans						
	i) Loans from LIC	28.01	26.70	18.79	10.75	9.06	3.51
	ii) Loans from RBI	0.73	0.49	0.18	-	-	-
	iii) Loans from REC	10.93	10.85	10.89	1.55	1.34	3.03
	iv) Other Loans	-	-	1.74	-	-	-
	TOTAL - VII	39.67	38.04	31.60	12.30	10.40	6.54
VIII.	Market Borrowings and Negotiated Loans (VI + VII)	62.44	61.78	57.06	33.44	32.49	30.13
IX.	States' Total Resources (V + VIII)	39.00	13.98	-11.11	0.50	-52.45	-118.71
X.	Central Assistance						
	i) Normal	196.00	243.21	248.54	209.50	293.61	291.19
	ii) For Externally aided projects	-	-	-	-	-	-
	iii) Adjt. of A.P.A.	-	-	-	-	-	-
	TOTAL - X	196.00	243.21	248.54	209.50	293.61	291.19
XI.	Aggregate Resources (IX + X)	235.00	257.19	237.43	210.00	241.16	172.48
XII.	Surplus (+)/Deficit - with R.B.I.	-	-5.19	-24.09		+17.35	-54.86

(Contd.) TABLE-IV-25 : STATES' FINANCIAL RESOURCES - SIXTH FIVE YEAR PLAN 1980-85

	TOTAL-I- SPL CATEGORY STATES		
	Originaliy Approved	Total of Annual Plans	L.E.
1	26	27	28
I. Plan Outlay	3627.00	3939.36	3989.67
II. State Govt.'s Budgetary Rescurces at 1979-80 rates			
i) Balance from Current Revenues	-682.00	-970.31	-1089.10
ii) Share of Small Savings	218.46	255.03	294.71
iii) State Provident Fund	134.44	153.75	173.18
iv) Misc. Capital Receipts	-361.84	-385.51	-483.20
v) Others	94.16	60.60	-287.94
TOTAL - II	-596.78	-886.44	-1387.35
III. Contribution of State Enterprises at 1979-80 rates			
i) State Elec. Boards	-125.69	-140.01	-189.61
ii) Road Transport Corpns.	-28.99	-55.48	-87.51
TOTAL - III	-154.68	-195.49	277.12
IV. Additional Resource Mobilisation	580.00	541.26	462.52

V.	States' Budgetary Resources and contribution of Public Enterprises at current rates (II + III + IV)	-171.46	-540.67	-1201.95
VI.	Market Borrowings (Net)	332.66	346.80	351.69
VII.	Negotiated Loans			
	i) Loans from LIC	127.99	113.20	87.52
	ii) Loans from RBI	15.18	13.88	36.58
	iii) Loans from REC	79.63	79.44	19.68
	iv) Other Loans	-	0.88	19.68
	<u>TOTAL - VII</u>	<u>222.80</u>	<u>207.40</u>	<u>220.05</u>
VIII.	Market Borrowings and Negotiated Loans (VI + VII)	555.46	554.20	571.74
IX.	States' total Resources (V + VIII)	384.00	13.53	-650.21
X.	Central assistance			
	i) Normal	3236.83	3907.58	3956.75
	ii) For Externally aided Projects	6.17	17.99	24.89
	iii) Adjt. of A.P.A.	-	-7.13	-8.03
	<u>TOTAL - X</u>	<u>3243.00</u>	<u>3918.44</u>	<u>3973.61</u>
XI.	Aggregate Resources (IX + X)	3627.00	3931.97	3443.40
XII.	Surplus (+)/Deficit-with RBI		-7.39	-646.27

Contd.) TABLE-IV-25 : STATES' FINANCIAL RESOURCES - SIXTH FIVE YEAR PLAN 1980-85

(Rs. Crores)

		ANDHRA PRADESH			BIHAR		
		Originally approved	Total of Annual Plans	L.E.	Originally approved	Total of Annual Plans	L.E.
	1	2	3	4	5	6	7
I.	Plan Outlay	3100.00	3381.62	3190.00	3225.00	3138.61	2972.68
II.	State Govt.'s Budgetary Resources at 1979-80 rates						
	i) Balance from Current Revenues.	968.06	993.40	568.93	478.15	-127.26	-319.52
	ii) Share of Small Savings	137.14	241.94	242.00	359.74	403.52	489.19
	iii) State provident Fund	82.43	117.84	123.36	187.12	182.68	171.95
	iv) Misc.Capital Receipts	-268.27	-299.01	-311.24	-420.10	-433.92	-929.45
	v) Others	43.79	20.25	184.02	228.35	85.05	320.00
	TOTAL - II	963.15	1074.42	807.07	833.26	110.07	-267.83
III.	Contribution of State Enterprises at 1979-80 rates						
	i) State Elec. Boards	220.30	83.44	-31.52	-36.46	-338.38	-493.79
	ii) Road Transport Corons.	-16.88	-128.89	-161.96	-8.64	-25.22	-43.07
	TOTAL - III	203.42	-45,45	-193.48	-45.10	-363.60	-536.86
IV.	Additional Resource Mobilisation	532.70	827.16	758.79	600.00	1230.05	1168.19

V.	States' Budgetary Resources and contribution of Public Enterprises at current rates (II + III + IV)	1699.27	1856.13	1372.38	1388.16	976.52	363.50
VI.	Market Borrowings (Net)	321.90	332.97	334.02	463.44	476.36	480.92
VII.	Negotiated Loans						
	i) Loans from LIC	99.77	94.98	82.46	65.51	64.47	6228
	ii) Loans from RBI	17.71	17.71	9.75	3.04	3.03	1.55
	iii) Loans from R.E.C.	31.24	31.43	56.49	44.35	45.21	55.07
	iv) Other Loans	24.41	12.40	33.30	-	-	3.40
	TOTAL - VII	173.13	156.52	182.00	112.90	112.71	122.30
VIII.	Market Borrowings and Negotiated Loans (VI+VII)	495.03	489.49	516.02	576.34	589.07	603.22
IX	States' Total resources (V + VIII)	2194.30	2345.62	1888.40	1964.50	1565.59	966.72
X.	Central Assistance						
	i) Normal	806.35	936.16	935.98	1227.93	1416.65	1415.14
	ii) For externally aided Projects	99.35	119.13	109.45	32.57	37.80	34.48
	iii) Adjt. of A.P.A.	-	-34.29	-37.92	-	-11.97	-14.98
	TOTAL - X	905.70	1021.00	1007.51	1260.50	1442.48	1434.64
XI.	Aggregate Resources (IX + X)	3100.00	3366.62	2895.91	3225.00	3008.07	2401.30
XII.	Surplus (+)/Deficit- with R.B.I.		-15.00	-294.09		-130.54	-571.32

(Contd.) TABLE-IV-25 : STATES' FINANCIAL RESOURCES - SIXTH FIVE YEAR PLAN 1980-85

(Rs. crores)

		GUJARAT			HARYANA		
		Originally approved	Total of Plans	L.E.	Originally approved	Total of Plans	L.E.
		8	9	10	11	12	13
I.	Plan Outlay	3680.00	3751.63	3900.62	1800.00	1697.12	1595.88
II.	State Govt.'s Budgetary Resources at 1979-80 rates						
	i) Balance from Current Revenues	1431.05	1230.73	980.33	726.88	685.58	479.15
	ii) Share of Small Savings	370.53	483.76	604.23	106.85	110.50	139.01
	iii) State Provident Fund	69.94	68.74	71.28	93.04	90.31	105.93
	iv) Misc. Capital Receipts	26.97	211.10	486.15	-10.64	13.31	26.90
	v) Others	330.35	90.36	-24.23	-10.95	6.05	-133.28
	TOTAL - II	2228.84	2084.69	2117.90	905.18	905.75	617.57
III.	Contribution of State Enterprises at 79-80 rates						
	i) S.E.Bs.	-63.23	-415.95	-788.62	23.71	-149.08	-119.11
	ii) R.T.Cs.	-21.74	-139.53	-151.44	-	-	-
	TOTAL - III	-84.97	-555.48	-940.06	23.71	-149.08	-119.11
IV.	Additional Resources Mobilisation	500.00	1146.87	1482.31	416.11	489.27	380.15

V.	States' Budgetary Resources and contribution of Public Enterprises at current rates (II + III + IV)	2643.87	2676.08	2660.15	1345.00	1245.94	878.61
VI.	Market Borrowings (Net)	239.70	252.04	255.06	114.00	120.27	121.43
VII.	Negotiated Loans						
	i) Loans from LIC	139.66	133.00	118.68	82.85	78.04	66.96
	ii Loans from RBI	25.64	11.80	1.86	9.17	9.17	6.60
	iii) Loans from REC	31.45	30.91	50.20	14.13	14.15	36.80
	iv) Other Loans	-	-	-	-	-	-
	Total - VII	196.75	175.71	170.74	106.15	101.36	110.36
VIII.	Market Borrowing and Negotiated Loans (VI+VII	436.45	427.75	425.80	220.15	221.63	231.79
IX.	States' total Resources (V + VIII)	3080.32	3103.83	3085.95	1565.15	1467.57	1110.40
X.	Central Assistance						
	i) Normal	387.74	450.71	443.11	187.42	220.67	218.63
	ii) For Externally aided Projects	211.94	180.47	208.49	47.43	68.35	81.36
	iii) Adjt. of A. P.A.	-	-8.38.	-5.58	-	-8.44	-8.44
	TOTAL - X	599.68	622.80	646.02	234.85	280.58	291.55
XI.	Aggregate Resources (IX + X)	3680.00	3726.63	3731.97	1800.00	1748.15	1401.95
XII.	Surplus (+)/Deficit with R.B.I.		-25.00	-168.65		51.03	-193.93

(Contd.) TABLE-IV-25 : STATES' FINANCIAL RESOURCES - SIXTH FIVE YEAR PLAN 1980-85

(Rs. Crores)

	KARNATAKA			KERALA		
	Originally approved	Total of Annual Plans	L.E.	Originally approved	Total of Annual Plans	L.E.
	14	15	16	17	18	19
I. Plan Outlay	2265.00	2503.55	2583.91	1550.00	1498.00	1669.85
II. State Govt.'s Budegtary Resources at 1979.80 rates						
i) Balance from Current Revenues	992.67	942.61	1006.75	329.16	218.63	33.31
ii) Share of Small Savings	171.52	196.74	280.94	47.02	63.69	73.45
iii) State Provident Fund	116.50	129.10	135.14	147.27	151.11	223.18
iv) Misc. Capital Receipts	-242.42	-251.14	-253.28	-119.52	-86.93	-79.09
v) Others	112.94	143.02	-76.27	233.67	22.34	1.48
TOTAL - II	1151.21	1160.33	1093.28	-637.60	368.84	252.30
III. Contribution of State Enterprises at 79.80 rates						
i) S.E.Bs.	-191.98	-264.60	-300.52	-103.70	-67.72	0.51
ii) R.T.Cs.	-44.08	-147.01	-198.63	-41.17	-141.72	134.46
TOTAL - III	-236.06	-411.61	-499.15	144.87	-209.44	-133.95
IV. Additional Resources Mobilisation	457.71	839.43	789.95	310.91	479.32	369.26

V.	States' Budgetary Resources and contribution of Public Enterprises at current rates (II + III + IV)	1372.86	1588.15	1384.08	803.64	638.72	487.61
VI.	Market Borrowings (Net)	215.12	228.30	232.69	194.81	205.20	206.20
VII.	Negotiated Loans						
	i) Loans from LIC	104.24	105.58	117.76	103.82	100.23	72.07
	ii) Loans from RBI	15.27	7.62	3.59	8.85	8.88	4.84
	iii) Loans from REC	18.31	18.31	16.74	8.72	10.40	9.17
	iv) Other Loans	-	2.00	2.65	-	-	-
	TOTAL - VII	137.82	133.51	140.74	121.39	119.51	86.68
VIII.	Market Borrowings and Negotiated Loans (VI+VII)	352.94	361.81	373.43	316.20	324.71	292.88
IX.	States' Total Resources (V + VIII)	1725.80	1949.96	1757.51	1119.84	963.43	780.49
X.	Central Assistance						
	i) Normal	416.82	482.34	485.72	380.04	443.77	442.34
	ii) For Externally aided Projects	122.38	117.27	95.16	50.12	54.41	44.24
	ii) Adjt. of A.P.A.	-	-18.61	-18.61	-	-3.61	-3.61
	TOTAL - X	539.20	589.00	564.27	430.16	494.57	482.97
XI.	Aggregate Resources (IX + X)	2265.00	2538.96	2321.78	1550.00	1458.00	1263.46
XII.	Surplus (+)/Deficit with R.B.I		35.41	-262.13		-40.00	-406.39

(Contd.) TABLE-IV-25 : STATES' FINANCIAL RESOURCES - SIXTH FIVE YEAR PLAN 1980-85

(Rs. Crores)

	MADHYA PRADESH			MAHARASHTRA		
	Originally approved	Total of Annual Plans	L.E.	Originally approved	Total of Annual Plans	L.E.
	20	21	22	23	24	25
I. Plan Outlay	3800.00	3821.43	3903.61	6175.00	6435.00	6481.20
II. State Govt.'s Budgetary Resources at 1979-80 rates						
i) Balance from Current Revenues	1142.36	957.18	247.90	2254.21	2106.79	2539.94
ii Share of Small Savings	177.05	171.40	209.08	824.18	946.50	216.53
iii) State Provident Fund	331.63	315.89	256.33	292.39	320.10	303.63
iv) Misc. Capital Receipts	-79.74	-128.80	-456.31	-232.21	-277.63	-590.11
v) Others	48.26	61.98	17.30	155.90	168.81	38.09
TOTAL - II	1619.56	1377.65	1274.39	3294.47	3264.57	3607.30
III. Contribution of State Enterprises at 79-80 rates						
i) S.E. Bs.	66.50	-198.04	-377.64	653.45	103.43	-231.02
ii) R.T.Cs.	-20.68	-71.63	-97.59	-94.39	289.92	-310.83
TOTAL - III	45.82	-269.67	-475.23	559.06	-186.49	-541.85
IV. Additional Resource Mobilisation	600.00	1138.81	1167.46	900.00	1755.26	1669.82

V.	States Budgetary Resources and contribution of Public Enterprises at current rates (II+III+IV)	2265.38	2246.79	1966.62	4753.53	4383.34	4735.27
VI.	Market. Borrowing (Net)	333.13	343.33	346.75	331.52	349.34	353.94
VII.	NEGOTIATED LOANS						
	i) Loans from LIC	108.36	103.19	91.43	169.74	161.75	156.73
	ii) Loans from RBI	8.07	7.85	5.47	5.15	5.15	1.38
	iii) Loans from REC	71.67	71.65	84.73	39.15	39.16	31.67
	iv) Other Loans	-		-	-		
	TOTAL - VII	188.10	182.69	181.63	214.04	205.86	189.78
VIII.	Market Borrowings and Negotiated Loans (VI+VII)	521.23	526.02	528.38	545.56	555.20	543.72
IX.	States total Resources (V+VIII)	2786.61	2772.81	2495.00	5299.09	5388.54	5278.99
X.	Central Assistance						
	i) Normal	861.06	998.73	996.61	624.44	767.25	764.25
	ii) For Externally aided projects	152.33	132.66	119.70	251.47	295.82	320.61
	iii) Adjt. of A.P.A.	-	-26.48	-31.89	-	-16.61	-16.61
	TOTAL - X	1013.39	1104.91	1084.42	875.91	1046.46	1068.98
XI.	Aggregate Resources (IX + X)	3800.00	3877.72	3579.42	6175.00	6435.00	6347.90
XII.	Surplus (+)/Deficit with R.B.I		56.29	-324.19			-133.31

(Contd.) TABLE-IV-25 : STATES' FINANCIAL RESOURCES - SIXTH FIVE YEAR PLAN 1980-85

(Rs. Crores)

	ORISSA			PUNJAB		
	Originally approved	Total of Annual Plans	L.E.	Originally approved	Total of Annual Plans	L.E.
	26	27	28	29	30	31
I. Plan Outlay	1500.00	1570.16	1557.42	1957.00	1905.34	1973.33
II. State Govt.'s Budgetary Resources at 1979-80 rates						
i) Balance from Current Revenues	48.11	-62.53	16.69	734.81	515.91	44.12
ii) Share of Small Savings	82.39	94.65	90.94	175.00	146.50	186.71
iii) State Provident Fund	80.00	86.00	98.33	58.30	55.60	53.38
iv) Misc. Capital Receipts	-146.75	-121.87	-128.53	94.00	59.84	120.61
v) Others	140.25	17.20	-40.40	-16.63	10.00	378.33
TOTAL - II	204.00	13.45	37.14	1045.48	787.85	783.15
III. Contribution of State Enterprises at 1979.80 rates						
i) S.E.Bs..	-35.04	-81.53	-111.53	23.14	-161.07	-213.01
ii) R.T.Cs.	-8.55	-23.75	-30.51	-39.34	-48.45	-56.57
TOTAL - III	-43.59	105.28	-142.04	-16.20	-209.52	-269.58
IV. Additional Resource Mobilisation	350.00	574.45	423.41	400.00	727.72	647.07

V.	States' Budgetary Resources and contribution of Public Enterprises at current rates (II + III + IV)	510.41	482.62	318.51	1429.28	1306.05	1160.64
VI.	Market Borrowings (Net)	198.03	204.65	206.09	97.70	102.90	104.00
VII.	Negotiated Loans						
	i) Loans from LIC	80.70	77.18	75.11	85.47	75.48	117.76
	ii) Loans from RBI	16.97	35.97	34.36	31.74	32.21	43.76
	iii) Loans from REC	34.36	35.97	34.36	31.74	32.21	43.76
	iv) Other Loans		-	-	-	2.30	-
	TOTAL - VII	132.03	130.10	121.71	130.02	122.78	169.43
VIII.	Market Borrowing and Negotiated Loans (VI + VII)	330.06	334.75	327.80	227.72	225.68	273.43
IX.	States' Total Resources (V + VIII)	840.47	817.37	646.31	1657.00	1531.73	1434.07
X.	Central Assistance						
	i) Normal	586.66	676.96	676.45	233.14	273.10	272.44
	ii) For Externally aided projects	72.87	94.23	95.56	66.86	72.36	65.49
	iii) Adjt. of A.P.A.		-11.82	-13.93			
	TOTAL - X	659.53	759.37	758.98	300.00	345.46	337.93
XI.	Aggregate Resources (IX + X)	1500.00	1576.74	1404.39	1957.00	1877.19	1772.00
XII.	Surplus(+)/ Deficit-		6.58	-153.03		-28.15	-201.33

(Contd.) TABLE-IV-25 : STATES' FINANCIAL RESOURCES - SIXTH FIVE YEAR PLAN 1980-85

(Rs. Crores)

		RAJASTHAN			TAMIL NADU		
		Originally approved	Total of Annual Plans	L.E.	Originally approved	Total of Annual Plans	L.E.
		32	33	34	35	36	37
I.	Plan Outlay	2025.00	1801.86	1867.97	3150.00	3405.43	3623.79
II.	State Govt.'s Budgetary Resources at 1979-80 rates						
	i) Balance from Current Revenues	276.26	-94.55	-109.12	682.32	1075.72	1017.95
	ii) Share of Small Savings	114.17	133.40	206.21	241.77	225.96	244.13
	iii) State Provident Fund	99.93	102.91	11.21	87.70	89.31	87.43
	iv) Misc. Capital Receipts	-114.05	206.08	-385.27	-101.40	-81.89	86.13
	v) Others	-34.00	72.30	82.04	245.64	33.19	61.01
	TOTAL - II	342.31	7.98	94.43	1156.03	1342.29	1496.65
III.	Contribution of State Enterprises at 1979.80 rates				*12.0		
	i) S.E.Bs..	-95.44	-191.17	-231.50	-195.03	-417.46	-564.94
	ii) R.T.Cs.	-63.82	-31.29	-111.41	-38.74	-134.83	-195.86
	TOTAL - III	-159.26	-272.46	-342.91	-221.77	-552.29	-760.80
IV.	Additional Resource Mobilisation	750.70	742.53	735.13	1101.65	1407.56	1538.57

V.	States' Budgetary Resources and contribution of Public Enterprises at current rates (II + III + IV)	933.75	478.05	297.79	2035.91	2197.56	2274.42
VI.	Market Borrowings (Net)	303.61	315.17	315.69	258.07	274.78	271.45
VII.	Negotiated Loans						
	i) Loans from LIC	104.03	101.08	97.67	161.15	151.07	131.12
	ii) Loans from RBI	11.60	11.23	10.21	12.21	12.21	4.15
	iii) Loans from REC	44.70	44.67	46.90	17.86	17.86	46.25
	iv) Other Loans	1.00	23.67	65.82	-	-	-
	TOTAL - VII	161.33	180.65	220.60	121.22	181.14	181.52
VIII.	Market Borrowing and Negotiated Loans (VI + VII)	464.94	495.82	536.29	449.29	455.92	452.97
IX.	States' Total Resources (V + VIII)	1398.69	973.87	834.08	2485.20	2653.48	2727.39
X.	Central Assistance						
	i) Normal	567.23	690.00	694.78	606.31	698.82	698.82
	ii) For Externally aided projects	59.03	73.16	62.55	58.49	81.10	84.10
	iii) Adjt. of A.P.A.	-	-31.81	-33.82	-	-25.56	-25.56
	TOTAL - X	626.31	731.35	723.51	664.80	754.36	757.36
XI.	Aggregate Resources (IX + X)	2025.00	1705.22	1557.59	3150.00	3407.84	3484.75
XII.	Surplus(+)/ Deficit with RBI		-96.64	-310.38		+2.36	-139.04

* Others

(Contd.) TABLE-IV-25 : STATES' FINANCIAL RESOURCES - SIXTH FIVE YEAR PLAN 1980-85

(Rs. Crores)

		UTTAR PRADESH			WEST BENGAL		
		Originally approved	Total of Annual Plans	L.E.	Originally approved	Total of Annual Plans	L.E.
		38	39	40	41	42	43
I.	Plan Outlay	5850.00	5840.08	6041.99	3500.00	2662.31	2276.78
II.	State Govt.'s Budgetary Resources at 1979-80 rates						
	i) Balance from Current Revenues	957.34	735.70	884.16	908.95	-111.60	-530.87
	ii) Share of Small Savings	483.41	605.00	724.45	842.00	979.00	931.96
	iii) State Provident Fund	160.32	169.22	167.70	100.73	172.65	153.18
	iv) Misc. Capital Receipts	-217.84	-59.88	-309.34	-151.67	-344.91	-572.43
	v) Others	494.51	67.01	59.63	174.74	53.02	-10.81
	TOTAL - II	1877.74	1517.05	1526.60	1874.75	748.16	-28.37
III.	Contribution of State Enterprises at 1979.80 rates						
	i) S.E.Bs..	-40.37	-377.42	-670.23	-121.74	-229.07	-374.76
	ii) R.T.Cs.	8.14	-95.94	-160.74	-87.35	-58.87	-41.31
	TOTAL - III	-32.23	-473.36	-830.97	-209.09	-287.94	-416.07
IV.	Additional Resource Mobilisation	1000.00	1459.49	1450.77	512.33	836.20	746.40

V.	States' Budgetary Resources and contribution of Public Enterprises current rates (II + III + IV)						
VI.	Market Borrowings (Net)	2845.51	2503.18	2146.40	2177.99	1296.42	301.96
VII.	Negotiated Loans	695.00	714.97	717.23	403.00	424.37	427.98
	i) Loans from LIC	309.36	296.13	288.39	150.06	134.87	116.55
	ii) Loans from RBI	6.60	6.71	6.83	16.65	14.65	5.19
	iii) Loans from REC	64.49	64.49	64.49	70.04	69.98	65.15
	iv) Other Loans	-	1.65	-	2.00	-	-
	TOTAL - VII	380.45	363.98	359.71	238.75	219.50	186.89
VIII.	Market Borrowing and Negotiated Loans (VI + VII)	1075.45	1083.95	1076.94	641.75	643.87	614.87
IX.	States' Total Resources (V+VIII)	3920.96	3587.13	3223.34	2819.74	1940.29	916.83
X.	Central Assistance						
	i) Normal	1827.12	2115.43	2119.36	583.17	674.95	678.62
	ii) For Externally aided projects	101.91	104.70	113.56	97.09	96.93	91.02
	iii) Adjt. of A.P.A.	-	-19.15	-25.53	-	-8.70	-8.70
	TOTAL - X	1929.04	2200.98	2207.39	680.26	763.18	760.94
XI.	Aggregate Resources (IX+X)	5850.00	5788.11	5430.73	3500.00	2703.47	1677.77
XII.	Surplus(+)/ Deficit with R.B.I		-51.97	611.26		+41.16	-599.01

(Contd.) TABLE-IV-25 : STATES' FINANCIAL RESOURCES - SIXTH FIVE YEAR PLAN 1980-85

(Rs. Crores)

		TOTAL - II - NON-SPL. CATEGORY		
		Originally	Total of Annual Plans	L.E
		44	45	46
I.	Plan Outlay	43577.00	43412.19	43639.11
II.	State Govt.'s Budgetary Resources at 1979-80 rates			
	i) Balance from Current Revenues	11930.33	9066.31	7859.72
	ii) Share of Small Savings	4132.77	4802.56	5737.69
	iii) State Provident Fund	1907.30	2051.46	2062.23
	iv) Misc. Capital Receipts	-1983.64	-2007.81	-3295.26
	v) Others	2146.82	850.58	858.34
	TOTAL - II	18133.58	14763	13222.72
III.	Contribution of State Enterprises at 1979.80 rates			
	i) S.E.Bs..	116.11	-2704.62	-450.68
	ii) R.T.Cs.	-477.24	-1387.05	-1694.38
	TOTAL - III	-361.13	-4091.67	-6202.06
IV.	Additional Resource Mobilisation	8432.11	13654.12	13327.28
V.	States' Budgetary Resources contribution of Public Enterpri current rates (II +III + IV)	26204.56	24325.55	20347.94
VI.	Market Borrowings (Net)	4169.03	4344.65	4373.45
VII.	Negotiated Loans			
	i) Loans from LIC	1764.72	1676.85	1594.97
	ii) Loans from RBI	169.74	145.75	81.57
	iii) Loans from REC	522.21	526.40	642.38
	iv) Other Loans	27.41	42.02	105.17
	TOTAL - VII	2484.08	2391.02	2424.09
VIII.	Market Borrowing and Negotiated Loans (VI + VII)	6653.11	6735.67	6797.54
IX.	States' Total Resources (V+VIII)	32857.67	31061.22	27145.48
X.	Central Assistance			
	i) Normal	9295.48	10848.54	10839.98
	ii) For Externally aided projects	1423.85	1523.39	1525.77
	iii) Adjt. of A.P.A.	-	-220.43	-240.18
	TOTAL - X	10719.33	12156.50	12125.57
XI.	Aggregate Resources (IX + X)	43577.00	43217.72	39271.05
XII.	Surplus(+)/ Deficit with R.B.I		-194.47	-4368.06

(Contd.) TABLE-IV-25 : STATES' FINANCIAL RESOURCES - SIXTH FIVE YEAR PLAN 1980-85

(Rs. Crores)

		GRAND TOTAL - (I + II)		
		Originally	Total of Annual Plans	L.E
		47	48	49
I.	Plan Outlay	47204.00	47351.55	47628.78
II.	State Govt.'s Budgetary Resources at 1979-80 rates			
	i) Balance from Current	11248.33	8096.00	6770.62
	ii) Share of Small Savings	4351.23	5057.59	6032.40
	iii) State Provident Fund	2041.74	2205.21	2235.41
	iv) Misc. Capital Receipts	-2345.48	-239.32	-3778.46
	v) Others	2240.98	911.18	598.40
	TOTAL - II	17536.80	13876.66	11835.37
III.	Contribution of State Enterprises at 1979.80 rates			
	i) S.E.Bs.	-9.58	-2844.63	-4697.29
	ii) R.T.Cs.	-306.23	+1442.53	-1781.89
	TOTAL - III	-515.81	-4287.16	-6479.80
IV.	Additional Resource Mobilisation	9012.11	14195.38	13789.80
V.	States' Budgetary Resources contribution of Public Enterpr current rates (II + III + IV)	26033.10	23784.88	19145.99
VI.	Market Borrowings (Net)	4501.69	4691.45	4725.14
VII.	Negotiated Loans			
	i) Loans from LIC	1892.71	1790.05	1682.49
	ii) Loans from RBI	184.92	159.63	118.15
	iii) Loans from REC	601.84	605.84	718.65
	iv) Other Loans	27.41	42.90	124.85
	TOTAL - VII	2706.88	2598.42	2644.14
VIII.	Market Borrowing an Negotiated Loans (VI + VII)	7208.88	2598.42	2644.14
IX.	States' Total Resources (VI+VIII)	33241.67	31074.75	26315.27
X.	Central Assistance			
	i) Normal	12532.31	14756.12	42614.45
	ii) For Externally aided projects	1430.02	1546.38	1550.66
	iii) Adjt. of A.P.A.	-	-227.56	-248.21
	TOTAL - X	13962.33	16074.94	16099.18
XI.	Aggregate Resources (IX + X)	47204.00	47149.69	42614.45
XII.	Surplus(+)/ Deficit with R.B.I		-201.86	-5014.33

* Includes opening cash balance of Rs. 161.82 crores.

Source: Government of India, Ministry of Finance, 'Statistical Statements on Finances : and Plans of states and Union Territories, 1985

TABLE-IV-26: STATES FINANCIAL RESOURCES - 7TH FIVE YEAR PLAN 1985-90 (SUMMARY) (Rs. in Crores)

	STATES	State's budgetary resources and contribution of Public enterprises at current rates	Market Borrowing and negotiated loans	Central Assistance (Net)	Drawal from R.B.I	Aggregate Resources/ Plan Outlay
I. <u>SPL. CATEGORY STATES</u>						
1.	Assam	-344.75	379.67	2065.08	-	2100.00
2.	Himachal Pradesh	55.10	131.88	863.02	-	1050.00
3.	Jammu & Kashmir	-664.26	225.58	1830.68		-1400.00
4.	Manipur	-157.36	42.36	545.00	-	430.00
5.	Meghalaya	-104.73	103.45	441.28	-	440.00
6.	Nagaland	-324.12	57.24	666.38	-	400.00
7.	Sikkim	-36.11	18.49	247.62	-	230.00
8.	Tripura	-173.70	72.49	541.21	-	440.00
	TOTAL (I)	-1749.13	1031.16	7208.77	-	6490.00
II. <u>NON-SPL. CATEGORY STATES</u>:						
1.	Andhra Pradesh	2557.13	1022.55	1620.32	-	5200.00
2.	Bihar	1564.37	1245.67	-2289.96	-	5100.00
3.	Gujarat	4157.69	790.64	1051.67	-	6000.00
4.	Haryana	2103.57	407.44	388.99 *	-	2900.00
5.	Karnataka	1942.53	683.74	873.73	-	3500.00
6.	Kerala	201.63	761.46	1136.91	-	2100.00
7.	Madhya Pradesh	4025.58	1050.36	1879.06	-	7000.00
8.	Maharashtra	7672.33	1050.99	1776.68	-	10500.00
9.	Orissa	383.89	672.35	1143.76	-	2700.00
10.	Punjab	2425.03	393.04	466.93	-	3285.00
11.	Rajashthan	971.75	888.48	1139.77	-	3000.00
12.	Tamil Nadu	3199.20	1112.94	1437.86	-	5750.00
13.	Uttar Pradesh	4687.96	2151.49	3607.55	-	10447.00
14.	West Bengal	1737.27	1173.84	1289.89	-	4125.00
	TOTAL (II)	38129.93	13449.99	20027.08	-	71607.00
	GRAND TOTAL (I+II)	36380.00	14481.15	27235.85	-	78097.00

TABLE IV.27 : STATES FINANCIAL RESOURCES FOR 7TH PLAN 1985-90

(Rs. Crores)

	ITEMS	I-SPECIAL Assam	CATEGORY Himachal-Pradesh	STATES Jammu &-Kashmir	Manipur	Meghalaya
	1.	2.	3.	4.	5.	6.
I.	PLAN OUTLAY	2100.00	1050.00	1400.00	430.00	440.00*
II.	State's budgetary resources at 1984-85 rates					
i)	Balance from current revenues	-95.75	-198.92	-455.05	-128.93	-87.42
ii)	Share of Small savings	268.60	141.04	79.36	2.36	18.47
iii)	State Provident Fund	85.40	80.59	78.07	8.11	7.29
iv)	Misc. Capital Receipts	-563.62	-58.47	-423.21	-41.41	-19.58
v)	Adjustment of Overdraft	-151.34	-2.63	-	-	-
	Total (II):	-456.71	-38.39	-720.83	-159.89	-81.24
III.	Contribution of State enterprises at 1984-85 rates					
i)	S.E.Bs.	-137.98	-19.54	-79.93	-	-27.21
ii)	R.T.Cs.	-7.06	-11.97	-7.05	-6.09	-4.46
	Total (III)	-145.04	-31.51	-86.98	-6.09	-31.67
IV.	Addl. Resource Mobilisation	257.00	125.00	143.55	8.62	8.18
V.	State's budgetary resources and-contribution of public enterprises at current rates (II+III+IV):	-344.75	55.10	-664.26	-157.36	-104.73

VI.	Market Borrowing (Net)	291.94	81.48	141.86	32.71	45.47
VII.	Negotitated Loans					
i)	Loans from LIC	30.26	13.29	34.26	5.10	27.18
ii)	Loans from R.B.I	13.64	0.25	2.41	0.65	0.29
iii)	Loans from REC	28.76	30.26	30.00	1.15	16.98
iv)	Others (IDBI)	15.07	6.60	17.05	2.75	13.53
	Total (VII) :	87.73	50.40	83.72	9.65	57.98
VIII.	Market Borrowing + Negotiated-loans (VI + VIII)	379.67	131.88	225.58	42.36	103.45
IX.	State's total resources (V + VIII) :	34.92	186.98	-433.63	-115.00	-1.28
X.	Central Assistance:					
i)	Normal	2057.08	781.93	1820.68	545.00	441.28
ii)	Externally aided projects	8.00	85.00	18.00	-	-
iii)	APA adjustments	-	-3.91	-	-	-
	Total (X) :	2065.08	863.02	1838.68	545.00	441.28
XI.	Aggregate Resoruces (IX+X) :	2100.00	1020.00	1400.00	430.00	440.00

(Contd.) TABLE IV.27 : STATES FINANCIAL RESOURCES FOR 7TH PLAN 1985-90

(Rs.Crores)

	ITEMS	Nagaland	Sikkim	Tripura	Total-Spl. Cat. States
		7.	8.	9.	10.
I.	PLAN OUTLAY	400.00	230.00	440.00	6490.00
II.	State's budgetary resources 1984-85 rates				
i)	Balance from current revenues	-330.29	-33.23	-184.02	-1513.61
ii)	Share of Small savings	1.70	0.50	16.80	528.83
iii)	State Provident Fund	20.70	4.17	16.59	300.92
iv)	Misc. Capital Receipts	-11.61	-12.13	-23.86	-1153.91
v)	Adjustment of Overdraft	-8.83	-	-	-162.80
	Total (II):	-388.33	-40.69	-174.49	-2000.57
III.	Contribution of State enterprises at 1984-85 rates				
i)	S.E.Bs.	-	-	-	-264.66
ii)	R.T.Cs.	-	-	-5.21	-41.84
	Total (III)	-	-	-5.21	-306.50
IV.	Addl. Resource Mobilisation	4.21	4.58	6.00	557.14
V.	State's budgetary resources contribution of public enterprises at current rates (II+III+IV):	-324.12	-36.11	-173.70	-1749.93

VI.	Market Borrowing (Net)	42.53	5.60	38.20	679.79
VII.	Negotitated Loans				
i)	Loans from LIC	6.71	1.70	13.22	131.72
ii)	Loans from R.B.I	-	-	2.26	19.50
iii)	Loans from REC	4.70	10.09	12.21	134.15
iv)	Others (IDBI)	3.30	1.10	6.60	66.00
	Total (VII) :	14.71	12.89	34.29	351.37
VIII.	Market Borrowing + Negotitated loans (V + VII)	57.24	18.49	72.49	1031.16
IX.	State's total resources (V + VIII) :	-266.88	-17.62	-101.21	-718.77
X.	Central Assistance:				
i)	Normal	666.88	247.62	541.58	7102.05
ii)	Externally aided projects	-	-	-	111.00
iii)	APA adjustments	-	-	-0.37	-4.28
	Total (X) :	666.88	247.62	541.21	7208.77
XI.	Aggregate Resoruces (IX+X) :	400.00	230.00	440.00	6490.00

(Contd.) TABLE IV.27 STATES FINANCIAL RESOURCES - 7TH FIVE YEAR PLAN -1985-90

(RS.CRORES)

	ITEMS	II - NONSPECIAL Andhra Pr.	CATEGORY Bihar	STATES Gujarat	Haryana	Karnataka
		11.	12.	13.	14.	15.
I.	PLAN OUTLAY	5200.00	5100.00	6000.00	2900.00	3500.00
II.	State's budgetary resources 1984-85 rates					
i)	Balance from current revenues	106.90	-215.48	816.36	1333.52	1436.57
ii)	Share of Small savings	671.56	1007.35	1220.00	235.13	493.17
iii)	State Provident Fund	289.81	434.26	109.72	151.51	285.42
iv)	Misc. Capital Receipts	-397.82	-922.08	152.82	-138.33	-385.38
v)	Adjustment of Overdraft	-229.98	-46.68	-6.76	-83.26	-245.85
	Total (II): 440.47	257.37	2292.14	1498.57	1583.93	
III.	Contribution of State enterprises at 1984-85 rates					
i)	S.E.Bs.	380.01	-249.14	239.77	55.00	-1026.83
ii)	R.T.Cs.	24.85	-45.67	-115.60	-	-152.28
iii)	Others	-	-	-	-	-
	Total (III)	404.86	-294.81	174.17	55.00	-1179.11
IV.	Addl. Resource Mobilisation	1711.80	1601.81	1691.38	550.00	1537.71
V.	State's budgetary resources contribution of public enter prises at current rates (II+III+IV):	2557.13	1564.37	4157.69	303.57	1942.53

VI.	Market Borrowing (Net)	749.15	1053.64	479.56	228.71	431.03
VII.	Negotiated Loans					
i)	Loans from LIC	129.53	73.45	169.10	102.54	145.25
ii)	Loans from R.B.I	28.60	4.83	7.33	14.77	5.71
iii)	Loans from REC	50.81	77.23	50.50	22.81	29.48
iv)	Others (IDBI)	64.46	36.52	84.15	38.61	72.27
	Total (VII) :	273.40	192.03	311.08	178.73	252.71
VIII.	Market Borrowing + Negotiated loans (VI + VIII)	1022.55	1245.67	790.64	407.44	683.74
IX.	State's total resources (V + VIII) ·	3579.68	2810.04	4948.33	2511.01	2626.27
X.	Central Assistance:					
i)	Normal	1483.47	2134.74	687.63	323.46	767.72
ii)	Externally aided projects	158.00	170.00	358.00	71.00	114.00
iii)	APA adjustments	-21.15	-14.78	-3.96	-5.47	-7.99
	Total (X) :	1620.32	2289.96	1051.67	388.99	873.73
XI.	Aggregate Resoruces (IX+X) :	5200.00	5100.00	6000.00	2900.00	3500.00

(Contd.) TABLE IV.27 : STATES FINANCIAL RESOURCES FOR 7TH PLAN 1985-90

(Rs.Crores)

	ITEMS	Kerala	Madhya Pr.	Maharashtra	Orissa
		16.	17.	18.	19.
I.	PLAN OUTLAY	2100.00	7000.00	10500.00	2700.00
II.	State's budgetary resources 1984-85 rates				
i)	Balance from current revenues	-739.53	1108.32	2670.92	-282.44
ii)	Share of Small savings	141.03	402.95	2283.00	213.69
iii)	State Provident Fund	332.58	1075.56	610.09	183.15
iv)	Misc. Capital Receipts	-308.25	-189.72	-694.94	-296.96
v)	Adjustment of Overdrafts	-174.50	-30.48	-	-50.13
	Total (II):	-748.67	2366.63	4869.07	-232.69
III.	Contribution of State enterprises at 1984-85 rates				
i)	S.E.Bs.	96.11	667.35	-551.76	173.47
ii)	R.T.Cs.	-148.77	-8.40	122.66	-99.72
iii)	Others	-	-	-	-
	Total (III)	-52.66	658.95	-429.10	73.75
IV.	Addl. Resource Mobilisation	1002.96	1000.00	3232.36	1042.83
V.	State's budgetary resources contribution of public enter prises at current rates (II+III+IV):	201.63	4025.58	7672.33	883.89

VI.	Market Borrowing (Net)	524.71	759.39	664.48	441.82
VII.	Negotitated Loans				
i)	Loans from LIC	135.65	138.60	210.43	94.21
ii)	Loans from R.B.I	14.30	13.02	8.26	27.30
iii)	Loans from REC	19.48	115.38	63.10	62.16
iv)	Others (IDBI)	67.32	68.97	104.72	46.86
	Total (VII) :	236.75	335.97	386.51	230.53
VIII.	Market Borrowing + Negotiated loans (V + VIII)	761.46	1095.36	1050.99	672.35
IX.	State's total resources (V + VIII) :	963.09	5120.94	8723.32	1556.24
X.	Central Assistance:				
i)	Normal	923.51	1400.35	1169.82	910.43
ii)	Externally aided projects	217.00	496.00	620.00	242.00
iii)	APA adjustments	-3.60	-17.29	-13.14	-8.67
	Total (X) :	1136.91	1879.06	1776.68	1143.76
XI.	Aggregate Resoruces (IX+X) :	2100.00	7000.00	10500.00	2700.00

(Contd.) TABLE IV.27 : STATES FINANCIAL RESOURCES FOR 7TH PLAN 1985-90

(Rs.Crores)

	ITEMS	Punjab	Rajasthan	Tamil Nadu
		20.	21.	22.
I.	PLAN OUTLAY	3285.00	3000.00	5750.00
II.	State's budgetary resources 1984-85 rates			
i)	Balance from current revenues	79.62	-280.39	2097.50
ii)	Share of Small savings	310.25	503.63	436.50
iii)	State Provident Fund	77.90	397.87	145.91
iv)	Misc. Capital Receipts	264.03	-247.16	-140.94
v)	Adjustment of Overdraft	-78.19	-	-19.62
	Total (II): 653.61	373.95	2519.75	
III.	Contribution of State enterprises at 1984-85 rates			
i)	S.E.Bs.	-146.04	-404.71	-513.13
ii)	R.T.Cs.	-82.54	2.51	177.63
iii)	Others	-	-	15.00
	Total (III)	-228.58	-402.20	-320.55
IV.	Addl. Resources Mobilisation	2000.00	1000.00	1000.00
V.	State's budgetary resources and contribution of public enterprises at current rates (II+III+IV):	2425.03	971.75	3192.20

VI.	Market Borrowing (Net)	195.67	627.18	750.28
VII.	Negotitated Loans			
i)	Loans from LIC	91.24	115.26	209.76
ii)	Loans from R.B.I	20.70	16.70	19.67
iii)	Loans from REC	40.00	71.92	28.84
iv)	Others (IDBI)	45.43	57.42	104.39
	Total (VII) :	197.37	261.30	362.66
VIII.	Market Borrowing + Negotiated loans (VI + VII)	393.04	888.48	1112.94
IX.	State's total resources (V + VIII) :	2818.07	1860.23	4312.14
X.	Central Assistance:			
i)	Normal	383.73	1096.46	1238.49
ii)	Externally aided projects	84.00	58.00	216.00
iii)	APA adjustments	-0.80	-14.69	-16.63
	Total (X) :	466.93	1139.77	1437.86
XI.	Aggregate Resoruces (IX+X) :	3285.00	3000.00	5750.00

(Contd.) TABLE IV.27 : STATES FINANCIAL RESOURCES FOR 7TH PLAN 1985-90

(Rs.Crores)

	ITEMS	Uttar Pradesh	West Bengal	Total-Non-Spl.-Category States	Grand Total
		23.	24.	25.	26.
I.	PLAN OUTLAY	10447.00	4125.00	71607.00	78097.00
II.	State's budgetary resources 1984-85 rates				
i)	Balance from current revenues	870.61	-826.88	8176.00	6662.39
ii)	Share of Small savings	1343.10	1749.00	11010.36	11539.19
iii)	State Provident Fund	261.90	370.00	4725.68	5026.60
iv)	Misc. Capital Receipts	-274.61	-885.43	-4464.77	-5618.68
v)	Adjustment of Overdraft	-372.40	-228.88	-1566.73	-1729.53
	Total (II): 1828.60	177.81	17880.54	15879.97	
III.	Contribution of State enterprises at 1984-85 rates				
i)	S.E.Bs.	-131.45	57.25	-1304.15	-1568.81
ii)	R.T.Cs.	120.59	-168.79	-373.53	-415.37
iii)	Others	-	-	15.00	15.00
	Total (III)	-10.86	-111.54	-1662.68	-1969.18
IV.	Addl. Resource Mobilisation	2870.22	1671.00	21912.07	22469.21
V.	State's budgetary resources and contribution of public enterprises at current rates (II+III+IV):	4687.96	1737.27	38129.93	36380.00

VI.	Market Borrowing (Net)	1550.05	806.54	9262.21	9942.00
VII.	Negotitated Loans				
i)	Loans from L.I.C	324.94	162.82	2102.78	2234.50
ii)	Loans from R.B.I	10.79	10.74	202.72	222.22
iii)	Loans from R.E.C	103.90	112.67	848.28	982.43
iv)	Others (IDBI)	161.81	81.07	1034.00	1100.00
	Total (VII) :	601.44	367.30	4187.78	4539.15
VIII.	Market Borrowing + Negotiated loans (VI + VII):	2151.49	1173.84	13449.99	14481.15
IX.	State's total resources (V + VIII) :	6839.45	2911.11	51579.92	50861.15
X.	Central Assistance:				
i)	Normal	2944.85	1007.65	16482.31	23584.36
ii)	Externally aided projects	670.00	215.00	3689.00	3800.00
iii)	APA adjustments	-7.30	-8.76	-144.23	-148.51
	Total (X) :	3607.55	1213.89	20027.08	27235.85
XI.	Aggregate Resoruces (IX+X) :	10447.00	4125.00	71607.00	78097.00

Source: Government of India, Ministry of Finance, 'Statistical Statements on Finances and plans of States and Union Territories 1985.

TABLE V.1 : CENTRAL TRANSFERS TO THE STATES OTHER HAN THOSE BY THE FINANCE COMMISSION AND THE PLANNING COMMISSION

1980-81 to 1986-87 (Rs. Crores)

PURPOSE 1980-81	1981-82 (RE)	1982-83 (RE)	1983-84 (RE)	1984-85 (RE)	1985-86 (RE)	1986-87 (RE)	(RE)
I. GRANTS							
1. Relief on account of natural calamities	143.00	103.00	250.00	250.00	230.00	320.00	100.00
2. Gandak, Western Kosi canal and Jalpapur flood control works	2.02	1.06	0.62	0.60	2.15	7.31	3.00
3. Handloom Industries	36.00	51.75	57.00	57.97	77.10	85.88	110.55
4. Improvement in the salary scales of University and college teachers and youth welfare schemes	15.63	13.14	11.97	12.36	12.50	13.79	15.05
5. Modernisation of Police force	3.75	4.00	3.75	3.75	4.07	5.00	5.00
6. Compensation for loss of revenue due to prohibition	20.00	3.12	-	0.50	0.50	-	-
7. Police Grants	5.39	1.33	4.40	3.37	11.37	10.25	2.75
8. Payment for Home guards	-	-	-	10.77	15.80	17.00	17.00
9. Improvement of Roads including border roads	29.48	32.92	38.72	45.30	55.58	58.94	62.41
10. Rehabilitation of displaced persons	3.65	3.65	2.68	2.60	3.36	10.40	11.50
11. Compensation to State Govt. for exemption from sales tax on aviation turbine fuel	6.35	5.48	5.48	5.48	5.00	5.48	30.00
12. Other items	17.23	7.17	7.25	13.02	35.38	-	
II. LOANS							
1. Fertiliser and other inputs	200.00	200.00	250.00	260.00	260.00	250.00	255.00
2. Loans against small savings	715.00	860.00	1100.00	1400.00	2000.00	2900.00	3200.00
3. Pre-1974 arrear assistance towards relief on damage caused by natrual calamities	2.00	2.00	2.00	2.00	2.00	-	-
4. Ways and Means Advances	300.00	500.00	600.00	800.00	800.00	1200.00	800.00
5. Loans to clear overdrafts	76.34	-	1743.46	@500.00	@440.00	1628.01	-
6. Other Purposes	24.53	29.21	28.17	46.44	63.54	517.40	48.93
TOTAL: LOANS	1317.87	1591.21	3723.63	3008.44	3565.54	6495.41	4303.93
GRAND TOTAL (I + II)	1600.37	1817.83	4105.50	3414.16	4018.35	7029.46	4661.19

\# It represent loans to eover gap in resources

Source: Explanatory Memoranda to the Central Budgets.

TABLE V.2 : DISCRETIONARY TRANSFERS TO STATES

(Rs. Crores)

	1974-75 to 1978-79			1979-80			1980-81 to 1984-85		
	GRANTS	LOANS	TOTAL	GRANTS	LOANS	TOTAL	GRANTS	LOANS	TOTAL
GROUP 'A' STATES	189.69	505.17	694.86	27.22	248.82	276.04	268.25	2305.41	2573.66
1. Punjab	79.96	115.99	195.95	2.08	28.37	30.45	15.13	73.84	88.97
2. Haryana	42.44	40.75	83.19	0.91	18.24	19.15	17.07	218.24	235.31
3. Maharashtra	45.75	222.87	268.62	16.18	136.55	152.73	102.10	1350.10	1452.20
4. Gujarat	21.54	125.56	147.10	8.05	65.66	73.71	133.95	663.23	797.18
GROUP 'B' STATES	127.49	889.30	1016.79	50.42	462.06	512.48	340.90	2341.70	2682.60
5. West Bengal	44.01	486.88	530.89	8.10	110.71	118.81	100.85	1141.87	1242.72
6. Karnataka	8.85	94.94	103.79	2.40	30.71	33.11	33.82	353.60	387.42
7. Tamil Nadu	21.99	133.21	155.20	16.39	36.60	52.99	98.86	345.25	444.11
8. Kerala	7.20	73.30	80.50	2.19	9.21	11.40	25.39	150.04	175.43
9. Rajasthan	45.44	100.97	146.41	21.34	274.83	296.17	81.98	350.94	432.92
GROUPS 'C' STATES	288.09	1285.22	1573.31	95.22	267.49	362.71	958.29	2871.99	3830.28
10. Andhra Pradesh	49.33	127.83	177.16	47.16	38.96	86.12	133.01	649.53	782.54
11. Orissa	94.13	76.60	170.73	4.82	16.97	21.79	328.17	189.13	517.30
12. Madhya Pradesh	19.88	168.90	188.78	4.50	35.47	39.97	76.40	333.83	410.23
13. Uttar Pradesh	90.49	563.69	654.18	30.95	109.67	140.62	333.31	941.17	1274.48
14. Bihar	34.26	348.20	382.46	7.79	66.42	74.21	87.40	758.33	845.73
TOTAL 14 STATES	605.27	2679.69	3284.96	172.86	978.37	1151.23	1567.44	7519.10	9086.54
SPL. CATEGORY STATES	134.72	187.35	322.07	30.63	34.04	64.67	301.31	525.24	826.55
ALL STATES	739.99	2867.04	3607.03	203.49	1012.41	1215.90	1868.75	8044.34	9913.09

Source: Various Issues of Reserve Bank of India Bulletin.

TABLE V.3 : PERCAPITA DISCRETIONARY TRANSFERS TO STATES

(Rs. Crores)

	1974-75 to 1978-79			1979-80			1980-81 to 1984-85		
	Grants	Loans	Total	Grants	Loans	Total	Grants	Loans	Total
GROUP 'A' STATES	16.80	44.74	61.54	2.25	20.56	22.81	21.19	182.10	203.29
1. Punjab	52.95	76.81	129.76	1.29	17.62	18.91	9.01	43.95	52.96
2. Haryana	37.23	35.75	72.98	0.74	14.83	15.57	13.23	169.18	182.41
3. Maharashtra	8.14	39.66	47.80	2.69	22.72	25.41	16.26	214.98	231.24
4. Gujarat	7.13	41.58	48.71	2.48	20.20	22.68	39.28	194.50	233.78
GROUP 'B' STATES	7.01	49.43	56.52	2.63	24.10	26.73	17.05	117.14	134.19
5. West Bengal	8.95	98.96	107.91	1.55	21.13	22.68	18.47	209.13	227.60
6. Karnataka	2.68	28.77	31.45	0.68	8.68	9.36	9.12	95.31	104.43
7. Tamil Nadu	4.93	29.87	34.80	3.49	7.80	11.29	20.43	71.33	91.76
8. Kerala	3.09	31.46	34.55	0.89	3.74	4.63	9.96	58.84	68.80
9. Rajasthan	15.25	33.88	49.13	6.59	84.82	91.41	23.90	102.31	126.21
GROUPS 'C' STATES	10.26	45.77	56.03	3.18	8.93	12.11	30.63	91.79	122.42
10. Andhra Pradesh	10.23	26.52	36.75	9.19	7.59	16.78	24.86	121.41	146.27
11. Orissa	39.05	31.78	70.83	4.65	1.90	6.68	8.58	124.31	195.95
12. Madhya Pradesh	4.26	36.17	40.43	0.90	7.11	8.01	14.64	63.95	78.59
13. Uttar Pradesh	9.14	56.94	66.08	2.92	10.35	13.27	30.06	84.87	114.93
14. Bihar	5.46	55.45	60.91	1.16	9.91	11.07	12.50	108.49	120.99
TOTAL 14 STATES	10.55	46.72	57.27	2.82	15.98	18.80	24.51	117.60	142.11
SPL. CATEGORY STATES	43.04	59.86	102.90	8.98	9.98	18.96	83.47	145.50	228.97
ALL STATES	12.23	47.40	59.63	3.15	15.66	18.81	27.66	119.09	146.75
POP		1976			1979			1981	

Source: Worked out on the basis of figures presented in Table-2

TABLE V.4 : LOANS TO STATES AGAINST SMALL SAVINGS COLLECTIONS

(Rs. Crores)

		1979-80 Accounts	1980-81 Accts.	1981-82 Accts.	1982-83 Accts.	1983-84 Accts.	1984-85 Accts.	1980-85 Accts.	1980-85 Original Estimates	1980-85 Annual approvel	1985-90 Approved estimates	1985-86 Approved estimates
1.	Andhra Pradesh	20.42	24.05	30.06	42.54	56.27	89.08	242.00	137.14	241.94	671.56	110.00
2.	Assam	16.50	21.74	30.30	26.77	36.67	36.57	152.05	127.98	133.04	268.60	44.00
3.	Bihar	53.57	64.26	65.59	99.88	75.03	184.43	489.10	359.74	403.52	1007.35	165.00
4.	Gujarat	55.17	65.57	85.13	106.67	162.58	184.32	604.27	370.53	483.76	1220.00	200.00
5.	Haryana	11.17	9.58	33.46	16.18	37.17	42.62	139.01	106.85	110.50	235.13	38.50
6.	Himachal Pradesh	6.93	9.64	12.52	14.66	16.68	22.67	76.17	43.85	59.20	141.04	23.10
7.	Jammu & Kashmir	5.20	8.04	7.57	8.88	7.60	12.19	44.28	38.14	49.74	79.36	13.00
8.	Karnataka	24.65	26.33	36.83	52.68	68.79	96.31	280.94	171.52	196.74	493.17	89.20
9.	Kerala	6.74	10.81	10.57	14.83	13.33	23.91	73.45	47.02	63.69	141.03	23.10
10.	Madhya Pradesh	25.93	33.50	25.91	32.69	42.19	74.79	209.08	177.05	171.40	402.95	66.00
11.	Maharashtra	129.13	163.04	179.26	219.27	317.32	435.96	1314.85	824.18	946.50	2283.00	380.00
12.	Manipur	0.07	0.17	0.09	0.09	0.16	0.40	0.91	0.50	0.89	2.36	0.30
13.	Meghalaya	0.50	1.10	1.10	1.53	1.88	2.78	8.39	3.40	4.98	18.47	3.00
14.	Nagaland	0.08	0.15	0.12	0.16	0.20	0.33	0.96	0.92	1.02	1.70	0.20
15.	Orissa	11.80	15.45	15.44	20.92	28.03	11.10	90.94	82.39	94.65	213.69	350.00
16.	Punjab	21.17	21.80	25.82	34.07	31.64	73.38	186.71	175.00	146.50	310.25	55.00
17.	Rajasthan	23.56	7.50	32.27	33.89	48.95	84.10	206.71	114.17	133.40	503.63	82.50
18.	Sikkim	0.02	0.04	0.04	1.24	0.47	0.07	1.86		0.15	0.50	0.05
19.	Tamil Nadu	36.20	45.70	36.05	41.43	42.56	78.39	244.13	241.77	225.96	436.50	71.50
20.	Tripura	0.78	1.57	1.14	1.61	2.64	3.13	10.09	3.67	6.01	16.80	2.50
21.	Uttar Pradesh	83.85	70.69	108.33	132.52	189.23	223.68	724.45	483.41	605.00	1343.10	220.00
22.	West Bengal	91.11	111.53	144.53	201.51	219.88	254.51	931.96	842.00	979.00	1749.00	283.00
	TOTAL:	624.55	712.26	882.13	1104.02	1399.27	1984.72	6682.40	4351.23	5057.59	11539.19	1905.00

Source: Govt. of India, Ministry of Finance, Statistical Statements on Finances and Plans of States and Union Territories 1985.

TABLE VI.1: STATE-WISE CUMULATIVE ASSISTANCE SANCTIONED BY ALL-INDIA FINANCIAL INSTITUTIONS AT THE END OF ACCOUNTING YEAR 1984

(Rs. Crores)

Sl. No.	State	% of Population 1981	NABARD (June 1984)		L. I. C. (March 1984)		I. F. CI (June 1984)	
			Amount	%	Amount	%	Amount	%
1.	Andhra Pradesh	7.8	530.79	12.1	279.17	5.9	214.04	9.9
2.	Assam	2.9	34.02	0.8	81.46	1.7	22.51	1.0
3.	Bihar	10.2	275.85	6.3	268.04	5.6	60.07	2.8
4.	Gujarat	5.0	233.37	5.3	473.92	9.9	239.73	11.1
5.	Haryana	1.9	350.76	8.0	183.24	3.8	71.64	3.3
6.	Himachal Pradesh	0.6	13.20	0.3	19.96	0.4	20.99	1.0
7.	Jammu & Kashmir	0.9	14.02	0.3	44.50	0.9	6.85	0.3
8.	Karnataka	5.4	274.19	6.3	246.62	5.2	160.17	7.4
9.	Kerala	3.7	112.01	2.6	234.34	4.9	67.51	3.1
10.	Madhya Pradesh	7.6	324.24	7.4	219.33	4.6	84.36	3.9
11.	Maharastra	9.2	402.94	9.2	710.88	14.9	329.57	15.3
12.	Orissa	3.8	161.42	3.7	165.97	3.5	68.33	3.2
13.	Punjab	2.4	457.77	10.5	186.24	3.9	91.40	4.2
14.	Rajasthan	5.0	209.73	4.8	276.61	5.8	124.11	5.8
15.	Tamil Nadu	7.1	231.54	5.3	409.81	8.6	188.26	8.7
16.	Uttar Pradesh	16.2	645.81	14.8	516.78	10.8	234.70	10.9
17.	West Bengal	8.0	85.02	1.9	371.28	7.8	121.50	5.6
18.	Other	0.2	8.36	0.2	0.52	0.1	5.72	0.3
19.	Union Territories	9.8	10.26	0.2	0.31	0.1	44.78	2.1
	ALL INDIA TOTAL	100.0	4376.23	100.00	4772.14	100.00	2156.75	100.00

(Contd.) TABLE VI.1 : STATE WISE CUMULATIVE ASSISTANCE SANCTIONED BY ALL INDIA INANCIAL INSTITUTIONS AS AT THE END OF ACCOUNTING YEAR 1984

Sl. No.	State	I.D.B.I. (June 1984) Amount	%	I.C.I.C.I. (December) Amount	%	H U D C O (March, 1984) Amount	%	Total Amount	%
1.	Andhra Pradesh	1047.10	8.4	219.09	7.3	101.66	9.1	2391.85	8.6
2.	Assam	109.00	0.9	16.56	0.5	4.07	0.4	267.62	1.0
3.	Bihar	351.80	2.8	109.07	3.6	24.31	2.4	1089.14	3.9
4.	Gujarat	1783.10	14.4	418.63	14.0	122.69	11.0	3272.44	11.8
5.	Haryana	399.30	3.2	80.81	2.7	42.71	3.8	1128.46	4.0
6.	Himachal Pradesh	121.50	1.0	-	-	5.41	0.5	181.06	0.6
7.	Jammu & Kashmir	123.00	1.0	-	-	9.79	0.9	198.16	0.7
8.	Karnataka	932.50	7.5	212.20	7.1	72.61	7.0	1898.29	6.8
9.	Kerala	401.90	3.2	47.61	1.6	56.71	5.1	920.98	3.3
10.	Madhya Pradesh	440.20	3.6	119.09	4.0	48.30	4.1	1235.52	4.4
11.	Maharastra	1804.40	14.6	759.23	25.2	117.10	10.4	4124.12	14.8
12.	Orissa	410.70	3.4	89.28	3.0	32.97	3.0	934.67	3.4
13.	Punjab	422.60	3.4	81.34	2.7	43.55	3.9	1282.90	4.6
14.	Rajasthan	622.60	5.0	127.67	4.2	112.14	10.8	1472.86	5.3
15.	Tamil Nadu	135.10	10.9	269.91	9.0	100.33	9.0	2544.95	9.1
16.	Uttar Pradesh	977.70	7.9	188.80	6.3	121.18	10.9	2684.97	9.6
17.	West Bengal	644.50	5.2	151.32	5.0	32.92	3.6	1406.54	5.0
18.	Other	38.70	0.3	114.00	3.8	3.66	0.3	170.96	0.6
19.	Union Territories	407.10	3.3	-	-	45.11	4.0	507.56	1.8
	ALL INDIA TOTAL	12389.20	100.00	3005.61	100.00	1115.40	100.00	27815.33	100.00

Source: Government of Andhra Pradesh, Finance and Planing (Plg.Wing) Department, Seventh Five Year Plan 1985-90.

TABLE VI.2 : FINANCIAL ASSISTANCE DISBURSED BY PUBLIC SECTOR NON-BANKING FINANCIAL INSTITUTIONS* CUMALATIVE UP TO THE END OF MARCH, 1981 AND 1983

	States	Disbursement (Rs. crores)		% to total		Percapita assistance Rs.	
		1981	1983	1981	1983	1981	1983
		1	2	3	4	5	6
1.	Andhra Pradesh	502.16	862.23	6.3	7.0	94	161
2.	Assam	101.11	117.64	1.3	1.0	51	59
3.	Bihar	255.59	380.12	3.2	3.1	37	54
4.	Gujarat	1,006.80	1,555.82	12.7	12.8	296	456
5.	Haryana	207.49	327.54	2.6	2.7	161	253
6.	Karnataka	613.33	935.73	7.7	7.7	166	252
7.	Kerala	253.28	391.66	3.2	3.2	100	154
8.	Madhya Pradesh	221.30	369.87	2.8	3.0	42	71
9.	Maharastra	1,727.89	2,421.24	21.8	19.9	276	386
10.	Orissa	151.26	304.67	1.9	2.5	58	116
11.	Punjab	232.71	415.66	2.9	3.4	140	248
12.	Rajasthan	298.07	534.66	3.8	4.4	87	156
13.	Tamil Nadu	782.38	1,161.80	9.9	9.5	162	240
14.	Uttar Pradesh	571.54	894.46	7.2	7.3	52	81
15.	West Bengal	628.70	895.79	7.9	7.3	115	164
	Other States						
1.	Himachal Pradesh	35.58	95.72	0.4	0.8	85	224
2.	Jammu & Kashmir	62.75	104.98	0.8	0.9	105	175
3.	Manipur	0.93	3.25	-	-	7	23
4.	Meghalaya	12.92	16.79	0.2	0.1	99	126
5.	Nagaland	6.12	7.66	0.1	0.1	77	99
6.	Sikkim	0.62	1.22	-	-	21	39
7.	Tripura	4.27	8.94	0.1	0.1	20	44
8.	Union Territories	252.92	387.98	3.2	3.2	254	394
	ALL INDIA	7,929.92	12,195.63	100.00	100.00	116	178

Note * Institutions covered here are; IDBI, IFCI, ICICI, LIC, UTI, GIC, IRCI, SFCS AND SIDCS.

Source: Basic Statistics relating to Indian Economy Vol. 2 States September, 1984.

TABLE VI.3 : VALUE OF PROPERTY (GROSS BLOCK) INVESTED BY CENTRAL GOVT. PUBLIC SECTOR UNDERTAKINGS

(Rs. in Crores)

		1st, 2nd and 3rd Plans	1966-67 to 1968-69	Fourth Plan 1969-74	Fifth Plan 1974-78	1978-79 to 1980-81	1981-82 to 1983-84	Cummulative as on 31.3.1984 Amount	Percapita (Rs.)
1.	Andhra Pradesh	45.6	41.3	116.1	286.7	497.9	2099.4	3087	576
2.	Assam	27.9	36.2	93.1	213.5	296.2	1263.1	1930	970
3.	Bihar	324.1	297.1	847.1	1347.0	726.1	1610.6	5152	737
4.	Gujarat	26.6	60.1	163.1	377.1	441.6	443.5	1512	444
5.	Haryana	-	7.1	3.8	133.8	116.4	99.9	361	279
6.	Himachal Pradesh	0.1	1.6	(-)1.1	86.9	60.3	27.2	175	409
7.	Jammu & Kashmir	-	-	6.2	(-)0.4	4.2	18.0	28	47
8.	Karnataka	55.5	24.1	80.6	254.2	430.2	354.4	1199	323
9.	Kerala	38.1	63.3	71.8	152.3	156.5	233.0	715	281
10.	Madhya Pradesh	444.0	99.2	186.3	1064.1	841.1	1876.3	4511	865
11.	Maharastra	60.1	40.8	103.0	705.3	917.6	4091.2	5918	943
12.	Manipur	-	-	-	-	-	-	-	-
13.	Meghalaya	-	-	-	-	-	-	-	-
14.	Nagaland	-	-	-	-	-	-	-	-
15.	Orissa	290.4	132.8	107.4	123.8	384.6	1126.0	2165	821
16.	Punjab	39.0	(-)6.4	9.9	183.2	192.9	118.4	537	320
17.	Rajasthan	4.2	23.0	88.3	161.6	84.5	281.4	643	188
18.	Sikkim	-	-	-	-	-	-	-	-
19.	Tamil Nadu	174.6	87.6	103.0	198.2	359.0	1204.4	2127	439
20.	Tripura	-	-	-	-	-	-	-	-
21.	Uttar Pradesh	49.7	87.3	80.5	269.5	530.9	1076.1	2094	189
22.	West Bengal	329.3	82.1	239.5	407.9	672.3	1178.9	2910	533
Unallocated and others* (including UTs)		335.8	140.9	613.9	1365.0	754.0	574.4	3784	
	TOTAL	2245.0	1218.1	2912.5	7329.7	7466.5	17676.2	38848	567

* Represents besides unallocated expenditure during construction, value of other miscellaneous assets like exploration, equipments, storage, installations etc., for which Statewise figures are not readily available and value of aircrafts, ships etc., not assigned to any particular State.

Source: Annual Reports of the working of Industrial and Commercial undertakings.

TABLE VI.4 : STATEWISE DISTRIBUTION OF INVESTMENTS UPTO 31st MARCH, 1983 BY THE LIFE INSURANCE CORPORATION OF INDIA (Rs. in Crores)

	States	State Electricity Boards	State Govts. for Housing Schemes	Co-Op Housing Finance Societies	Municipal Committees and State ovt. for urban water Supply	ZPs for Rural Piped Water Supply
1.	Andhra Pradesh	68.52	41.47	33.20	11.96	3.45
2.	Assam	28.59	6.45	1.00	1.68	-
3.	Bihar	73.44	29.01	14.50	-	-
4.	Gujarat	100.69	30.30	189.47	44.16	1.06
5.	Haryana	91.62	8.83	4.75	15.82	-
6.	Himachal Pradesh	8.38	5.09	-	2.13	-
7.	Jammu & Kashmir	5.51	7.15	-	3.53	-
8.	Karnataka	20.20	30.36	15.90	56.33	-
9.	Kerala	71.60	23.91	32.00	33.08	4.98
10.	Madhya Pradesh	67.64	23.43	21.40	24.55	-
11.	Maharashtra	104.38	28.35	163.18	66.68	44.89
12.	Maharastra	104.38	28.35	163.18	66.68	44.89
12.	Manipur	-	1.42	-	1.86	-
13.	Meghalaya	14.28	1.49	0.75	2.50	-
14.	Nagaland	-	0.34	-	2.11	-
15.	Orissa	71.07	33.12	2.00	6.80	-
16.	Punjab	75.16	19.90	7.50	20.42	-
17.	Rajasthan	92.08	22.61	15.20	27.08	-
18.	Sikkim	-	0.43	-	-	-
19.	Tamil Nadu	100.65	42.75	83.92	62.62	-
20.	Tripura	-	2.49	-	0.43	-
21.	Uttar Pradesh	241.15	51.03	11.55	45.21	1.75
22.	West Bengal	117.38	41.64	25.10	1.27	-
	Union Territories	-	12.12	7.95	3.07	-
	Grand Total	1,352.34	463.69	631.37	433.29	56.13

Source: 26th Annual Report of the Life Insurance Corporation of India for the year ended 31st March, 1983.

TABLE VI.4 : STATEWISE DISTRIBUTION OF INVESTMENTS UPTO 31ST MARCH, 1983 BY THE LIFE INSURANCE CORPORATION OF INDIA

(Rs. Crores)

	States	Sugar co-operative Societies	Industrial Estates	State Transport Corporations	Companies and Industrial Co-op. Societies	Total (Col 2-10)	Stock Exchange Investements
1.	Andhra Pradesh	4.23	0.40	7.93	24.58	195.74	116.96
2.	Assam	-	-	4.50	2.86	45.08	44.56
3.	Bihar	-	-	-	22.81	139.76	142.32
4.	Gujarat	2.64	13.73	8.42	65.41	455.88	110.98
5.	Haryana	1.75	-	-	3.66	126.43	70.30
6.	Himachal Pradesh	-	-	-	2.21	17.81	3.67
7.	Jammu & Kashmir	-	-	-	1.19	17.38	23.39
8.	Karnataka	3.79	-	8.72	77.95	213.25	76.52
9.	Kerala	0.40	-	5.64	8.04	179.65	75.29
10.	Madhya Pradesh	0.40	-	12.62	6.57	156.61	71.38
11.	Maharastra	12.52	14.28	16.91	75.83	527.02	271.80
12.	Manipur	-	-	-	-	3.28	3.62
13.	Meghalaya	-	-	-	1.40	20.42	7.53
14.	Nagaland	-	-	-	1.44	3.89	7.28
15.	Orissa	0.60	-	5.35	10.12	129.06	69.81
16.	Punjab	0.15	-	5.60	7.77	136.50	71.50
17.	Rajasthan	0.40	0.04	6.90	12.26	177.57	133.09
18.	Sikkim	-	-	-	-	0.43	-
19.	Tamil Nadu	2.65	0.15	5.57	32.27	330.58	125.47
20.	Tripura	-	-	-	0.20	3.12	2.56
21.	Uttar Pradesh	7.51	-	17.35	35.58	411.13	200.68
22.	West Bengal	-	-	-	34.22	220.61	186.91
	Union Territories	-	-	-	3.82	26.96	10.42
	Grand Total	37.05	28.61	105.51	430.19	3,538.18	1,826.04

Source: 26th Annual Report of the Life Insurance Corporation of India for the year ended 31st March, 1983.

TABLE VI.5 : STATEMENT SHOWING STATE-WISE DISTRIBUTION OF COMMERCIAL BANK OFFICES IN INDIA

	July 19	As at the end of December							June, 30
	1969	1975	1976	1977	1978	1979	1980	1981	1982
I. NORTHERN REGION	1,268	3,493	4,055	4,583	4,985	5,274	5,636	6,159	6,289
1. Haryana	174	492	585	660	695	732	779	850	871
2. Himachal Pradesh	41	198	235	283	311	320	362	398	412
3. Jammu & Kashmir	53	227	274	325	356	386	426	535	546
4. Punjab	354	1,062	1,231	1,379	1,461	1,509	1,566	1,655	1,672
5. Rajasthan	369	853	984	1,121	1,277	1,421	1,567	1,737	1,785
6. Chandigarh	21	57	66	72	75	78	79	84	89
7. Delhi	274	604	680	748	810	828	857	900	914
II. NORTH-EASTERN REGION	91	337	476	561	653	696	739	828	844
1. Assam	74	253	339	386	437	465	492	550	562
2. Manipur	2	11	21	25	33	35	36	39	39
3. Meghalaya	7	28	37	43	53	54	59	66	67
4. Nfagaland	3	13	22	24	32	35	39	45	45
5. Tripura	5	22	42	67	69	76	81	86	86
6. Arunachal Pradesh	-	9	11	11	17	19	20	24	25
7. Mizoram	-	1	4	5	12	12	12	12	13
8. Sikkim	-	-	-	-	-	-	-	6	7
III. EASTERN REGION	880	2,495	3,122	3,673	4,074	4,548	5,326	6,202	6,512
1. Bihar	274	891	1,092	1,306	1,498	1,775	2,233	2,660	2,807
2. Orissa	100	356	477	616	698	767	914	1,142	1,228
3. West Bengal	505	1,243	1,546	1,741	1,856	1,994	2,162	2,388	2,465
4. Andaman & Nicobar Islands	1	5	7	10	12	12	12	12	12

IV. CENTRAL REGION	1,097	3,097	3,739	4,289	4,824	5,398	6,038	6,870	7,257
1. Madhya Pradesh	344	999	1,176	1,373	1,578	1,769	2,058	2,358	2,510
2. Uttar Pradesh	753	2,098	2,563	2,916	3,246	3,629	3,980	4,512	4,747
V. WESTERN REGION	1,970	4,154	4.585	5,094	5,432	5,692	6,113	6,503	6,592
1. Gujarat	758	1,666	1,848	2,043	2,143	2,204	2,318	2,425	2,452
2. Maharastra	1,125	2,335	2,562	2,839	3,062	3,255	3,548	3,826	3,888
3. Goa, Daman & Diu	87	149	171	208	223	229	241	246	246
4. Dadra & Nagar Haveli	-	4	4	4	4	4	6	6	6
VI. SOUTHERN REGION	3,015	6,878	7,678	8,791	9,536	9,949	10,740	11,485	11,683
1. Andhra Pradesh	571	1,494	1,723	2,041	2,314	2,433	2,676	2,945	2,998
2. Karnataka	761	1,857	2,056	2,278	2,480	2,598	2,751	2,907	2,973
3. Kerala	605	1,435	1,617	1,945	2,059	2,128	2,306	2,397	2,428
4. Tamil Nadu	1,066	2,058	2,240	2,481	2,635	2,740	2,952	3,177	3,224
5. Pondicherry	12	30	37	41	43	45	50	54	55
6. Lakshadweep	-	4	5	5	5	5	5	5	5
ALL INDIA	8,321	20,454@	23,655@	26,996@	29,504@	31,557@	34,587@	38,047	39,177

@ Excludes one branch of S.B.I. in Sikkim

Source: Government of India, Ministry of Finance, Department of Economic Affairs. "Current Banking Statistics - December, 1982".

TABLE VI.6 : STATE-WISE DISTRIBUTION OF BANK OFFICES, AGGREGATE DEPOSITS AND TOTAL CREDIT OF PUBLIC SECTOR BANKS@ AND PERCENTAGE SHARE OF ADVANCES TO PRIORITY SECTORS

State/Union Territory	No. of offices at the end of		Deposits (Rs. crores)		Bank credit (Rs. cores)		Share of sectors credit	priority in bank (per cent)
	June 1969	June 1985*	June 1969	Dec. 1984*	June 1969	Dec. 1984*	June 1969	December 1983*
1	2	3	4	5	6	7	8	9
STATES								
1. Andhra Pradesh	444	4062	121.11	3937	122.00	3053	24.4	56.7
2. Assam	67	852	33.20	752	12.85	381	10.3	44.3
3. Bihar	269	3959	168.67	3112	52.05	1199	9.1	57.2
4. Gujarat	750	3021	401.31	4650	194.89	2552	15.9	46.3
5. Haryana	140	1090	48.78	1267	23.15	886	28.2	69.7
6. Himachal Pradesh	41	518	12.38	432	3.49	186	2.7	68.2
7. Jammu & Kashmir	17	670	17.95	346	0.86	134	30.3	69.9
8. Karnataka	510	3832	187.79	3285	143.04	2776	24.8	45.5
9. Kerala	331	2694	116.79	2103	76.95	1430	27.6	49.5
10. Madhya Pradesh	332	3611	107.43	2404	63.14	1405	22.3	56.9
11. Maharashtra	946	4797	902.67	11434	911.79	10832	12.4	21.1
12. Manipur	2	60	1.06	26	0.15	16	..	55.6
13. Meghalaya	7	122	8.87	102	2.52	26	50.0	68.8
14. Nagaland	2	65	1.07	58	0.06	22	40.0	66.5
15. Orissa	96	1672	29.49	819	14.60	642	11.2	58.0
16. Punjab	290	1986	185.41	3717	50.29	1816	27.9	70.3
17. Rajasthan	311	2580	73.73	1563	38.20	1088	16.8	56.2
18. Tamil Nadu	721	3892	233.48	3930	311.32	3785	25.5	39.3
19. Tripura	5	104	3.76	63	0.16	39	9.5	87.0
20. Uttar Pradesh	639	7046	337.15	6761	153.74	3033	16.9	58.6
21. West Bengal	428	3167	456.45	6641	525.80	3717	4.4	23.2

UNION TERRITORIES									
1.	Chandigarh	19	104	34.55	517	64.13	1011	4.2	27.0
2.	Delhi	207	1029	359.80	6280	244.90	3669	10.2	14.7
3.	Goa, Daman & Diu	83	259	48.68	600	19.63	211	12.6	41.2
4.	Pondichery	11	62	5.06	93	4.74	54	12.9	69.3
5.	All others**	1	131	0.33	115	0.01	27	..	73.8
	TOTAL	6,669	51,385	3,896.97	65007	3,034.60	43990	14.9	38.3

@ Include State Bank of India and its subsidiaries and 20 Nationalised Banks.
* Data are provisional
** Include Andaman & Nicobar Islands, Arunachal Pradesh, Dadra and Nagar Haveli, Lakshadweep, Mizoram and Sikkim.

Notes:1. Deposits excludes Inter-bank deposit.
2. Bank credit excludes dues from banks but includes amount of bills rediscounted with R.B.I/I.D.B.I/ other financial institutions and value of participation certificates.
3. The data relating of deposit and bank credit relate to the last Friday of the month and are based on monthly return on aggregate deposit and gross bank credit.

TABLE VI.7 : STATEWISE DISTRIBUTION OF DEPOSITS OF SCHDULED COMMERCIAL BANKS

(Rs. Crores)

Region/State/ Union Territory	As at the end of the December							
	1969	1975	1976	1977	1978	1979	1980	1981
I.NORTHERN REGION	966.21	2,666.58	3,591.27	4,348.29	5,610.04	6,655.91	8,024.78	9,537.64
1. Haryana	64.10	196.30	264.85	343.77	427.10	526.64	657.64	810.69
2. Himachal Pradesh	17.51	71.98	89.30	105.51	139.91	169.27	216.65	258.57
3. Jammu & Kashmir	26.70	98.03	132.57	182.98	278.58	295.28	375.89	389.15
4. Punjab	230.36	669.45	839.52	1,010.72	1,279.76	1,595.76	1,963.56	2,400.52
5. Rajasthan	93.55	261.64	365.81	440.31	564.04	688.15	845.37	1,024.36
6. Chandigarh	40.35	89.08	131.86	143.20	193.63	261.20	277.33	351.99
7. Delhi	493.14	1,280.15	1,767.36	2,121.80	2,727.02	3,119.61	3,688.34	4,302.36
II. NORTH-EASTERN REGION	53.55	169.64	222.60	276.56	347.88	440.07	500.13	619.37
1. Assam	47.78	123.79	164.84	207.43	256.56	308.58	350.29	442.39
2. Manipur	-	4.18	6.49	7.10	9.81	19.93	14.78	20.30
3. Meghalaya	-	18.73	24.70	26.76	34.36	47.53	54.27	56.82
4. Nagaland	1.24	5.59	5.73	8.96	12.44	15.15	20.04	24.23
5. Sikkim	-	1.87	2.55	3.44	3.40	5.16	4.92	7.36
6. Tripura	4.53	12.20	13.38	16.97	21.50	26.82	37.26	43.99
7. Arunachal Pradesh	-	2.08	2.97	3.72	5.74	8.42	9.64	13.19
8. Mizoram	-	1.20	1.94	2.24	4.07	8.38	8.93	11.09
III. EASTERN REGION	934.29	2,584.83	3,166.10	3,612.36	4,485.20	5,196.58	6,049.15	7,455.47
1. Bihar	186.08	630.73	784.40	877.66	1,067.60	1,286.80	1,558.69	1,932.40
2. Orissa	35.96	127.82	162.31	201.04	263.62	323.09	426.54	543.94

3. West Bengal	712.25	1,823.66	2,215.91	2,529.39	3,148.30	3,579.24	4,055.28	4,969.89
4. Andaman and Nichobar Islands	-	2.62	3.48	4.27	5.68	7.45	8.64	9.24
IV. CENTRAL REGION	551.98	1,630.23	2,118.17	2,526.44	3,174.94	3,836.57	4,782.30	5,779.97
1. Madhya Pradesh	126.38	394.12	531.83	634.74	791.64	966.79	1,174.78	1,408.24
2. Uttar Pradesh	425.60	1,236.11	1,586.34	1,891.70	2,383.30	2,869.78	3,607.52	4,371.73
V. WESTERN REGION	1,740.99	3,982.66	5,086.08	6,121.97	7,384.06	8,480.48	9,822.82	11,522.57
1. Gujarat	459.06	983.74	1,255.02	1,524.30	1,882.04	2,204.74	2,576.81	3,042.33
2. Maharastra	1,229.77	2,872.96	3,671.52	4,413.94	5,284.80	6,007.91	6,923.59	8,102.90
3. Dadra, Nagar Haveli	-	0.31	0.41	0.50	0.86	1.17	1.42	1.88
4. Goa, Daman & Diu	52.16	125.65	159.13	183.23	216.36	266.66	321.00	375.46
VI. SOUTHERN REGION	899.72	2,677.35	3,443.50	4,328.46	5,507.35	6,615.60	7,817.86	9,344.45
1. Andhra Pradesh	173.05	596.60	804.79	993.81	1,279.13	1,591.60	1,863.35	2,293.51
2. Karnataka	255.22	670.85	877.21	1,117.70	1,341.26	1,598.23	1,933.51	2,302.28
3. Kerala	152.72	442.27	568.46	760.52	1,042.22	1,211.27	1,462.33	1,706.44
4. Tamil Nadu	313.21	949.96	1,169.23	1,426.30	1,806.12	2,168.41	2,499.45	2,972.91
5. Pondicherry	5.52	17.28	22.91	29.00	37.73	45.00	58.00	67.88
6. Lakshadweep	-	0.39	0.90	1.13	0.89	1.09	1.22	1.43
VII. OTHERS	1.63	-	-	-	-	-	-	-
ALL INDIA	5,148.27	13,711.29	17,627.72	21,214.08	26,509.47	31,225.21	36,997.05	44,259.47

Note:

i) Data for 1981 are provisional

ii) Data for 1975 to 1981 relate to last friday of December.

iii) Deposits are exclusive of inter bank transactions.

Source: Government of India, Ministry of Finance, Department of Economic affairs, "Current Banking Statistics" December, 1982.

TABLE VI-8: STATEWISE DISTRIBUTION OF ADVANCES (ACCORDING TO SANCTION) OF SCHEDULED COMMERCIAL BANKS

(Rs. Crores)

Region/State/ Union Territory	As at the end of the December 1969	1975	1976	1977	1978	1979	1980	1981
I.NORTHERN REGION	385.88	1,957.33	3,503.41	4,024.35	4,782.47	5,546.16	5,616.19	6,905.82
1. Haryana	30.27	123.13	163.89	211.39	296.20	373.55	462.88	611.39
2. Himachal Pradesh	3.90	13.46	15.75	25.73	37.75	49.23	68.99	110.46
3. Jammu & Kashmir	2.45	37.02	48.63	52.29	84.96	97.99	115.54	179.53
4. Punjab	76.41	254.78	316.26	427.62	586.45	671.72	830.86	1,122.18
5. Rajasthan	46.04	155.54	227.42	273.07	348.32	467.11	570.01	706.31
6. Chandigarh	26.08	187.01	333.64	406.29	398.50	501.88	580.07	643.60
7. Delhi	200.13	1,186.59	2,399.82	2,627.96	3,030.29	3,384.68	2,987.84	3,532.35
II. NORTH-EASTERN REGION	20.62	63.57	94.16	111.76	141.17	163.04	225.85	253.06
1. Assam	20.25	55.91	81.62	94.41	115.77	130.62	186.67	192.01
2. Manipur	-	1.64	2.70	3.39	4.19	5.33	5.46	7.25
3. Meghalaya	-	2.67	4.40	4.98	6.31	7.02	8.18	11.46
4. Nagaland	0.10	0.81	1.58	2.31	3.62	3.68	5.13	8.43
5. Sikkim	-	0.03	0.07	0.11	0.14	0.17	0.21	0.79
6. Tripura	0.27	2.36	3.82	6.12	9.90	14.81	18.33	29.04
7. Arunachal Pradesh	-	0.10	0.24	0.30	0.65	0.85	1.00	1.98
8. Mizoram	-	0.05	0.09	0.14	0.59	0.56	0.87	2.10
III. EASTERN REGION	784.39	1,669.49	1,983.76	2,211.10	2,664.51	3,023.42	3,383.43	4,039.86
1. Bihar	50.56	279.58	336.90	346.25	455.26	530.62	642.86	761.16
2. Orissa	17.79	59.98	84.62	115.62	153.56	183.83	249.56	357.12

3. West Bengal	716.54	1,329.37	1,561.49	1,748.40	2,054.32	2,302.10	2,488.76	2,918.36
4. Andaman and Nichobar	-	0.56	0.75	0.83	1.37	1.87	2.25	3.22
IV. CENTRAL REGION	260.09	750.67	959.11	1.179.49	1,511.86	1,789.43	2,206.95	2,903.42
1. Madhya Pradesh	70.52	197.18	270.15	347.62	431.12	513.09	648.27	866.30
2. Uttar Pradesh	189.57	553.49	688.96	831.87	1,080.74	1,276.34	1,558.68	2,037.12
V. WESTERN REGION	1,388.28	3,134.10	3,852.37	4,257.49	5,124.78	5,906.98	7,087.37	8,466.00
1. Gujarat	232.31	600.06	743.37	824.31	1,027.66	1,183.46	1,481.60	1,753.95
2. Maharastra	1,132.46	2,470.60	3,029.91	3,359.15	3,998.45	4,610.29	5,475.63	6,543.91
3. Dadra, Nagar Haveli	..	0.36	0.55	0.68	0.64	1.04	1.52	1.95
4. Goa, Daman & Diu	23.51	63.08	73.54	73.45	93.03	112.19	128.62	166.19
VI. SOUTHERN REGION	876.71	2,500.15	3,166.15	3,519.38	4,346.19	5,129.92	6,240.61	7,586.75
1. Andhra Pradesh	163.02	462.35	609.51	720.62	951.57	1,171.05	1,384.60	1,727.56
2. Karnataka	185.55	671.00	859.92	932.48	1,091.27	1,268.20	1,459.67	1,771.93
3. Kerala	105.14	317.08	385.13	466.11	655.33	779.03	996.41	1,219.73
4. Tamil Nadu	418.20	1,036.26	1,294.25	1,379.56	1,624.17	1,884.46	2,366.57	2,826.24
5. Lakshadweep	-	0.04	0.06	0.06	0.07	0.06	0.09	0.13
6. Pondicherry	4.80	13.42	16.98	20.55	23.78	27.12	33.27	41.16
VII. OTHERS	0.23	..	-	-	-	-	-	-
All India	3,716.70	10,075.51	13,558.96	15,303.57	18,570.98	21,558.95	24,760.40	30,154.91

Note:

i) Data for 1981 are provisional.

ii) Data from 1975 to 1981 relate to last Friday of December.

iii) Advances include bills rediscounted.

Source: Government of India, Ministry of Finance, "Current Banking Statistics December, 1982".

TABLE-VI.9: STATEWISE DISTRIBUTION OF ADVANCES OF SCHEDULED COMMERCIAL BANKS
(According to Sanction and utilisation)

(Rs. Crores).

Region/State Union territory	According to sanction End-December				Accordding to utilisation End-Deecember			
	1972	1975	1979	1980	1972	1975	1979	1980
I. NORTHERN REGION	729.10	1,957.53	5,546.16	5,616.19	712.51	1,833.24	5,490.21	5,546.80
1. Haryana	61.14	123.13	373.55	462.88	115.72	221.98	549.68	625.10
2. Himachal Pradesh	4.78	13.46	49.23	68.99	5.32	13.60	49.60	70.23
3. Jammu & Kashmir	12.60	37.02	97.99	115.54	12.95	34.75	81.93	101.85
4. Punjab	124.73	254.78	671.72	830.36	129.47	395.07	1,033.37	1,348.77
5. Rajasthan	80.19	155.54	467.11	570.01	89.98	165.38	504.76	615.74
6. Chandigarh	71.16	187.01	501.88	580.07	74.19	17.97	89.36	153.16
7. Delhi	374.50	1,186.59	3,384.68	2,987.84	284.88	984.49	3,181.51	2,631.95
II. NORTH-EASTERN REGION	34.93	63.57	163.04	225.85	68.78	111.45	232.72	312.38
1. Assam	30.15	55.91	130.62	186.67	63.61	103.15	196.03	268.29
2. Manipur	1.11	1.64	5.33	5.46	1.52	2.65	6.13	6.33
3. Meghalaya	2.46	2.67	7.02	5.18	2.00	1.18	7.33	8.30
4. Nagaland	0.43	0.81	3.68	5.13	0.43	0.86	4.60	5.89
5. Sikkim	-	0.03	0.17	0.21	-	0.02	0.17	0.21
6. Tripura	0.75	2.36	14.81	18.33	1.29	2.81	15.69	19.05
7. Arunachal Pradesh	0.03	0.10	0.85	1.00	0.32	0.73	2.05	2.19
8. Mizoram	-	0.05	0.56	0.87	0.01	0.05	0.72	2.12
III. EASTERN REGION	1,005.33	1,669.49	3,023.42	3,383.43	1,001.17	1,687.78	3,009.63	3,326.76
1. Bihar	104.27	279.58	530.62	642.86	196.34	422.21	674.40	767.95
2. Orissa	27.67	59.58	188.83	249.56	43.53	80.67	214.38	282.13
3. West Bengal	873.39	1,329.37	2,302.10	2,488.76	761.24	1184.33	2,118.27	2,274.26
4. Andaman & Nicobar Islands	0.05	0.56	1.87	2.25	0.06	0.57	2.58	2.42

TABLE-VI.9(Contd.)

Region/State/ Union Territory	According to Sanction End December 1972	1975	1979	1980	According to Utilisation End December 1972	1975	1979	1980
IV. CENTRAL REGION	375.02	750.67	1,789.43	2,006.95	425.72	878.90	1,945.41	2,360.12
1. Madhya Pradesh	103.41	197.18	513.09	648.27	114.84	213.29	544.58	673.43
2. Uttar Pradesh	271.61	533.49	1,276.34	1,558.68	310.88	665.61	1,400.83	1,683.69
V. Western Region	2,030.11	3,134.10	5,906.98	7,087.37	1,912.53	3,002.29	5,683.74	6,890.62
1. Gujarat	372.34	600.06	1,183.46	1,481.60	426.73	665.94	1,270.96	1,574.17
2. Maharastra	1,617.06	2,470.60	4,610.29	5,475.63	1,443.47	2,269.22	4,272.91	5,181.09
3. Dadra & Nagar Haveli	0.11	0.36	1.04	1.52	0.16	0.48	1.82	1.87
4. Goa, Daman & Diu	40.60	63.08	112.19	128.62	42.17	66.65	138.05	133.49
VI. SOUTHERN REGION	1,378.53	2,500.15	5,129.92	6,240.61	1,432.36	2,559.80	5,197.24	6,323.72
1. Andhra Pradesh	250.98	462.35	1,171.05	1,384.60	270.14	484.75	1,194.30	1,407.56
2. Karnataka	352.92	671.00	1,268.20	1,459.67	372.31	700.63	1,294.94	1,488.05
3. Kerala	172.15	317.08	779.03	996.41	183.45	330.05	797.45	1,012.78
4. Tamil Nadu	594.26	1,036.26	1,884.46	2,366.57	596.79	1,028.14	1,880.53	2,378.31
5. Lakshadweep	0.01	0.04	0.06	0.09	0.01	0.04	0.07	0.10
6. Pondicherry	8.21	13.42	27.12	33.27	9.66	16.19	29.95	36.92
ALL-INDIA	5,553.60	10.075.51	21,558.95	24,760.40	5,553.07	10,073.46	21,558.95	24,760.40

Source: Govt. of India, Ministry of Finance "CURRENT BANKING STATISTICS-Dec. 1982".

TABLE-VI.10 : STATEWISE CREDIT DEPOSIT RATIO OF SCHEDULED COMMERCIAL BANKS (CREDIT ACCORDING TO SANCTION) (Percent).

Region/State/ Union Territory	As at the end of December 1969	1975	1976	1977	1978	1979	1980	1981
I. Northern region	39.9	73.4	97.6	92.6	85.2	83.3	70.0	72.4
1. Haryana	47.2	62.7	61.1	61.5	69.4	70.9	70.4	75.4
2. Himachal Pradesh	22.3	18.7	17.6	24.4	27.0	29.1	31.8	42.7
3. Jammu & Kashmir	9.2	37.8	36.7	28.6	30.5	33.2	30.7	46.1
4. Punjab	33.2	38.1	37.7	42.3	45.8	42.1	42.3	46.7
5. Rajasthan	49.9	59.4	62.2	62.0	61.8	67.9	67.4	68.9
6. Chandigarh	63.8	209.9	253.0	283.7	205.8	192.1	209.2	182.8
7. Delhi	40.6	92.7	135.8	123.9	111.1	108.5	81.0	82.1
II. NORTH-EASTERN REGION	38.5	37.5	42.3	40.4	40.6	37.0	45.2	40.8
1. Assam	42.4	45.2	49.5	45.5	45.1	42.3	53.3	43.4
2. Manipur	-	39.2	41.6	47.7	42.7	26.7	36.9	35.7
3. Meghalaya	-	14.3	16.4	18.7	18.4	14.8	15.1	20.2
4. Nagaland	8.1	14.5	27.6	26.8	29.1	24.3	25.6	34.8
5. Sikkim	-	1.6	2.7	3.2	4.1	3.3	4.3	10.7
6. Tripura	6.0	19.3	28.6	36.1	46.0	55.2	49.2	66.0
7. Arunachal Pradesh	-	4.8	8.1	8.1	11.3	10.1	10.4	15.0
8. Mizoram	-	4.2	4.6	6.2	14.5	6.7	9.7	18.9
III. EASTERN REGION	84.0	64.6	62.7	61.2	59.4	58.2	55.9	54.2
1. Bihar	27.2	44.3	43.0	39.5	42.6	41.2	41.2	39.4
2. Orissa	49.5	46.9	52.1	57.5	58.3	58.4	58.5	65.6
3. West Bengal	100.6	72.9	70.5	69.1	65.3	64.3	61.4	58.7

4. Andaman and Nicobar Island		21.4	21.6	19.4	24.1	25.1	26.0	34.8
IV. CENTRAL REGION	47.1	46.0	45.3	46.7	47.6	46.6	46.2	50.2
1. Madhya Pradesh	55.8	50.0	50.8	54.8	54.5	53.1	55.2	61.5
2. Uttar Pradesh	44.5	44.8	43.4	44.0	45.3	44.5	43.2	46.6
V. WESTERN REGION	79.7	78.7	.75.7	69.5	69.4	69.6	72.2	73.5
1. Gujarat	50.6	61.0	59.6	54.1	54.6	53.7	57.5	57.6
2. Maharastra	92.1	86.0	82.5	76.1	75.7	76.7	79.1	80.7
3. Dadra & Nagar Haveli	-	116.1	134.1	116.0	74.4	88.9	107.0	103.7
4. Goa, Daman & Diu	45.1	50.2	46.2	40.1	45.3	42.1	40.1	44.2
VI. SOUTHERN REGION	97.4	93.4	91.9	81.3	78.9	77.5	79.8	81.2
1. Andhra Pradesh	94.2	77.5	75.7	72.5	74.4	73.6	74.3	75.3
2. Karnataka	72.7	100.0	98.0	83.4	81.4	79.3	75.5	76.9
3. Kerala	68.8	71.7	67.8	61.3	62.9	64.3	68.1	71.5
4. Tamil Nadu	193.5	109.1	110.7	96.7	89.9	86.9	94.7	95.1
5. Lakshadweep	-	10.3	6.7	5.3	7.9	5.5	7.4	9.1
6. Pondicherry	87.0	77.7	74.1	70.9	63.0	60.3	57.4	60.6
ALL-INDIA	72.7	73.5	76.9	72.1	70.1	69.0	66.9	68.1

Note:1. Data from 1975 to 1981 are as on the last Friday of December.
2. Data for 1981 are provisional

Source: Ministry of Finance, Department of Economic Affairs, "Current Banking Statistics" - December,1982".

TABLE-VII-1: YEAR-WISE MARKET BORROWINGS BY THE STATES DURING FOURTH PLAN PERIOD.

	States	Market Borrowing (Rs. Crores).						Per Capita Market Borrowing (In Rupees.)					
		1969-70	1970-71	1971-72	1972-73	1973-74	Total Fourth Plan	1969-70	1970-71	1971-72	1972-73	1973-74	Total Fourth Plan
	1	2	3	4	5	6	7	8	9	10	11	12	13
1.	Andhra Pradesh	11.80	11.34	12.64	21.16	21.01	77.95	2.71	2.61	2.91	4.86	4.48	0.92
2.	Assam	7.95	6.89	7.16	8.60	11.31	41.91	5.30	4.59	4.77	5.73	7.5	0.93
3.	Bihar	8.88	6.88	7.68	16.62	24.56	64.62	1.58	1.22	1.36	2.95	4.3	0.47
4.	Gujarat	27.46	18.02	20.92	20.08	21.77	108.25	10.28	6.75	7.84	7.52	8.1	0.54
5.	Haryana	11.02	8.75	8.33	10.49	11.61	50.20	11.02	8.75	8.33	10.49	11.6	0.20
6.	Himachal Pradesh	-	-	-	2.12	3.03	5.15	-	-	-	6.06	8.8	0.72
7.	Jammu & Kashmir	-	-	-	2.20	6.60	8.80	-	-	-	4.78	14.35	0.13
8.	Karnataka	20.33	16.52	17.55	17.22	22.02	93.64	6.94	5.64	5.99	5.88	7.58	0.97
9.	Kerala	5.07	8.49	11.48	19.52	19.82	64.38	2.37	3.97	5.36	9.12	9.2	0.08
10.	Madhya Pradesh	8.43	12.71	12.43	12.65	19.32	65.54	2.02	3.05	2.98	3.03	4.63	0.71
11.	Maharashtra	35.70	27.73	31.16	36.71	31.73	163.03	7.08	5.50	6.18	7.28	6.30	0.34
12.	Manipur	-	-	-	1.11	1.38	2.49	-	-	-	10.09	12.55	0.64
13.	Meghalaya	-	-	-	1.10	1.10	2.20	-	-	-	11.00	11.00	0.00
14.	Nagaland	-	-	-	1.11	1.98	3.09	-	-	-	22.20	39.60	0.80
15.	Orissa	5.03	7.97	10.20	6.60	12.70	42.50	2.30	3.64	4.68	3.01	5.80	0.43
16.	Punjab	10.40	9.38	9.01	9.94	9.94	48.67	7.70	6.67	7.36	7.36	7.36	0.04
17.	Rajasthan	6.50	9.65	9.68	20.59	22.70	69.12	2.52	3.74	3.75	7.98	8.80	0.79
18.	Tamilnadu	18.54	21.45	19.38	20.53	26.25	106.15	4.49	5.19	4.69	4.97	6.36	23.70
19.	Tripura	-	-	-	-	-	-	-	-	-	-	-	-
20.	Uttar Pradesh	13.60	13.40	17.48	26.20	38.32	109.00	1.54	1.52	1.98	2.97	4.34	12.35
21.	West Bengal	7.89	17.99	19.72	35.13	41.03	121.76	1.78	4.06	4.45	7.93	9.26	27.48
	Total:	198.60	197.17	214.82	289.68	348.18	1,248.45	3.67*	3.64*	3.97*	5.35*	6.43*	23.06*

* Average for all States.

Source: Planning Commission.

TABLE-VII-2: YEAR-WISE MARKET BORROWINGS BY THE STATES DURING FIFTH PLAN PERIOD.

	States	Market borrowing(Rs. Crores).						Per capita Market Borrowing (In Rs.)				
		1974-75	1975-76	1976-77	1977-78	1978-79	Total	1974-75	1975-76	1976-77	1977-78	1978-79
	1	2	3	4	5	6	7	8	9	10	11	12
1.	Andhra Pradesh	21.98	22.60	23.11	25.42	27.96	121.07	5.05	5.19	5.31	5.84	6.43
2.	Assam	11.36	11.48	12.44	13.68	15.06	64.02	7.57	7.65	8.29	9.12	10.03
3.	Bihar	24.57	24.69	27.02	29.72	32.70	138.70	4.36	4.38	4.80	5.28	5.80
4.	Gujarat	24.63	24.27	26.70	29.37	32.31	137.28	9.22	9.08	10.00	11.00	12.10
5.	Haryana	14.70	11.65	12.77	14.05	15.45	68.62	14.70	11.65	12.77	14.05	15.45
6.	Himachal Pradesh	3.02	3.03	3.33	3.66	4.03	17.07	8.62	8.65	9.51	10.46	11.51
7.	Jammu & Kashmir	6.61	6.66	7.31	8.04	8.85	37.47	14.36	14.47	15.89	17.47	19.22
8.	Karnataka	22.21	21.96	24.20	26.62	29.28	124.27	7.58	7.49	8.26	9.08	9.99
9.	Kerala	19.39	20.50	21.80	23.98	26.38	112.05	9.06	9.57	10.19	11.21	12.32
10.	Madhya Pradesh	19.08	19.38	21.27	23.40	25.73	108.86	4.57	4.64	5.10	5.61	6.17
11.	Maharashtra	31.98	33.90	37.09	40.80	44.88	188.65	6.34	6.72	7.36	8.10	8.90
12.	Manipur	3.54	1.37	1.52	1.67	1.84	9.94	32.14	12.45	13.82	15.20	16.71
13.	Meghalaya	3.88	2.20	2.42	2.67	2.94	14.11	38.80	22.00	24.20	26.52	29.28
14.	Nagaland	5.79	1.98	2.18	2.40	2.64	14.99	115.80	39.60	43.60	47.95	52.75
15.	Orissa	13.12	12.70	13.97	15.37	16.90	72.06	5.99	5.79	6.38	7.01	7.72
16.	Punjab	14.14	10.59	10.93	12.02	13.23	60.91	10.39	7.78	8.04	8.84	9.72
17.	Rajasthan	22.83	24.01	24.97	27.47	30.21	129.49	8.84	9.30	9.68	10.65	11.71
18.	Tamil Nadu	24,24	26.42	28.87	31.76	34.93	146.22	5.88	6.41	7.01	7.71	8.48
19.	Tripura	1.66	1.38	1.52	1.67	1.84	8.07	10.37	8.62	9.50	10.45	11.48
20.	Uttar Pradesh	36.68	39.91	42.17	46.39	51.02	215.17	4.15	4.40	4.78	5.25	5.78
21.	West Bengal	40.92	41.20	45.13	49.64	54.61	231.50	9.23	9.30	10.19	11.30	12.44
	Total:	366.33+	360.88+	390.72	429.80	472.79	2,020.52	6.76*	6.66*	7.21*	7.93*	8.73*

+ Ecludes additional market borrowing for repayment of Hyderabad Development loan in 1974-75 & of Centralised market borrowing in 1975-76.

* Average for all States.

Source: Planning Commission.

TABLE-VII-3: DISTRIBUTION OF MARKET BORROWINGS DURING 1980-85(Original Allocation and Actuals)

(Rs. Crores)

	States	Original Sixth Plan (1980-85) Allocation			1980-81 Actuals			1981-82 Actuals			1982-83 Actuals		
		Normal	Special	Total	Normal	Special	Total	Normal	Special	Total	Normal	Special	Total
	1.	2.	3.	4.	5.	6.	7.	8.	9.	10.	11.	12.	13
I.	SPL. CATEGORY STATES:												
1.	Assam	112.00	30.00	142.00	17.81	-	17.81	20.59	2.00	22.59	22.78	8.19	30.97
2.	Himachal Pradesh	29.53	10.00	39.53	5.06	-	5.06	5.33	1.00	6.33	5.85	3.50	9.35
3.	Jammu & Kashmir	65.57	5.00	70.57	10.75	-	10.75	11.85	0.50	12.35	2.38	1.75	14.13
4.	Manipur	15.11	1.00	16.11	2.52	-	2.52	2.80	0.25	3.05	3.05	0.25	3.30
5.	Meghalaya	21.77	1.00	22.77	4.81	-	4.81	3.99	0.25	4.24	4.35	0.25	4.60
6.	Nagaland	20.14	1.00	21.14	3.33	-	3.33	3.91	0.25	4.16	4.15	0.25	4.40
7.	Sikkim	-	2.00	2.00	-	-	-	-	0.25	0.25	-	0.50	0.50
8.	Tripura	13.54	5.00	18.54	2.49	-	2.49	2.53	0.50	3.03	2.69	2.00	4.69
	TOTAL: I	277.66	55.00	332.66	46.77	-	46.77	51.00	5.00	56.00	55.25	16.69	71.94
II.	OTHER STATES:												
1.	Andhra Pradesh	206.90	115.00	321.90	31.81	-	31.88	40.70	17.40	58.10	41.31	23.20	64.51
2.	Bihar	241.44	222.00	463.44	41.37	-	41.37	45.43	34.80	80.23	48.45	46.39	94.84
3.	Gujarat	239.70	-	239.70	39.41	-	39.41	43.81	-	43.81	47.50	-	47.50
4.	Haryana	114.00	-	114.00	19.34	-	19.34	21.16	-	21.16	22.64	-	22.64
5.	Karnataka	215.12	-	215.12	35.86	-	35.86	41.44	-	41.44	44.44	-	44.44
6.	Kerala	194.81	-	194.81	32.75	-	32.75	35.52	-	35.52	38.59	-	38.59
7.	Madhya Pradesh	190.13	143.00	333.13	32.14	-	32.14	35.39	21.30	56.69	38.75	28.40	67.15
8.	Maharastra	331.52	-	331.52	55.11	-	55.11	62.29	-	62.29	65.87	-	65.87
9.	Orissa	126.03	72.00	198.03	21.67	-	21.67	22.93	10.60	33.53	24.98	14.13	39.11
10.	Punjab	97.70	-	97.70	16.50	-	16.50	18.01	-	18.01	19.38	-	19.38
11.	Rajasthan	223.61	80.00	303.61	36.43	-	40.40	36.43	12.60	53.00	44.38	16.80	61.18
12.	Tamil Nadu	258.07	-	258.07	42.32	-	42.32	45.55	-	45.55	51.41	-	51.41
13.	Uttar Pradesh	377.00	318.00	695.00	64.30	-	64.30	67.96	48.30	116.26	74.87	64.40	139.27
14.	West Bengal	403.00	-	403.00	67.15	-	67.15	74.40	-	74.40	79.66	-	79.66
	TOTAL : II	3219.03	950.00	4169.03	536.16		536.16	594.99	145.00	739.99	642.23	193.32	835.55
III.	GRAND TOTAL:	3496.69	1005.00	4501.69	582.93		582.93	645.99	150.00	795.99	697.48	210.01	907.49

(Contd.) TABLE-VII-3: DISTRIBUTION OF MARKET BORROWINGS DURING 1980-85(Original Allocation and Actuals)

STATES	1983-84 Pre-Actuals			1984-85 Latest Estimates			Total 1980-85 Latest Estimates		
	Normal 14.	Special 15.	Total 16.	Normal 17.	Special 18.	Total 19.	Normal 20.	Special 21.	Total 22.
I. SPL. CATEGORY STATES									
1. Assam	26.83	9.50	36.33	30.61	10.31	40.92	118.62	30.00	148.62
2. Himachal Pradesh	7.60	2.75	10.35	8.06	2.75	10.81	31.90	10.00	41.90
3. Jammu & Kashmir	15.81	1.42	17.23	17.86	1.33	19.19	68.65	5.00	73.65
4. Manipur	3.65	0.25	3.90	4.45	0.25	4.70	16.47	1.00	17.47
5. Meghalaya	5.43	0.25	5.68	5.88	0.25	6.13	24.46	1.00	25.46
6. Nagaland	4.70	0.25	4.95	6.50	0.25	6.75	22.59	1.00	23.59
7. Sikkim	-	-	-	-	0.70	0.70	-	1.45	1.45
8. Tripura	3.15	1.25	4.40	3.69	1.25	4.94	14.55	5.00	19.55
TOTAL:I	67.17	15.67	82.84	77.05	17.09	94.14	297.24	54.45	351.69
II. OTHER STATES									
1. Andhra Pradesh	48.60	30.92	79.52	56.60	43.48	100.08	219.02	115.00	334.02
2. Bihar	57.72	61.85	119.57	65.95	78.96	144.91	258.92	222.00	480.92
3. Gujarat	58.88	-	58.88	65.46	-	65.46	255.06	-	255.06
4. Haryana	26.39	-	26.39	31.90	-	31.90	121.43	-	121.43
5. Karnataka	52.14	-	52.14	58.81	-	58.81	232.69	-	232.69
6. Kerala	46.07	-	46.07	53.27	-	53.27	206.20	-	206.20
7. Madhya Pradesh	45.40	37.77	83.17	52.07	55.53	107.60	203.75	143.00	346.75
8. Maharastra	79.98	-	79.98	90.69	-	90.69	353.94	-	353.93
9. Orissa	29.98	18.83	48.81	34.53	28.44	62.97	134.09	72.00	206.09
10. Punjab	23.24	-	23.24	26.87	-	26.87	104.00	-	104.00
11. Rajasthan	53.36	24.03	77.39	61.12	26.57	87.69	235.69	80.00	315.69
12. Tamil Nadu	60.47	-	60.47	71.70	-	71.70	271.45	-	271.45
13. Uttar Pradesh	89.10	85.86	174.96	103.00	119.44	222.44	399.23	318.00	717.23
14. West Bengal	96.59	-	96.59	110.18	-	110.18	427.98	-	427.98
TOTAL: II	767.92	259.26	1027.18	882.15	352.42	1234.57	3423.45	950.00	4373.45
GRAND TOTAL:	835.09	274.93	1110.02	959.20	369.51	1328.71	3720.69	1004.45	4725.14

Source: Govt of India, Ministry of Finance, 'Statistical Statements on Finances and Plans of States and Union Territories' 1985.

TABLE VII.4 : DISTRIBUTION OF MARKET BORROWINGS - 1980-85

(SUMMARY)

(Rs. Crores)

	STATES	ORIGINALLY APPROVED		LATEST ESTIMATES			
		Normal	Special	Total	Normal	Special	Total
	1	2	3	4	5	6	7
I.	SPECIAL CATEGORY STATES						
1.	Assam	112.00	30.00	142.00	118.62	30.00	148.62
2.	Himachal Pradesh	29.53	10.00	39.53	31.90	10.00	41.90
3.	Jammu & Kashmir	65.57	5.00	70.57	68.65	5.00	73.65
4.	Manipur	15.11	1.00	16.11	16.47	1.00	17.47
5.	Meghalaya	21.77	1.00	22.77	24.46	1.00	25.46
6.	Nagaland	20.14	1.00	21.14	22.59	1.00	23.59
7.	Sikkim	-	2.00	2.00	-	1.45	1.45
8.	Tripura	13.54	5.00	18.54	14.55	5.00	19.55
	TOTAL (I):	277.66	55.00	332.66	297.24	54.45	351.69
II.	NON-SPECIAL CATEGORY STATES						
1.	Andhra Pradesh	206.90	115.00	321.90	219.02	115.00	334.02
2.	Bihar	241.44	222.00	463.44	258.92	222.00	480.92
3.	Gujarat	239.70	-	239.70	255.06	-	255.06
4.	Haryana	114.00	-	114.00	121.43	-	121.43
5.	Karnataka	215.12	-	215.12	232.69	-	232.69
6.	Kerala	194.81	-	194.81	206.20	-	206.20
7.	Madhya Pradesh	190.13	143.00	333.13	203.75	143.00	346.75
8.	Maharashtra	331.52	-	331.52	353.94	-	353.94
9.	Orissa	126.03	72.00	198.03	134.09	72.00	206.09
10.	Punjab	97.70	-	97.70	104.00	-	104.00
11.	Rajasthan	223.61	80.00	303.61	235.69	80.00	315.69
12.	Tamil Nadu	258.07	-	258.07	271.45	-	271.45
13.	Uttar Pradesh	377.00	318.00	695.00	399.23	318.00	717.23
14.	West Bengal	403.00	-	403.00	427.98	-	427.98
	TOTAL (II):	3219.03	950.00	4169.03	3423.45	950.00	4373.45
GRAND TOTAL (I+II):		3496.69	1005.00	4501.69	3720.69	1004.45	4725.14

Source: Government of India, Ministry of Finance, Statistical Statements on Finances and Plans of States and Union Territories. 1985

TABLE VII.5 : DISTRIBUTION OF MARKET BORROWINGS DURING THE SEVENTH FIVE YEAR PLAN 1985-90 AND ANNUAL PLAN 1985-86

(Rs. Crores)

		1985-90			1985-86		
	STATES 1	Normal 2	Special 3	Total 4	Normal 5	Special 6	Total 7
I.	SPECIAL CATEGORY STATES						
1.	Assam	224.61	67.33	291.94	36.79	12.37	49.16
2.	Himachal Pradesh	59.04	22.44	81.48	9.67	3.30	12.97
3.	Jammu & Kashmir	130.64	11.22	141.86	21.40	1.50	22.90
4.	Manipur	30.47	2.24	32.71	4.99	0.30	5.29
5.	Meghalaya	43.23	2.24	45.47	7.08	0.30	7.38
6.	Nagaland	40.29	2.24	42.53	6.60	0.30	6.90
7.	Sikkim	0.48	5.12	5.60	-	0.84	0.84
8.	Tripura	26.98	11.22	38.20	4.42	1.50	5.92
	TOTAL (I) :	555.74	124.05	679.79	90.95	20.41	111.36
II.	NON-SPECIAL CATEGORY STATES						
1.	Andhra Pradesh	414.65	334.50	749.15	67.92	54.79	122.71
2.	Bihar	483.76	569.88	1053.64	79.24	93.35	172.59
3.	Gujarat	479.56	-	479.56	78.55	-	78.55
4.	Haryana	228.71	-	228.71	37.46	-	37.46
5.	Karnataka	431.03	-	431.03	70.60	-	70.60
6.	Kerala	390.24	134.47	524.71	63.92	22.03	85.95
7.	Madhya Pradesh	381.02	378.37	759.39	62.41	61.98	124.39
8.	Maharashtra	664.48	-	664.48	108.84	-	108.84
9.	Orissa	252.63	189.19	441.82	41.38	30.99	72.37
10.	Punjab	195.67	-	195.67	32.05	-	32.05
11.	Rajasthan	448.05	179.13	627.18	73.39	29.34	102.73
12.	Tamil Nadu	525.28	225.00	750.28	86.04	-	86.04
13.	Uttar Pradesh	754.59	795.46	1550.05	123.60	130.30	253.90
14.	West Bengal	806.54	-	806.54	132.11	-	132.11
	TOTAL (II) :	6456.21	2806.00	9262.21	1057.51	422.78	1480.29
	GRAND TOTAL (I+II)	7011.95	2930.05	9942.00	1148.46	443.19	1591.65

Source: Government of India, Ministry of Finance, Statistical Statements on Finance and Plans of States and Union Territories 1985.

TABLE VII.6 : PERCAPITA MARKET BORROWINGS

(In Rs.)

	FOURTH PLAN	FIFTH PLAN	SIXTH PLAN	SEVENTH PLAN	TOTAL
GROUP 'A' STATES	36.82	40.34	65.91	123.89	255.01
1. Punjab	36.45	40.33	61.90	116.47	243.60
2. Haryana	50.20	60.19	94.13	177.29	363.53
3. Maharashtra	32.34	33.56	56.36	105.81	218.17
4. Gujarat	40.54	45.46	74.80	140.63	287.43
GROUP 'B' STATES	28.11	41.33	72.74	157.07	289.76
5. West Bengal	27.48	47.05	78.38	147.72	290.80
6. Karnataka	31.97	37.66	62.72	116.18	237.64
7. Tamil Nadu	25.70	32.78	56.09	155.02	263.25
8. Kerala	30.08	48.09	80.86	205.77	355.82
9. Rajasthan	26.79	43.45	92.04	182.85	332.79
GROUP 'C' STATES	14.28	23.36	66.64	145.54	244.63
10. Andhra Pradesh	17.92	25.12	62.43	140.03	239.66
11. Orissa	19.43	29.90	78.06	167.36	288.81
12. Madhya Pradesh	15.71	23.31	66.43	145.48	245.31
13. Uttar Pradesh	12.35	21.73	64.67	139.77	233.67
14. Bihar	11.47	22.09	68.80	150.74	248.62
Per Capita for 14 States	32.69	30.29	68.40	144.86	260.80
SPECIAL GATEGORY STATES	23.48	52.93	97.42	188.31	349.25
ALL STATES	23.06	33.40	74.80	147.18	265.52
POPULATION	1971	1976	1981	1981	1981

Source: Worked out on the basis of the figures presented in the tables 1 to 5.

TABLE-VIII-1 : DEBT POSITION OF STATES

(Rs. Crores)
Outstanding as on March 31

	ITEMS	1971	1976	1980	1981	1982	1983	1984 Revised Estimates	1985 Budget) Estimates
I.	Internal Debts (a to c)	1,847	2,893	3,731	4,452	5,639	5,221	5,959	6,922
a)	Market Loans and Bonds (i+ii)	1,233	2,107	2,838	3,033	3,369	3,758	4,318	5,094
	i Market Loans	1,143	2,033	2,775	2,973	3,313	3,706	4,269	5,044
	ii Compensation and other Bonds	90	74	63	60	56	52	49	50
b)	Ways and Means Advances from the RBI	375	287	177	487	1,182	359	322	319
c)	Loans from Banks and other Institutions	239	499	716	932	1,088	1,104	1,319	1,509
II.	Loans and Advances from the Central Government	6,365	9,682	15,739	17,071	19,071	23,550 @	26722 @	29,609 @
III.	Provident Funds, etc*	537	1,142	2,108	2,450	2,912	3,642	4,503	5,328
	(of which State Provident Funds)	(471)	(1,022)	(1,893)	(2,177)	(2,551)	(3,144)	(3,872)	(4,554)
IV.	Total Debt (I to III)	8,749	13,717	21,578	23,973	27, 622	32,413	37,184	41,859

Notes: (1) Figures are revised (2) Since the data have been presented as per the revised budgetary classification beginning the financial year 1974-75, the various components of State Debt and other liabilities for 1971 are not strictly comparable with those for subsequent years. (3) During 1984-85 State Government have raised till November 7, 1984, Rs. 768 crores (net) approximately through market loans. (4) Figures for Assam for 1982 relate to Revised Estimates. * Figures shown here include transactions on account of insurance and Pension Funds and trusts & Endowments. @ Includes medium term loan of Rs. 1,743 crores given by the Centre to States to clear their overdrafts outstanding with the Reserve Bank of India as at the end of March, 1982.

Source: Report on Currency and Finance 1983-84. Reserve Bank of India.

TABLE-VIII-2 : STATEWISE COMPOSITION OF OUTSTANDING DEBT

(Rs. Crores)

	States	As at the end of March 1983 (Account)				As at the end of March 1984 (Revised Estimates)				As at the end of March 1985 (Budget Estimates)			
		Internal Debt	Loans and Advances	Provident Funds from Central Govt.@	Total Debt (1+2+3) etc.	Internal Debt	Loans and Advances from	Provident Funds etc. Central Govt.@	Total Debt (5+6+7)	Internal Debt	Loans and Advances	Provident Funds from Central Govt. @	Total Debt (9+10+11) etc.
	1.	2.	3.	4.	5.	6.	7.	8.	9.	10.	11.	12.	13.
1.	Andhra Pradesh	440	1639	158	2237	502	1847	196	2545	611	2053	230	2894
2.	Assam	(-)4	998	47	1041	9	1274	75	1358	20	1528	91	1639
3.	Bihar	313	2214	348	2875	357	2424	449	3230	407	2638	568	3613
4.	Gujarat	303	1187	176	1666	331	1423	213	1967	361	1664	241	2266
5.	Haryana	160	570	147	877	179	624	182	985	199	667	208	1074
6.	Himachal Pradesh	32	190	74	296	37	219	90	346	42	245	109	396
7.	Jammu & Kashmir	55	779	88	922	75	914	114	1103	87	1059	144	1290
8.	Karnataka	293	989	176	1458	331	1093	215	1639	383	1218	258	1859
9.	Kerala	251	769	238	1258	289	964	278	1531	332	1022	319	1673
10.	Madhya Pradesh	198	1445	529	2172	239	1615	684	2538	284	1761	847	2892
11.	Maharashtra	450	2184	414	3048	465	2583	460	3508	501	2987	508	3996
12.	Manipur	29	121	8	158	34	128	10	172	40	126	13	179
13.	Meghalaya	29	38	7	74	33	46	8	87	37	50	9	96
14.	Nagaland	48	45	29	122	55	52	37	144	62	58	38	158
15.	Orissa	260	1082	156	1498	304	1195	195	1694	367	1322	232	1921
16.	Punjab	392	671	132	1195	446	736	163	1345	480	775	177	1432
17.	Rajasthan	361	1639	190	2190	421	1736	256	2413	485	1779	315	2579
18.	Sikkim	1	15	1	17	2	19	2	23	3	23	2	28
19.	Tamil Nadu	417	1213	136	1766	443	1335	159	1937	472	1452	184	2108
20.	Tripura	30	62	21	113	40	76	35	151	52	88	29	169
21.	Uttar Pradesh	825	3101	404	4330	972	3479	484	4935	1129	3812	578	5519
22.	West Bengal	338	2599	163	3100	395	2940	198	3533	568	3282	228	4078
	TOTAL	5221	23550	3642	32413	5959	26722	4503	37184	6922	29609	5328	41859

@ Includes medium term loan of Rs. 1,743 crores given by the Centre to States to clear their overdrafts Outstanding with the Reserve Bank of India as at the end of March 1982.

Source: Report on Currency and Finance 1983-84, Reserve Bank of India.

TABLE-VIII-3 :RATIO OF LOAN OUTSTANDINGS, REPAYMENTS, ETC. TO STATE DOMESTIC PRODUCT

(Rs. crores)

	STATE	Total debt out-standings *	Central loans out-standings *	Repay-ment of Central loans (1984-89)	Non-Plan Capital gap (1984-89)	Total out stand-ing as % of S.D.P.@	Central loans out-stand-ing as % of SDP@	Repay-ment of Cen-tral loans as % of SDP@	Non-Plan capital gap as % of SDPO
	1	2	3	4	5	6	7	8	9
1.	Andhra Pradesh	2575.10	1860.21	509.82	432.88	52.00	37.56	10.30	8.74
2.	Assam	1495.29	1306.47	410.05	365.11	86.63	75.69	23.76	21.15
3.	Bihar	3270.04	2611.53	949.60	865.29	67.26	53.72	19.53	17.80
4.	Gujarat	2056.61	1419.25	369.60	226.18	41.67	28.76	7.49	4.58
5.	Haryana	973.39	635.95	238.49	209.50	43.92	28.69	10.76	9.45
6.	Himachal Pradesh	336.97	214.88	55.72	49.61	69.07	44.04	11.42	10.17
7.	Jammu & Kashmir	1087.21	912.64	278.28	259.10	179.57	150.73	45.96	42.79
8.	Karnataka	1612.31	1077.24	343.98	220.53	39.77	26.57	8.49	5.44
9.	Kerala	1440.83	859.02	320.55	249.81	50.95	30.37	11.33	8.83
10.	Madhya Pradesh	2509.20	1642.87	585.29	503.28	57.09	37.38	13.32	11.45
11.	Maharashtra	3545.69	2544.99	632.44	328.74	36.69	26.34	6.55	3.40
12.	Manipur	180.94	123.51	50.32	46.47	160.72	109.71	44.70	41.28
13.	Meghalaya	84.49	45.30	16.08	16.62	66.59	35.70	12.69	13.10
14.	Nagaland	126.16	51.57	21.93	20.44	175.64	71.79	30.53	28.46
15.	Orissa	1692.68	1214.67	354.13	340.99	73.29	52.59	15.33	14.76
16.	Punjab	1161.09	682.05	327.83	259.17	33.74	19.82	9.53	7.53
17.	Rajasthan	2679.98	1802.61	701.20	668.61	77.10	51.86	20.17	19.23
18.	Sikkim	16.73	15.63	4.99	3.64	62.59	58.47	18.67	13.62
19.	Tamil Nadu	1915.60	1399.34	472.84	199.13	36.03	26.32	8.89	3.75
20.	Tripura	133.02	69.00	25.47	19.47	65.20	33.82	12.48	9.54
21.	Uttar Pradesh	4989.98	3532.12	1002.12	800.37	57.04	40.38	11.46	9.15
22.	West Bengal	3522.72	3037.89	1017.31	721.25	54.74	47.20	15.81	11.21
	TOTAL	37406.03	27058.74	8688.04	6806.19	52.69	38.11	12.24	9.59

* As at the end of 1983-84.

@ Average for 1976-79.

Source: Report of the VIII, Finance Commission

TABLE-VIII-4 : CENTRAL LOANS OUTSTANDING AS PERCENTAGE OF STATE DOMESTIC PRODUCT

(Rs. Crores)

	STATE Net State	Central Loans Domestic Product (Average 1976-79) (Rs. crores)	Percentage of outstanding (excluding Small Savings & over-draft loans) (Rs. crores)	loans Outstanding to State Domestic Pro-Product (Percent)
	1.	2.	3.	4.
1.	Punjab	3440.83	370.42	10.8
2.	Maharashtra	9662.69	1165.84	12.1
3.	Gujarat	4935.29	754.34	15.3
4.	Haryana	2216.25	379.58	17.1
5.	Tamil Nadu	5316.56	930.76	17.5
6.	Karnataka	4053.78	773.57	19.1
7.	West Bengal	6435.61	1385.52	21.5
8.	Kerala	2828.06	625.48	22.1
9.	Madhya Pradesh	4395.27	1210.41	27.5
10.	Uttar Pradesh	8747.70	2592.08	29.6
11.	Andhra Pradesh	4952.00	1549.89	31.3
12.	Bihar	4861.82	1630.78	33.5
13.	Rajasthan	3476.06	1261.77	36.3
14.	Orissa	2309.66	1004.27	43.5
15.	Assam	1726.03	977.41	56.6
16.	Tripura	204.02	29.49	14.5
17.	Meghalaya	126.89	21.05	16.6
18.	Himachal Pradesh	487.89	87.98	18.0
19.	Nagaland	71.83	28.15	39.2
20.	Manipur	112.58	55.93	49.7
21.	Sikkim	26.73*	15.05	56.3
22.	Jammu & Kashmir	605.46	851.20	140.6
	TOTAL	70993.01	17700.97	24.9

* Estimated by the Secretariat of the Finance Commission.

Source: Report of the VIII, Finance Comission.

TABLE-VIII-5 : SUMMARY OF DEBT RELIEF RECOMMENDED BY THE EIGHTH FINANCE COMMISSION. (Rs. Crores)

	STATE	Non-Plan Capital Gap* during 1984-89	Debt relief during 1984-89: On the basis of rescheduling	On the basis of write off repayment	Total	Percentage of debt relief to non-plan capital gap
	1.	2.	3.	4.	5.	6.
1.	Maharashtra	82.37	27.83	-	27.83	33.8
2.	Punjab	118.86	38.71	-	38.71	32.6
3.	Gujarat	81.78	17.80	-	17.80	21.8
4.	Haryana	93.79	31.79	-	31.79	33.9
5.	Tamil Nadu	95.59	28.19	-	28.19	29.5
6.	Karnataka	177.32	48.45	-	48.45	27.3
7.	Uttar Pradesh	653.44	337.92	-	337.92	51.7
8.	Madhya Pradesh	294.07	143.65	-	143.65	48.8
9.	Andhra Pradesh	384.97	204.64	-	204.64	53.2
10.	Kerala	107.78	53.80	-	53.80	49.9
11.	Bihar	441.30	254.53	76.45	330.98	75.0
12.	Rajasthan	319.20	141.56	97.85	239.41	75.0
13.	West Bengal	161.12	116.14	4.70	120.84	75.0
14.	Orissa	260.81	119.12	76.50	195.62	75.0
15.	Assam	274.00	155.75	49.75	205.50	75.0
16.	Jammu & Kashmir	250.24	127.62	85.10	212.72	85.0
17.	Himachal Pradesh	19.44	10.92	5.60	16.52	85.0
18.	Tripura	3.05	2.17	0.40	2.57	84.3
19.	Manipur	13.13	7.63	3.55	11.18	85.1
20.	Meghalaya	7.54	3.49	2.90	6.39	84.8
21.	Nagaland	9.21	6.01	1.80	7.81	84.8
22.	Sikkim	3.63	2.47	0.60	3.07	84.6
	All States	3852.64	1880.19	405.20	2285.39@	59.3

* Excluding repayment of small savings and overdraft loans

@ Excluding relief of Rs.117.08 crores in the repayment or small savings loans in 1984-85.

Source : Report of the VIII Finance Cimmission.

TABLE-VIII-6 : LIABILITIES OF THE CENTRAL GOVERNMENT AS AT THE END OF

(Rs. crores)

		1950-51	1960-61	1965-66	1977-78	Revised 1984-85	Budget 1985-86
A.	Internal Debt						
1.	Market Loans	1,438.46	2,555.72	3,415.27	9,212.22	30,367.50	35,467.40
2.	Market Loans in course of repayment	6.49	22.73	33.72	50.48	53.51	53.51
3.	Special Bearer Bonds	-	-	-	-	964.27	964.27
4.	Treasury Bills	358.02	1,106.29	1,611.82	8,618.83	19,256.47	22,915.47
5.	Compensation & other Bonds	-	19.08	15.13	125.20	548.24	588.85
6.	Special floting and Other Loans	212.60	274.18	340.70	1,018.56	2,553.66	3,061.18
7.	Treasury Deposit receipts and other Floating Loans	6.73	-	-	-	-	-
8.	Special Securities issued to the Reserve Bank	-	-	-	-	4,750.00	5,009.90
	Total - Internal Debt	2,022.30	3,978.00	5,416.64	19,025.29	58,493.65	68,060.58
B.	External Debt	32.03	760.96	2,590.62	8,984.74	16,857.22	19,001.39
	Total - Public Debt	2,054.33	4,738.96	8,007.26	28,010.03	75,350.87	87,061.97
C.	Small Savings Schemes	336.87	969.99	1,538.21	4,902.82	16,806.36	20,706.36
D.	Provident Fund						
1.	State Provident Fund	95.05	289.14	527.02	1,853.56	3,508.04	3,773.09
2.	Public Provident Fund	-	-	-	61.07	591.87	696.87
	Total - Provident Funds	95.05	289.14	527.02	1,914.63	4,099.91	4,469.96
E.	Other Accounts						
1.	Special Deposits of Non-Government Provident Fund	-	-	-	617.26	5,871.79	7,221.79
2.	Other Items	16.10	262.23	694.57	1,704.83	2,519.22	3,302.32
	Total - Other Accounts	16.10	262.23	694.57	2,322.09	8,391.01	10,524.11
	RESERVE FUND AND DEPOSITS						
1.	Bearing Interest	260.85	142.19	275.03	1,236.40	6,339.73	8,604.10
2.	Not Bearing Interest	102.20	141.73	285.02	1,817.98	1,823.77	1,866.08
	Total - Reserve Fund and Deposits	363.05	283.92	560.05	3,054.38	8,163.50	10.470.18
	Total - Liabilities	2,865.40	6,544.24	11,327.11	40,203.95	1,12,811.65	1,33,232.58
	Amount due from Pakistan on account of her share of pre-partition debt(approx.)	-300.00	-300.00	-300.00	-300.00	-300.00	-300.00
	Net Liabilities of the Central Government	2,565.40	6,244.24	11,027.11	39,903.95	1,12,511.65	1,32,932.58
	Excess of Capital outlay and Loan over Liabilities	-	-	937.12	996.41	-	-
	Total - Capital Outlay and Loans	2,565.40	6,244.24	11,964.23	40,900.36	1,05,251.07	1,19,825.93

Source : Explanatory Memorandum to Central Budget 1985-86.

TABLE VIII.7 : OWNERSHIP OF CENTRAL AND STATE GOVERNMENT SECURITIES

(Rs. Crores)

	Category of Holders	CENTRAL GOVERNMENT SECURITIES End March 1981		End March 1982		End March 1983		STATE GOVERNMENT SECURITIES End March 1981		End March 1982		End March 1983	
		Amount	percent to total	Amount	percent to total	Amount	percent to total	Amount	percent to total	Amount	percent to total	Amount	percent
	Total of which:	15,660.8	100.0	18,579.0	100.0	22,359.0	100.0	3,022.8	100.0	3,383.1	100.0	3,779.7	100.0
I.	State Govts.	234.8	1.5	209.7	1.1	220.6	1.0	9.2	0.3	5.9	0.2	4.5	0.1
II.	Reserve Bank of India (own Account)	3,858.4	24.6	5,126.0	27.6	6,333.7	28.4	-	-	-	-	-	
III.	Commercial Banks (a+b)	6,842.6	43.7	7,727.7	41.6	8,704.1	38.9	1,680.8	55.6	1,960.7	58.0	2,317.3	61.3
a.	Scheduled Commercial Banks (i to iii)	6,842.3	43.7	7,727.3	41.6	8,703.6	38.9	1,679.6	55.6	1,959.1	57.9	2,315.2	61.2
i.	State Bank of India & Associates	2,098.0	13.4	2,530.5	13.6	3,003.0	13.4	449.5	14.9	553.8	16.4	593.4	15.7
ii.	Nationalised Bank	4,224.1	27.0	4,602.7	24.8	4,966.5	22.2	1,011.7	33.5	1,171.9	34.6	1,442.1	38.1
iii.	Other Scheduled Commercial Banks	520.2	3.3	594.1	3.2	734.1	3.3	218.4	7.2	233.4	6.9	279.7	7.4
b.	Non-Scheduled Commercial Banks	0.3	-	0.4	-	0.5	-	1.2	-	1.6	0.1	2.1	0.1
IV.	L I C of India	1,784.8	11.4	2,011.5	10.8	2,464.0	11.0	465.2	15.4	466.7	13.8	447.3	11.8
V.	Employees Provident fund scheme	740.0	4.7	737.0	4.0	755.8	3.4	115.8	3.8	122.7	3.6	133.9	3.5
VI.	Provident Funds of exempted Establishment	1,332.4	8.5	1,453.6	7.8	1,591.7	7.1	646.5	21.4	763.2	22.5	901.0	23.8
VII.	Coal Mines Provident fund scheme	168.9	1.1	196.2	1.1	224.7	1.0	30.8	1.0	39.7	1.2	54.5	1.4
VIII.	Assam Tea Plantations Provident Fund Scheme	3.7		4.0	-	3.8	-	7.6	0.3	7.7	0.2	7.7	0.2
IX.	Other Catogeries of holders	695.2	4.5	1,113.3	6.0	2,060.6	9.2	66.9	2.2	16.5	0.5	-	-

TABLE IX.1 : ANDHRA PRADESH, REVENUE RECEIPTS

(Rs. Crores)

		1961-62 Accts.	1985-86 B.E.	% share in 1961-62	% share in 1985-86	Compound growth 1976-71	Compound growth 1971-84
I.	Total Revenue Receipts	85.76	2847.48	100.00	100.00	13.14	17.02
1.	Share of Central Taxes	14.64	521.33	17.07	18.31	15.55	16.33
2.	States' Own tax Revenues	45.97	1444.59	53.60	50.73	11.69	16.34
3.	States' Own Non-Tax Revenues	11.15	511.62	13.00	17.97	15.12	13.03
4.	Grants from the Centre	14.00	369.94	16.33	12.99	13.19	15.58
II.	States' Own Tax Revenues	45.97	1444.59	100.00	100.00		
1.	Land Revenue	10.12	57.99	22.01	4.01	0.51	
2.	Stamps & Registration	2.35	61.94	5.13	4.29	15.70	12.29
3.	State Excise	8.73	387.00	18.99	26.79	14.77	17.31
4.	Sales Tax	14.81	743.55	32.21	51.47	15.29	19.46
5.	Motor Vehicles Tax	2.76	112.68	6.00	7.80	19.72	13.79
6.	Entertainment Tax	1.19	45.00	2.58	3.12	17.55	17.98

Source: Various issues of Reserve Bank of India, Bulletin.

TABLE IX.2 : ASSAM, REVENUE RECEIPTS

(Rs. Crores)

		1961-62 Accts.	1985-86 B.E.	%share in 1961-62	1985-86	Compound growth Rate 1961-71	1971-84
I.	Total Revenue Receipts	40.36	809.36	100.00	100.00	12.13	15.16
1.	Share in Central Taxes	7.68	224.33	19.03	27.72	9.01	15.97
2.	State's Own Tax Revenue	13.82	150.49	34.24	18.59	10.60	13.55
3.	State's Own Non-Tax Revenues	5.52	86.56	13.68	10.69	5.33	19.24
4.	Grants from the Centre	13.34	347.98	33.05	43.00	17.17	11.73
II.	State's Own Tax Revenues	13.82	150.49	100.00	100.00		
1.	Land Revenue	2.86	4.00	20.69	2.66	10.78	
2.	Stamps & Registration	0.47	6.06	3.40	4.03	12.88	9.75
3.	State Excise	2.04	6.42	14.76	4.27	4.38	6.22
4.	Sales Tax	3.45	101.10	24.96	67.18	15.37	13.60
5.	Motor Vehicles Tax	0.77	8.66	5.57	5.75	9.39	12.34
6.	Entertainment Tax	0.30	3.88	2.17	2.58	14.01	18.51

Source: Various issues of Reserve Bank of India, Bulletin

TABLE IX.3 : BIHAR, REVENUE RECEIPTS

(Rs. Crores)

		1961-62 Accts.	1985-86 B. E.	% share in 1961-62	% share in 1985-86	Compound Growth Rate 1961-71	Compound Growth Rate 1971-84
I.	Total Revenue Receipts	79.81	1988.84	100.00	100.00	12.21	15.57
1.	Share in Central Taxes	16.35	711.04	20.49	35.75	18.30	16.13
2.	State's Own Tax Revenue	35.84	529.74	44.91	26.64	9.77	14.39
3.	State's Own Non-Tax Revenues	10.63	344.31	13.32	17.31	10.62	15.22
4.	Grants from the Centre	16.99	403.75	21.28	20.30	10.33	16.99
II.	State's Own Tax Revenues	35.84	529.74	100.00	100.00		
1.	Land Revenue	9.11	22.50	25.42	4.25	-5.33	8.64
2.	Stamps & Registration	3.83	30.45	10.69	5.75	8.99	10.84
3.	State Excise	6.31	42.80	17.61	8.08	8.63	8.65
4.	Sales Tax	11.34	368.44	31.64	69.55	15.27	17.62
5.	Motor Vehicles Tax	0.14	38.88	0.39	7.34	47.97	18.05
6.	Entertainment Tax	1.11	10.65	3.10	2.01	11.78	9.18

Source: Various issues of Reserve Bank of India, Bulletin.

TABLE IX.4 : GUJARAT, REVENUE RECEIPTS

		1961-62	1985-86	% share in		Compound growth rate	
		Accts.	B. E.	1961-62	1985-86	1961-71	1971-84
I.	Total Revenue Receipts	62.70	1855.62	100.00	100.00	13.89	16.22
1.	Share of Central Taxes	18.01	247.66	28.72	13.35	10.51	14.78
2.	State's Own tax Revenues	28.86	1077.54	46.03	58.06	15.57	17.49
3.	State's Own Non-Tax Revenue	8.85	336.66	14.12	18.14	15.41	14.16
4.	Grants from the Centre	6.98	193.76	11.13	10.45	12.78	16.18
II.	State's Own Tax Revnues	28.86	1077.54	100.00	100.00		
1.	Land Revenue	4.64	14.00	16.08	1.30	4.86	4.64
2.	Stamps & Registration	2.13	48.25	7.38	4.48	12.65	14.44
3.	State Excise	0.31	6.09	1.07	0.57	12.65	14.26
4.	Sales Tax	13.82	662.35	47.89	61.47	18.87	18.10
5.	Motor Vehicles Tax	3.39	108.43	11.75	10.06	8.20	24.44
6.	Entertainment Tax	0.97	43.00	3.36	3.99	16.18	19.50

Source: Various issues of Reserve Bank of India, Bulletin

TABLE IX.5 : HARYANA REVENUE RECEIPTS

(Rs. Crores)

		1961-62 Accts.	1985-86 B. E.	% share in 1961-62	% share in 1985-86	Compound growth rate 1961-71	Compound growth rate 1971-84
I.	Total Revenue Receipts	14.56	901.27	100.00	100.00	26.44	16.20
1.	Share of Central Taxes	1.99	75.47	13.67	8.37	21.81	15.59
2.	State's Own Tax Revenues	4.25	495.63	29.19	54.99	34.35	17.72
3.	State's own Non-Tax Revenues	4.23	243.62	29.05	27.03	27.56	13.79
4.	Grants from the Centre	4.09	86.55	28.09	9.61	11.17	16.89
II.	State's Own Tax Revenue	4.25	495.63	100.00	100.00		
1.	Land Revenue	0.64	4.17	15.06	0.84	9.31	6.79
2.	Stamps & Registration	0.54	48.95	12.71	9.88	33.15	13.57
3.	State Excise	0.59	100.06	13.88	20.19	43.12	17.05
4.	Sales Tax	1.32	226.38	31.06	45.67	37.20	19.02
5.	Motor Vehicles Tax	0.14	78.01	3.29	15.74	32.98	34.87
6.	Entertainment Tax	0.11	9.50	2.59	1.92	32.92	15.63

Source: Various issues of Reserve Bank of India, Bulletin

TABLE IX.6 : JAMMU AND KASHMIR, REVENUE RECEIPTS

(Rs. Crores)

		1961-62 Accts.	1985-86 B. E.	% share in 1961-62	% share in 1985-86	Compound growth rate 1961-71	Compound growth rate 1971-84
I.	Total Revenue Receipts	22.07	579.41	100.00	100.00	14.51	14.31
1.	Share in Central Taxes	1.96	133.10	8.88	22.97	14.17	15.08
2.	State's Own Tax Revenues	1.82	88.31	8.25	15.24	16.55	19.45
3.	State's Own Non-Tax Revenues	8.81	74.49	39.92	12.86	9.44	8.25
4.	Grants from the Centre	9.48	283.51	42.95	48.93	19.26	15.65
II.	State's Own Tax Revenue	1.82	88.31	100.00	100.00		
1.	Land Revenue	0.63	0.89	34.62	1.01	-2.46	4.72
2.	Stamps & Registration	0.16	3.25	8.79	3.68	15.17	10.23
3.	State Excise	0.55	21.00	30.22	23.78	18.82	17.50
4.	Sales Tax	0.28	32.56	15.38	36.87	25.65	19.95
5.	Motor Vehicles Tax	0.12	24.75	6.59	28.03	17.11	32.81
6.	Entertainment Tax	0.08	3.00	4.40	3.40	12.38	18.24

Source: Various issues of Reserve Bank of India, Bulletin

TABLE IX.7 : KARNATAKA, REVENUE RECEIPTS

(Rs. Crores)

		1961-62 Accts.	1985-86 B. E.	% share in 1961-62	% share in 1985-86	Compound growth rate 1961-71	Compound growth rate 1971-84
I.	Total Revenue Receipts	84.30	2012.66	100.00	100.00	14.06	14.84
1.	Share of Central Taxes	9.60	312.66	11.39	15.53	16.19	16.02
2.	State's own tax revenues	44.50	1071.44	52.79	53.23	12.36	16.86
3.	State's Own Non-Tax Revenues	15.62	407.43	18.53	20.24	18.47	10.60
4.	Grants from the Centre	14.58	221.13	17.29	11.00	8.32	15.56
II.	State's own tax Revenue	44.50	1071.44	100.00	100.00		
1.	Land Revenue	4.51	9.00	10.14	0.84	-0.39	4.72
2.	Stamps & Registration	2.09	58.00	4.70	5.41	12.61	14.58
3.	State Excise	2.88	190.00	6.47	17.73	26.37	17.16
4.	Sales Tax	9.45	551.00	21.24	51.43	20.18	17.54
5.	Motor Vehicles Tax	4.59	125.18	10.32	11.68	6.52	17.73
6.	Entertainment Tax	0.82	40.27	1.84	3.76	16.28	19.65

Source: Various issues of Reserve Bank of India, Bulletin

BLE IX.8 : KERALA REVENUE RECEIPTS

(Rs. Crores)

		1961-62 Accts.	1985-86 B. E.	% share in 1961-62	% share in 1985-86	Compound growth rate 1961-71	Compound growth rate 1971-84
I.	Total Revenue Receipts	47.20	1156.30	100.00	100.00	13.27	15.06
1.	Share of Central Taxes	8.73	234.51	18.50	20.28	14.54	15.14
2.	State's Own Tax Revenues	24.50	638.59	51.90	55.23	13.13	16.79
3.	States' Own Non-Tax Revenues	6.46	121.37	13.69	10.50	11.03	11.75
4.	Grants from the Centre	7.51	161.83	15.91	13.99	16.06	12.92
II.	State's Own Tax Revenues	24.50	638.59	100.00	100.00		
1.	Land Revenue	1.58	6.19	6.45	0.97	2.20	11.56
2.	Stamps & Registration	1.73	45.87	7.06	7.18	14.12	14.37
3.	State Excise	3.27	100.85	13.35	15.79	15.04	17.42
4.	Sales Tax	10.56	385.00	43.10	60.29	15.27	17.56
5.	Motor Vehicles Tax	2.68	51.56	10.94	8.07	10.07	12.45
6.	Entertainment Tax	0.12	0.32	0.49	0.05	27.96	

ɔurce: Various issues of Reserve Bank of India, Bulletin

TABLE IX-9 :MADHYA PRADESH REVENUE RECEIPTS

(Rs. Crores)

		1961-62 Accts.	1985-86 B. E.	% share in 1961-62	% share in 1985-86	Compound growth rate 1961-71	Compound growth rate 1971-84
I.	Total Revenue Receipts	78.31	2357.07	100.00	100.00	13.19	17.22
1.	Share of Central Taxes	11.65	525.70	14.88	22.30	17.45	16.78
2.	State's Own Tax Revenues	39.60	831.10	50.57	35.26	11.12	16.67
3.	State's Own Non-Tax Revenue	10.44	576.62	13.33	24.46	17.83	17.61
4.	Grants from the Centre	16.62	423.65	21.22	17.98	8.53	18.79
II.	State's Own Tax Revenues	39.60	831.10	100.00	100.00		
1.	Land Revenue	8.78	18.19	22.17	2.19	-3.62	6.49
2.	Stamps & Registration	1.74	43.23	4.39	5.20	14.20	15.26
3.	State Excise	5.71	124.70	14.42	15.00	13.08	14.38
4.	Sales Tax	8.06	426.48	20.35	51.32	20.25	18.01
5.	Motor Vehicles Tax	2.11	129.29	5.33	15.56	7.71	26.45
6.	Entertainment Tax	0.82	24.54	2.07	2.95	13.29	16.91

Source: Various issues of Reserve Bank of India, Bulletin

TABLE IX.10 : MAHARASHTRA, REVENUE RECEIPTS

(Rs. Crores)

		1961-62 Accts.	1985-86 B. E.	% share in 1961-62	% share in 1985-86	Compound growth rate 1961-71	Compound growth rate 1971-84
I.	Total Revenue Receipts	118.75	3817.14	100.00	100.00	15.44	16.3
1.	Share of Central Taxes	14.47	455.65	12.19	11.94	18.19	14.16
2.	State's Own Tax Revenues	72.17	2130.97	60.77	55.83	15.08	16.31
3.	State's Own Non- Tax Revenues	19.70	855.69	16.59	22.41	16.34	17.13
4.	Grants from the Centre	12.41	374.92	10.45	9.82	11.38	18.60
II.	State's Own Tax Revenues	72.17	2130.97	100.00	100.00		
1.	Land Revenue	6.18	25.50	8.56	1.20	3.75	7.11
2.	Stamps & Registration	5.61	70.95	7.77	3.33	9.32	12.39
3.	State Excise	1.26	176.64	1.75	8.43	22.33	27.04
4.	Sales Tax	35.03	1338.60	48.54	62.82	17.16	16.99
5.	Motor Vehicles Tax	5.86	173.71	8.12	8.15	11.19	19.70
6.	Entertainment Tax	2.82	100.71	3.91	4.73	16.57	15.66

Source: Various issues of Reserve Bank of India, Bulletin

TABLE IX.11 : ORISSA, REVENUE RECEIPTS

(Rs. Crores)

		1961-62 Accts.	1985-86 B. E.	1961-62	% share in 1985-86	Compound growth rate 1961-71	Compound growth rate 1971-84
I.	Total Revenue Receipts	37.15	1069.50	100.00	100.00	13.50	14.43
1.	Share of Central Taxes	6.57	312.00	17.69	29.17	15.41	16.51
2.	State's Own Tax Revenues	13.39	297.34	36.04	27.80	10.55	14.86
3.	State's Own Non-Tax Revenues	8.25	129.68	22.21	12.13	13.20	10.86
4.	Grants from the Centre	8.94	330.48	24.06	30.90	15.54	14.74
II.	State's own Tax Revenues	13.39	297.34	100.00	100.00		
1.	Land Revenue	2.42	7.50	18.07	2.52	-6.96	13.78
2.	Stamps & Registration	0.74	14.90	5.53	5.01	12.90	12.65
3.	State Excise	1.67	22.30	12.47	7.50	12.28	10.43
4.	Sales Tax	4.02	153.96	30.04	51.78	15.63	15.49
5.	Motor Vehicles Tax	1.03	32.00	7.69	10.76	11.50	15.27
6.	Entertainment Tax	0.15	6.08	1.12	2.04	12.47	17.44

Source: Various issues of Reserve Bank of India, Bulletin.

TABLE IX.12 : PUNJAB REVENUE RECEIPTS

(Rs. Crores)

		1961-62 Accts.	1985-86 B. E.	% share in 1961-62	% share in 1985-86	Compound growth rate 1961-71	Compound growth rate 1971-84
I.	Total Revenue Receipts	63.40	1158.40	100.00	100.00	9.52	13.45
1.	Share of Central Taxes	6.19	107.16	9.76	9.25	8.94	14.95
2.	State's Own Tax Revenues	27.15	671.51	42.82	57.97	13.00	15.25
3.	State's Own Non-Tax Revenues	22.00	197.61	34.70	17.06	5.93	8.84
4.	Grants from the Centre	8.06	182.12	12.72	15.72	6.70	12.70
II.	State's own Tax Revenues	27.15	671.51	100.00	100.00		
1.	Land Revenue	2.35	3.20	8.66	0.48	-8.13	3.15
2.	Stamps & Registration	3.91	62.20	14.40	9.26	7.69	12.89
3.	State Excise	5.13	159.02	18.90	23.68	20.62	15.56
4.	Sales Tax	7.59	321.32	27.96	47.85	18.27	15.95
5.	Motor Vehicles Tax	0.96	72.26	3.54	10.76	5.18	30.83
6.	Entertainment Tax	0.74		2.73		10.34	

Source: Various issues of Reserve Bank of India, Bulletin.

TABLE IX.13 : RAJASTHAN REVENUE RECEIPTS

(Rs. Crores)

		1961-62	1985-86	% share in		Compound growth rate	
		Accts.	B. E.	1961-62	1985-86	1961-71	1971-84
I.	Total Revenue Receipts	46.21	1423.95	100.00	100.00	15.17	15.85
1.	Share of Central Taxes	7.16	289.82	15.49	20.35	17.28	16.06
2.	State's Own Tax Revenues	21.96	567.95	47.52	39.89	11.77	16.52
3.	State's Own Non-Tax Revenues	7.21	291.73	15.60	20.49	16.92	17.06
4.	Grants from the Centre	9.88	274.45	21.39	19.27	18.37	13.08
II.	State's own Tax Revenues	21.96	567.95	100.00	100.00		
1.	Land Revenue	8.68	19.18	39.53	3.38	0.67	5.32
2.	Stamps & Registration	1.91	26.30	8.70	4.63	8.47	15.97
3.	State Excise	4.42	85.00	20.13	14.97	7.94	16.51
4.	Sales Tax	4.62	325.50	21.04	57.31	21.32	18.35
5.	Motor Vehicles Tax	1.10	79.69	5.01	14.03	13.94	24.03
6.	Entertainment Tax	0.32	11.26	1.46	1.98	16.11	17.75

Source: Various issues of Reserve Bank of India, Bulletin.

TABLE IX.14 : TAMILNADU REVENUE RECEIPTS

(Rs. Crores)

		Accts.	1961-62 B. E.	1985-86 1961-62	% share in 1985-86	Compound growth rate 1961-71	Compound growth rate 1971-84
I.	Total Revenue Receipts	92.18	2368.47	100.00	100.00	14.32	15.14
1.	Share of Central Taxes	16.24	428.61	17.62	18.10	15.56	15.88
2.	State's Own Tax Revenues	44.71	1461.73	48.50	61.72	14.07	17.12
3.	State's Own Non-Tax Revenues	20.54	215.41	22.28	9.09	15.17	6.67
4.	Grants from the Centre	10.69	262.72	11.60	11.09	11.39	18.08
II.	State's own Tax Revenues	44.71	1461.73	100.00	100.00		
1.	Land Revenue	4.43	21.26	9.91	1.45	-3.89	3.31
2.	Stamps & Registration	5.22	82.45	11.68	5.64	12.91	11.27
3.	State Excise	0.33	222.23	0.74	15.20	17.37	47.55
4.	Sales Tax	21.26	963.01	47.55	65.88	16.55	17.97
5.	Motor Vehicles Tax	7.03	100.40	15.72	6.87	11.32	11.56
6.	Entertainment Tax	2.28	54.70	5.10	3.74	15.76	13.52

Source: Various issues of Reserve Bank of India, Bulletin.

TABLE IX.15 : UTTAR PRADESH REVENUE RECEIPTS

(Rs. Crores)

		1961-62 Accts.	1985-86 B. E.	% share in 1961-62	% share in 1985-86	Compound growth rate 1961-71	Compound growth rate 1971-84
I.	Total Revenue Receipts	153.99	3429.29	100.00	100.00	13.14	13.97
1.	Share of Central Taxes	29.98	1126.27	19.47	32.84	18.03	13.73
2.	State's Own Tax Revenues	65.68	1163.40	42.65	33.93	10.59	11.52
3.	State's Own Non-Tax Revenues	35.46	438.34	23.03	12.78	14.19	7.82
4.	Grants from the Centre	22.87	701.28	14.85	20.45	11.02	20.24
II.	State's own Tax Revenues	65.68	1163.40	100.00	100.00		
1.	Land Revenue	21.12	35.24	32.16	3.03	-0.24	3.59
2.	Stamps & Registration	4.19	120.39	6.38	10.35	13.81	16.79
3.	State Excise	8.42	180.00	12.82	15.47	13.86	13.74
4.	Sales Tax	13.02	626.63	19.82	53.86	17.54	19.91
5.	Motor Vehicles Tax	3.43	117.59	5.22	10.11	9.91	20.66
6.	Entertainment Tax	1.72	55.41	2.62	4.76	17.45	15.99

Source: Various issues of Reserve Bank of India, Bulletin.

TABLE IX.16 : WEST BENGAL REVENUE RECEIPTS

(Rs. Crores)

		1961-62 Accts.	1985-86 B. E.	% share in 1961-62	% share in 1985-86	Compound growth rate 1961-71	Compound growth rate 1971-84
I.	Total Revenue Receipts	101.70	2197.23	100.00	100.00	12.17	14.36
1.	Share of Central Taxes	17.10	548.45	16.81	24.96	15.32	15.90
2.	State's Own Tax Revenues	53.51	1059.77	52.62	48.23	10.41	14.67
3.	State's Own Non-Tax Revenues	12.81	183.15	12.60	8.34	12.04	14.02
4.	Grants from the Centre	18.28	405.86	17.97	18.47	14.54	10.74
II.	State's own Tax Revenues	53.51	1059.77	100.00	100.00		
1.	Land Revenue	6.20	103.29	11.59	9.75	1.28	17.20
2.	Stamps & Registration	4.20	52.26	7.85	4.93	8.35	12.24
3.	State Excise	6.96	91.40	13.01	8.62	10.35	11.42
4.	Sales Tax	21.45	610.00	40.09	57.56	13.53	15.66
5.	Motor Vehicles Tax	2.35	97.39	4.39	9.19	10.74	21.17
6.	Entertainment Tax	1.86	35.16	3.48	3.32	9.95	14.94

Source: Various issues of Reserve Bank of India, Bulletin.

TABLE IX.17 : TOTAL 16 STATES <u>REVENUE RECEIPTS</u>

	1961-62 Accts.	1985-86 B. E.	% share in 1961-62	% share in 1985-86	(Rs. Crores) Compound growth rate 1961-71	1971-84
I. Total Revenue Receipts	1128.45	29971.99		100.00	100.00	13.62
1. Share of Central Taxes	188.32	6253.76		16.69	20.87	15.86
2. State's Own Tax Revenues	537.73	13680.10		47.65	45.64	12.71
3. State's Own Non-Tax Revenues	207.68	5014.20		18.40	16.73	14.28
4. Grants from the Centre	194.72	5023.93		17.26	16.76	13.03
II. State's own Tax Revenues	537.73	13680.10		100.00	100.00	
1. Land Revenue	94.25	352.10		17.53	2.57	0.15
2. Stamps & Registration	40.82	775.45		7.59	5.67	12.00
3. State Excise	58.68	1918.51		10.89	14.02	15.08
4. Sales Tax	180.08	7835.88		33.49	57.28	17.23
5. Motor Vehicles Tax	38.46	1350.25		7.15	9.87	11.45
6. Entertainment Tax	15.41	443.48		2.87	3.24	15.28

Source: Various issues of Reserve Bank of India, Bulletin.

TABLE-IX-18: RATES OF GROWTH OF PRINCIPAL TAXES 1970-82 (As worked out by N.I.P.F.P.)

	STATE 1	Stamps & registration 2	Stae Excise 3	Sales Tax 4	Vehicle Taxes 5	Electricity Duty 6	Entertain-ment Tax 7
I.	Non-Hill States						
1.	Andhra Pradesh	13.18	18.43	17.87	11.56	*	12.23
2.	Assam (1972-82)	7.00	7.17	12.47	10.73	12.96	13.49
3.	Bihar	4.68	9.50	16.67	13.10	5.82	4.58
4	Gujarat	12.60	18.42	16.58	8.83	21.10	15.13
5.	Haryana	12.37	16.03	18.23	18.88	23.51	13.12
6.	Karnataka	10.34	13.54	15.35	11.92	6.71	13.94
7.	Kerala	15.41	20.95	14.53	8.29	19.57	##
8.	Madhya Pradesh	11.30	12.19	14.66	18.42	19.30	12.12
9.	Maharashtra	6.78	18.88	15.89	8.92	13.09	11.28
10.	Orissa	11.52	5.59	16.72	9.14	22.31	17.01
11.	Punjab	9.90	13.54	12.99	13.26	18.76	9.34
12.	Rajasthan	7.95	4.04	16.74	14.32	18.65	12.67
13.	Tamil Nadu	9.24	**	16.61	6.95	*	11.94
14.	Uttar Pradesh	15.15	9.61	17.35	11.87	13.50	13.38
15.	West Bengal	7.49	8.18	13.99	13.69	6.69	11.78
II.	Hill States						
1.	Himachal Pradesh (1972-82)	7.31	10.87	16.04	7.62	24.76$	1.05
2.	Jammu & Kashmir (1971-82)	10.91	4.04	18.11	22.04	21.64	11.27
3.	Manipur	3.12	15.20	10.66	12.57	N.A	10.32
4.	Meghalaya	7.92	18.15	15.24	15.82	16.03	5.40
5.	Nagaland	21.43	11.78	19.34	15.20	N.A.	18.56
6.	Sikkim (1976-82)	5.00	18.71	15.86	15.09	N.A.	16.77#
7.	Tripura	6.72	9.42	33.00₵ -	5.74	N.A.	13.87

* In these States Electricity Duty has been merged in Electricity Tariff.
** There was more or less complete prohibition in this State upto July 1981.
$ This is for the period 1976-82.
# This is for the period 1976-81.
₵ This is for the period 1977-82.
This tax has been transferred to Local Bodies for levy since 1.8.75.
N A. Not avallable.
N B. The above rates are at constant rates of taxation.
Source: Report of National Insititute of Public Finance and Policy (N.I.P.F.P.)
Source: Report of the VIII Finance Commission.

TABLE IX.19 : RATES OF GROWTH OF PRINCIPAL TAXES AS ADOPTED BY THE EIGHTH FINANCE COMMISSION

(Percent)

STATE	Stamps Regist-ration	State Excise	Sales Tax	Vehicles Taxes	Extertainment Tax
1	2	3	4	5	6
I. Non-Hill States					
1. Andhra Pradesh	9.5	10.0	10.5	7.0	8.0
2. Assam	5.0	7.0	7.0	6.0	7.0
3. Bihar	5.0	7.0	9.5	8.0	8.0
4. Gujarat	8.5	7.0	9.5	7.0	10.0
5. Haryana	8.0	10.0	10.5	11.0	8.0
6. Karnataka	6.0	10.0	8.5	7.0	9.0
7. Kerala	10.0	7.0	8.0	7.0	-
8. Madhya Pradesh	6.5	7.0	8.0	10.0	8.0
9. Maharastra	7.0	10.0	9.5	7.0	8.0
10. Orissa	7.0	7.0	9.0	7.0	8.0
11. Punjab	7.0	10.0	10.0	8.0	8.0
12. Rajasthan	5.0	7.0	9.0	9.0	8.0
13. Tamil Nadu	5.5	10.0	10.0	7.0	8.0
14. Uttar Pradesh	10.0	7.0	9.0	7.0	8.0
15. West Bengal	5.0	7.0	8.0	8.5	8.0
II. Hill States					
1. Himachal Pradesh	4.0	7.0	9.0	6.0	6.0
2. Jammu & Kashmir	5.5	10.0	10.0	11.0	6.0
3. Manipur	4.0	7.0	7.0	6.0	6.5
4. Meghalaya	4.0	7.0	7.0	6.0	6.0
5. Nagaland	5.0	7.0	7.0	6.0	6.0
6. Sikkim	4.0	7.0	7.0	6.0	6.0
7. Tripura	5.0	7.0	7.0	6.0	7.0

Source : Report of the Eighth Finance Commission, 1984

TABLE IX-20 : ESTIMATED YIELD FROM ADDITIONAL RESOURCE MOBILISATION MEASURES ADOPTED IN DIFFERENT STATES (Rs. in Crores)

	First Plan 1951-1956	Second Plan 1956-1961	Third Plan 1961-1966	Fourth Plan 1969-1974	Fifth Plan 1974-1979 Budget Proposals	Annual Plan 1979-1980 Budget Proposals	Sixth Plan 1980-1985 Budget Proposals
1. Andhra Pradesh	-	22.2	47.4	115.4	1.2	-	
2. Assam	-	4.2	13.2	8.2	-4.7	4.3	-
3. Bihar	-	15.3	24.0	36.8	44.2	12.0	1.00
4. Gujarat	-	28.2#	44.1	66.9	36.7	8.3	295.9
5. Haryana	-	-	-	16.8	5.0	9.9	77.7
6. Himachal Pradesh	-	-	-	5.6	6.8	3.7	22.5
7. Jammu & Kashmir	-	3.7	6.1	10.5	8.0	3.0	-
8. Karnataka	-	15.4	38.3	88.8	49.4	30.0	16.7
9. Kerala	-	13.7	26.2	43.8	30.3	-	133.2
10. Madhya Pradesh	-	13.7	32.3	103.9	40.9	11.3	93.4
11. Maharastra	-	##	79.2	129.8	78.3	29.9	91.5
12. Meghalaya	-	-	-	-	-	0.6	72.4
13. Manipur	-	-	-	0.2	-	-	1.1
14. Nagaland	-	-	-	2.7	-	-	-
15. Orissa	-	5.1	32.7	40.3	20.6	17.1	-
16. Punjab	-	16.0	52.4	42.7	25.8	-	72.7
17. Rajasthan	-	14.1	31.2	37.6	22.0	30.0	122.4
18. Sikkim	-	-	-	-	-	-	66.3
19. Tamil Nadu	-	20.1	56.8	155.9	53.4	2.0	0.7
20. Tripura	-	-	-	0.3	0.5	-	135.4
21. Uttar Pradesh	-	31.8	89.6	99.3	67.6	37.5	-
22. West Bengal	-	40.6	41.4	52.7	66.6	34.0	170.2
Total	80.4*	244.1	615.7	1058.2	552.6	242.6	1373.1

* State wise figures for re-organised states are not available

\# Relates to composite state of Bombay

\## Included in Gujarat.

Source : Government of India, Ministry of Finance, 'Indian Economics Statistics' December 1978 and 1984

TABLE IX-21 : ESTIMATED YIELD FROM ADDITIONAL RESOURCE MOBILISATION MEASURES BY THE CENTRE AND STATES

Rs. Crores

Plan period	Centre	States	Total
First Plan	314	80	394
Second Plan	991	244	1235
Third Plan	2,276	616	2,892
Fourth Plan	3,261	1,058	4,319
Fifth Plan (1974-79)	8,289	5,738	14,027
Sixth Plan			
1980-81 (Actuals)	501	425	926
1981-82 (Actuals)	2,597	1,557	4,154
1982-83 (Actuals)	4,038	2,784	6,822
1983-84 (Actuals)	5,598	4,125	9,723
1984-85 (R.E)	6,099	5,246	11,345
Total 1980-85	18,833	14,137	32,970
Sixth Plan Target	12,290	9,012	21,302
Seventh Plan Target	22,490	22,212	44,702

Note : Estimated yield during the first, second, third and Fourth Plan in respect of the Centre is nEt of States share in Central Taxes. For the fifth plan it is gross of States share. In respect of the States the estimated yield relates to States own tax efforts only, i.e., excluding their share in Centre's efforts of additional resources mobilisation, upto the Fifth Plan period. For the Sixth Plan period it includes share in the yield from Central measures.

Source: 1. Government of India, Ministry of Finance,'Indian Economic Statistics-December 1985'.

2. Government of India, 'Planning Commission, 'Seventh Five year Plan Vol.I'1985.

TABLE IX.22 : ADDITIONAL RESOURCES MOBILIZATION BY STATES - YIELD IN 1980-85 FROM MEASURES TAKEN DURING 1980-85

Rs.Crores.

STATE	TARGET Original	Total of annually approved	State Govt. Tax measures	Non tex measures	Public a/c Impounding of
1	2	3	4	5	6
I. Spl. Category States					
1. Assam	348.00	247.61	71.74	3.21	17.35
2. Himachal Pradesh	53.13	82.68	28.17	-	11.23
3. Jammu & Kashmir	137.47	140.79	51.20	8.14	63.08
4. Manipur	15.03	20.85	3.24	1.29	4.65
5. Meghalaya	13.85	28.30	5.53	1.70	-
6. Nagaland	3.97	9.16	1.93	3.36	8.94
7. Sikkim	3.55	5.19	2.16	1.62	-
8. Tripura	5.00	6.68	4.03	-	-
Total-(I)	580.00	541.26	168.00	19.32	105.25
II. Non-Spl. Category States					
1. Andhra Pradesh	532.70	827.16	209.79	33.90	-
2. Bihar	600.00	1230.05	232.83	394.27	214.47
3. Gujarat	500.00	1146.87	429.55	31.02	39.34
4. Haryana	416.11	489.27	93.73	79.53	33.30
5. Karnataka	457.71	839.43	298.81	36.70	-
6. Kerala	310.91	479.32	94.55	10.86	-
7. Madhya Pradesh	600.00	1139.81	112.71	89.62	338.24
8. Maharashtra	900.00	1755.26	634.18	15.50	-
9. Orissa	350.00	574.45	149.71	53.35	36.47
10. Punjab	400.00	727.72	219.51	44.02	59.45
11. Rajasthan	750.70	742.53	201.96	160.24	98.82
12. Tamil Nadu	1101.65	1407.56	927.06	--	--
13. Uttar Pradesh	1000.00	1459.49	511.41	53.65	83.18
14. West Bengal	512.33	836.20	387.02	2.50	-
Total-II	8432.11	13654.12	4502.82	1005.16	903.37
GRAND TOTAL:	9012.11	14195.38	4670.82	1024.48	1008.82

(Contd.) TABLE IX.22 : ADDITIONAL RESOURCES MOBILIZATION BY STATES - YIELD IN 1980-85 FROM MEASURES TAKEN DURING 1980-85

Rs.Crores.

	STATE	TOTAL 4, 5 & 6	State electricity	State Road Transport Board	Total 7, 8 & 9 Corporation
		7	8	9	10
I. Spl. Category States					
1.	Assam	92.30	61.32	13.16	166.78
2.	Himachal Pradesh	39.40	22.96	24.31	86.67
3.	Jammu & Kashmir	122.42	7.56	16.70	146.68
4.	Manipur	9.18	-	0.95	10.13
5.	Meghalaya	7.23	20.80	2.19	30.22
6.	Nagaland	14.23	-	-	14.23
7.	Sikkim	3.78	-	-	3.78
8.	Tripura	4.03	-	-	4.03
Total-I	292.57	112.64	57.31	462.52	
II.	Non-Spl. Category States				
1.	Andhra Pradesh	243.69	299.12	215.98	758.79
2.	Bihar	841.57	306.04	20.58	1168.19
3.	Gujarat	499.91	817.97	164.43	1482.31
4.	Haryana	206.56	173.59	-	380.15
5.	Karnataka	335.51	287.73	166.71	789.95
6.	Kerala	105.41	155.81	108.04	369.26
7.	Madhya Pradesh	540.57	542.02	84.87	1167.46
8.	Maharashtra	649.68	628.23	391.91	1669.82
9.	Orissa	239.53	166.89	16.99	423.41
10.	Punjab	322.98	287.20	36.89	647.07
11.	Rajasthan	461.02	178.29	95.82	735.13
12.	TamilNadu	927.06	310.42	301.09	1538.57
13.	Uttar Pradesh	648.24	628.94	173.59	1450.77
14.	West Bengal	389.52	324.21	32.67	746.40
TOTAL-I		6411.25	5106.46	1800.07	13327.28
GRAND TOTAL:		6703.82	5219.10	1857.38	13789.80

Source: Government of India, Ministry of Finance, Statistical Statements on Finance and Plans of States and Union Territories 1985.

TABLE IX.23 : STATE TARGETS OF ADDITIONAL RESOURCES MOBILISATION

(Rs. Crores)

STATES	A. R. M. TARGETS 1985-86	1985-90
SPECIAL CATEGORY STATES		
1. Assam	41.32	257.00
2. Himachal Pradesh	13.00	125.00
3. Jammu & Kashmir	21.81	143.55
4. Manipur	0.69	8.62
5. Meghalaya	0.88	8.18
6. Nagaland	0.39	4.21
7. Sikkim	0.34	4.58
8. Tripura	0.50	6.00
TOTAL: (I):	78.93	557.14
11.NON-SPECIAL CATEGORY STATES:		
1. Andhra Pradesh	204.42	1711.80
2. Bihar	85.60	1601.81
3. Gujarat	106.82	1691.38
4. Haryana	60.90	550.00
5. Karnataka	189.13	1537.71
6. Kerala	106.74	1002.96
7. Madhya Pradesh	184.03	1000.00
8. Maharashtra	341.58	3232.36
9. Orissa	77.27	1042.83
10. Punjab	100.00	2000.00
11. Rajasthan	103.51	1000.00
12. Tamil Nadu	100.00	1000.00
13. Uttar Pradesh	163.81	2870.22
14. West Bengal	91.18	1671.00
TOTAL II:	1914.99	21912.07
GRAND TOTAL(I&II):	1993.92	22469.21

Source: Government of India, Ministry of Finance, Statistical Statements on Finances and Plans of STATES and Union Territories 1985.

TABLE-IX-24 6.1 : ESTIMATED YIELD FROM ADDITIONAL TAXATION OF THE CENTRE

(Rs. crores)

	Measures during															
	1971-72	1972-73	1973-74	1974-75 Regular Budget	Suppl. Budget	1975-76	1976-77	1977-78	1978-79	1979-80	1980-81	1981-82	1982-83	1983-84	1984-85	1985-86
1. Income-tax (including corporation tax)	34.5	16.5	18.6	-	-	1.5	-	78.4	16.7	53.6	-	-115.0	-59.2	69.6	-75.0	48.0 (54.0)
2. Wealth Tax	-	-	-	-	-	-	-	9.9	-	-	-	-	-	-	-	-
3. Custom duties	72.0	20.4	154.2	20.0	1.0	34.1	36.7	-5.0	10.4	139.3	24.8	282.7	390.6	393.0	458.1	285.0 $ (287.1)
4. Union Excise duties	141.1	134.8	117.4	190.9	110.0	280.2	8.3	43.3	472.4	432.5	147.7	28.4	192.7	315.3 (259.5)	-189.3	314.7
5. Central Sales Tax Union Territory of Delhi		-	-	-		1.7	-	-	-	-	-	-	-	-	-	-
6. Tax on Foreign Traval	3.4	-	-	-		-	-	-	-	-	-	-	-	-	-	-
7. Interest Tax	-	-	-	-	25.0	-	-	-	-108.0	-	80.0	-	-	104.0	-	-170.0
8. Stamp duty & Excise duty on medical & toilet preparations in Union Territories	-	-	-	-		-	0.9	-	-	-	-	-	-	-	-	-8.2
9. Hotel Receipts Tax	-	-	-	-		-	-	-	-	-	5.0	-	-6.0	-	-	-
10. Total	251.0	171.7	290.2	210.9	236.0	257.5	49.9	126.6	391.5	625.4	257.5	196.1	151.1	673.9	193.8	477.9 (430.9)
11. Increase in Railway fares & freight	26.2	17.0	43.2	136.4	140.1	39.0	87.4	-	-	160.0	204.2	252.9	257.5	431.4	114.2	495.0
12. Step-up in postal rates	7.2	-	-	42.8	-	-	141.0#	-	11.4	48.3	13.0	25.0**	26.##	10.0	-	-
13. Licence fee for Radio/ Transistor with one and two bands	-	-	-	-		-	-	-	-	-	-4.0	-	-	-	-	-

Source: Government of Inida, Ministry of Finance, 'Inidan Economics Statistics 1985'.

(Contd.) TABLE-IX-24 6.1: ESTIMATED YIELD FROM ADDITIONAL TAXATION OF THE CENTRE

(Rs. crores)

	Measures during 1971-72	1972 73	1973-74	1974-75	Regular Budget	1975-76 Suppl. Budget	1976-77	1977-78	1978-79	1979-80	1980-81	1981-82	1982-83	1983-84	1984-85	1985-86
14. Special Levels from refugees from Bangladesh	10.7	-	-	-	-	-	-	-	-	-	-	-	-	-	-	-
15. TOTAL (10 to 14)	295.1	188.7	333.4	390.1	276.1	296.5	274.3	126.6	402.9	833.7	470.7	574.0	801.6	1115.3	308.0	972.9$ (925.9)
16. Deduct: States Share of Taxes	40.1	48.1	42.5	25.9	13.0	40.2	5.2	9.2	91.5	195.8	59.0	-74.9	53.4	90.0	-79.1	134.1 (120.0)
a) Income Tax	-	2.4	4.7	-	-	-6.7	-	-3.5	-3.4	12.0	-	-85.6	-44.4	-34.7	-38.7	-2.5
b) Estate Duty	-	-	-	-	-	-	-	-	-	-	-	-	-	-	-	-
c) Union Excise	40.1	45.7	37.8	25.9	13.0	46.9	5.2	12.6	94.9	xx	59.0	10.7	98.6	124.7	-40.4	136.6 (120.0)
d) Hotel Receipt	-	-	-	-	-	-	-	-	-	-	-	-	-0.8	-	-	-
17. Total Net of States Share (15-16)	255.0	140.6	290.9	364.2	263.1	256.3	269.1	117.4	311.4	637.9	411,7	648.9	748.2	1025.33	87.1	838.8$ (806.0)

f Excluding States' Share of Rs. 38.25 crores in 1975-76
/ Excluding States Share of Rs. 25.94 crores in 1976-77
$ After the Budget's approval by Parliament.
* Measures effective from January 1, 1982 are expected to yield an additional Rs. 60 croors during the remaining periodof 1981-82 which became effective from March 1,1982.
** Does not include the effect of measures
# Became effective from Ist March,1976
Does not include the effect of measures which became effctive from March 1, 1983. Note: Estimated yield during first, second and third plan periods is net of States share.
Source: Government of India. Ministry of Finance, Indian Economics Statistics 1985

TABLE IX.25 : TOTAL REVENUE RECEIPTS-1961-62 to 1985-86

(Rs. Crores)

STATE	1961-62 Accts	1962-63 Accts	1963-64 Accts	1964-65 Accts	1965-66 Accts	1966-67 Accts	1967-68 Accts	1968-69 Accts	1969-70 Accts	1970-71 Accts	1971-72 Accts	1972-73 Accts	1973-74 Accts
Andhra Pradesh	85.76	112.88	136.36	142.69	163.36	172.36	184.27	238.60	248.20	296.26	333.44	346.23	454.92
Assam	40.36	45.45	49.56	58.24	70.63	77.72	87.21	87.41	111.05	101.19	117.58	116.11	114.24
Bihar	79.81	93.37	100.00	111.39	127.24	133.96	161.06	170.94	210.21	229.31	267.45	319.65	335.60
Gujarat	62.70	83.32	90.97	103.64	120.70	135.59	152.21	163.74	192.80	221.89	260.21	291.13	340.97
Haryana	14.56	16.26	20.14	21.87	25.85	24.27	61.77	78.61	84.95	99.18	114.91	137.38	153.98
Jammu & Kashmir	22.07	25.32	26.55	26.53	31.67	49.49	47.84	55.61	64.84	66.05	76.95	94.35	88.73
Karnataka	84.30	91.81	102.09	111.06	127.69	156.40	170.99	223.91	234.72	246.57	264.00	316.84	368.32
Kerala	47.20	66.02	72.26	80.88	91.09	108.69	125.41	142.54	136.92	150.79	179.19	196.49	217.72
Madhya Pradesh	78.31	81.60	104.70	110.46	122.43	137.87	167.46	179.15	214.84	228.15	269.48	314.90	351.83
Maharashtra	118.75	149.60	187.25	202.61	227.39	272.03	309.69	363.90	395.53	456.31	521.38	621.44	743.66
Orissa	37.15	62.27	69.29	74.98	80.39	106.80	109.03	116.62	131.13	135.83	151.32	168.13	174.62
Punjab	63.40	75.04	93.07	101.65	113.58	117.00	105.46	122.98	144.12	170.36	174.28	214.24	233.50
Rajasthan	46.21	58.66	68.03	73.87	96.88	96.75	121.38	130.46	157.01	168.85	185.11	223.75	264.36
Tamil Nadu	92.18	117.97	134.77	153.88	172.80	194.55	233.39	277.92	280.91	313.89	400.34	445.67	490.36
Uttar Pradesh	153.99	190.00	213.46	234.15	263.97	300.87	350.16	380.34	435.79	485.40	525.89	575.36	674.96
West Bengal	101.70	107.51	125.91	141.33	169.82	185.33	198.99	224.53	261.68	268.02	425.43	351.22	378.93
TOTAL	1128.45	1377.08	1594.41	1749.23	2005.47	2269.68	2586.32	2957.26	3304.70	3638.05	4266.96	4732.89	5386.70

STATE	1974-75 Accts	1975-76 Accts	1976-77 Accts	1977-78 Accts	1978-79 Accts	1979-80 Accts	1980-81 Accts	1981-82 Accts	1982-83 Accts	1983-84 Accts	1984-85 R.E.	1985-86 B.E.
Andhra Pradesh	526.25	652.19	727.84	811.52	944.35	1136.22	1264.54	1466.29	1639.07	1953.35	2407.41	2847.48
Assam	169.69	202.00	219.57	270.78	305.05	269.28	522.20	365.47	439.04	550.72	700.06	809.36
Bihar	376.63	492.26	518.44	588.20	686.13	870.57	988.08	1160.08	1318.84	1504.37	1815.11	1988.84
Gujarat	378.28	453.27	535.35	616.17	674.39	836.56	1024.99	1159.46	1349.29	1565.14	1771.64	1855.62
Haryana	187.09	228.53	257.79	295.84	334.83	402.12	459.94	536.07	611.62	698.59	795.68	901.27
Jammu & Kashmir	123.29	148.53	160.30	179.13	222.83	203.88	258.09	298.57	325.02	375.83	438.36	579.41
Karnataka	413.10	514.12	559.11	598.49	688.55	819.30	953.46	1166.64	1280.66	1489.46	1806.76	2012.66
Kerala	287.97	351.55	386.18	444.94	522.15	519.62	640.38	850.48	810.17	934.24	1032.32	1156.30
Madhya Pradesh	423.37	546.78	614.05	653.58	772.32	958.63	1133.94	1344.06	1516.14	1800.00	2042.83	2357.07
Maharashtra	802.72	1049.38	1204.83	1290.20	1533.44	1794.33	2038.06	2385.40	2838.20	3251.98	3550.52	3817.14
Orissa	227.37	277.46	325.79	368.86	447.44	467.59	621.33	601.53	801.62	783.07	819.67	1069.50
Punjab	250.02	304.41	376.41	406.12	481.00	519.35	567.66	682.61	786.04	879.13	911.86	1158.40
Rajasthan	327.49	394.92	452.59	486.54	595.88	653.37	752.85	857.08	1009.06	1143.12	1233.85	1423.95
Tamil Nadu	523.98	567.57	631.19	681.75	801.48	944.85	1279.96	1441.55	1678.02	1962.51	2239.90	2368.47
Uttar Pradesh	730.65	968.12	1115.41	1164.66	1361.81	1684.47	1898.73	2259.67	2556.08	2655.41	3158.01	3429.29
West Bengal	460.19	562.35	621.11	699.27	828.19	963.14	1091.70	1223.75	1379.26	1533.13	1796.77	2197.23
TOTAL	6199.19	7713.44	8705.96	9556.35	11199.84	13043.28	15495.91	17798.71	20338.13	23080.05	26520.75	29971.99

CONTD. TABLE IX.25: SHARE IN CENTRAL TAXES. 1961-62 TO 1985-86. (Rs. Crores).

STATE	1961-62	1962-63	1963-64	1964-65	1965-66	1966-67	1967-68	1968-69	1969-70	1970-71	1971-72	1972-73	1973-74
	Accts	Accts	Accts	Accts	Accts	Accts	Accts	Accts	Accts	Accts	Accts	Accts	Accts
Andhra Pradesh	14.64	17.50	20.35	20.19	21.65	28.31	31.59	37.33	47.19	57.16	71.27	79.98	88.41
Assam	7.68	11.79	12.61	12.20	11.94	13.53	15.33	15.24	20.41	20.04	25.81	28.57	27.38
Bihar	16.35	21.40	23.79	24.50	26.54	34.08	37.23	44.72	69.96	84.48	103.79	111.51	128.12
Gujarat	18.01	13.73	15.71	15.45	16.57	20.63	22.70	26.98	31.16	37.79	47.19	53.06	58.67
Haryana	1.99	2.86	3.32	3.29	3.53	3.96	7.20	8.73	10.16	12.28	13.32	17.73	18.90
Jammu & Kashmir	1.96	3.28	3.46	3.29	3.63	5.90	6.38	7.65	5.78	7.00	8.67	8.77	10.65
Karnataka	9.60	12.13	13.72	14.15	15.76	20.55	23.56	27.06	32.47	39.28	49.37	55.53	58.92
Kerala	8.73	11.72	13.12	12.74	13.88	17.43	19.55	22.68	27.82	33.51	40.41	47.15	47.38
Madhya Pradesh	11.65	15.48	18.09	17.80	19.27	25.07	27.59	33.34	46.65	56.31	69.64	78.46	86.28
Maharashtra	14.47	25.41	28.80	30.41	30.83	44.40	50.61	58.11	66.49	80.45	101.33	113.24	124.57
Orissa	6.57	10.46	12.20	11.88	13.07	15.13	16.57	20.05	25.31	30.54	37.66	42.15	46.42
Punjab	6.19	9.28	10.69	10.53	11.44	12.92	10.57	12.82	15.01	18.24	22.88	25.84	28.46
Rajasthan	7.16	10.07	11.77	11.57	12.55	16.37	17.97	21.77	28.87	34.93	43.31	48.81	53.77
Tamil Nadu	16.24	18.07	20.86	20.88	21.89	30.81	35.21	40.73	48.90	59.18	74.19	83.26	86.15
Uttar Pradesh	29.98	30.85	35.40	35.31	37.58	55.13	61.06	72.18	106.65	128.15	157.39	176.49	193.64
West Bengal	17.10	20.62	23.65	24.13	25.50	34.74	40.16	46.21	52.14	63.75	79.28	88.61	96.26
Total	188.32	234.65	267.54	268.32	285.63	378.96	423.28	495.60	634.97	763.09	945.51	1059.16	1153.98

STATE	1974-75	1975-76	1976-77	1977-78	1978-79	1979-80	1980-81	1981-82	1982-83	1983-84	1984-85	1985-86
	Accts	Accts	Accts	Accts	*Accts	Accts	Accts	Accts	Accts	Accts	R.E.	B.E.
Andhra Pradesh	98.48	128.04	135.85	144.78	157.55	264.29	295.75	333.48	360.88	408.32	439.18	521.33
Assam	31.94	41.55	44.04	46.86	51.06	88.07	98.32	113.10	121.95	137.47	146.96	224.33
Bihar	127.10	165.09	176.10	187.22	204.74	382.59	423.85	480.74	522.37	590.51	630.44	711.04
Gujarat	63.48	83.16	87.03	92.90	97.04	173.33	189.67	208.10	211.17	226.71	287.82	247.66
Haryana	20.77	27.14	19.58	37.58	33.06	54.06	61.23	68.03	72.61	80.78	90.88	75.47
Jammu & Kashmir	10.29	13.37	13.67	14.82	15.45	26.13	28.97	35.02	38.25	43.48	47.86	133.10
Karnataka	66.55	86.65	91.54	97.89	106.30	177.75	197.73	222.53	240.09	271.15	298.88	312.66
Kerala	47.14	61.70	64.95	69.06	75.16	136.65	151.41	170.81	185.94	209.48	233.28	234.51
Madhya Pradesh	93.23	121.50	129.67	136.65	149.83	271.72	302.88	341.37	372.17	423.07	463.70	525.70
Maharashtra	123.25	161.53	168.37	180.74	194.71	301.59	336.40	368.54	421.93	449.92	515.49	455.65
Orissa	47.24	61.46	65.21	69.37	75.68	144.36	159.98	180.74	197.26	222.76	243.21	312.00
Punjab	28.93	38.18	39.53	42.21	45.67	73.35	82.21	92.24	99.23	111.65	122.18	107.16
Rajasthan	57.12	74.49	79.04	83.99	91.71	157.23	174.52	196.36	213.61	242.01	266.97	289.82
Tamil Nadu	97.36	122.37	128.51	136.39	148.55	262.97	291.76	329.48	356.38	402.03	435.05	428.61
Uttar Pradesh	197.25	256.85	273.45	291.24	317.62	569.12	632.22	711.87	775.33	682.11	961.65	1126.27
West Bengal	101.68	134.14	140.05	149.08	161.73	277.57	309.89	348.09	379.25	433.92	472.43	548.45
Total	1211.81	1577.22	1656.59	1780.78	1925.86	3360.78	3736.79	4200.50	1568.42	4935.37	5655.98	6253.76

(CONTD.) TABLE IX.25:STATES OWN TAX REVENUES 1961-62 TO 1985-86. (Rs. Crores).

STATE	1961-62 Accts	1962-63 Accts	1963-64 Accts	1964-65 Accts	1965-66 Accts	1966-67 Accts	1967-68 Accts	1968-69 Accts	1969-70 Accts	1970-71 Accts	1971-72 Accts	1972-73 Accts	1973-74 Accts
Andhra Pradesh	45.97	50.29	63.91	66.98	69.13	73.14	79.48	105.55	107.04	135.01	138.10	130.72	201.24
Assam	13.82	11.63	13.50	15.88	18.86	19.35	22.93	24.05	27.50	26.01	28.99	32.01	32.14
Bihar	35.84	40.96	45.28	48.49	54.69	55.63	74.13	73.80	77.67	76.90	85.12	104.91	114.56
Gujarat	28.56	34.48	39.17	47.71	53.08	60.71	69.95	78.93	92.94	108.09	125.10	140.97	151.19
Haryana	4.25	4.61	6.04	6.99	7.68	8.38	26.34	34.72	37.69	43.89	51.11	60.50	76.14
Jammu & Kashmir	1.82	2.20	2.72	3.15	3.16	3.77	4.72	6.00	6.70	7.09	7.91	11.85	15.92
Karnataka	44.50	31.44	39.31	41.55	44.56	51.50	61.23	76.69	86.72	100.19	111.61	128.88	150.38
Kerala	24.50	22.56	27.08	33.77	37.32	42.47	50.46	53.65	57.85	64.70	71.05	79.68	95.46
Madhya Pradesh	39.60	32.59	39.66	46.96	48.64	53.48	63.54	69.85	79.92	86.59	94.90	110.83	128.35
Maharashtra	72.17	78.06	100.37	111.54	108.73	152.08	168.23	127.61	215.48	255.51	274.27	302.81	382.26
Orissa	13.39	13.23	16.54	18.92	20.08	21.11	24.19	25.99	28.34	33.19	34.69	39.88	42.20
Punjab	27.15	29.42	38.56	44.58	48.11	53.45	50.20	56.22	75.83	86.00	92.21	109.58	123.16
Rajasthan	21.96	25.25	28.39	32.45	35.07	38.93	46.60	49.32	53.79	60.46	65.66	74.90	90.67
Tamil Nadu	44.71	51.09	60.74	71.82	80.39	91.60	107.91	114.11	129.58	146.71	188.41	220.30	273.11
Uttar Pradesh	65.68	70.10	77.45	80.13	91.00	102.65	122.84	133.35	141.19	152.67	155.57	177.77	225.61
West Bengal	53.51	60.01	77.19	81.89	92.46	97.82	106.70	112.91	126.24	129.75	145.12	172.83	191.18
TOTAL	537.73	557.92	669.91	752.81	812.96	926.13	1079.45	12[illegible]2.75	1344.48	1512.76	1669.82	1898.42	2293.57

STATE	1974-75 Accts	1975-76 Accts	1976-77 Accts	1977-78 Accts	1978-79 Accts	1979-80 Accts	1980-81 Accts	1981-82 Accts	1982-83 Accts	1983-84 Accts	1984-85 R.E.	1985-86 B.E.
Andhra Pradesh	251.82	325.55	342.84	368.21	420.94	492.71	582.08	702.89	808.39	965.37	1127.88	1444.59
Assam	38.44	59.33	63.21	78.64	87.65	72.06	65.78	90.27	108.35	135.67	142.47	150.49
Bihar	144.23	186.36	208.46	213.98	203.92	233.59	276.54	338.12	381.48	441.49	487.88	529.74
Gujarat	201.15	235.98	298.19	329.26	372.61	448.88	531.02	660.62	763.03	879.05	990.58	1077.54
Haryana	99.11	116.95	138.07	147.68	170.57	197.30	233.91	290.62	336.68	365.87	411.87	495.63
Jammu & Kashmir	18.86	25.31	26.88	30.61	34.64	29.00	37.80	60.26	61.89	71.44	78.90	88.31
Karnataka	198.59	236.73	269.25	297.27	334.00	404.86	474.86	607.04	674.10	759.52	941.40	1071.44
Kerala	123.56	159.70	186.50	213.36	254.24	290.80	336.54	374.18	438.35	486.77	573.20	638.59
Madhya Pradesh	172.83	231.46	249.56	260.25	283.13	320.25	385.88	475.86	558.25	642.99	730.94	831.10
Maharashtra	497.89	585.96	679.97	712.80	850.81	980.85	1130.34	1383.68	1647.98	1822.49	1945.28	2130.79
Orissa	50.43	68.41	80.82	83.77	98.38	112.10	132.08	159.72	173.62	200.93	225.56	297.34
Punjab	151.61	172.80	201.98	235.12	267.08	309.06	343.84	432.18	490.47	544.13	528.50	671.51
Rajasthan	106.15	130.80	151.67	172.71	229.79	216.79	230.23	311.98	389.47	441.18	490.17	567.95
Tamil Nadu	305.68	319.10	346.34	361.41	504.32	486.36	639.11	842.40	1011.53	1145.24	1350.64	1461.73
Uttar Pradesh	297.96	393.36	453.76	467.31	508.16	562.27	645.19	822.83	929.30	992.10	1107.36	1163.40
West Bengal	224.84	280.97	314.21	344.64	408.16	467.76	514.08	616.09	637.88	768.63	963.67	1059.77
Total	2883.15	3528.77	4011.71	4317.02	5028.40	5624.64	6564.10	8168.74	9410.77	10662.87	12141.30	13680.10

(ONTD.)TABLE IX.25:STATES OWN NON-TAX REVENUES (Rs. Crores).

STATE	1961-62	1962-63	1963-64	1964-65	1965-66	1966-67	1967-68	1968-69	1969-70	1970-71	1971-72	1972-73	1973-74
	Accts	Accts	Accts	Accts	Accts	Accts	Accts	Accts	Accts	Accts	Accts	Accts	Accts
Andhra Pradesh	11.15	27.38	30.68	32.37	48.68	44.46	43.30	48.77	52.50	62.96	69.55	69.49	98.60
Assam	5.52	5.93	6.99	9.94	14.03	9.39	8.96	10.00	10.68	7.91	7.96	9.78	14.86
Bihar	10.67	17.31	18.34	23.33	23.30	23.25	20.17	30.92	30.23	36.33	38.20	43.56	42.42
Gujarat	8.85	23.44	24.88	26.58	30.00	37.04	37.41	37.69	45.94	52.21	61.15	57.48	74.53
Haryana	4.23	5.89	6.98	7.34	8.00	8.39	21.97	28.57	29.67	33.49	32.32	44.00	43.56
Jammu & Kashmir	8.81	12.16	12.08	11.58	12.97	14.80	16.03	18.94	19.72	21.78	23.18	27.94	23.53
Karnataka	15.62	33.62	33.18	38.11	49.10	52.50	51.54	80.67	94.97	85.36	75.26	95.93	117.61
Kerala	6.46	19.65	20.28	21.37	25.11	20.03	23.79	27.75	27.83	27.91	39.54	34.19	39.53
Madhya Pradesh	10.44	18.83	32.30	26.84	35.00	40.13	44.50	52.56	58.20	57.54	65.71	73.70	89.42
Maharashtra	19.70	32.76	43.82	42.34	62.88	48.47	63.46	86.62	87.82	90.81	100.35	107.86	119.77
Orissa	8.25	19.06	18.43	21.74	26.64	27.45	27.26	31.37	36.56	33.17	34.75	37.83	41.82
Punjab	22.00	30.62	36.35	38.17	40.96	43.66	33.67	34.84	42.48	51.96	38.28	41.07	45.78
Rajasthan	7.21	12.08	14.06	13.67	30.79	19.01	27.85	28.10	31.07	34.52	34.16	45.89	54.21
Tamil Nadu	20.54	33.95	36.47	42.21	46.82	49.04	61.51	81.67	75.91	82.04	101.32	95.61	88.86
Uttar Pradesh	35.46	65.46	75.33	83.74	95.10	94.53	11.68	126.94	137.37	152.07	149.74	137.45	162.31
West Bengal	12.81	17.09	19.44	19.89	28.97	34.11	31.87	44.32	39.41	28.72	31.22	35.01	42.64
Total	207.68	375.24	429.61	458.77	578.35	566.26	629.70	769.73	819.59	858.78	908.69	956.79	1099.45

STATE	1974-75	1975-76	1976-77	1977-78	1978-79	1979-80	1980-81	1981-82	1982-83	1983-84	1984-85	1985-86
	Accts	Accts	Accts	Accts	Accts	Accts	Accts	Accts	Accts	Accts	R.E	B.E
Andhra Pradesh	96.54	105.18	133.74	155.05	172.86	195.06	228.83	263.23	259.78	309.42	519.46	511.62
Assam	17.77	22.27	26.86	40.98	43.04	43.73	264.70	56.66	73.63	77.89	88.35	86.56
Bihar	39.97	61.18	51.18	81.35	83.38	91.15	95.41	156.45	194.99	229.24	347.42	344.31
Gujarat	78.69	86.77	106.87	133.01	124.14	152.59	185.56	188.45	245.11	292.15	311.23	336.66
Haryana	55.13	64.75	78.16	78.46	93.39	11.78	119.31	137.98	159.88	179.54	203.32	243.62
Jammu & Kashmir	28.87	36.49	37.23	42.63	55.11	54.28	77.74	76.77	62.50	61.03	57.20	74.49
Karnataka	125.37	155.80	155.06	145.35	183.19	177.62	201.77	243.69	265.59	316.37	363.00	407.43
Kerala	55.17	62.87	67.79	80.64	92.03	122.01	100.05	232.33	116.39	118.26	123.91	121.37
Madhya Pradesh	117.86	145.84	169.29	176.89	216.23	253.67	263.90	350.00	394.98	473.99	513.30	576.62
Maharashtra	143.72	252.94	303.67	321.57	368.02	392.99	437.34	502.71	585.91	708.99	758.11	855.60
Orissa	48.04	58.12	77.98	81.30	94.88	61.27	134.03	98.84	104.39	126.73	122.13	129.68
Punjab	50.68	62.01	77.59	76.92	124.54	104.48	92.56	114.86	147.06	156.37	158.20	197.61
Rajasthan	77.71	97.73	113.82	106.50	92.40	146.24	198.36	175.93	232.63	267.45	277.42	291.73
Tamil Nadu	93.81	93.64	102.23	110.48	66.19	121.78	232.57	144.01	167.53	190.00	215.22	215.41
Uttar Pradesh	148.55	188.02	217.60	187.57	217.32	259.88	242.96	294.06	374.85	404.75	396.30	438.34
West Bengal	54.68	65.84	73.60	88.33	90.14	138.78	153.37	139.51	164.67	158.10	174.15	183.15
TOTAL	1232.56	1559.96	1803.33	1907.03	2116.86	2427.31	3022.46	3175.48	3549.89	4070.28	4628.72	5014.20

(CONTD.) TABLE IX.25: GRANTS FROM THE CENTRAL 1961-62 TO 1985-86 (Rs. Crores).

STATE	1961-62	1962-63	1963-64	1964-65	1965-66	1966-67	1967-68	1958-69	1969-70	1970-71	1971-72	1972-73	1973-74
	Accts	Accts	Accts	Accts	Accts	Accts	Accts	Accts	Accts	Accts	Accts	Accts	Accts
Andhra Pradesh	14.00	17.71	21.42	23.15	23.90	26.35	29.90	46.95	41.47	41.13	54.52	66.04	66.67
Assam	13.34	16.10	16.46	20.67	25.80	35.45	39.99	38.12	52.46	47.23	54.82	45.75	39.86
Bihar	16.99	13.70	12.59	15.07	22.11	21.00	29.53	21.50	32.35	31.60	40.34	59.67	50.50
Gujarat	6.98	11.67	11.21	13.90	21.05	17.21	22.15	20.14	22.76	23.80	26.77	39.62	56.58
Haryana	4.09	2.90	3.80	4.25	6.64	3.54	6.26	6.59	7.43	9.52	12.16	15.15	15.38
Jammu & Kashmir	9.48	7.68	8.29	8.51	11.91	25.02	20.11	23.02	32.64	30.18	37.19	45.79	38.63
Karnataka	14.58	14.62	15.88	17.25	18.25	31.85	34.66	39.49	20.56	21.74	27.76	36.50	41.41
Kerala	7.51	12.09	11.78	13.00	14.78	28.76	31.61	38.46	23.42	24.67	28.19	35.47	35.35
Madhya Pradesh	16.62	14.70	14.65	18.86	19.52	19.19	31.83	23.40	30.01	27.71	39.23	51.91	47.78
Maharashtra	12.41	13.37	14.26	18.32	24.95	27.08	27.39	31.56	26.24	29.54	45.43	97.53	117.06
Orissa	8.94	19.52	22.12	22.44	20.60	43.11	41.01	39.21	40.92	38.93	44.22	48.27	44.18
Punjab	8.06	5.72	7.47	8.37	13.07	6.97	11.02	9.10	10.80	14.16	20.91	37.75	36.10
Rajasthan	9.88	11.26	13.81	16.18	18.47	22.44	29.23	31.27	43.28	38.94	41.98	54.15	65.71
Tamil Nadu	10.69	14.86	16.70	18.97	23.70	23.10	28.76	41.41	26.52	25.96	36.42	46.50	42.24
Uttar Pradesh	22.87	23.59	25.28	34.97	40.29	48.56	49.58	47.87	50.58	52.51	63.19	83.65	93.40
West Bengal	18.28	9.79	11.63	15.42	22.89	18.60	20.26	21.09	44.16	45.80	169.81	54.77	48.85
Total	194.72	209.28	227.35	269.33	328.53	398.23	453.89	479.18	505.66	503.42	742.94	818.52	839.70

STATE	1974-75	1975-76	1976-77	1977-78	1978-79	1979-80	1980-81	1981-82	1982-83	1983-84	1884-85	1985-86
	Accts	Accts	Acct	Accts	Accts	Accts	Accts	Accts	Accts	Accts	R.E.	B.E.
Andhra Pradesh	79.51	93.42	115.41	143.48	193.00	184.16	163.88	166.69	210.02	270.24	275.89	369.94
Assam	81.54	78.35	85.46	104.30	123.30	65.42	93.40	105.44	135.11	199.69	322.28	347.98
Bihar	56.33	79.63	72.04	105.65	194.09	163.24	192.28	184.77	220.00	243.13	349.37	403.75
Gujarat	34.96	47.36	43.26	61.00	80.60	61.76	118.74	102.29	129.98	167.23	182.01	193.76
Haryana	12.08	19.69	21.98	32.12	37.81	38.98	45.49	39.44	42.45	72.40	89.61	86.55
Jammu & Kashmir	65.27	73.36	82.52	91.07	117.63	94.47	113.58	126.52	162.38	199.88	254.40	283.51
Karnataka	22.59	34.94	43.26	57.98	65.06	59.07	79.28	93.38	100.88	142.42	203.48	221.13
Kerala	62.10	67.28	66.96	81.88	100.72	42.16	52.38	73.16	69.49	119.73	101.93	161.83
Madhya Pradesh	39.45	47.98	65.53	79.79	123.13	112.99	181.28	176.83	190.74	259.95	334.89	423.65
Maharashtra	37.86	48.94	52.82	75.09	119.90	118.90	133.93	130.47	182.38	270.58	331.64	374.92
Orissa	81.66	89.47	101.78	134.42	178.50	149.86	195.24	162.23	326.35	232.65	228.77	330.48
Punjab	18.80	31.42	57.31	51.87	43.71	71.87	44.05	43.33	49.28	66.98	102.98	182.12
Rajasthan	86.51	91.90	108.06	123.34	181.98	133.11	149.74	172.81	173.35	192.48	199.29	274.45
Tamil Nadu	27.13	32.46	54.11	73.47	82.42	73.74	116.52	125.66	142.58	225.24	238.99	262.72
Uttar Pradesh	86.89	129.89	170.60	218.54	318.71	293.20	378.36	430.91	476.60	576.45	692.70	701.28
West Bengal	78.99	81.40	93.25	117.22	168.16	79.03	112.36	120.06	197.46	172.48	186.52	405.86
TOTAL	871.67	1047.49	1234.33	1551.22	2128.72	1741.96	2170.56	2253.99	2809.05	3411.53	4094.75	5023.93

(CONTD.) TABLE IX.25: LAND REVENUE 1961-62 TO1985-86. (Rs. Crores).

STATE	1961-62 Accts	1962-63 Accts	1963-64 Accts	1964-65 Accts	1965-66 Accts	1966-67 Accts	1967-68 Accts	1968-69 Accts	1969-70 Accts	1970-71 Accts	1971-72 Accts	1972-73 Accts	1973-74 Accts
Andhra Pradesh	10.12	16.49	20.18	18.05	14.12	11.07	7.90	20.16	11.34	20.12	19.91	11.26	41.90
Assam	2.86	3.20	3.15	3.96	5.49	4.86	5.21	5.04	7.34	6.98	6.75	9.25	3.38
Bihar	9.11	15.41	12.52	12.07	12.05	5.46	3.24	13.26	11.26	6.98	7.73	10.74	11.55
Gujarat	4.64	6.80	5.98	7.60	7.32	6.32	7.81	7.26	7.81	8.99	11.02	5.84	6.72
Haryana	0.64	1.00	1.08	0.89	0.85	0.64	1.43	1.45	1.73	1.60	1.62	1.58	0.68
Jammu & Kashmir	0.63	0.69	0.60	0.75	0.44	0.38	0.58	0.69	0.61	0.45	0.73	0.59	0.56
Karnataka	4.51	5.19	8.23	7.11	5.57	3.86	7.41	7.09	5.14	4.72	4.60	5.41	5.27
Kerala	1.58	1.12	0.77	2.45	2.65	2.00	1.85	1.61	1.95	1.15	1.83	2.62	3.08
Madhya Pradesh	8.78	9.63	10.62	10.92	6.99	5.50	7.26	7.87	7.81	7.30	7.64	7.46	11.32
Maharashtra	6.18	7.29	8.13	7.27	5.58	7.26	8.74	8.82	7.97	9.89	12.02	10.26	15.26
Orissa	2.42	2.79	3.01	2.99	2.87	2.51	1.61	1.58	1.73	1.67	1.79	2.06	2.31
Punjab	2.35	3.66	3.95	3.27	3.13	2.34	1.85	1.87	1.72	1.69	1.19	1.35	1.13
Rajasthan	8.68	9.41	7.53	8.81	6.98	6.98	10.14	7.23	8.15	10.71	8.57	7.24	12.81
Tamil Nadu	4.43	4.41	6.05	5.51	6.76	3.88	5.28	3.29	3.21	4.15	4.49	3.68	7.83
Uttar Pradesh	21.12	25.13	25.19	20.31	24.10	20.49	25.33	24.31	21.44	22.05	6.00	9.96	25.11
West Bengal	6.20	7.84	6.42	7.82	7.02	6.00	8.28	7.47	10.11	5.90	5.19	5.23	7.41
Total	94.25	120.06	123.41	119.78	11.92	89.55	103.92	119.00	109.32	114.35	101.08	94.53	156.32

STATE	1974-75 Accts	1975-76 Accts	1976-77 Accts	1977-78 Accts	1978-79 Accts	1979-80 Accts	1980-81 Accts	1981-82 Accts	1982-83 Accts	1983-84 Accts	1984-85 R.E.	1985-86 B.E.
Andhra Pradesh	26.09	48.47	25.49	27.73	32.38	31.86	32.76	34.15	25.62	14.47	25.72	57.99
Assam	3.02	7.17	3.18	2.51	2.96	2.97	2.89	2.97	3.33	4.26	4.00	4.00
Bihar	12.08	21.76	20.81	23.64	15.10	11.70	11.35	16.76	12.08	20.50	21.00	22.50
Gujarat	6.38	8.67	7.53	9.47	6.90	8.80	12.92	14.52	13.62	16.22	14.70	14.00
Haryana	6.25	6.54	5.76	5.02	4.75	3.15	3.93	3.64	3.38	3.76	3.82	4.17
Jammu & Kashmir	0.64	0.80	0.65	0.73	0.77	0.72	0.72	0.75	0.81	0.82	0.87	0.89
Karnataka	6.95	7.09	4.25	4.94	6.95	6.92	6.47	8.80	7.31	8.60	8.50	9.00
Kerala	2.92	3.50	3.20	2.88	3.78	3.32	3.20	3.13	3.47	4.77	6.19	6.19
Madhya Pradesh	15.88	25.01	19.78	21.78	11.08	7.94	9.64	11.83	13.09	16.54	17.10	18.19
Maharashtra	21.32	15.64	18.59	14.19	20.85	19.66	16.01	21.82	29.57	24.16	25.47	25.50
Orissa	2.43	3.19	4.39	4.83	5.47	4.68	6.47	5.26	4.99	8.94	5.78	7.50
Punjab	1.83	1.32	1.18	1.27	2.61	30.18	2.42	3.19	3.37	2.53	3.11	3.20
Rajasthan	7.47	15.65	11.79	9.02	12.43	7.67	9.64	25.00	24.33	21.00	20.80	19.18
Tamil Nadu	1.72	11.53	5.09	5.55	6.85	8.08	4.34	9.66	10.17	6.34	16.17	21.26
Uttar Pradesh	32.76	40.37	38.66	20.71	46.86	25.95	22.73	35.56	28.43	34.86	30.07	35.24
West Bengal	8.34	10.96	10.15	10.75	20.07	5.85	7.47	6.33	4.69	46.46	101.76	103.29
TOTAL:	156.08	227.65	180.50	165.02	199.81	179.45	152.96	203.37	188.26	234.23	305.06	352.10

(CONTD.) TABLE IX.25: STAMPS AND REGISTRATION 1961-62 TO 1985-86.

(Rs. Crores) >

STATE	1961-62 Accts	1962-63 Accts	1963-64 Accts	1964-65 Accts	1965-66 Accts	1966-67 Accts	1967-68 Accts	1968-69 Accts	1969-70 Accts	1970-71 Accts	1971-72 Accts	1972-73 Accts	1973-74 Accts
Andhra Pradesh	2.35	3.75	4.57	5.47	6.21	6.48	8.14	9.18	9.20	10.02	12.27	7.84	14.61
Assam	0.47	0.65	0.75	0.83	0.84	0.98	1.42	1.30	1.43	1.42	1.54	1.69	1.82
Bihar	3.83	4.49	5.62	6.40	7.37	8.00	8.53	7.51	8.16	8.94	9.94	11.26	12.80
Gujarat	2.13	2.84	3.09	3.40	3.53	4.00	4.65	5.31	6.05	6.91	7.97	8.59	8.40
Haryana	0.54	0.84	0.85	0.95	0.85	0.99	3.60	4.75	6.05	5.37	6.84	6.47	7.02
Jammu & Kashmir	0.16	0.24	0.26	0.27	0.27	0.32	0.43	0.46	0.60	0.64	0.60	0.78	0.70
Karnataka	2.09	2.94	3.44	3.65	4.39	4.89	5.54	5.65	6.11	6.81	7.63	9.01	7.52
Kerala	1.73	2.64	3.02	3.76	4.37	4.60	5.14	5.25	6.17	6.63	7.03	8.11	10.06
Madhya Pradesh	1.74	2.12	2.52	2.79	3.19	3.52	4.36	4.84	5.32	5.76	6.49	7.31	8.04
Maharashtra	5.61	7.16	8.43	8.68	9.08	9.89	11.26	11.86	13.26	13.36	15.31	17.82	17.90
Orissa	0.74	1.10	1.39	1.49	1.64	1.70	2.05	2.13	2.37	2.66	3.21	3.28	3.47
Punjab	3.91	4.93	5.69	6.30	5.66	6.65	6.21	6.83	7.99	9.31	10.01	11.38	12.63
Rajasthan	1.91	1.28	1.59	1.58	1.75	1.85	2.35	2.67	2.78	3.03	3.47	4.33	4.12
Tamil Nadu	5.22	6.72	8.19	9.37	9.96	11.02	13.35	13.51	15.53	16.78	17.72	19.23	25.62
Uttar Pradesh	4.19	5.42	6.28	7.47	8.01	8.95	10.46	10.93	13.18	14.59	17.97	14.80	20.51
West Bengal	4.20	5.83	6.55	7.55	8.63	8.67	10.54	9.14	9.31	9.43	9.51	11.35	15.29
Total	40.82	52.95	62.24	69.96	75.75	82.51	98.03	101.32	113.51	121.66	137.06	143.20	170.51

STATE	1974-75 Accts	1975-76 Accts	1976-77 Accts	1977-78 Accts	1978-79 Accts	1979-80 Acct	1980-81 Accts	1981-82 Accts	1982-83 Accts	1983-84 Accts	1984-85 R.E.	1985-86 B.E.
Andhra Pradesh	15.87	16.83	19.68	21.64	25.12	28.24	35.28	40.81	44.49	45.22	49.25	61.94
Assam	2.00	2.29	2.35	2.44	2.80	2.64	2.62	3.52	3.40	4.76	5.62	6.06
Bihar	16.15	17.07	16.03	18.62	15.27	17.95	14.51	17.15	30.99	34.07	29.43	30.45
Gujarat	9.48	13.54	12.91	17.38	21.75	25.80	29.49	37.69	38.40	39.88	46.76	48.25
Haryana	7.72	9.14	7.89	10.15	13.09	15.21	18.35	25.37	25.18	28.08	33.00	48.95
Jammu & Kashmir	0.76	0.73	0.72	0.97	1.16	1.38	1.84	2.97	3.14	2.27	2.99	3.25
Karnataka	12.85	10.79	10.78	14.95	17.91	22.15	29.08	29.31	32.64	39.97	50.00	58.00
Kerala	11.94	13.31	15.29	17.25	22.05	22.99	25.83	29.53	32.62	38.00	41.74	45.87
Madhya Pradesh	9.71	13.08	12.57	14.48	16.52	17.66	22.21	28.73	30.14	36.49	40.59	43.23
Maharashtra	18.96	20.19	22.43	27.67	37.40	34.25	42.88	49.32	54.06	61.00	67.72	70.95
Orissa	4.38	5.25	5.16	5.63	6.56	7.21	7.82	9.28	10.79	12.51	11.72	14.90
Punjab	17.65	18.48	17.28	21.51	27.67	30.18	35.83	46.75	50.12	45.01	40.66	62.20
Rajasthan	5.12	5.15	6.08	7.90	9.26	11.39	13.86	15.24	17.95	20.79	23.90	26.30
Tamil Nadu	25.77	23.89	22.22	27.62	30.92	39.12	44.92	54.29	62.73	67.27	80.12	82.45
Uttar Pradesh	28.05	25.96	37.75	55.19	56.70	64.23	68.96	87.04	110.40	109.70	117.39	120.39
West Bengal	17.55	19.67	20.95	21.11	22.91	25.00	28.72	34.47	39.31	42.32	47.11	52.26
TOTAL	203.96	215.37	230.09	284.51	327.09	365.40	422.21	511.47	586.36	627.34	688.00	775.45

(CONTD.) TABLE IX.25: STATE EXCISE 1961-62 TO 1985-86.

(Rs. Crores).

STATE	1961-62 Accts	1962-63 Accts	1963-64 Accts	1964-65 Accts	1965-66 Accts	1966-67 Accts	1967-68 Accts	1968-69 Accts	1969-70 Accts	1970-71 Accts	1971-72 Accts	1972-73 Accts	1973-74 Accts
Andhra Pradesh	8.73	9.04	11.86	12.42	13.74	14.40	16.00	18.02	25.36	35.47	34.71	34.19	43.43
Assam	2.04	2.13	2.00	1.84	2.16	2.51	2.96	2.90	2.62	2.60	2.55	2.14	2.85
Bihar	6.31	6.37	6.77	6.49	8.18	9.16	10.76	11.06	11.40	11.88	12.65	14.11	17.93
Gujarat	0.31	0.37	0.39	0.45	0.49	0.50	0.62	0.73	0.83	0.73	0.82	0.72	0.90
Haryana	0.59	0.61	0.76	1.11	1.37	1.49	6.26	8.40	7.44	8.84	9.54	12.46	14.99
Jammu & Kashmir	0.55	0.66	0.67	0.79	0.89	1.29	1.65	2.08	2.05	2.15	2.37	5.03	4.56
Karnataka	2.88	2.93	3.52	3.73	4.04	4.41	7.11	13.11	17.97	19.73	23.55	29.65	37.64
Kerala	3.27	3.59	3.91	4.56	5.01	5.59	9.27	9.27	8.70	10.01	9.99	9.42	12.06
Madhya Pradesh	5.71	5.78	6.75	7.99	8.94	10.13	11.83	13.02	1449	15.78	17.44	19.56	22.64
Maharashtra	1.26	1.47	1.72	3.05	3.26	3.77	4.15	5.47	7.26	6.82	7.89	10.12	25.16
Orissa	1.67	1.81	1.95	2.13	2.23	2.45	2.87	4.16	4.22	4.25	17.48	21.21	22.47
Punjab	5.13	5.34	6.64	9.62	11.89	12.95	15.15	21.94	22.52	22.83	26.91	31.40	34.63
Rajasthan	4.42	5.11	5.64	6.36	7.80	8.38	7.79	939	8.09	8.77	9.38	12.02	12.93
Tamil Nadu	0.33	0.38	0.41	0.40	0.49	0.51	0.76	0.84	1.17	1.40	22.23	39.15	56.46
Uttar Pradeh	8.42	9.53	11.09	12.60	14.23	17.58	20.10	24.45	23.31	24.43	27.28	30.89	36.57
West Bengal	6.96	7.69	8.81	10.55	11.64	13.40	13.19	13.68	16.08	17.08	18.44	18.90	20.26
Total	58.58	62.81	72.89	84.54	96.36	108.88	130.47	158.99	173.51	193.17	243.23	290.97	365.48

STATE	1974-75 Accts.	1975-76 Accts.	1976-77 Accts.	1977-78 Accts.	1978-79 Accts.	1979-80 Accts.	1980-81 Accts.	1981-82 Accts.	1982-83 Accts.	1983-84 Accts.	1984-85 R. E.	1985-86 B. E.
Andhra Pradesh	58.11	75.93	96.52	103.38	119.90	141.12	153.02	194.38	235.47	282.48	335.00	387.00
Assam	2.77	2.95	3.87	4.37	4.09	3.95	3.62	4.74	4.28	5.70	6.00	6.42
Bihar	22.74	25.80	25.01	24.23	19.51	3.69	17.92	24.92	28.56	34.95	40.00	42.80
Gujarat	0.97	1.26	2.52	2.53	2.74	3.16	3.45	3.96	4.91	5.26	5.43	6.09
Haryana	19.04	21.06	23.52	25.35	23.69	34.52	42.???	51.99	61.91	68.40	87.38	100.06
Jammu & Kashmir	5.49	6.64	7.50	7.87	9.10	9.55	10.70	14.64	14.57	17.50	19.00	21.00
Karnataka	47.54	52.01	52.20	56.24	02.60	73.80	93.71	117.74	131.69	154.67	186.53	190.00
Kerala	15.55	21.54	31.03	39.03	42.30	60.99	65.23	53.99	73.37	80.73	85.04	100.85
Madhya Pradesh	29.64	35.41	38.03	41.37	45.31	48.53	59.34	68.41	80.47	91.63	110.00	124.70
Maharashtra	29.36	34.92	40.99	47.88	53.75	70.???	88.70	113.04	139.80	153.18	169.47	179.64
Orissa	27.31	38.04	47.07	47.13	55.18	7.82	9.17	11.02	13.07	15.44	18.28	22.30
Punjab	39.88	45.50	49.05	62.30	66.36	88.23	93.12	116.03	136.57	149.59	150.36	159.02
Rajasthan	17.01	19.54	22.94	27.55	24.48	20.45	13.46	33.64	53.55	63.95	72.00	85.00
Tamil Nadu	25.22	3.10	4.66	4.19	3.33	5.18	12.57	110.38	152.13	219.88	220.82	222.23
Uttar Pradesh	49.19	48.78	64.07	73.49	51.45	70.44	89.86	119.26	130.78	130.19	170.00	180.00
West Bengal	22.55	26.55	26.44	31.86	35.60	43.91	51.75	58.06	60.36	69.66	76.37	91.40
TOTAL	412.37	459.03	535.48	599.32	619.39	685.62	808.60	1096.20	1321.49	1543.21	1751.68	1918.51

(CONTD.) TABLE IX.25 : SALES TAX 1961-62 TO 1985-86 (Rs. Crores)

STATE	1961-62	1962-63	1963-64	1964-65	1965-66	1966-67	1967-68	1968-69	1969-70	1970-71	1971-72	1972-73	1973-74
	Accts	Accts	Accts	Accts	Accts	Accts	Accts	Accts	Accts	Accts	Accts	Accts	Accts
Andhra Pradesh	14.81	15.36	19.03	23.01	24.59	30.09	34.77	41.36	43.09	49.91	50.01	54.70	73.86
Assam	3.45	4.15	5.41	6.81	7.99	8.39	10.21	11.77	12.24	11.54	14.16	14.90	16.18
Bihar	11.34	12.45	16.75	17.63	21.42	26.65	34.54	33.03	35.70	36.17	40.10	48.30	52.39
Gujarat	13.82	15.39	19.60	24.81	26.98	35.13	39.22	45.89	54.57	63.83	73.62	87.42	93.97
Haryana	1.32	1.48	2.08	2.62	2.94	3.46	9.54	12.84	14.19	17.42	21.62	24.59	31.05
Jammu & Kashmir	0.28	0.41	0.76	0.84	0.76	1.09	1.33	1.85	2.22	2.49	2.60	3.68	3.49
Karnataka	9.45	11.22	13.52	16.48	19.54	26.43	28.25	34.20	40.51	48.87	51.59	58.01	68.22
Kerala	10.56	12.01	14.52	15.99	18.30	22.78	26.29	28.87	32.24	37.42	42.37	46.14	53.80
Madhya Pradesh	8.06	9.60	12.66	16.86	20.00	23.56	28.24	31.20	37.65	40.97	44.21	52.66	59.03
Maharashtra	35.03	40.57	54.90	62.40	70.59	87.47	96.09	106.45	125.34	155.59	156.98	174.66	231.16
Orissa	4.02	5.50	7.44	8.99	9.93	10.97	12.56	13.06	14.50	17.54	17.48	21.21	22.47
Punjab	7.59	8.49	11.97	15.07	16.95	19.91	18.06	24.85	30.71	37.28	37.69	46.09	52.51
Rajasthan	4.62	6.45	9.77	11.61	14.17	15.91	19.76	22.51	26.13	27.97	33.10	37.05	44.82
Tamil Nadu	21.26	24.80	27.02	35.30	40.95	48.77	56.48	61.12	72.15	81.86	98.97	114.02	132.25
Uttar Pradesh	13.02	14.63	18.67	21.11	24.85	30.13	38.03	41.95	47.13	52.02	58.42	70.40	101.18
West Bengal	21.45	24.68	32.18	36.89	45.38	48.65	52.30	56.89	63.30	67.93	74.18	91.24	101.69
TOTAL	180.08	207.19	266.28	316.42	365.34	439.39	505.67	567.34	651.67	748.81	817.10	945.13	1138.13

STATE	1974-75	1975-76	1976-77	1977-78	1978-79	1979-80	1980-81	1981-82	1982-83	1983-84	1984-85	1985-86
	Accts.	Accts.	Accts.	Accts.	Accts.	Accts.	Accts.	Accts.	Accts.	Accts.	R. E.	B. E.
Andhra Pradesh	110.27	141.08	152.64	162.71	181.44	217.41	278.79	341.67	401.88	503.38	615.74	743.55
Assam	20.75	27.18	28.54	28.44	34.32	35.08	31.49	53.26	75.44	93.89	95.98	101.10
Bihar	69.77	92.70	114.00	121.65	129.10	154.99	191.73	240.08	263.75	298.41	336.60	368.44
Gujarat	134.52	155.85	198.35	211.93	235.25	289.37	353.85	462.41	504.01	554.87	620.00	226.38
Haryana	39.05	49.50	63.95	69.62	79.20	88.12	104.83	138.37	160.48	167.46	187.70	226.38
Jammu & Kashmir	4.22	6.57	6.80	8.86	10.49	12.80	17.88	22.89	23.67	26.50	29.15	32.56
Karnataka	93.63	117.87	137.30	151.09	164.49	199.78	237.36	318.86	344.78	399.30	492.00	551.00
Kerala	75.31	97.92	107.60	118.74	146.88	162.64	203.94	245.49	275.20	306.61	350.00	385.00
Madhya Pradesh	85.73	117.38	126.58	126.74	139.64	161.04	200.00	260.96	307.65	352.78	387.78	426.48
Maharashtra	308.72	370.04	439.10	460.85	537.27	604.24	731.83	924.11	1026.94	1196.71	1234.57	1338.60
Orissa	27.31	38.04	47.07	47.13	55.18	65.95	76.63	94.29	102.05	114.00	127.02	153.96
Punjab	63.35	73.16	96.12	107.51	119.31	129.79	155.93	191.82	219.93	255.33	250.00	321.32
Rajasthan	57.54	67.60	84.29	100.25	113.68	135.86	147.31	186.21	222.23	249.98	278.00	325.50
Tamil Nadu	187.88	208.93	229.34	243.04	293.52	324.77	456.88	547.33	655.49	701.52	860.60	963.01
Uttar Pradesh	141.66	208.26	243.17	246.03	272.25	280.78	335.10	453.33	486.98	551.14	605.37	626.63
West Bengal	125.07	159.12	182.47	198.02	237.20	281.07	299.55	379.04	389.63	450.06	550.00	610.00
TOTAL	1542.78	1931.20	2257.32	2402.61	2749.22	3143.69	3823.10	4860.12	5460.11	6221.94	7020.51	7835.88

(CONTD.) TABLE IX.25 : TAXES ON VEHICLES AND TAXES ON GOODS AND PASSENGERS - 1961-62 TO 1985-86 (Rs. Crores)

STATE	1961-62	1962-63	1963-64	1964-65	1965-66	1966-67	1967-68	1968-69	1969-70	1970-71	1971-72	1972-73	1973-74
	Accts	Accts	Accts	Accts	Accts	Accts	Accts	Accts	Accts	Accts	Accts	Accts	Accts
Andhra Pradesh	2.76	3.32	6.81	6.47	8.33	8.31	9.45	13.12	14.10	14.87	15.82	15.83	20.31
Assam	0.77	0.76	1.19	1.28	1.18	1.34	1.62	1.55	1.66	1.71	1.98	1.98	2.70
Bihar	0.14	0.17	0.20	0.18	0.20	0.25	0.33	2.37	3.33	3.68	4.48	5.22	7.52
Gujarat	3.39	4.27	3.21	3.43	3.84	4.20	4.76	5.52	6.28	6.99	7.45	8.55	21.73
Haryana	0.14	0.15	0.14	0.15	0.16	0.18	0.58	0.80	1.11	1.31	1.64	2.34	15.76
Jammu & Kashmir	0.12	0.13	0.21	0.27	0.51	0.34	0.36	0.42	0.49	0.50	0.69	0.77	6.15
Karnataka	3.59	5.56	7.20	5.43	5.70	6.10	6.89	7.70	8.29	9.46	10.20	11.16	15.81
Kerala	2.68	3.02	3.75	3.91	4.15	4.40	5.15	5.43	5.90	6.82	7.02	7.15	10.39
Madhya Pradesh	2.11	2.18	2.28	2.58	2.85	2.93	3.14	3.27	3.68	4.19	4.53	4.76	14.60
Maharashtra	5.86	6.02	6.47	7.38	7.76	9.58	10.41	11.83	13.06	13.98	15.39	16.33	41.29
Orissa	1.03	1.29	1.50	1.65	1.71	1.87	2.17	2.59	2.60	2.93	3.07	3.33	4.80
Punjab	0.96	1.06	0.99	1.09	1.16	1.28	0.96	1.24	1.44	1.74	1.91	2.89	14.57
Rajasthan	1.10	1.21	1.52	1.59	1.71	2.11	2.41	2.75	3.17	3.48	3.78	4.96	11.94
Tamil Nadu	7.03	10.19	12.34	13.00	13.31	14.96	16.83	18.65	19.47	21.84	22.99	26.15	27.63
Uttar Pradesh	3.43	3.71	3.84	4.17	4.42	4.45	5.29	5.79	6.89	8.80	9.41	10.26	24.92
West Bengal	2.35	2.70	4.89	5.34	5.60	5.76	6.18	6.24	6.25	6.58	6.98	8.71	23.02
TOTAL	38.46	45.74	56.54	57.92	62.59	68.06	76.53	89.27	97.72	108.88	117.34	130.39	263.14

STATE	1974-75	1975-76	1976-77	1977-78	1978-79	1979-80	1980-81	1981-82	1982-83	1983-84	1984-85	1985-86
	Accts.	Accts.	Accts.	Accts.	Accts.	Accts.	Accts.	Accts.	Accts.	Accts.	R. E.	B. E.
Andhra Pradesh	25.35	27.98	30.77	33.82	37.73	48.79	52.90	57.57	64.35	79.78	94.54	112.68
Assam	2.61	3.32	3.89	4.05	4.59	4.73	4.87	6.12	7.34	7.76	8.17	8.66
Bihar	10.09	13.28	14.58	13.26	9.16	26.16	23.17	24.14	28.50	31.83	35.78	38.88
Gujarat	27.92	31.23	36.79	39.69	45.79	52.71	56.27	42.61	85.07	119.92	111.15	108.43
Haryana	18.83	20.61	24.06	26.08	31.92	37.68	42.67	50.40	57.80	63.99	68.92	78.01
Jammu & Kashmir	7.11	9.30	9.71	10.50	11.28	3.14	3.95	15.82	15.72	20.00	22.55	24.75
Karnataka	18.96	24.19	27.52	30.04	29.64	44.46	47.51	60.32	70.27	79.01	104.00	125.18
Kerala	10.14	11.75	17.64	19.15	20.95	19.22	20.04	21.67	26.02	31.34	40.64	51.56
Madhya Pradesh	17.15	21.08	33.94	37.56	46.32	53.57	60.26	63.38	75.88	88.53	107.30	129.29
Maharashtra	50.02	53.61	54.93	58.03	67.78	79.88	69.40	80.40	161.39	144.78	160.41	173.71
Orissa	6.13	7.67	7.75	8.69	9.93	11.05	12.04	13.39	15.56	18.58	26.45	32.00
Punjab	18.64	20.24	22.66	26.20	30.55	33.48	37.13	48.82	52.61	57.23	55.44	72.26
Rajasthan	14.34	16.43	18.12	19.10	8.86	30.42	31.72	36.44	46.98	57.18	64.81	79.69
Tamil Nadu	39.07	44.01	48.59	49.45	57.11	68.57	01.33	73.28	77.94	90.58	101.42	100.40
Uttar Pradesh	29.70	40.59	43.86	44.51	48.87	61.00	67.14	84.14	110.62	101.08	112.17	117.59
West Bengal	25.89	28.99	37.42	38.50	42.70	58.46	69.58	75.76	75.88	79.85	92.58	97.39
TOTAL	321.95	374.28	432.28	458.63	503.18	633.32	679.98	754.26	971.93	991.66	1206.39	1350.25

(CONTD.) TABLE IX.25 : ENTERTAINMENT TAX - 1961-62 TO 1985-86 (Rs. Crores)

STATE	1961-62	1962-63	1963-64	1964-65	1965-66	1966-67	1967-68	1968-69	1969-70	1970-71	1971-72	1972-73	1973-74
	Accts	Accts	Accts	Accts	Accts	Accts	Accts	Accts	Accts	Accts	Accts	Accts	Accts
Andhra Pradesh	1.19	1.27	1.42	1.53	2.11	2.76	3.18	3.67	3.79	4.42	4.88	4.88	6.35
Assam	0.30	0.33	0.36	0.41	0.45	0.52	0.49	0.67	1.06	0.88	1.05	1.20	1.35
Bihar	1.11	0.85	1.17	1.37	1.47	1.60	1.58	1.92	2.43	2.71	4.03	6.97	3.57
Gujarat	0.97	1.12	1.33	1.54	1.75	2.35	2.48	2.70	3.17	3.76	4.70	6.03	6.81
Haryana	0.11	0.13	0.15	0.18	0.19	0.22	0.58	0.77	0.90	1.21	1.55	2.35	2.76
Jammu & Kashmir	0.08	0.07	0.21	0.23	0.29	0.35	0.11	0.15	0.34	0.30	0.41	0.41	0.27
Karnataka	0.82	1.02	1.20	1.31	1.52	1.88	2.10	2.42	3.05	3.14	3.69	4.27	5.18
Kerala	0.12	0.03	0.12	0.25	0.34	0.40	0.39	0.49	0.45	0.52	0.63	0.71	0.71
Madhya Pradesh	0.82	0.92	1.11	1.30	1.67	1.76	1.79	1.99	2.23	2.62	2.70	3.48	4.66
Maharashtra	2.82	4.04	4.89	4.98	6.13	7.86	7.72	8.98	11.01	12.90	14.34	15.41	18.94
Orissa	0.15	0.22	0.23	0.26	0.30	0.39	0.36	0.39	0.44	0.49	0.60	0.79	0.71
Punjab	0.74	0.88	1.06	1.26	1.32	1.55	1.19	1.55	1.80	2.09	2.62	2.81	3.26
Rajasthan	0.32	0.41	0.50	0.55	0.66	0.73	0.87	1.01	1.19	1.24	1.53	1.80	2.20
Tamil Nadu	2.28	2.68	3.89	4.41	5.12	5.81	6.70	7.58	7.77	8.63	9.82	10.92	12.94
Uttar Pradesh	1.72	1.95	2.52	2.76	3.27	4.11	4.54	5.44	6.10	7.28	8.27	8.82	12.31
West Bengal	1.86	2.42	2.63	3.01	3.19	3.37	3.25	3.75	4.65	5.07	5.56	7.22	6.80
TOTAL	15.41	18.34	22.79	25.35	29.78	35.66	37.33	43.48	50.38	57.26	66.38	78.07	88.82

STATE	1974-75	1975-76	1976-77	1977-78	1978-79	1979-80	1980-81	1981-82	1982-83	1983-84	1984-85	1985-86
	Accts.	Accts.	Accts.	Accts.	Accts.	Accts.	Accts.	Accts.	Accts.	Accts.	R. E.	B. E.
Andhra Pradesh	11.97	14.84	17.07	18.38	18.98	21.95	25.17	29.55	30.75	37.93	42.33	45.00
Assam	1.40	1.59	1.88	2.51	2.69	3.22	-	-	3.15	3.78	3.63	3.88
Bihar	3.99	4.68	7.81	5.12	7.52	7.67	5.87	5.83	7.41	8.49	9.80	10.65
Gujarat	8.73	10.03	12.31	14.41	16.59	18.59	21.25	28.31	32.21	38.12	39.98	43.00
Haryana	3.43	5.74	4.00	5.43	5.09	5.51	5.92	7.29	8.16	7.99	8.05	9.50
Jammu & Kashmir	0.33	0.90	1.15	1.17	1.21	1.24	1.41	1.72	2.33	2.65	2.60	3.00
Karnataka	7.61	11.55	14.59	15.65	14.31	19.05	22.61	25.56	29.67	32.33	35.95	40.27
Kerala	0.63	0.86	0.28	0.29	0.19	0.10	0.13	0.16	0.22	0.29	0.30	0.32
Madhya Pradesh	6.08	7.18	7.94	8.00	9.22	10.37	11.27	14.00	18.39	19.98	21.80	24.54
Maharashtra	22.49	31.39	34.66	35.54	36.03	47.30	54.62	65.45	80.61	85.52	95.91	100.71
Orissa	1.16	1.32	1.74	1.90	2.10	2.82	3.03	3.44	3.89	3.96	4.12	6.08
Punjab	5.45	6.20	6.56	6.62	7.88	8.51	8.78	9.46	-	-	-	-
Rajasthan	2.87	3.68	4.44	4.76	5.44	6.17	7.31	8.32	-	10.37	10.72	11.26
Tamil Nadu	15.93	18.59	21.73	23.55	23.80	27.88	33.69	37.15	-	44.88	50.08	54.70
Uttar Pradesh	14.28	17.62	20.17	20.70	24.83	30.19	33.05	41.88	45.97	50.10	52.97	55.41
West Bengal	9.08	13.97	15.41	16.55	18.04	19.00	20.19	25.02	25.40	30.97	33.49	35.16
TOTAL	115.43	148.14	171.74	180.58	193.92	229.57	254.30	303.14	288.16	377.36	411.73	443.48

TABLE X.1 : AGGREGATE RECEIPTS OF CENTRE AND TRANSFER TO STATES

	1.	Gross Revenue Receipts (Rs.Crs) 2.	Gross Capital Receipts (Rs.Crs) 3.	Aggregate Receipts (Rs. Crs. Col. 2+3) 4.	Transfer of Resources from Centre to States (Crores) 5.	Percentage of Col.5 to Col.4 6.
1.	First Plan	2559	1077	3636	1287	35.40
2.	Second Plan	4274	3157	7431	2785	37.48
3.	Third Plan	9907	7091	16998	5600	32.94
4.	Three Annual Plans	9066	6802	15868	5371	33.85
5.	Fourth Plan					
	1969-70	3689	2508	6197	2182	35.21
	1970-71	4097	2524	6621	2301	34.75
	1971-72	4972	3031	8003	2989	37.35
	1972-73	5645	2974	8619	3931	45.60
	1973-74	6247	3646	9893	3691	37.31
	Total	24650	14683	39333	15094	38.37
	Fifth Plan					
	1974-75	7782	3297	11079	3320	29.97
	1975-76	9557	4815	14372	4092	28.47
	1976-77	10429	5607	16036	4685	29.21
	1977-78	11581	5588	17169	5583	32.52
	Total	39349	19307	58656	17680	30.14
7.	Annual Plan					
	1978-79	13197	6938	20135	7750	38.49
	1979-80	14745	6125	20871	8391	40.20
8.	Sixth Plan					
	1980-81	16621	9432	26053	9532	36.59
	1981-82	19849	10156	30005	10523	35.07
	1982-83	22731	13286	36017	14202	39.43
	1983-84	25738	16659	42397	15062	35.53
	1984-85(RE)	30708	18766	49474	17148	34.66
	1985-86(BE)	33365	22048	55413	19997	36.09

Notes: 1. Figures in column 2 are inclusive of States' Share of Central Taxes.
2. Figures in respect of transfer of resources from the centre to the states are Revised Estimates for the years 1981-82 to 1984-85.

Source: Various Issues of RBI Bulletin and Central Budgets.

TABLE X.2 : COMPOSITION OF TRANSFER OF RESOURCES FROM CENTRE TO THE STATES 1951-52 tO 1985-86:

(Rs. Crores)

Period	Share in Taxes	Grants	Loans	Total
First Plan	344	288	799	1431
Second Plan	668	789	1411	2868
Third Plan	1196	1304	3100	5600
Three Annual Plans	1282	1389	2676	5347
Fourth Plan				
1969-70	622	531	1029	2182
1970-71	755	544	1002	2301
1971-72	944	854	1191	2989
1972-73	1067	944	1926	3937
1973-74	1174	958	1560	3692
Total:	4562	3831	6708	15101
Fifth Plan				
1974-75	1224	1020	1076	3320
1975-76	1599	1219	1274	4092
1976-77	1690	1549	1460	4699
1977-78(R.E)	1799	1948	1972	5719
Total:	6312	5736	5782	17830
Annual Plans				
1978-79(R.E)	1957	2594	3326	7877
1979-80(R.E)	3406	2319	2732	8457
Sixth Plan				
1980-81(R.E)	3791	2775	3238	9804
1981-82(R.E)	4274	2727	3522	10523
1982-83(R.E)	4474	3487	6074	14035
1983-84(R.E)	5246	4286	5530	15062
1984-85(R.E)	5777	5080	6291	17148
Total:	23562	18355	24655	66572
Seventh Plan				
1985-86(R.E)	6592	6301	7103	19996

Source: Report of the Seventh Finance Commission (upto 1977-78) and the Central Budgets.

TABLE-X-3: TRANSFER OF RESOURCES FROM THE CENTRE AND THE EXPENDITURE OF THE STATES

(Rs. Crores)

Period	Resources from the Centre Share in Taxes	Grants	Loans Gross	Net	Total 2+3+5	Expenditure of States Revenue	Capital	Total	Percentage of 2+3to7	5to8	6to9
1	2	3	4	5	6	7	8	9	10	11	12
First Plan	352	215	720	638	1205	2354	997	3351	24.1	64.0	36.0
Second Plan	710	700	1375	1038	2448	3938	1908	5846	35.8	54.4	41.7
Third Plan	1196	1303	3101	2151	4650	7272	3448	10720	34.4	62.4	43.4
Annual Plans	1279	1399	2693	1453	4131	7176	2736	9912	37.3	53.1	41.7
Fourth Plan											
1969-70	622	531	1029	398 (RE)	1551	3101	1687	4788	37.2	23.6	32.4
1970-71	755	544	1002	347 (RE)	1646	3390	1784	5174	38.3	19.4	31.8
1971-72	944	854	1191	357 (RE)	2155	4136	2179	6615	40.5	16.4	32.6
1972-73	1067	944	1926	893	2904	4943	2318	7261	40.7	38.5	40.0
1973-74	1174	958	1560	207	2339	5669	2558	8227	37.6	8.1	28.4
TOTAL	4562	3831	6708	2202	10595	21539	10526	32065	39.0	20.9	33.0
Fifth Plan											
1974-75	1224	1020	1076	202	2446	5982	2584	8566	37.5	7.8	28.5
1975-76	1599	1219	1274	80	2898	6966	3493	10459	40.4	2.3	27.7
1976-77	1690	1549	1447	407	3645	7940	3932	11872	40.8	10.3	30.7
1977-78	1799	1877	1908	444	4120	8911	4447	13358	41.2	10.0	30.8
TOTAL	6312	5736	5705	1133	13181	29799	14456	44255	40.4	7.8	20.8
Annual Plans											
1978-79	1957	2533	3260	1786	6276	10511	5267	15778	42.7	33.9	39.8
1979-80	3406	2288	2697	1365	7059	12081	6008	18089	47.1	27.7	39.0
Sixth Plan											
1980-81	3792	2666	3074	365	6823	14808	7856	22664	43.6	4.6	30.1
1981-82 (RE)	4274	2727	3522	1290	8264	17074 (RE)	7797	24871	41.0	16.5	33.2
1982-83 (RE)	4474	3487	6074	3397	11358	18848 (BE)	7640	26488	42.2	44.5	42.8

Note: Figures relating to capital expenditure of states up to 1968-69 are excluding to appropriations contingency and other funds state trading tran-saction and all debt and and deposit items except loans and advances by states.

Source: 1. RBI Bulletin, June 1973 2. RBI Bulletin August 1982 3. Various issue of Report currency and Finance.

TABLE X.4 AGGREGATE (GROSS) BUDGETARY TRANSFERS 1956-81

States	Rupees Per Capita				Index Numbers			
	Statu-tory	Plan	Discre-tionary	Total	Statu-tory	Plan	Discre-tionary	Total
A. High Income States								
Punjab	405	443	604	1452	78	101	159	109
Haryana	389	498	490	1377	75	113	129	103
Mahrastra	461	291	397	1149	89	66	104	86
Gujarat	466	355	398	1219	90	81	105	91
West Bengal	524	314	486	1324	102	71	128	99
GROUP-A	471	338	449	1258	91	77	118	94
B. Middle Income States								
Tamil Nadu	446	350	274	1070	86	80	72	80
Kerala	611	445	335	1391	118	101	88	104
Orissa	708	536	476	1720	137	122	125	129
Assam	742	675	659	2076	144	153	173	155
Karnataka	465	374	384	1223	90	85	101	92
Andhra Pradesh	504	427	381	1312	98	97	100	98
GROUP-B	542	436	386	1364	105	99	102	102
C. Low Income States								
Uttar Pradesh	446	390	264	1100	86	89	69	82
Rajasthan	553	451	734	1738	107	103	193	130
Madhya Pradesh	428	434	248	1110	83	99	65	83
Bihar	456	363	318	1137	88	83	84	85
GROUP-C	459	398	332	1189	89	90	87	89
D. Special Category States								
Himachal Pradesh	1102	1405	498	3005	214	319	131	225
Jammu & Kashmir	1304	2058	1466	4828	253	468	386	361
Tripura	1519	1125	381	3025	294	256	100	226
Manipur	2302	1331	925	4558	446	303	243	341
Nagaland	6080	3896	2758	12734	1178	885	726	953
Meghalaya	1702	1764	845	4311	330	401	222	323
Sikkim	722	3271	1071	5064	140	743	282	379
GROUP-D	1701	1902	1086	4689	330	432	286	351
ALL STATES	516	440	380	1336	100	100	100	100

Source: George KK, 'Centre-State Financial Flows and Inter-State

TABLE-X.5: TRANSFER OF RESOURCES FROM CENTRE TO STATES 1978-79 (ACCOUNTS) (Rs. Crores).

STATES	Share in Central Taxes				Plan Grants			Non-Plan Grants			Total Grants (6to11)
	Income Tax	Estate Duty	Union Excise	Total (2to4)	State Plan Schemes	Central Plan Schemes	Centrally sponsered Schemes	Statutory Grants	Grants for Natural calamities	Others	
1	2	3	4	5	6	7	8	9	10	11	12
1. Andhra Pradesh	54.83	0.88	101.84	157.55	78.09	18.83	31.06	47.88	-	17.14	193.00
2. Assam	17.95	0.27	32.86	51.08	123.30	-	-	-	-	-	123.30
3. Bihar	67.91	1.04	135.79	204.74	81.09	38.28	45.22	3.75	6.90	19	194.09
4. Gujarat	39.22	0.50	57.32	97.04	28.41	13.03	31.80	-	-	1.50	80.29
5. Haryana	12.51	0.35	20.20	33.06	19.60	6.05	8.49	-	-	3.67	37.81
6. Himachal Pradesh	4.24	0.06	7.69	11.99	61.68	-	13.47	32.65	-	1.74	109.54
7. Jammu & Kashmir	4.73	0.08	10.64	15.45	39.50	-	8.23	47.41	-	22.49	117.63
8. Karnataka	37.66	0.57	68.07	106.30	30.32	11.55	21.14		-	2.05	65.06
9. Kerala	27.70	0.46	47.00	75.16	32.81	3.68	14.10	49.12	-	1.00	100.71
10. Madhya Pradesh	51.58	0.77	97.48	149.83	69.81	26.78	22.29	-	-	4.26	123.14
11. Maharastra	78.08	1.00	115.63	194.71	56.60	17.36	28.13	-	-	17.82	119.91
12. Manipur	1.27	-	2.48	3.75	22.44	1.62	2.07	26.51	-	0.18	52.82
13. Meghalaya	1.27	0.02	2.29	3.58	22.87	0.77	2.35	17.52	0.18	0.21	43.90
14. Nagaland	0.63	0.01	1.27	1.91	25.00	-	4.82	29.56	-	4.14	63.52
15. Orissa	26.36	0.42	48.90	75.68	61.03	13.24	20.68	-	-	83.55	178.50
16. Punjab	13.55	0.49	31.64	45.68	17.39	11.63	10.23	-	-	4.45	43.70
17. Rajasthan	31.80	0.48	59.46	91.74	37.76	55.11	21.51	59.43	-	8.17	181.98
18. Sikkim	0.12	-	-	0.12	14.07	-	1.71	4.21	-	3.40	82.42
19. Tamil Nadu	56.10	0.83	91.61	148.54	48.88	9.45	20.08	0.98	-	3.03	82.42
20. Tripura	1.91	0.03	3.57	5.51	20.21	3.07	1.60	25.66	-	0.30	50.84
21. Uttar Pradesh	107.62	1.73	208.28	317.63	150.01	21.07	45.25	75.53	-	26.85	318.71
22. West Bengal	62.82	0.82	98.10	161.74	69.42	5.98	18.65	63.45	-	10.66	168.16
TOTAL (22 States)	699.86	10.81	1242.12	1952.79	987.75	237.31	489.24	525.13	3.93	229.37	2472.73

(Contd.) TABLE-X.5: TRANSFER OF RESOURCES FROM CENTRE TO STATES 1978-79 (ACCOUNTS) (Rs. Crores).

STATES	Plan State Plan	Loans from the Centre Central Plan	Centrally Sponsered	Share of Small Savings	Natural calamities	Non-Plan Others	Way and Means	Total Loans (13 to 19)
1	13	14	15	16	17	18	19	
1. Andhra Pradesh	174.15	7.02	3.64	11.40	-	12.93	-	209.14
2. Assam								99.21
3. Bihar	166.20	1.31	3.79	40.59	-	93.85	-	305.74
4. Gujarat	51.36	1.89	1.33	28.38	-	5.61	10.00	98.57
5. Haryana	44.44	0.75	0.69	12.14	-	3.15	-	61.17
6. Himachal Pradesh	5.91	-	2.08	5.74	-	0.06	-	13.79
7. Jammu & Kashmir	50.60	-	11.43	1.75	-	32.55	-	96.33
8. Karnataka	68.63	21.27	2.18	13.79	-	4.43	15.00	125.30
9. Kerala	74.92	6.53	2.46	6.22	-	19.77	-	109.90
10. Madhya Pradesh	109.01	7.08	3.11	18.73	-	75.47	-	213.40
11. Maharastra	128.10	10.76	2.64	61.78	-	6.96	30.00	240.24
12. Manipur	2.15	0.20	0.65	0.09	-	4.51	-	7.60
13. Meghalaya	1.48	0.21	0.06	0.52	-	0.06	-	2.33
14. Nagaland	7.73	-	2.00	0.14	-	8.80	-	18.67
15. Orissa	69.47	3.62	2.94	7.54	-	17.33	-	100.90
16. Punjab	45.74	0.58	-	15.86	-	81.08	32.00	175.26
17. Rajasthan	75.05	4.70	3.49	20.37	-	19.65	-	123.26
18. Sikkim	0.69	-	0.95	-	-	-	-	1.64
19. Tamil Nadu	111.05	11.96	4.43	36.98	-	0.92	-	165.34
20. Tripura	0.80	0.22	0.10	0.52	-	1.49	-	3.13
21. Uttar Pradesh	314.72	7.95	4.96	93.58	-	222.39	-	643.60
22. West Bengal	146.86	2.34	7.42	67.95	-	145.50	45.10	415.17
TOTAL (22 States)	1748.27	88.39	60.35	444.07	-	756.51	132.10	3229.69

Source: RBI Bulletin.

TABLE-X-6 TRANSFER OF RESOURCES FROM CENTRE TO STATES 1979-80 (ACCOUNTS)

	Share in Central Taxes				Plan Grants				Non-Plan Grants	Total	
STATES	Income Tax	Estate Duty	Union Excise	Total (2to4)	State Plan Schemes	Central Plan Schemes	Centrally sponsered Schemes	Statutory Grants	Grants for Natural calamities	Others	Grants (6to11)
1	2	3	4	5	6	7	8	9	10	11	12
1. Andhra Pradesh	69.39	0.79	194.11	264.29	70.14	37.82	27.09	1.95	35.18	11.98	184.16
2. Assam	21.82	0.12	66.13	88.07	44.56	3.35	8.50	2.48	-	6.53	9.01
3. Bihar	82.51	0.31	299.77	382.59	75.86	30.57	44.18	4.84	-	7.79	12.63
4. Gujarat	51.54	1.02	120.77	173.33	30.21	2.46	21.04	-	10.00	-1.95	61.76
5. Haryana	15.73	0.16	38.17	54.06	23.59	-	14.48	-	-	0.91	38.98
6. Himachal Pradesh	5.15	-	14.39	19.54	68.00	-	14.00	37.60	1.00	1.50	40.10
7. Jammu & Kashmir	5.08	-	21.05	26.13	34.54	6.16	1.83	42.11	-	9.83	94.47
8. Karnataka	47.07	0.88	129.80	177.75	30.97	11.30	14.40	-	-	2.40	59.07
9. Kerala	34.16	0.37	102.12	136.65	26.27	2.04	11.41	0.25	-	2.19	42.16
10. Madhya Pradesh	63.62	0.18	207.92	271.72	68.71	18.97	20.81	-	-	4.50	112.99
11. Maharastra	94.73	3.21	203.65	301.59	55.13	20.54	27.05	-	-	16.18	118.90
12. Manipur	1.16	-	5.55	6.71	27.66	0.86	1.92	26.19	-	3.20	59.83
13. Meghalaya	1.54	-	4.98	6.52	25.50	0.31	1.87	17.13	-	1.38	46.19
14. Nagaland	0.74	-	2.39	3.13	25.80		4.51	38.29	-	3.27	41.56
15. Orissa	32.34	0.12	111.90	144.36	54.18	34.03	15.28	41.55	-	4.82	46.37
16. Punjab	23.47	0.33	49.55	73.35	13.24	10.40	6.74	-	-	2.08	32.46
17. Rajasthan	37.74	0.19	119.30	157.23	40.96	34.74	34.26	1.81	10.34	11.00	133.11
18. Sikkim	0.31	-	0.08	0.39	16.34	-	0.70	6.34	-	2.80	26.18
19. Tamil Nadu	69.62	1.21	192.14	262.97	36.70	7.24	13.24	13.24	0.17	9.40	6.99
20. Tripura	2.23	-	8.51	10.74	24.41	2.40	1.75	24.75	-	1.12	54.43
21. Uttar Pradesh	133.44	0.87	434.81	569.12	133.36	66.26	52.21	10.42	0.53	30.42	293.20
22. West Bengal	69.35	1.28	206.94	277.57	47.79	5.46	17.53	0.15	-	8.10	79.03
TOTAL	862.74	11.04	2534.03	3407.81	973.92	299.42	350.29	256.03	66.45	137.04	2083.15

(Contd.) TABLE-X-6 TRANSFER OF RESOURCES FROM CENTRE TO STATES 1979-80 (ACCOUNTS)

	STATES	Plan State Plan	Loans from the Centre Central Plan	Centrally Sponsered	Share of Small Savings	Natural calamities	Non-Plan Others	Way and Means	Total Loans (13 to 19)
	1	13	14	15	16	17	18	19	20
1.	Andhra Pradesh	151.93	1.53	3.27	20.42	-	18.54	0.32	196.01
2.	Assam	79.41	11.31	0.33	-	-	17.56	-	108.61
3.	Bihar	145.96	2.97	3.94	53.57	-	12.85	-	219.29
4.	Gujarat	66.11	1.18	1.48	55.17	-	10.49	-	134.43
5.	Haryana	30.79	0.56	0.48	11.17	-	7.07	10.00	60.07
6.	Himachal Pradesh	6.51	-	2.42	6.93	-	-	-	15.86
7.	Jammu & Kashmir								
8.	Karnataka	68.35	13.72	1.36	24.65	-	6.06	20.00	134.14
9.	Kerala	58.50	3.58	2.12	6.74	-	2.47	-	73.41
10.	Madhya Pradesh	105.81	1.98	1.60	25.93	-	9.54	-	144.86
11.	Maharastra	118.13	1.51	1.50	129.13	-	7.42	0.08	257.77
12.	Manipur	2.54	2.20	1.14	0.03	-	8.00	-	13.91
13.	Meghalaya	1.32	-	0.04	0.50	-	0.04	-	1.90
14.	Nagaland	2.10	-	0.94	0.08	-	-	5.00	8.12
15.	Orissa	95.65	3.94	1.82	11.80	-	5.17	-	118.38
16.	Punjab	30.48	0.02	-	21.17	-	7.20	0.87	59.74
17.	Rajasthan	-146.61	-6.03	-7.64	-23.26	-	298.09	77.00	191.55
18.	Sikkim	1.69	-	1.04	-	-	-	-	2.73
19.	Tamil Nadu	81.21	5.67	2.81	36.20	-	0.40	30.02	156.31
20.	Tripura	1.28	0.11	0.09	0.67	-	0.23	-	2.38
21.	Uttar Pradesh	269.76	0.33	6.34	83.85	-	25.82	-	386.10
22.	West Bengal	96.67	0.68	2.44	91.11	-	19.60	75.00	285.50
	TOTAL:	1267.59	45.26	27.52	555.86	-	554.01	218.29	2668.53

TABLE-X.7 TRANSFER OF RESOURCES FROM CENTRE TO STATES 1980-81 (ACCOUNTS)

STATES	Share in Central Taxes Income Tax	Estate Duty	Union Excise	Total (2to4)	Plan Grants State Plan Schemes	Central Plan Schemes	Centrally sponsered Schemes	Statutory Grants	Non-Plan Grants Grants for Natural calamities	Others	Total Grants (6to11)
1	2	3	4	5	6	7	8	9	10	11	12
1. Andhra Pradesh	80.44	1.27	214.04	295.75	75.24	40.38	34.07	5.86	2.04	6.29	163.88
2. Assam	25.29	0.17	72.86	98.32							93.40
3. Bihar	95.52	0.08	328.25	423.85	94.33	20.16	46.40	-	16.90	14.49	192.28
4. Gujarat	59.95	0.66	129.06	189.67	35.55	18.98	31.34	-	28.94	3.93	118.74
5. Haryana	18.25	1.05	41.93	61.23	16.90	7.69	11.88	9.02	-		45.49
6. Himachal Pradesh	5.96	0.01	15.73	21.70	79.05	-	14.63	40.54	-	1.45	135.67
7. Jammu & Kashmir	8.84	-	20.13	28.97	61.75	1.54	5.89	37.10	-	7.30	113.58
8. Karnataka	54.57	0.50	142.66	197.73	31.94	23.84	19.49	-	1.01	3.00	79.38
9. Kerala	39.64	0.38	111.39	151.41	25.00	9.34	11.93	0.08	4.00	2.03	52.38
10. Madhya Pradesh	73.83	0.41	228.64	302.88	75.92	46.04	30.11	-	13.97	15.24	181.28
11. Maharastra	109.67	2.32	224.32	336.40	60.85	27.44	30.71	-	-	14.93	133.98
12. Manipur	1.89	-	5.63	7.52							70.52
13. Meghalaya	1.78	-	5.41	7.19	32.83	0.64	2.75	18.32	-	1.40	55.94
14. Nagaland	0.85	-	2.65	3.50	31.63	-	7.80	41.45	-	4.23	85.11
15. Orissa	37.48	0.15	122.35	159.98	56.36	45.56	18.73	37.74	28.20	8.65	195.24
16. Punjab	27.27	0.67	54.27	82.21	18.56	11.87	8.41	-	-	5.21	44.05
17. Rajasthan	43.77	0.33	130.42	174.52	53.47	58.48	22.30	3.88	-	11.61	149.74
18. Sikkim	0.18	-	0.10	0.28	18.15	-	1.18	6.81	0.01	3.16	29.31
19. Tamil Nadu	80.67	0.34	210.75	291.76	43.89	29.30	30.61	3.77	-	8.95	116.52
20. Tripura	2.60		9.33	11.93	43.41	3.12	1.89	26.56	-	0.48	75.46
21. Uttar Pradesh	154.46	0.50	477.26	632.22	131.66	105.56	40.75	23.93	-	76.46	378.36
22. West Bengal	80.10	2.84	226.95	309.89	67.08	3.22	18.68	3.90	9.84	9.64	112.36
TOTAL:	1003.01	11.68	2774.22	3788.91	1217.49	453.16	389.55	249.94	104.91	207.52	2622.57

(Contd.)TABLE-X.7 TRANSFER OF RESOURCES FROM CENTRE TO STATES 1980-81 (ACCOUNTS)

STATES	Plan State Plan	Loans from the Centre Central Plan	Centrally Sponsered	Share of Small Savings	Natural calamities	Non-Plan Others	Way and Means	Total Loans (13 to 19)
1	13	14	15	16	17	18	19	20
1. Andhra Pradesh	156.41	1.65	4.85	24.05	-	26.58	-	213.54
2. Assam								157.62
3. Bihar	173.90	3.83	3.29	64.26	-	14.58	-	157.62
4. Gujarat	67.64	1.12	0.73	65.57	-	8.44	20.00	163.50
5. Haryana	41.39	0.73	0.49	9.58	-	12.48	-	64.67
6. Himachal Pradesh	8.62	-	2.28	9.64	-	-	-	20.54
7. Jammu & Kashmir	113.83	0.13	0.54	8.04	-	1.60	-	124.14
8. Karnataka	72.34	4.45	2.14	26.33	-	12.24	30.00	147.50
9. Kerala	55.58	3.65	2.42	10.81	-	2.36	-	74.82
10. Madhya Pradesh	140.02	2.49	5.45	33.50	-	19.69	10.00	211.15
11. Maharastra	134.80	0.31	1.86	163.04	-	12.07	-0.08	312.00
12. Manipur	-	-	-		-			42.07
13. Meghalaya	2.14	-	-	1.10	-	0.52	0.29	4.05
14. Nagaland	3.46	-	0.68	0.15	-	7.74	-	12.03
15. Orissa	108.32	4.05	1.94	15.45	-	8.40	-	138.16
16. Punjab	43.32	0.01	1.43	21.76	-	11.29	15.00	92.81
17. Rajasthan	102.51	10.75	1.97	7.50	-	17.53	35.00	175.26
18. Sikkim	2.02	-	0.84	-	-	-	-	2.86
19. Tamil Nadu	97.38	4.14	4.82	45.70	-	2.54	-	154.58
20. Tripura	3.38	0.18	0.34	1.56	-	0.14	-	5.60
21. Uttar Pradesh	257.96	5.89	6.85	70.69	-	39.96	-	381.35
22. West Bengal	95.26	2.03	3.02	111.53	-	26.90	25.00	263.74
TOTAL:	1879.97	45.41	45.94	690.26	-	225.06	135.21	3021.85

Source: RBI Bulletin

TABLE-X.8 TRANSFER OF RESOURCES FROM CENTRE TO STATES 1981-82 (ACCOUNT)

STATES	Share in Central Taxes Income Tax	Estate Duty	Union Excise	Total (2to4)	Plan Grants State Plan Schemes	Central Plan Schemes	Centrally sponsered Schemes	Statutory Grants	Non-Plan Grants Grants for Natural calamities	Others	Total Grants (6to11)
1	2	3	4	5	6	7	8	9	10	11	12
1. Andhra Pradesh	81.79	1.22	250.47	333.48	60.46	50.56	41.94	5.08	-	8.65	166.69
2. Assam	27.07	0.18	85.85	113.10	98.86*	-	-	6.58*	-	-	105.44
3. Bihar	97.30	0.89	382.55	480.74	85.58	75.68	16.02	-	-	7.49	184.77
4. Gujarat	60.88	3.06	144.16	208.10	29.52	25.58	42.98	-	-	4.21	102.29
5. Haryana	18.54	0.91	48.58	68.03	15.50	4.71	16.16	-	-	3.07	39.44
6. Himachal Pradesh	6.06	0.25	18.36	24.67	74.20	-	15.54	41.63	-	5.94	137.31
7. Jammu & Kashmir	8.33	-0.04	26.73	35.02	63.38	4.33	8.77	48.71	-	1.33	126.52
8. Karnataka	55.44	0.83	166.26	222.53	35.82	22.93	27.28	-	-	7.35	93.38
9. Kerala	40.21	1.01	129.59	170.81	34.58	11.57	16.61	0.73	-	9.67	73.16
10. Madhya Pradesh	74.89	-0.51	266.99	341.37	98.54	19.90	41.51	-	-	16.88	176.83
11. Maharastra	111.42	6.60	250.52	368.54	54.90	28.35	34.47	0.03	-	12.72	130.47
12. Manipur	1.91	0.01	6.61	8.53							80.27*
13. Meghalaya	1.80	-0.02	6.24	8.02	35.56	0.64	4.59	20.27	-	0.15	61.81
14. Nagaland	0.86	-0.01	3.09	3.94	36.18	-	5.37	44.41	-	6.69	92.65
15. Orissa	38.06	-0.29	142.97	180.97	55.02	26.53	30.59	29.03	1.56	19.50	162.23
16. Punjab	28.90	0.52	62.82	92.24	19.06	11.18	10.61	-	-	2.48	43.33
17. Rajasthan	44.35	-0.07	152.08	196.36	70.32	-	59.29	5.33	-	37.87	172.81
18. Sikkim	0.37	-	0.12	0.49	30.75	-	-	-	-	-	30.75
19. Tamil Nadu	81.98	2.14	245.36	329.48	54.21	26.27	30.53	-	-	14.65	125.66
20. Tripura	2.62	-	10.89	13.51	35.83	2.48	3.25	27.59	-	0.51	69.66
21. Uttar Pradesh	158.24	-0.81	554.44	711.87	178.24	114.80	61.07	27.22	25.99	23.59	430.91
22. West Bengal	81.14	1.19	265.76	348.09	73.17	5.00	22.71	1.54	5.00	12.64	120.06
TOTAL:	1022.16	17.06	3220.44	4259.66	1319.95	430.51	489.29	250.84	32.55	203.30	2726.44

@ Figures for Assam relate to revised estimates.

* Represents total. Break up not available.

Source: RBI Bulletin, October, 1983

(Contd.)TABLE-X.8 TRANSFER OF RESOURCES FROM CENTRE TO STATES 1981-82 (ACCOUNTS)

STATES	Plan State Plan	Loans from the Centre Central Plan	Centrally Sponsered	Share of Small Saving	Natural calamities	Non-Plan Others	Way and Means	Total Loans (13 to 19)
1	13	14	15	16	17	18	19	20
1. Andhra Pradesh	131.13	3.73	5.30	30.06	-	19.68	-	189.90
2. Assam	-	143.56	-			27.67*		171.23
3. Bihar	164.90	1.83	5.23	65.59	-	17.02	4.00	258.57
4. Gujarat	73.09	2.38	1.77	85.13	-	10.49	47.00	219.86
5. Haryana	34.32	0.08	3.60	33.46	-	13.72	5.00	90.18
6. Himachal Pradesh	7.66	-	1.69	12.52	-	-		21.87
7. Jammu & Kashmir	115.50*	-	-	24.80*	-	-	-	140.31
8. Karnataka	77.19	5.07	2.31	36.83	-	11.90	1.00	134.30
9. Kerala	73.15	3.90	2.38	10.57	-	3.48	-	93.48
10. Madhya Pradesh	131.70	2.19	7.83	25.91	-	13.26	-	180.89
11. Maharastra	122.87	2.96	1.55	179.26	-	10.63	41.00	358.27
12. Manipur								21.99*
13. Meghalaya	2.67	-	0.07	1.10	-	1.22	-	5.06
14. Nagaland	3.72	-	0.51	0.12	-	-	-	4.35
15. Orissa	90.69	5.98	3.67	15.44	-	7.55	-	123.33
16. Punjab	44.48	-	1.61	25.82	-	14.97	49.50	136.38
17. Rajasthan	112.95	1.20	2.43	32.27	-	21.19	83.00	253.04
18. Sikkim								
19. Tamil Nadu	107.06	5.74	4.90	36.05	-	0.87	-	154.62
20. Tripura	3.43	0.14	0.62	1.14	-	0.74	-	6.07
21. Uttar Pradesh	256.42	5.81	2.34	108.33	-	43.10	4.26	420.26
22. West Bengal	89.89	1.33	6.27	144.53	-	29.85	114.00	385.87
TOTAL:	1667.45	185.90	54.08	844.13	-	272.15	348.76	3372.47

@ Figures for Assam relate to Revised Estimates. * Represents total. Break up not available.

Source: RBI Bulletin, October, 1983.

TABLE-X.9 TRANSFER OF RESOURCES FROM CENTRE TO STATES 1982-83 (ACCOUNTS)

STATES	Share in Central Taxes Income Tax	Estate Duty	Union Excise	Total (2to4)	Plan Grants State Plan Schemes	Central Plan Schemes	Centrally sponsered Schemes	Statutory Grants	Non-Plan Grants Grants for Natural calamities	Others	Total Grants (6to11)
1	2	3	4	5	6	7	8	9	10	11	12
1. Andhra Pradesh	90.69	1.07	269.12	360.88	86.95	23.56	83.96	-	-	15.55	210.02
2. Assam	28.55	0.35	93.05	121.95	98.73	6.14	17.94	3.99	-	8.31	135.11
3. Bihar	108.00	0.39	413.98	522.37	100.86	52.51	31.42	-	14.03	21.18	220.00
4. Gujarat	67.28	2.40	141.49	211.17	38.64	5.19	26.75	-	35.63	23.77	129.98
5. Haryana	20.57	0.28	51.76	72.61	16.89	-	24.32	-	-	1.24	42.45
6. Himachal Pradesh	6.74	0.01	19.72	26.47	89.14	0.50	21.65	43.00	3.01	2.18	159.48
7. Jammu & Kashmir	9.26	0.03	28.96	38.25	52.50	2.19	14.55	39.40	-	53.74	162.38
8. Karnataka	61.55	0.70	177.84	240.09	32.11	16.16	47.29	-	-	5.32	100.88
9. Kerala	44.69	1.45	139.80	185.94	33.18	3.46	29.66	0.06	-	3.13	69.49
10. Madhya Pradesh	83.23	0.42	288.52	372.17	93.72	17.38	66.86	-	-	12.78	190.74
11. Maharastra	124.00	2.85	295.08	421.93	60.88	24.10	73.19	-	-	24.21	182.38
12. Manipur	2.13	0.03	7.17	9.33	96.45	-	-	-	-		96.45
13. Meghalaya	2.01	0.01	6.71	8.73	46.82	0.59	3.68	21.32	0.19	2.11	74.71
14. Nagaland	0.96	-	3.35	4.31	51.35	7.51	-	49.48	-	5.43	113.77
15. Orissa	42.31	0.12	154.83	197.26	65.11	20.86	44.31	19.16	121.58	55.33	326.35
16. Punjab	30.73	2.17	66.33	99.23	-	-	-	-	-	-	49.28*
17. Rajasthan	49.45	0.22	163.94	213.61	91.94	-	72.01	2.02	8.99-	1.61	173.35
18. Sikkim	0.50	-	0.14	0.64	-	-	-	-	-	-	36.58*
19. Tamil Nadu	91.06	1.32	264.00	356.68	50.76	17.11	55.81	0.64	-	18.26	142.58
20. Tripura	2.93	0.03	11.82	14.78	49.86	3.45	4.08	33.48	-	0.62	91.49
21. Uttar Pradesh	174.54	0.84	599.95	775.33	206.31	51.15	127.11	28.08	39.01	24.94	476.60
22. West Bengal	91.10	1.26	286.89	379.25	142.61	5.48	33.78	1.15	0.62	13.82	197.46
TOTAL:	132.28	15.95	3484.45	4632.68	1590.67	249.83	785.38	241.78	223.06	290.31	3381.53

* Break up not available

Source: RBI Bulletin, October, 1984.

(Contd.)TABLE-X.9 TRANSFER OF RESOURCES FROM CENTRE TO STATES 1981-82 (ACCOUNTS)

STATES	Plan State Plan	Loans from the Centre Central Plan	Centrally Sponsered	Share of Small Savings	Natural calamities	Non-Plan Others	Way and Means	Total Loans (13 to 19)
1	13	14	15	16	17	18	19	20
1. Andhra Pradesh	168.45	3.04	5.06	42.54	-	10.66	-	229.75
2. Assam	152.13	13.78	1.48	26.77	-	4.35	-	198.51
3. Bihar	196.60	1.22	5.28	99.88	-	21.86	23.00	347.84
4. Gujarat	121.29	0.95	1.46	106.67	-	14.00	38.00	356.97
5. Haryana	44.48	1.66	1.13	16.18	-	15.94	40.00	119.39
6. Himachal Pradesh	11.83	0.07	3.55	14.66	-	-	-	30.11
7. Jammu & Kashmir	-	-	-	-	-	144.07	-	144.07
8. Karnataka	78.00	1.03	2.22	52.68	-	14.48	27.00	175.41
9. Kerala	69.21	4.04	1.56	14.83	-	3.83	15.00	108.47
10. Madhya Pradesh	160.25	3.11	6.79	32.69	-	21.61	6.00	230.45
11. Maharastra	172.20	0.40	1.75	219.27	-	16.33	44.00	453.95
12. Manipur	15.56	-	-	-	--	-	-	15.56
13. Meghalaya	4.77	-	0.31	1.53	-	1.65	-	8.26
14. Nagaland	5.37	-	0.80	0.16	-	-	-	6.33
15. Orissa	111.46	6.81	3.43	20.92	-	13.43	-	156.05
16. Punjab	-	-	-	-	-	-	-	162.99*
17. Rajasthan	158.68	1.94	3.53	33.89	-	22.38	21.00	241.42
18. Sikkim	-	-	-	-	-	-	-	3.83*
19. Tamil Nadu	100.57	18.99	3.85	41.43	-	10.73	33.00	208.57
20. Tripura	4.90	0.28	0.47	1.61	-	0.56	-	7.82
21. Uttar Pradesh	286.71	4.34	6.89	132.52	-	42.02	12.00	483.63
22. West Bengal	238.78	0.45	5.00	201.51	-	30.56	74.32	550.62
TOTAL:	2268.06	62.11	54.56	1059.74	-	337.61	333.32	4165.40@

* Break up not available **Source:** RBI Bulletin, October, 1984.

@ Excludes the medium term loan of Rs. 1743.46 crores given by the centre in July 1982 to the States to clear their overdrafts outstanding with the RBI as at the end of March, 1982.

TABLE-X.10: TRANSFER OF RESOURCES FROM THE CENTRE TO STATES 1983-84 (ACCOUNTS) (Rs. Crores)

STATES	Share in Central Taxes Income Tax	Estate Duty	Union Excise	Total (2to4)	Plan Grants State Plan Schemes	Central Plan Schemes	Centrally sponsered Schemes	Statutory Grants	Non-Plan Grants Grants for Natural calamities	Others	Total Grants (6to11)
1	2	3	4	5	6	7	8	9	10	11	12
1. Andhra Pradesh	94.00	1.93	312.39	408.32	78.62	31.08	97.36	1.10	55.88	6.20	270.24
2. Assam	29.55	-	107.92	137.47	144.48	10.14	34.82	3.66	-	6.59	199.69
3. Bihar	111.78	0.77	477.96	590.51	109.84	36.30	68.90	17.44	0.50	10.15	243.13
4. Gujarat	60.44	1.37	164.90	226.71	52.91	16.16	65.20	-	-	32.96	167.23
5. Haryana	22.01	0.16	58.61	80.78	21.99	7.78	31.10	-	9.46	2.07	72.40
6. Himachal Pradesh	6.97	0.04	23.03	30.04	106.58	0.29	27.73	44.30	-	5.42	184.32
7. Jammu & Kashmir	9.58	0.08	33.82	43.48	55.70	-	32.53	39.08	-	72.77	199.88
8. Karnataka	63.76	0.43	206.96	271.15	48.70	29.43	57.79	-	-	6.50	142.42
9. Kerala	46.28	0.60	162.60	209.48	52.58	13.88	48.36	2.05	-	2.86	119.73
10. Madhya Pradesh	89.01	0.24	333.82	423.07	117.10	25.34	77.94	30.96	-	8.61	259.95
11. Maharastra	132.54	0.49	317.87	449.92	115.27	32.97	86.73	-	16.96	18.65	270.58
12. Manipur	1.83	0.04	7.88	9.75	111.45	-	-	-	-	-	111.45
13. Meghalaya	2.09	-	7.77	9.86	63.76	0.95	8.26	23.18	0.28	1.96	98.39
14. Nagaland	1.00	0.01	3.88	4.89	67.56	-	11.09	52.52	-	5.31	136.48
15. Orissa	43.81	0.12	178.83	222.76	71.81	23.46	57.34	9.44	15.25	55.35	232.65
16. Punjab	31.80	1.20	78.65	111.65	-	-	-	-	-	-	66.98
17. Rajasthan	51.13	0.24	190.64	242.01	59.64	-	110.06	6.08	6.62	10.08	192.48
18. Sikkim	1.00	-	0.13	1.13	43.32	-	-	-	-	-	43.32
19. Tamil Nadu	94.32	1.03	306.68	402.03	76.45	22.80	84.55	-	22.97	18.47	225.24
20. Tripura	3.02	0.03	15.73	16.78	36.67	5.10	6.61	36.10	-	2.69	107.17
21. Uttar Pradesh	180.15	1.02	500.94	682.11	237.76	77.31	179.72	-	-	81.66	576.45
22. West Bengal	93.94	5.73	334.25	433.92	89.38	12.38	56.02	2.02	-	12.68	172.48
TOTAL:	1170.01	14.55	3823.36	5007.82	1848.35	345.37	1142.11	267.93	127.92	360.98	4092.66

(Contd.)TABLE-X.10 TRANSFER OF RESOURCES FROM CENTRE TO STATES 1983-84 (ACCOUNTS) CONTD..

STATES	Plan State Plan	Loans from the Centre Central Plan	Centrally Sponsered	Share of Small Savings	Natural calamities	Non-Plan Others	Way and Means	Total Loans (13 to 19)
1	13	14	15	16	17	18	19	20
1. Andhra Pradesh	171.01	2.49	4.04	56.27	-	12.61	-	246.42
2. Assam	241.61	10.71	-	36.67	-	5.50	1.14	295.63
3. Bihar	210.31	0.76	2.81	75.03	-	200.96	25.05	514.92
4. Gujarat	92.94	2.13	1.84	162.58	-	10.74	20.00	290.23
5. Haryana	51.04	0.12	1.53	37.17	-	16.96	73.43	180.25
6. Himachal Pradesh	10.60	0.03	4.42	16.68	-	-	-	31.73
7. Jammu & Kashmir	129.50	-	-	12.00	-	36.40	-	177.90
8. Karnataka	84.42	0.13	4.20	68.79	-	20.74	47.40	225.68
9. Kerala	97.45	4.03	3.69	13.33	-	65.73	15.45	199.68
10. Madhya Pradesh	170.62	2.87	4.97	42.19	-	44.94	-	265.59
11. Maharastra	173.34	3.50	1.76	268.80	-	61.69	60.00	569.17
12. Manipur	-	-	-	-	-	-	-	9.77
13. Meghalaya	6.40	-	0.10	1.88	-	1.50	-	9.88
14. Nagaland	7.12	-	0.90	2.0	-	-	9.72	17.94
15. Orissa	124.66	0.54	7.93	28.03	-	53.26	-	214.42
16. Punjab	-	-	-	-	-	-	-	304.93
17. Rajasthan	116.75	3.23	4.40	48.95	-	69.49	1.00	243.82
18. Sikkim	-	-	-	-	-	-	-	7.66
19. Tamil Nadu	153.02	4.41	3.50	98.34	-	16.29	38.35	313.91
20. Tripura	6.54	0.42	0.58	2.76	-	-	-	10.30
21. Uttar Pradesh	334.45	6.10	7.82	189.23	-	47.46	95.00	680.06
22. West Bengal	128.64	0.30	4.83	219.88	-	95.78	43.25	492.68
TOTAL:	2632.78	41.77	59.32	1378.86	-	360.05	429.79	4902.57

Source: Reserve Bank of India, Bulletin, November, 1985.

TABLE-X.11: TRANSFER OF RESOURCES FROM THE CENTRE TO STATES 1984-85 (REVISED) (Rs. Crores).

STATES	Share in Central Taxes Income Tax	Estate Duty	Union Excise	Total (2to4)	Plan Grants State Plan Schemes	Central Plan Schemes	Centrally sponsered Schemes	Statutory Grants	Non-Plan Grants Grants for Natural calamities	Others	Total Grants (6to11)
1	2	3	4	5	6	7	8	9	10	11	12
1. Andhra Pradesh	95.19	1.92	342.07	439.18	88.16	41.36	107.97	-	34.32	4.08	275.89
2. Assam	30.90	-	116.06	146.96	154.68	27.08	50.32	38.17	26.74	25.29	322.28
3. Bihar	113.19	0.74	516.51	630.44	135.44	2.42	208.85	-	-	2.66	349.37
4. Gujarat	73.38	1.84	212.60	287.82	62.46	-	115.04	-	-	4.51	182.01
5. Haryana	22.40	0.49	67.99	90.88	25.28	-	63.10	-	-	1.23	89.61
6. Himachal Pradesh	7.29	0.03	28.88	36.20	116.09	1.77	35.31	91.15	2.88	0.84	248.04
7. Jammu & Kashmir	10.07	0.10	37.69	47.86	70.50	-	43.94	114.85	1.86	23.25	254.40
8. Karnataka	67.02	0.59	231.27	298.88	57.27	47.32	88.25	-	-	10.64	203.48
9. Kerala	48.64	2.49	182.15	233.28	40.67	-	57.50	0.06	-	3.70	101.93
10. Madhya Pradesh	90.59	0.16	372.95	463.70	134.27	55.16	136.54	-	-	8.92	334.89
11. Maharastra	134.88	2.28	378.33	515.49	99.40	62.08	155.58	-	-	14.58	331.64
12. Manipur	2.85	-	8.44	11.29	70.88	3.74	5.90	56.08	-	2.18	138.78
13. Meghalaya	2.19	-	8.46	10.65	60.46	0.34	11.05	40.27	-	3.96	116.08
14. Nagaland	1.04	-	4.30	5.34	75.51	-	13.30	81.12	-	5.01	174.94
15. Orissa	46.07	-0.26	197.40	243.21	68.81	77.90	59.31	-	11.11	11.64	228.77
16. Punjab	33.42	1.96	86.80	122.18	24.72	7.00	49.44	-	-	21.82	102.98
17. Rajasthan	53.74	0.65	212.58	266.97	47.73	-	42.96	0.18	-	8.42	199.28
18. Sikkim	0.70	-	1.32	2.02	27.93	-	5.58	-	-	22.42	55.93
19. Tamil Nadu	98.63	1.12	335.30	435.05	68.74	22.16	132.53	-	-	15.56	238.99
20. Tripura	2.80	-	13.70	16.50	74.22	4.81	13.79	53.34	5.00	0.44	151.60
21. Uttar Pradesh	190.00	2.21	769.44	961.65	266.13	37.87	327.04	-	32.07	29.59	692.70
22. West Bengal	98.74	3.91	369.78	472.43	54.35	22.45	65.05	8.06	25.82	10.79	186.52
TOTAL 22 STATES:	1223.73	20.23	4494.02	5737.98	1823.70	413.46	1888.35	483.28	139.80	231.53	4980.12

(Contd..): TABLE-X.11 TRANSFER OF RESOURCES FROM CENTRE TO STATES 1984-85 (REVISED) (Rs. Crores)

STATES	Plan State Plan	Loans from the Centre Central Plan	Centrally Sponsered	Share of Small	Natural calamities	Non-Plan Others	Way and Means	Total Loans (13 to 19)
1	13	14	15	16	17	18	19	20
1. Andhra Pradesh	213.05	*12.07	-	100.00	-	327.08	-	652.20
2. Assam	249.80	32.39	10.18	40.00	-	5.96	28.00	366.33
3. Bihar	250.86	0.76	4.00	173.00	-	26.15	10.50	465.27
4. Gujarat	113.55	-	15.65	180.00	-	19.61	-	328.81
5. Haryana	58.98	0.02	1.94	46.00	-	16.75	-	123.69
6. Himachal Pradesh	12.46	-	12.08	21.00	-	-	-	45.54
7. Jammu & Kashmir	164.50	-	-	11.00	-	30.25	-	205.75
8. Karnataka	122.84	5.39	4.86	95.00	-	14.61	120.00	362.70
9. Kerala	89.90	-	12.77	21.00	-	4.10	110.00	237.77
10. Madhya Pradesh	198.67	5.91	5.62	74.79	-	25.25	17.00	327.24
11. Maharastra	196.11	-	5.84	400.00	-	19.00	70.00	690.95
12. Manipur	7.69	0.41	0.30	0.35	-	0.09	-	8.84
13. Meghalaya	6.68	-	0.25	2.75	-	2.08	2.00	13.76
14. Nagaland	8.39	-	0.98	0.25	-	-	-	9.62
15. Orissa	117.85	5.75	7.49	11.10	-	15.55	-	157.74
16. Punjab	-	-	-	-	-	-	-	614.51
17. Rajasthan	111.38	4.83	6.16	75.00	-	22.74	10.00	230.11
18. Sikkim	-	-	-	-	-	-	-	4.77
19. Tamil Nadu	135.91	2.24	3.97	65.00	-	28.30	5.00	240.42
20. Tripura	8.25	0.50	6.64	2.75	-	-	-	18.14
21. Uttar Pradesh	397.58	6.05	8.18	223.68	-	44.18	23.29	702.96
22. West Bengal	30.55	0.20	10.21	240.00	-	41.33	110.00	432.29
TOTAL (22 STATES)	3114.28	76.52	117.12	1782.67	=	643.03	505.79	6239.41

Source: Reserve Bank of India Bulletin, November. 1985.

TARLE-X.12: TRANSFER OF RESOURCES FROM THE CENTRE TO STATES 1985-86 (Budget) (Rs. Crores).

	Share in Central Taxes				Plan Grants			Non-Plan Grants			
STATES	Income Tax	Estate Duty	Union Excise	Total (2to4)	State Plan Schemes	Central Plan Schemes	Centrally sponsered Schemes	Statutory Grants	Grants for Natural calamities	Others	Total Grants (6to11)
1	2	3	4	5	6	7	8	9	10	11	12
1. Andhra Pradesh	109.78	2.88	408.67	521.33	110.10	79.48	139.58	17.96	12.25	10.57	369.94
2. Assam	35.00	-	189.33	224.33	153.42	30.76	43.71	66.92	3.62	49.55	347.98
3. Bihar	149.73	0.76	560.55	711.04	132.45	2.42	205.11	37.04	16.87	9.86	403.75
4. Gujarat	59.11	1.44	187.11	247.66	75.51	-	116.00	-	-	2.25	193.76
5. Haryana	14.40	0.29	60.78	75.47	24.42	-	60.42	-	-	1.71	86.55
6. Himachal Pradesh	7.44	0.05	84.74	92.23	147.50	1.47	32.77	59.60	0.88	23.25	265.47
7. Jammu & Kashmir	11.23	0.12	121.75	133.10	78.00	-	50.49	81.14	1.97	71.91	283.51
8. Karnataka	66.76	0.81	245.09	312.66	64.20	55.84	88.46	-	-	12.63	221.13
9. Kerala	50.41	2.35	181.75	334.51	50.64	-	103.32	0.06	2.50	5.31	161.83
10. Madhya Pradesh	112.35	0.38	412.97	525.70	161.06	63.46	161.44	28.09	2.38	7.22	423.65
11. Maharastra	112.54	3.49	339.62	455.65	93.46	37.69	211.86	-	3.62	28.29	374.92
12. Manipur	2.85	-	36.41	39.26	61.94	0.01	3.20	35.51	0.12	9.57	110.35
13. Megahalaya	2.47	-	39.22	41.69	64.12	2.09	11.00	36.38	-	5.19	118.78
14. Nagaland	1.10	-	50.38	51.48	110.98	-	15.08	50.07	-	4.47	180.60
15. Orissa	56.33	-	255.67	312.00	86.50	77.67	56.90	35.76	-	73.65	330.48
16. Punjab	23.38	1.23	82.55	107.16	58.28	14.74	56.76	-	-	52.34	182.12
17. Rajasthan	60.95	0.32	228.55	289.82	65.97	-	142.83	20.48	12.12	33.05	274.45
18. Sikkim	0.73	-	10.80	11.53	41.16	-	6.07	-	-	19.21	66.44
19. Tamil Nadu	98.74	1.14	328.73	428.61	63.55	24.21	154.35	4.38	-	16.23	262.72
20. Tripura	3.61	0.01	58.16	61.78	77.76	6.50	14.40	44.71	0.38	9.59	153.34
21. Uttar Pradesh	240.11	1.51	884.65	1126.27	293.50	47.07	328.12	-	-	32.59	701.28
22. West Bengal	104.59	1.06	442.80	548.45	103.56	47.14	80.45	155.33	7.99	11.39	405.86
TOTAL 22 STATES	1323.61	17.84	5210.28	2118.08	490.55	2082.32	12227.96	673.43	64.70	489.83	5918.91

(Contd.) TABLE-X.12 TRANSFER OF RESOURCES FROM CENTRE TO STATES 1985-86 (BUDGET) (Rs. Crores).

STATES	Plan State Plan	Loans from the Centre Central Plan	Centrally Sponsered	Share of Small Savings	Natural calamities	Non-Plan Others	Way and Means	Total Loans (13 to 19)
1	13	14	15	16	17	18	19	20
1. Andhra Pradesh	255.53	*15.58	-	110.00	-	6.82	-	387.93
2. Assam	246.85	37.85	22.06	44.00	-	5.98	50.51	407.25
3. Bihar	246.04	1.00	4.00	165.00	-	22.60	10.00	448.64
4. Gujarat	143.11	-	19.11	180.00	-	10.66	-	352.88
5. Haryana	56.98	0.02	2.26	60.00	-	10.64	-	129.90
6. Himachal Pradesh	15.59	-	12.30	23.10	-	-	-	50.99
7. Jammu & Kashmir	182.00	-	-	13.00	.66	67.59	-	263.25
8. Karnataka	138.69	4.44	4.93	110.00	-	14.50	50.00	322.56
9. Kerala	98.57	-	37.16	23.10	-	4.56	-	163.39
10. Madhya Pradesh	247.67	7.90	9.13	82.87	-	28.43	20.00	395.40
11. Maharastra	190.74	-	14.38	418.00	-	20.63	-	643.75
12. Manipur	6.88	-	0.02	0.39	-	0.05	-	7.34
13. Maghalaya	7.07	-	0.25	3.00	-	2.10	2.00	14.42
14. Nagaland	12.33	-	0.90	0.28	-	-	10.00	23.51
15. Orissa	154.44	1.94	9.70	35.00	-	15.40	-	216.48
16. Punjab	-	-	-	-	-	-	-	303.09
17. Rajasthan	153.93	3.45	4.18	92.50	-	22.64	-	276.70
18. Sikkim	-	-	-	-	-	-	-	5.49
19. Tamil Nadu	147.13	2.24	3.97	75.00	-	15.45	-	243.79
20. Tripura	8.64	0.70	9.81	2.75	-	-	-	21.90
21. Uttar Pradesh	450.86	6.40	9.51	300.00	-	41.72	-	808.49
22. West Bengal	135.14	0.80	11.07	300.00	-	46.47	-	493.48
TOTAL 22 STATES	3206.77	82.32	174.74	2037.39	0.66	336.24	142.51	5980.63

Source: Reserve Bank of India Bulletin, November, 1985.

TABLE-XI-1: ANALYSIS OF REVENUE RECEIPTS OF THE CENTRE (Rs. Crores).

		1978-79	1979-80	1980-81	1981-82	1982-83	1983-84	1984-85	1985-86
I.	Gross Tax Revenue (1+2+3)	10525	11974	13180	15847	17696	20722	23702	25514
1.	Taxes On Income	2453	2732	2907	3679	4020	4370	4829	4988
a)	Corporate Tax	1251	1392	1311	1970	2185	2493	2824	2804
b)	Income Tax	1177	1340	1506	1475	1570	1699	1810	1964
c)	Others	25	-	90	234	265	178	195	220
2.	Taxes on Property and Capital transactions	106	94	100	118	132	144	148	153
a)	Estate Duty	13	14	16	20	20	26	23	23
b)	Wealth Tax	55	64	67	78	90	93	100	104
c)	Stamps & Registration	31	8	9	12	13	15	16	16
d)	Others	7	8	8	8	9	10	9	10
3.	Taxes on Commodities & Services	7966	9148	10172	12050	13544	16209	18725	20373
a)	Customs	2449	2924	3409	4300	5119	5583	7100	7881
b)	Union Excise Duties	5342	6011	6500	7420	8059	10222	11167	11993
c)	Others	175	213	263	330	366	404	458	499
II.	States Share in Taxes	1957	3406	3792	4274	4639	5246	5777	6592
III.	Net Tax Revenue (I-II)	8568	8568	9388	11573	13056	15476	17925	18922
IV.	Non-Tax Revenue	2672	2772	3441	4001	5035	5016	7007	7851
a)	Fiscal Services	95	110	143	107	123	160	550	361
b)	Interest Receipts	1427	1360	1795	2215	2852	2668	3986	4657
c)	Devidends and Profits	264	302	292	321	419	451	382	449
d)	General Services	237	274	329	464	531	612	719	756
e)	Economic Services	314	289	330	375	486	554	662	880
f)	Grants-in-aid	223	313	373	320	299	281	394	376
g)	Others	112	124	179	199	325	290	314	372
V.	Total Revenue receipts (III+IV)	11240	11340	12829	15574	18091	20492	24932	26773

Source: Explanatory Memorandum to Central Budget 1985-86.

Sl.	Iteam	1950-51	1951-52	1952-53	1953-54	1954-55	1955-56	1956-57	1957-58	1958-59	1959-60
	1	2	3	4	5	6	7	8	9	10	11
1.	Total Tax Revenue All India (2x5)	6.56	7.37	6.95	6.43	7.43	7.48	7.53	8.72	8.10	8.70
	a) Direct Taxes	2.42	2.43	2.58	2.32	2.47	2.52	2.44	2.73	2.56	2.70
	b) Indirect Taxes	4.14	4.94	4.37	4.11	4.96	4.96	5.09	5.99	5.54	6.00
2.	Central Taxes (Gross)	4.24	5.11	4.56	4.02	4.70	4.73	4.82	5.77	5.21	5.68
	a) Direct Taxes	1.84	1.90	1.91	1.59	1.66	1.67	1.64	1.92	1.77	1.92
	b) Indirect Taxes	2.40	3.21	2.65	2.43	3.04	3.06	3.18	3.85	3.44	3.76
3.	States Share in Central Taxes	0.50	0.53	0.75	0.70	0.73	0.72	0.66	0.96	1.10	1.09
	a) Direct Taxes	0.50	0.53	0.57	0.56	0.59	0.56	0.43	0.63	0.56	0.56
	b) Indirect Taxes	-	-	0.18	0.14	0.14	0.16	0.23	0.33	0.54	0.53
4.	Central Taxes(net)(2-3)	3.74	4.58	3.81	3.32	3.97	4.01	4.16	4.81	4.11	4.59
	a) Direct Taxes	1.34	1.37	1.34	1.03	1.07	1.11	1.21	1.29	1.21	1.36
	b) Indirect Taxes	2.40	3.21	2.47	2.29	2.90	2.90	2.95	3.52	2.90	3.23
5.	States Own Taxes	2.32	2.26	2.39	2.41	2.73	2.75	2.71	2.95	2.89	3.02
	a) Direct Taxes	0.58	0.53	0.67	0.73	0.81	0.85	0.80	0.81	0.79	0.78
	b) Indirect Taxes	1.74	1.73	1.72	1.68	1.92	1.90	1.91	2.14	2.10	2.24
6.	States Tax Revenue Total (3x5)	2.82	2.79	3.14	3.11	3.46	3.47	3.37	3.91	3.99	4.11
	a) Direct Taxes	1.08	1.06	1.24	1.29	1.40	1.41	1.23	1.44	1.35	1.34
	b) Indirect Taxes	1.74	1.73	1.90	1.82	2.06	2.06	2.14	2.47	2.64	2.77

(Contd.) TABLE XI.2 : TAX GDP RATIOS : 1950-51 TO 1983-84

Sl.	Iteam	1960-61	1961-62	1962-63	1963-64	1964-65	1965-66	1966-67	1967-68	1968-69	1969-70
	1	2	3	4	5	6	7	8	9	10	11
1.	Total Tax Revenue - All India (2x5)	8.99	9.66	10.90	11.83	11.28	12.12	11.79	10.70	11.29	11.40
	a) Direct Taxes	2.68	2.81	3.27	3.53	3.22	3.04	2.77	2.48	2.52	2.61
	b) Indirect Taxes	6.31	6.85	7.63	8.30	8.06	9.08	9.02	8.28	8.77	8.79
2.	Central Taxes (Gross)	5.96	6.60	7.51	8.31	7.90	8.55	8.34	7.29	7.54	7.66
	a) Direct Taxes	1.95	2.11	2.47	2.80	2.60	2.48	2.38	2.03	2.10	2.24
	b) Indirect Taxes	4.01	4.49	5.04	5.51	5.30	6.07	5.96	5.26	5.44	5.42
3.	States Share in Central Taxes	1.10	1.12	1.31	1.32	1.12	1.15	1.35	1.29	1.47	1.68
	a) Direct Taxes	0.60	0.61	0.58	0.63	0.56	0.54	0.52	0.56	0.60	0.81
	b) Indirect Taxes	0.50	0.51	0.73	0.69	0.56	0.61	0.83	0.73	0.87	0.87
4.	Central Taxes (Net) (2-3)	4.86	5.48	6.20	6.99	6.78	7.40	6.99	6.00	6.07	5.98
	a) Direct Taxes	1.35	1.50	1.89	2.17	2.04	1.94	1.86	1.47	1.50	1.43
	b) Indirect Taxes	3.51	3.98	4.31	4.82	4.74	5.46	5.13	4.53	4.57	4.55
5.	States Own Taxes	3.03	3.06	3.39	3.52	3.38	3.57	3.45	3.41	3.75	3.74
	a) Direct Taxes	0.73	0.70	0.80	0.73	0.62	0.56	0.40	0.39	0.42	0.37
	b) Indirect Taxes	2.30	2.36	2.59	2.79	2.76	3.01	3.05	3.02	3.33	3.37
6.	States Tax Revenue - Total	4.13	4.18	4.70	4.84	4.50	4.72	4.80	4.70	5.22	5.42
	a) Direct Taxes	1.33	1.31	1.38	1.36	1.18	1.10	0.92	0.95	1.02	1.18
	b) Indirect Taxes	2.80	2.87	3.32	3.48	3.32	3.62	3.88	3.75	4.20	4.24

(Contd.) TABLE XI.2 : TAX GDP RATIOS : 1950-51 TO 1983-84

S1.	Iteam	1970-71	1971-72	1972-73	1973-74	1974-75	1975-76	1976-77	1977-78	1978-79	1979-80
	1	2	3	4	5	6	7	8	9	10	11
1.	Total Tax Revenue - All India	11.80	12.86	13.43	12.52	13.24	15.04	15.38	14.74	15.86	16.42
	a) Direct Taxes	2.50	2.70	2.81	2.63	2.63	3.35	3.23	2.98	2.91	2.88
	b) Indirect Taxes	9.30	10.16	10.62	9.89	10.61	11.69	12.15	11.76	12.95	13.54
2.	Central Taxes (gross)	7.96	8.93	9.40	8.59	9.08	10.23	10.32	9.86	10.75	11.12
	a) Direct Taxes	2.16	2.41	2.57	2.33	2.37	2.97	2.91	2.67	2.58	2.62
	b) Indirect Taxes	5.80	6.52	6.83	6.26	6.71	7.26	7.41	7.19	8.17	8.50
3.	States Share in Central Taxes	1.87	2.18	2.21	1.98	1.76	2.15	2.11	2.00	2.00	3.16
	a) Direct Taxes	0.91	1.08	1.03	0.91	0.75	1.00	0.83	0.76	0.73	0.81
	b) Indirect Taxes	0.96	1.10	1.18	1.07	1.01	1.15	1.28	1.24	1.27	2.35
4.	Central Taxes (Net) (2-3)	6.09	6.75	7.19	6.61	7.32	8.08	8.21	7.86	8.75	7.96
	a) Direct Taxes	1.25	1.33	1.54	1.42	1.62	1.97	2.08	1.91	1.85	1.81
	b) Indirect Taxes	4.84	5.42	5.65	5.19	5.70	6.11	6.13	5.95	6.90	6.15
5.	States Own Taxes	3.84	3.93	4.03	3.93	4.16	4.81	5.06	4.88	5.11	5.30
	a) Direct Taxes	0.34	0.29	0.24	0.30	0.26	0.38	0.32	0.31	0.33	0.26
	b) Indirect Taxes	3.50	3.64	3.79	3.63	3.90	4.43	4.74	4.57	4.78	5.04
6.	States Tax Revenue - Total	5.71	6.11	6.24	5.91	5.92	6.96	7.17	6.88	7.11	8.46
	a) Direct Taxes	1.25	1.37	1.27	1.21	1.01	1.38	1.15	1.07	1.06	1.07
	b) Indirect Taxes	4.46	4.74	4.97	4.70	4.91	5.58	6.02	5.81	6.05	7.39

(Contd.) TABLE XI.2 : TAX GDP RATIOS : 1950-51 TO 1983-84

Sl.	Item	1980-81	1981-82	1982-83	1983-84
	1	2	3	4	5
1.	Total Tax Revenue - All India	15.51	16.37	16.65	16.10
	a) Direct Taxes	2.55	2.80	2.74	2.50
	b) Indirect Taxes	12.96	13.57	13.91	13.60
2.	Central Taxes (gross)	10.30	10.75	10.82	10.59
	a) Direct Taxes	2.34	2.57	2.53	2.30
	b) Indirect Taxes	7.96	8.18	8.29	8.29
3.	States Share in Central Taxes	2.96	2.90	2.84	2.68
	a) Direct Taxes	0.79	0.70	0.70	0.61
	b) Indirect Taxes	2.17	2.20	2.14	2.07
4.	Central Taxes (Net)(2-3)	7.34	7.85	7.98	7.91
	a) Direct Taxes	1.55	1.87	1.83	1.69
	b) Indirect Taxes	5.79	5.98	6.15	6.22
5.	Statew Own Taxes	5.21	5.62	5.83	5.51
	a) Direct Taxes	0.21	0.23	0.21	0.20
	b) Indirect Taxes	5.00	5.39	5.62	5.31
6.	States Tax Revenue - Total	8.17	8.52	8.67	8.19
	a) Direct Taxes	1.00	0.93	0.91	0.81
	b) Indirect Taxes	7.17	7.59	7.76	7.38

Sources: Government of India, Ministry of Finance, Indian Economics Statistics 1985

TABLE XI-3 : GOVERNMENT EXPENDITURE (REVENUE & CAPITAL) AS PER CENT OF G.D.P

(Rs. Crores)

	1950-51	1955-56	1960-61	1965-66	1970-71	1975-76	1976-77	1977-78	1978-79	1979-80	1980-81	1981-82	1982-83	1983-84
1. G.D.P. at Market Prices (at current prices)	9564	10261	15018	24112	40263	74344	80198	89815	97860	107658	127926	147497	163576	195739
2. Development Expenditure (including loans and advances gross)	380	796	1599	3333	4554	11129	12611	14484	16719	18651	22672	26083	30356	34474
	(4.0)	(7.7)	(10.6)	(13.8)	(11.3)	(15.0)	(15.7)	(16.1)	(17.1)	(17.3)	(17.7)	(17.7)	(18.6)	(17.6)
3. Non-Developmental Expenditure	534	625	987	2074	3512	6935	7746	7857	9186	10515	12707	14463	17659	21220
	(5.6)	(6.2)	(6.6)	(8.6)	(8.7)	(9.3)	(9.7)	(8.8)	(9.4)	(9.8)	(9.9)	(9.8)	(10.8)	(10.8)
4. Total Expenditure (2+3)	914	1431	2586	5407	8066	18114	20357	22341	25905	29166	35379	40546	48015	55694
	(9.6)	(13.9)	(17.2)	(22.4)	(20.0)	(24.3)	(25.4)	(24.9)	(26.5)	(27.1)	(27.6)	(27.5)	(29.4)	28.4)
Expenditure incurred upon:														
i)Education, Medical and Health and family planning	89	163	13	???	1239	2645	3034	3360	3829	4345	25262	6184	7446	8683
	(0.9)	(1.6)	(2.1)	(2.5)	(3.1)	(3.6)	(3.8)	(3.7)	(3.9)	(4.0)	(4.1)	(4.2)	(4.6)	(4.4)
ii)Agriculture & Rural Development and Allied Service @	33	75	143	275	348	1150	1363	1752	1904	2276	2693	3097	3793	4500
	(0.3)	(0.7)	(1.0)	(1.1)	(0.9)	(1.5)	(1.7)	(2.0)	(1.9)	(2.1)	(2.1)	(2.1)	(2.3)	(2.3)
iii)Defence	168	190	281	885	1199	2472	2563	2634	2868	3356	3867	4652	5408	6309
	(1.8)	(1.9)	(1.9)	(3.7)	(3.0)	(3.3)	(3.2)	(2.9)	(2.9)	(3.1)	(3.0)	(3.2)	(3.3)	(3.2)

@ Includes Animal Husbandry, Community Development excluding Purchase and distribution of fertilizer and food respectively. However, due to the introduction of new classification of budgetary heads, figures from 1972-73 onwards are not strictly comparable with earlier figures.

Figures given in the brackets are percentage of G.D.P.,

Source: Government of India, Ministry of Finance, Indian Economics Statistics 1985.

TABLE XI.4 : TAX REVENUE OF THE CENTRE STATES AND UNION TERRITORIES AS PER CENT OF NATIONAL INCOME

(Rs. Crores)

		1950-51	1955-56	1960-61	1965-66	1968-69	1973-74	1975-76
1.	National Income at current prices	8,812	9,262	13,263	20,637	28,607	50,424	62,069
2.	Direct Taxes % of National Income	231	259	402	734	840	1,552	2,493
	of which:	(2.6)	(2.8)	(3.0)	(3.6)	(2.9)	(3.1)	(4.0)
a)	Income and Corporate tax	173	169	278	577	678	1,324	2,076
	% of National Income	(2.0)	(1.8)	(2.1)	(2.8)	(2.4)	(2.6)	(3.3)
b)	Land Revenue and Agri cultural Income Tax	55	87	107	130	136	160	263
	% of national Income	(0.6)	(0.9)	(0.8)	(0.6)	(0.5)	(0.3)	(0.4)
3.	Indirect Taxes	396	509	948	2,188	2,919	5,836	8,689
	% of national Income	(4.5)	(5.5)	(7.1)	(10.6)	(10.2)	(11.6)	(14.0)
	of which:							
a)	Union Excise Duty	68	145	416	898	1,321	2,602	3,845
	% of national Income	(0.8)	(1.6)	(3.1)	(4.4)	(4.6)	(5.2)	(6.2)
b)	Sales Tax	58	82	164	382	598	1,179	1,982
	% of national Income	(0.7)	(0.9)	(1.2)	(1.9)	(2.1)	(2.3)	(3.2)
4.	Total Taxes	627	768	1,350	2,922	3,759	7,389	11,182
	% of national Income	(7.1)	(8.3)	(10.2)	(14.2)	(13.1)	(14.7)	(18.0)
5.	Central Taxes	405	485	895	2,061	2,510	5,070	7,609
	% of national Income	(4.6)	(5.2)	(6.7)	(10.0)	(8.7)	(10.1)	(12.2)
6.	States Taxes	222	283	455	861	1,249	2,319	3,573
	% of national income	(2.5)	(3.1)	(3.4)	(4.2)	(4.3)	(4.6)	(5.8)

(Contd.) TABLE -11-4 : TAX REVENUE OF THE CENTRE STATES AND UNION TERRITORTIES AS PER CENT OF NATIONAL INCOME

(Rs. Crores)

		1976-77	1977-78	1978-79	1979-80	1980-81	1981-82	1982-83	1983-84	1984-85
1.	National income at current Prices	66,754	75,536	81,123	88,372	1,06,539	1,21,243	1,32,470	1,59,598	1,83,538*
2.	Direct Taxes % of	2,585	2,680	2,851	3,096	3,268	4,133	4,492	4,924	5,070
	National Income	(3.9)	(3.5)	(3.5)	(3.5)	(3.1)	(3.4)	(3.39)	(3.09)	(2.76)
	of Which:									
a)	Income and Corporation Tax	2,179	2,223	2,429	2,732	2,817	3,445	3,754	4,235	4,389
	% of national Income	(3.3)	(2.9)	(3.0)	(3.1)	(2.6)	(2.8)	(2.83)	(2.65)	(2.39)
b)	Land Revenue and Agricultural Income Tax	222	240	282	223	203	266	220	279	311
	% of national Income	(0.3)	(0.3)	(0.3)	(0.3)	(0.2)	(0.2)	(0.17)	(0.17)	(0.17)
3.	Indirect Taxes	9,747	10,557	12,677	14,587	16,576	20,009	22,750	26,893	30,362
	% of Nationa Income	(14.6)	(14.0)	(15.6)	(16.5)	(15.6)	(16.5)	(17.17)	16.85)	(16.54)
	of which:									
a)	Union Excise Duty	4,221	4,448	5,367	6,011	6,500	7,421	8,059	10,125	11,172
	% of National Income	(6.3)	(5.9)	(6.6)	(6.8)	(6.1)	(6.1)	(6.08)	6.34)	(6.09)
b)	Sales Tax	2,323	2,476	2,852	3,302	4,018	5,063	5,722	6,493	7,236
	% of National Income	(3.5)	(3.3)	(3.5)	(3.7)	(3.8)	(4.2)	(4.32)	(4.07)	(3.94)
4.	Total Taxes	12,332	13,237	15,528	17,683	19,844	24,142	27,242	31,817	35,432
	% of National Income	(18.5)	(17.5)	(19.1)	(20.0)	(18.7)	(19.9)	(20.56)	(19.94)	(19.30)
5.	Central Taxes	8,271	8,858	10,525	11,974	13,180	15,847	17,696	20,946	23,165
	% of National Income	(12.4)	(11.7)	(13.0)	(13.5)	(12.4)	(13.1)	(13.36)	(13.12)	(12.62)
6.	States Taxes	4,061	4,379	5,003	5,709	6,664	8,295	9,546	10,871	12,267
	% of national Income	(6.1)	(5.8)	(6.2)	(6.5)	(6.3)	(6.8)	(7.20)	(6.81)	(6.68)

Source: Government of India, Ministry of Finance, Indian Economic Statistics, Public Financem, December, 1983.

* Estimates on the assumption of a 15 per cent increase over the previous year.

T-XI.5 : RECEIPTS FROM INCOME TAX AND CORPOATION TAX (Rs. Crores)

Years	Income Tax (Inclusive of union surchage)	corporation Tax	Total	Percentage share in the total Income Tax	Percentage share in the total Corpn. Tax
FIRST FINANCE COMMISSION					
1952-53	143.2	43.8	187.0	76.6	23.4
1953-54	124.2	41.6	165.8	74.9	25.1
1954-55	123.2	37.3	160.5	76.8	23.2
1955-56	132.0	37.1	169.1	78.1	21.9
1956-57	151.2	51.2	202.4	74.7	25.3
Total 1952-57	673[illegible]	211.0	884.8	76.2	23.8
SECOND FINANCE COMMISSION					
1957-58	161.6	56.1	217.7	74.2	25.8
1958-59	172.0	54.3	227.1	76.1	23.9
1959-60	149.2	106.6	255.8	58.3	41.7
1960-61	168.7	110.7	279.4	60.4	39.6
1961-62	161.0	160.8	321.8	50.1	49.9
Total 1957-62	813.3	488.5	1,301.8	62.5	37.5
THIRD FINANCE COMMISSION					
1962-63	187.4	220.1	407.5	46.0	54.0
1963.64	245.6	287.3	532.9	46.1	53.9
1964-65	266.9	313.6	580.5	46.0	54.0
1965-66	271.9	304.8	576.7	47.2	52.8
Total 1962-66	971.8	1,125.8	2,097.6	46.3	53.7
FOURTH FINANCE COMMISSION					
1966-67	306.3	330.8	637.1	48.1	51.9
1967-68	325.9	310.5	636.4	51.2	48.8
1968-69	378.5	299.8	678.3	55.8	44.2
Total 1966-69	1,010.7	941.1	1,951.8	51.8	48.2

(Contd.) T-XI.5 : RECEIPTS FROM INCOME TAX AND CORPOATION TAX (Rs. Crores)

Years	Income Tax (Inclusive of union surchage)	corpora-tion Tax	Total	Percentage share in the total	
				Income Tax	Corpn. Tax
FIFTH FINANCE COMMISSION					
1969-70	448.4	353.4	801.8	55.9	44.1
1970-71	473.2	370.5	843.7	56.1	43.9
1971-72	536.7	472.1	1,008.8	53.2	46.8
1972-73	629.9	557.9	1,187.8	53.1	46.6
1973-74	745.2	582.6	1,327.8	56.1	43.9
Total 1969-74	2,833.4	2,336.5	5,169.9	54.8	45.2
SIXTH FINANCE COMMISSION					
SEVENTH FINANCE COMMISSION					
1979-80	1,340.3	1,391.9	2,732.2	49.1	50.9
1980-81	1,506.4	1,310.8	2,817.2	53.5	46.5
1981-82	1,475.5	1,970.0	3,445.5	42.8	57.2
1982-83	1,569.7	2,184.5	3,754.2	41.8	58.2
1983-84	1,699.1	2,492.7	4,191.8	40.5	59.5
Total 1979-84	7,591.0	9,349.9	16,940.9	44.8	55.2
1984-85 (R.E)	1,810.0	2,824.0	4,634.0	39.1	60.9
1985-86 (B.E)	1,964.0	2804.0	4,768.0	41.2	58.8

Source: Central Budget

TABLE XI.6 : 5.3 : Budgetary deficit of the Centre and States (1951-52 to 1984-85)

(Rs. Crores)

Year	Centre	States	Total
First Plan			
1951-52	-33	37	4
1952-53	46	-10	36
1953-54	81	-45	36
1954-55	142	-42	100
1955-56	160	-7	153
Total	396	-67	329
Second Plan			
1956-57	185	56	241
1957-58	458	39	497
1958-59	247	-67	180
1959-60	188	-1	187
1960-61	-177	24	-93
Total	961	51	1012
Third Plan			
1961-62	115	29	144
1962-63	156	-36	120
1963-64	167	-22	145
1964-65	172	-38	134
1965-66	173	196	369
Total	783	129	912
Three Annual Plans			
1966-67	295	-110	185
1967-68	206	84	290
1968-69	262	64	326
Total	763	38	801

<u>Fourth Plan</u>			
1969-70	46	-31	15
1970-71	285	134	419
1971-72	519	266	785
1972-73	869	-14	855
1973-74	328	175	503
Total	2047	530	2577
<u>Fifth Plan</u>			
1974-75	721	30	751
1975-76	366	-16	350
1976-77	131	3	134
1977-78	933	83	1016
1978-79	951	-320	631
Total*	3102	-220	2882
<u>Annual Plan</u>			
1979-80	2427	228	2655
<u>Sixth Plan</u>			
1980-81	2575	874	3450
1981-82	1392	1127	2519
1982-83	1655	694	2349
1983-84	1417	718	2135
1984-85 (RE)	3985	1892	5877
Total	11025	5305	16330
<u>Seventh Plan</u>			
1985-86 (BE)	3316	313	3629

* For the time period originally envisaged for the Fifth Plan.

Source:
Government of India, Ministry of Finance, Indian Economics Statestics 1985

TABLE XI.7 : 5.1 DEFICIT FINANCING DURING FIRST, SECOND & THIRD PLANS

(Rs. crores)

Year	CENTRE						STATES				
	Ad-hoc	Treasury Bills purchased & discounted by RBI	Withdrawal of cash balances	Adjustment for absorption (+) or liquidation (-) of treasury bills by State Govts.	RBI Support to long dated securities	Total (2 to 6)	Ways and Means advances from RBI	Withdrawal of cash balances	Adjustment for absorption (-)or liquidation (+) of treasury bills by State Govt.	Total (8 to 10)	Total deficit Financing by the Central & State Govt. (7 + 11)
1.	2.	3.	4.	5.	6.	7.	8.	9.	10.	11.	12.
First Plan											
1951-52	-7	-5	-1	-27	-12	-52	-1	11	27	37	-15
1952-53	-7	5	64	-2	-14	46	-	-12	2	-10	36
1953-54	-7	2	61	27	-56	27	-	-18	-27	-45	-18
1954-55	103	-	6	27	-37	99	-1	-14	-27	-42	57
1955-56	131	2	36	-3	41	207	-	-10	3	-7	200
Total	213	4	166	22	-78	327	-2	-43	-22	-67	260
Second Plan											
1956-57	226	-9	-56	27	53	241	6	77	-27	56	297
1957-58	476	5	-1	-17	-72	391	9	13	17	39	430
1958-59	132	-3	17	-58	-1	203	-6	-3	-58	-67	136
1959-60	149	28	-35	22	2	166	-2	23	-22	-1	165
1960-61	-84	6	25	-35	203	125	3	-4	25	24	149*
Total	899	27	-50	65	185	1126	10	106	-65	51	1177
Third Plan											
1961-62	76	15	-4	-13	78	152	11	5	13	29	181
1962-63	186	9	-19	1	39	216	-4	-31	-1	-36	180
1963-64	126	14	9	60	25	234	17	21	-60	-22	212
1964-65	98	42	60	32	-32	200	1	-5	-32	-38	162
1965-66	291	-3	-45	-108	67	202	14	74	108	196	398
Total	777	77	1	-28	177	1004	37	64	28	129	1133

Source : Government of India, Ministry of Finance, Indian Economics Statistics 1985.

TABLE XI.8 5.2: DEFICIT FINANCING DURING ANNUAL PLANS(1966-69) FOURTH PLAN, FIFTH PLAN AND ANNUAL PLAN1979-80

(Rs. crores)

Year	CENTRE						STATES				
	Ad-hoc	Treasury Bills purchased & discounted by RBI	Withdrawal of cash balances	Adjustment for absorption (+) or liquidation (-) of treasury bills by State Govts.	RBI Support to long dated securities	Total (2 to 6)	Ways and Means advances from RBI	Withdrawal of cash balances	Adjustment for absorption (-) or liquidation (+) of treasury bills by State Govts.	Total (8 to 10)	Total deficit Financing by the Central & State Govts. (7 + 11)
1.	2.	3.	4.	5.	6.	7.	8.	9.	10.	11.	12.
Annual Plan											
1966-67	256	112	-62	30	-37	299	-2	-78	-30	-110	189
1967-68	200	-40	40	-28	-32	140	20	36	28	84	224
1968-69	258	2	-48	37	-50	199	-5	106	-37	64	263
Fourth Plan											
1969-70	140	-56	-17	7	15	89	4	-28	-7	-31	58
1970-71	435	-35	-74	-36	-65	225	22	76	36	134	359
1971-72	331	-45	174	12	-28	444	2	276	-12	266	710
1972-73	615@	291	-75	35	-4	862@	4	17@	-35	-14@	848
1973-74	456	77	-121	-44	232	600	31	100	44	175	775
Total	1977	232	-113	-26	150	2220	63	441	26	530	2750
Fifth Plan											
1974-75	105	536	-82	102	-37	624	-12	144	-102	30	654
1975-76	540	-168	-480	101	-193	-190	-32	17	-101	-16	-206
1976-77	-495	558	472	-4	-194	337	3	-4	4	3	340
1977-78	-40	2297	-2546	47	-79	-321	35	95	-47	83	-238
1978-79	-735*	-333	2518	447	25	1922*	-97	224*	-447	-320*	1602
Total	-625	2900	-118	693	-478	2372	-103	576	-693	-220	2152
Annual Plan											
1979-80	1150	1400	-179	109	365	2845	38	299	-109	228	3073

@ Excludes book adjustment of Rs. 421 crores on account of centre's assistance to States for clearing their over drafts.
* Excludes book adjustment of Rs. 555 crores on account of centre's assistance to States for clearing their overdrafts.
? For the time period orginally envisaged for the Fifth Plan.
Source : Government of India, Ministry of Finance, 'Indian Economics Statistics 1985'

TABLE XI.9 : STATES' ADJUSTED OVERDRAFT

(Rs. Crores)

STATES	31.3. 1980	31.3. 1981	31.3. 1982	31.3. 1983	31.3. 1984	31.3. 1985
1	2	3	4	5	6	7
I. SPECIAL CATEGORY STATES :						
1. Assam	-	33.05	115.43	9.83	60.48	60.10
2. Himachal Pradesh	-	-	32.85	3.30	14.30	24.16
3. Jammu & Kashmir	*	*	*	*	*	*
4. Manipur	11.06	17.49	64.29	13.58	12.71	11.05
5. Meghalaya	-	-	14.11	0.18	2.59	-
6. Nagaland	6.81	0.64	19.96	14.94	33.59	27.73
7. Sikkim	*	*	*	*	*	*
8. Tripura	2.66	9.46	28.72	1.13	4.57	-
TOTAL : (I)	20.53	60.64	275.36	42.96	128.64	123.04
II. NON-SPECIAL CATEGORY STATES :						
1. Andhra Pradesh	-	-	-	-	13.00	172.21
2. Bihar	-	-	180.14	204.24	112.40	46.68
3. Gujarat	-	17.59	53.60	-	-	10.49
4. Haryana	1.95	36.01	66.79	48.87	12.63	91.16
5. Karnataka	-	14.37	-	4.84	37.26	214.57
6. Kerala	-	-	75.93	-	45.05	174.50
7. Madhya Pradesh	1.27	97.93	130.88	20.27	35.43	130.00
8. Maharashtra	-	-	36.40	-	-	-
9. Orissa	-	-	6.43	20.98	-	50.13
10. Punjab	9.53	64..01	79.35	-	47.34	78.19
11. Rajasthan	22.10	143.27	271.46	2.07	-	-
12. Tamil Nadu	-	-	-	-	-	19.62
13. Uttar Pradesh	-	-	-	2.00	36.61	372.40
14. West Bengal	41.16	93.91	316.96	38.69	62.90	140.72
TOTAL : (II)	76.01	457.09	1217.94	341.96	402.62	1500.67
GRAND TOTAL (I+II)	96.54	527.73	1493.30	384.92	531.26	1623.71

* Do not bank with R.B.I.

Source : Government of India, Ministry of Finance, Statistical Statements on Finances and Plans of States and Union Territories 1985.

TABLE XI.10 : STATES' ADJUSTED CASH BALANCE POSITION AS ON 31-3-1985

(Rs. Crores)

STATES	Treasury Bills holdings	Ways and Means advance availed of	Adjusted Cash balance	Net cash Position (2+3+4)	Surplus (+)/ Deficit(-) generated during 84-85
1	2	3	4	5	6
1. Andhra Pradesh	-	-59.58	-172.21	-231.79	-158.98
2. Assam	-	-21.37	-150.10	-171.47	-89.61
3. Bihar	+75.24	-	-152.85	-77.61	+65.74
4. Gujarat	-	-38.27	-10.49	-48.76	-38.21
5. Haryana	-	-18.00	-91.16	109.16	-78.53
6. Himachal Pradesh	+7.90	-	-40.13	-32.23	-9.47
7. Jammu & Kashmir*					
8. Karnataka	-	-40.74	-214.57	-255.31	-177.58
9. Kerala	-	-30.48	-174.50	-204.98	-129.74
10. Madhya Pradesh	-	-44.31	-130.00	-174.31	-94.81
11. Maharashtra	140.85	-	-67.97	-27.12	-20.39
12. Manipur	-	-5.93	-26.05	-31.98	-13.27
13. Meghalaya	+8.87	-	-7.16	+1.71	+8.70
14. Nagaland	-	4.00	-37.73	-41.73	-4.14
15. Orissa	-	-30.38	-54.51	-84.51	-136.42
16. Punjab	-	-	-110.19	-110.19	-27.00
17. Rajasthan	-	-12.25	-0.06	-12.31	-13.97
18. Sikkim*					
19. Tamil Nadu	-	-66.00	-19.62	-85.62	-43.19
20. Tripura	+9.65	-	-4.15	+5.50	+14.07
21. Uttar Pradesh	-	-102.00	-372.40	-474.40	-335.79
22. West Bengal	0.10	-43.86	-140.82	-184.58	-77.85
TOTAL	+142.61	-517.17	-1976.29	-2350.85	-1360.44
				-2358.06	-1448.95
				+7.21	+88.51

* DO NOT BANK WITH R.B.I.

Source : Government of India, Ministry of Finance, Statisticsl Statements on Finances and Plans of States and Union Territories 1985.

TABLE XI.11 : LIMITS FOR WAYS AND MEANS ADVANCES TO THE STATE GOVERNMENTS

(Rs. Crores)

STATES	31.3. 1980	31.3. 1981	31.3. 1982	31.3. 1983	31.3. 1984	31.3. 1985
1	2	3	4	5	6	7
I. SPECIAL CATEGORY STATES :						
1. Assam	12.00	12.00	12.00	21.04	21.38	21.37
2. Himachal Pradesh	4.06	4.06	4.06	8.06	8.06	8.07
3. Jammu & Kashmir	*	*	*	*	*	*
4. Manipur	2.00	2.00	2.00	4.00	6.00	5.93
5. Meghalaya	2.30	2.30	2.30	4.37	4.40	4.43
6. Nagaland	2.00	2.00	2.00	4.00	4.00	4.00
7. Sikkim	*	*	*	*	*	*
8. Tripura	2.00	2.00	2.00	4.00	4.00	4.00
TOTAL : (I)	24.36	24.36	24.36	45.47	47.84	47.80
II. NON-SPECIAL CATEGORY STATES :						
1. Andhra Pradesh	30.00	30.00	30.00	60.00	59.81	59.58
2. Bihar	17.25	17.25	17.25	31.12	30.95	30.93
3. Gujarat	21.00	21.00	21.00	42.00	42.00	38.27
4. Haryana	9.00	9.00	9.00	18.00	18.00	18.00
5. Karnataka	24.00	24.00	24.00	40.70	40.47	40.74
6. Kerala	18.00	18.00	18.00	30.19	30.19	30.48
7. Madhya Pradesh	24.00	24.00	24.00	44.18	44.07	44.31
8. Maharashtra	45.00	45.00	45.00	90.00	88.44	88.36
9. Orissa	18.00	18.00	18.00	34.98	34.43	34.38
10. Punjab	18.00	18.00	18.00	36.00	35.85	32.00
11. Rajasthan	12.00	12.00	12.00	24.00	24.00	24.00
12. Tamil Nadu	33.00	33.00	33.00	66.00	66.00	66.00
13. Uttar Pradesh	51.00	51.00	51.00	84.00	102.00	102.00
14. West Bengal	23.75	23.75	23.75	43.82	43.83	43.86
TOTAL : (II)	344.00	344.00	344.00	644.99	660.04	652.91
GRAND TOTAL (I+II)	368.36	368.36	368.36	690.46	707.88	700.71

* Do not bank with R.B.I.

Source : Government of India, Ministry of Finance, Statistical Statements on Finances and Plans of States Union Territories 1985'.

TABLE XI.12 : ADVANCE PLAN ASSISTANCE ALLOCATED/RELEASED TO THE STATE ON ACCOUNT OF NATURAL CALAMITIES RELIEF DURING 1974-75 TO 1978-89

(Rs. Crores)

	STATES	Calamity	Allocated	1974-75 Released	Allocated	Released	1975-86	
1.	Andhra Pradesh	Floods	-		-	-		-
		Cyclone	-		-	-		-
2.	Assam	Floods	2.00		1.84	-		-
3.	Bihar	Floods	4.00		4.00	9.75		9.75
4.	Gujarat	Drought	9.89		9.39	-		-
		Cyclone	-		-	4.15		4.15
		Floods	-		-	5.00		5.00
5.	Haryana	Drought	2.00		2.00	-		-
		Floods	-		-	-		-
		Hailstorm	-		-	-		-
6.	Himachal Pradesh	Earthquake	-		-	-		-
		Floods	-		-	-		-
7.	Jammu & Kashmir	Floods	-		-	-		-
8.	Karnataka	Drought	-		-	-		-
9.	Kerala	Floods	-		-	-		-
		Cyclone	-		-	-		-
		Drought	-		-	-		-
10.	Madhya Pradesh	Drought	6.50		6.50	-		-
		Floods	-		-	-		-
11.	Maharashtra	Drought	-		-	-		-
12.	Manipur	Floods	-		-	-		-
		Drought	-		-	-		-
13.	Orissa	Drought	7.91		7.91	-		-
		Floods	-		-	7.55		7.55
		Tornado	-		-	-		-
14.	Punjab	Floods	-		-	-		-
15.	Rajasthan	Drought	10.24		10.24	-		-
		Floods	-		-	2.50		2.50
16.	Sikkim	Drought	-		-	0.73		0.73
17.	Tamil Nadu	Drought	7.50		7.50	-		-
		Floods	-		-	-		-
		Cyclone	-		-	-		-
18.	Tripura	Floods	-		-	-		-
19.	Uttar Pradesh	Floods	-		-	6.20		5.65
		Drought	-		-	-		-
		Hailstorm	-		-	-		-
20.	West Bengal	Floods	2.25		-	-		-
	TOTAL		52.29		49.88	35.88		35.33
Total assistance sought by all State Govts. (Rs. Crores)				273.64			364.67	

(Contd.) TABLE XI.12

(Rs. Crores)

	STATES	Calamity	1976-77 Allocated	Released	1977-78 Allocated	Released	1978-79 Allocated	Released
1.	Andhra Pradesh	Floods	-	-	-	-	7.06	7.66
		Cyclone	3.53	3.53	56.52	56.52	11.46	11.46
2.	Assam	Floods	2.59	2.00	3.23	1.22	-	-
3.	Bihar	Floods	10.95	10.70	-	-	44.92	44.92
4.	Gujarat	Drought	-	-	-	-	-	-
		Cyclone	4.25	4.25	-	-	-	-
		Floods	-	-	10.43	9.77	-	-
5.	Haryana	Drought	-	-	-	-	-	-
		Floods	-	-	11.00	11.00	15.30	16.00
		Hailstorm	-	-	-	-	3.00	
6.	Himachal Pradesh	Earthquake	0.48	0.48	-	-	-	-
		Floods	-	-	2.70	2.70	6.99	6.89
7.	Jammu & Kashmir	Floods	-	-	-	-	0.26	0.26
8.	Karnataka	Drought	7.25	7.00	9.62	9.62	-	-
9.	Kerala	Floods	-	-	-	-	11.00	11.00
		Cyclone	-	-	3.64	3.64	-	-
		Drought	1.50	1.50	-	-	-	-
10.	Madhya Pradesh	Drought	6.15	5.00	-	-	6.45	6.45
		Floods	-	-	-	-	3.08	3.08
11.	Maharashtra	Drought	-	-	-	-	5.00	5.00
12.	Manipur	Floods	0.45	0.45	-	-	-	-
13.	Orissa	Drought	5.10	5.10	-	-	-	-
		Floods	-	-	8.52	8.40	6.65	7.56
		Tornado	-	-	-	-	1.92	7.56
14.	Punjab	Floods	-	-	-	-	6.75	6.75
15.	Rajasthan	Drought	-	-	-	-	-	-
		Floods	3.32	2.44	7.97	7.97	9.58	5.51
16.	Sikkim	Drought	-	-	-	-	-	-
17.	Tamil Nadu	Drought	15.70	15.70	-	-	-	-
		Floods	3.05	3.00	-	-	10.11	24.40
		Cyclone	-	-	29.31	29.31	14.40	
18.	Tripura	Floods	1.11	0.51	-	-	-	-
19.	Uttar Pradesh	Floods	11.25	11.23	10.00	7.04	74.92	74.13
		Drought	-	-				
		Hailstorm	-	-	-	-		
20.	West Bengal	Floods	-	-	4.41	1.88	38.93	88.93
TOTAL			76.68	72.91	157.35	149.07	329.20	323.75
Total assistance sought by all State Govts. (Rs. Crores)			495.15		749.69		1352.17	

Source: Government of India, Ministry of Finance, Statistical Statements on Finances and Plans of States and Union Territoris.

TABLE X1.13 : ADVANCE PLAN ASSISTANCE ALLOCATED / RELEASED TO STATES FOR DROUGHT 1979-80

(Rs. Lakhs).

STATES	Assistance sought by States	Ceilings of Additional Expenditure approved by the Govt. of India			Advance plan assistance special central assistance released		
		Non-Plan	Plan	Total	Loan	Grant	Total
1. Andhra Pr.	2807.00	177.00	2028.50	2205.50	1419.95	608.55	2028.50
2. Assam	868.00	178.47	461.50	639.97	245.00	105.00	350.00
3. Bihar	4307.00	102.00	1080.00	1182.00	382.20	163.80	546.00
4. Gujarat	-	-	-	-	-	-	-
5. Haryana	2532.00	-	450.00	450.00	140.00	60.00	200.00
6. Himachal Pr.	1502.00	12.00	358.00	370.00	30.00	270.00	300.00
7. J & K	2430.00	54.00	225.00	279.00	105.00	45.00	150.00
8. Karnataka	-	-	-	-	-	-	-
9. Kerala	-	-	-	-	-	-	-
10. Madhya Pr.	9100.00	155.00	2125.00	2280.00	1467.90	629.10	2097.00
11. Maharashtra	3271.00	169.00	685.00	854.00	479.50	205.50	685.00
12. Manipur	538.00	9.93	261.99	271.92	68.00	192.00	260.00
13. Meghalaya	300.00	4.38	72.32	76.70	5.78	52.04	57.82
14. Nagaland	405.00	7.00	60.00	67.00	5.30	47.70	53.00
15. Orissa	7214.00	375.00	1030.00	1405.00	706.00	324.00	1030.00
16. Punjab	-	-	-	-	-	-	-
17. Rajasthan	8067.00	190.00	1685.00	1875.00	1085.00	535.00	1620.00
18. Sikkim	-	-	-	-	-	-	-
19. Tamil Nadu		-	-	-	-	-	-
20. Tripura	347.00	12.00	121.00	133.00	10.00	90.00	100.00
21. Uttar Pr.	45617.00	370.00	3121.00	3491.00	2134.70	936.30	3121.00
22. West Bengal	9474.00	1360.00	1407.00	2767.00	885.137	379.773	1265.91
TOTAL ALL STATES	124093.00	3175.78	15171.31	18347.09	9220.467	4643.763	13864.23

Source: Government of India, Ministry of Finance, Statistical Statements on Finance and Plans of States and Union Territories,1985.

TABLE XI.14 : NON-PLAN GRANTS TO STATES FOR CYCLONE, SNOWSTORM, FLOODS ETC. 1979-80

STATES	Assistance sought by States	Ceilings of additional expenditure approved by Govt. of India	Non-Plan grant released
1	2	3	4
1. Andhra Pradesh	14500.00	6122.00	3518.25
2. Assam	1628.00	456.00	216.00
3. Bihar	-	-	-
4. Gujarat	13929.00	5060.00	3063.75
5. Haryana	-	-	-
6. Himachal Pradesh	353.00	210.00	100.00@
7. Jammu & Kashmir*	-	13.00	-(Covered b4y Margin Money)
8. Karnataka	-	-	-
9. Kerala	-	-	-
10. Madhya Pradesh	-	-	-
11. Maharashtra	-	-	-
12. Manipur	-	-	-
13. Meghalaya	-	-	-
14. Nagaland	-	-	-
15. Orissa	-	-	-
16. Punjab	-	-	
17. Rajasthan	11600.00	1685.00	1034.32
18. Sikkim*-	-	-	
19. Tamil Nadu	8270.83	2250.00	940.43
20. Tripura	-	-	-
21. Uttar Pradesh	-	-	-
22. West Bengal	-	-	-
TOTAL ALL STATES	50280.83	15796.00	8872.75

@ Non-Plan grants of Rs.27.14 lakhs released during 1980-81 as arrears for 1979-80.

Source : Environment of India, Ministry of Finance, Statistical Statements or Finances and Plans of States and Union Territories, 1985.

TABLE XI.15 : ASSISTANCE SOUGHT CEILING OF EXPENDITURE APPROVED AND ASSISTANCE RELEASED FOR DROUGHT DURING 1980-81 AND 1981-82

(Rs. Crores)

	STATES	1980-81			1981-82		
		Assistance sought by State Govt.	Ceilings approved	Central assistance released	Assistance sought by State Govt.	Ceilings approved	Central assistance released
	1	2	3	4	5	6	7
A.							
1.	Andhra Pradesh	227.00	42.97	39.23	105.03	26.25	14.94
2.	Assam	-	-	-	-	-	-
3.	Bihar	92.89	24.82	15.03	-	-	-
4.	Gujarat	42.98	6.12	2.68	-	-	-
5.	Haryana	38.79	4.02*	5.72@	760.63	8.25	6.94
6.	Himachal Pradesh	18.80	10.01	6.79	10.26	2.65	3.48
7.	Jammu & Kashmir	-	-	-	-	-	-
8.	Karnataka	250.00	6.65	4.00	60.04	13.81	12.65
8.	Kerala	-	-	-	-	-	-
10.	Madhya Pradesh	94.95	47.90	38.76	-	-	-
11.	Maharashtra	39.95	16.25	11.67	-	-	-
12.	Manipur	-	-	-	-	-	-
13.	Meghalaya	-	-	-	-	-	-
14.	Nagaland	-	-	-	-	-	-
15.	Orissa	56.68	17.39	10.56	-	-	-
16.	Punjab	-	-	-	-	-	-
17.	Rajasthan	120.84	40.31	24.40	451.06	87.83	65.04
18.	Sikkim	-	-	-	-	-	-
19.	Tamil Nadu	-	-	-	169.60	49.77	29.90
20.	Tripura	-	-	-	-	-	-
21.	Uttar Pradesh	122.23	47.52	26.42	-	-	-
22.	West Bengal	-	-	-	-	-	-
TOTAL ALL STATES		1111.11	263.96	188.26	1564.62	188.56	132.95
B.	Spillover of 1981-82 to 1982-83						
1.	Madhya Pradesh	-	-	-	-	-	-
2.	Orissa	-	-	-		-	-
C	Arrears for previous years						
1.	Karnataka	-	-	-	-	-	1.96

2. Madhya Pradesh	-	-	-	-	-	25.00
3. Rajasthan	-	-	-	-	-	-
4. Tamil Nadu	-	-	-	-	-	-
5. Haryana	-	-	-	-	-	-
D. Ad-hoc releases for 1983-84						
1. Rajasthan	-	-	-	-	-	-
E. Recovaries from State on account of 1982-83 drought						
1. Rajasthan	-	-	-	-	-	-
GRAND TOTAL (A TO E)	1111.11	263.96	183.26	1564.62	188.56	159.91

(Contd.) TABLE XI.15 : ASSISTANCE SOUGHT CEILING OF EXPENDITURE APPROVED AND ASSISTANCE RELEASED FOR DROUGHT 1982-83 AND 1983-84

(Rs. Crores)

STATES	1 9 8 2 - 8 3			1 9 8 3 - 8 4		
	Assistance sought by State Govt.	Ceilings approved	Central assistance released	Assistance sought by State Govt.	Ceilings approved	Central assistance released
1	2	3	4	5	6	7
A.						
1. Andhra Pradesh	220.24	68.77	65.80	165.12	26.26	26.19
2. Assam	-	-	-	-	-	-
3. Bihar	234.30	25.01	14.73	74.57	3.98	@@@
4. Gujarat	202.00	30.60	28.87	**	9.13	-7.60
5. Haryana	83.85	11.82	10.35	-	-	-
6. Himachal Pradesh	41.50	13.02	12.50	-	=-	3.00
7. Jammu & Kashmir	-	-	-	-	-	-
8. Karnataka	51.01	8.81	15.00@@	**	14.00	4.00Q
8. Kerala	23.56	4.10	2.00(L)	229.60	42.46	38.35Q
10. Madhya Pradesh	106.14	34.36	33.06	72.72	22.29	21.51
11. Maharashtra	131.14	56.89	42.94	27.41	11.66	5.00(b)
12. Manipur	-	-	-	-	-	-
13. Meghalaya	-	-	-	-	-	-
14. Nagaland	-	-	-	-	-	-
15. Orissa	251.43	15.98	14.48	149.65	24.65	22.05
16. Punjab	-	-	-	(C)	(C)	4.00
17. Rajasthan	398.94	74.00	65.10	105.67	39.85	19.79(g)
18. Sikkim	5.00	0.17	0.16	0.65	0.13(d)	

19. Tamil Nadu	190.00	18.39	15.00(LL)	219.45	59.15	47.96(h)
20. Tripura	4.22	2.01	1.86	-	-	-
21. Uttar Pradesh	-	-	-	36.00	1.57	1.57
22. West Bengal	278.22	74.27(f)	60.66	102.33	30.59	16.83
TOTAL ALL STATES	2221.55	438.20	382.57	1183.46	292.74	204.65
B. Spillover of 1981-82 to 1982-83						
1. Madhya Pradesh	27.56	6.63	6.37	-	-	-
2. Orissa	11.45	3.80	-	-	-	-
C. Arrears for previous years						
1. Karnataka	-	-	-	-	-	-
2. Madhya Pradesh	-	-	-	-	-	-
3. Rajasthan	-	-	21.02	-	-	-
4. Tamil Nadu	-	-	2.37	-	-	2.56
5. Haryana	-	-	-			
D. Ad-hoc releases for 1983-84						
1. Rajasthan	-	-	11.00	-	-	-
E. Recovaries from State on account of 1982-83 drough						
1. Rajasthan	-	-	-	-	-	-2.90
GRAND TOTAL (A+B+C+D+E)	2260.56	448.63	423.33	1183.46	292.74	204.31

1980-81: * Rs. 1.00 crores also approved for on going and other approved irrigation works but the expenditure will be not from the savings in the year marked Plan provision in the Annual Plan for Sutlaj-Jamuna Link Canal.

@ Arrears for 1979-80 drought.

1982-83: @@ Includes advance release of Rs. 6.66 crores for 1983-84.

(L) Includes Rs. 1.2 crores releases in advance for 1983-84.

(LL) Includes Rs. 6.42 crores for 1983-84 released in advance in 1982-83.

(f) Excludes Rs. 3.00 crores as short-term loan.

1983-84: @@@ Met out of the Margin Money.

** Demand included in 1982-83 demands.

QQ Excludes Rs. 6.66 crores released in 1982-83 in advance adjusted in 1983-84.

Q Excludes Rs. 1.22 crores released in 1982-83in advance adjusted in 1983-84.

(b) Rs. 5.00 crores [1982-83 in advance adjusted in 1983-84] had been released on ad-hoc basis during 1983-84. However on the basis of expenditure reported by the State Government, entitlement their works out to Rs. 3.15 crores. Hence the balance of Rs. 1.85 crores has been recovered from the Central assistance for State Plan Schemes for 1983-84.

(c) This relates to cotton crop damaged by pests, ceilings approved for 1984-85.

(g) Excludes Rs. 11.00 crores released in advance for 1983-84 during 1982-83.

(d) Rs. 0.04 crores for 1983-84 and Rs. 0.09 crores for 1984-85.

(h) Excludes Rs. 6.42 crores released in advance in 1982-83 adjusted in 1983-84.

Source: Government of India, Ministry of Finance, 'Statistical Statements on Finances and Plans of State and Union Territories, 1985'

TABLE-XI.16 : ASSISTANCE SOUGHT, CEILINGS OF EXPENDITURE APPROVED AND ASSISTANCE RELEASED FOR DROUGHT - RELIEF DURING 1984-85

	STATES	Assistance sought	Ceilings of Expenduture approved	Central Assistance Released
	1	2	3	4
1.	Andhra Pradesh	369.28	54.42	53.69
2.	Haryana (Cotton loss)	31.26	02.10	87.74
	(Breach in Canal)	47.70	06.60	
3.	Himachal Pradesh			
	(Pre-monsoon)	73.60	05.47	
	(Post-monsoon)	47.82	07.23@	09.46
4.	Karnataka	209.50	32.73	29.86(a)
5.	Madhya Pradesh	112.92	11.38	11.15
6.	Maharashtra (Drought)	117.06	30.63	30.41(b)
	(Cold wave)	16.60	01.20	
7.	Orissa	62.59	02.95@	05.00
8.	Punjab (Cotton loss)	24.45	06.35	*
9.	Rajasthan	141.79	05.43	met out from M.M.
10.	Uttar Pradesh	161.45	08.10	06.74
	TOTAL	1436.02	174.59	154.05

@ Based on recommendations.

(a) Includes Rs. 13 lakhs as arrears for 1983-84.

(b) Includes Rs. 6.09 crores as arrears for 1983-84.

* Rs. 4 crores was released as advance payment in 1983-84.

Source : Government of India, FMinistry of Finance, 'Statistical Statements on Finances and Plans of States and Union Territories 1985'.

TABLE XI.17 : ASSISTANCE SOUGHT, CEILINGS OF EXPENDITURE APPROVED FOR FLOOD, CYCLONE, HAILSTROM ETC. AND ASSISTANCE RELEASED DURING 1980-81. (Rs. Crores).

	STATES	Assistance sought by states	Approved Cellings of Expendi-ture.	Assistance released
1.	Andhra Pradesh	14.95	10.40	2.04
2.	Assam	34.37	12.72	5.59
3.	Bihar	89.80	23.47	10.90
4.	Gujarat	61.20	18.98	8.30
5.	Haryana	24.66	5.24	2.74
6.	Karnataka	28.57	3.48	1.01
7.	Kerala	19.89	9.09	4.00
8.	Orissa	112.30	42.89	28.20
9.	Uttar Pradesh	413.79	73.09	52.25*
10.	West Bengal	42.22	32.53	9.34
	TOTAL:	838.84	229.88	130.87

* In Addition, advance Plan assistance of Rs. 5.50 crores was also released for expenditure on Plan Works/Schemes.

(Contd.) TABLE-XI.17 ASSISTANCE SOUGHT, CEILINGS OF EXPENDITURE APPROVED FOR FLOOD, CYCLONE, HAIELSTORM ETC. AND ASSISTANCE REALESED DURING 1981-82. (Rs. Crores).

	STATES	Calamity	Assistance sought	Ceilings Approved	Amount Released
	1	2	3	4	5
1.	Andhra Pradesh	Hailstorm	2.65	0.82	-
2.	Bihar	Floods	78.60	20.74	2.00
3.	Himachal Pradesh	Hailstorm	0.00	2.41	0.80
4.	Jammu & Kashmir	Hailstorm	1.13	0.40	-
5.	Karnataka	Floods	14.11	2.31	1.18
6.	Kerala	Floods	40.10	8.43	5.13
7.	Manipur	Floods	1.89	1.60	1.00
8.	Orissa	Tormade	2.58	0.36	1.56
9.	Rajasthan	Floods	394.33	45.06	31.01
10.	Sikkim	Zersimatake	4.14	2.22	1.16
11.	Uttar Pradesh	Floods	300.55	45.46	26.99
12.	West Bengal	Cyclone	69.07	10.10	7.00
Arrears released					
1.	Kerala				1.24
	Ad-hoc advance realeased to Gujarat				5.00
TOTAL:			967.29	148.39	83.07

(Contd.) TABLE-XI-17 ASSISTANCE SOUGHT, CEILINGS OF EXPENDITURE APPROVED FOR FLOODS, CYCLONE, HAILSTORM ETC. AND ASSISTANCE RELEASED DURING 1982-83. (Rs. Crores).

STATES	Calamity	Assistance sought	Ceilings of expenditure approved	Amount released
1. Assam	Floods	24.84	9.47	4.51
2. Bihar	Floods	63.34	17.48	11.03
3. Gujarat	Cyclone	154.63	41.94	30.47
4. Haryana	Hailstrom	26.39	1.75	-
5. Himachal Pradesh	Hailstorm	21.07	4.03	3.01
6. Karnataka	Floods	20.80	4.42	-
7. Kerala	Floods	34.55	0.11	-
8. Madhya Pradesh	Floods	22.67	2.07	-
9. Meghalaya	Floods	1.00	0.33	0.19
10. Orissa	Floods	031.60	113.96	-
	Cyclone	125.44	90.53	129.20
11. Rajasthan	Hailstrom	32.20	0.32	-
12. Tripura	Floods	0.97	0.56	0.29
13. Uttar Pradesh	Floods	413.00	69.82	-
	Hailstrom	32.00	0.41	42.01
14. West Bengal	Cyclone	Included in the demand made in 1981-82	7.57	3.52
Sub-Total:		1607.66	327.80	224.33
Spillover of 1981-82 for 1982-83				
1. Gujarat	Flood & Cyclone	146.00	30.97	-
2. Madhya Pradesh	Hailstrom	38.16	0.14	-
Total:		1790.72	388.91	224.33
Arrears for the previous Years.				
1. Bihar				3.00
2. Manipur				0.08
3. Rajasthan				8.99
GRAND TOTAL:		1790.73	358.91	236.40

TABLE-XI-17 : ASSISTANCE SOUGHT, CEILINGS OF EXPENDITURE APPROVED FOR FLOOD, CYCLONE, HAILSTORM ETC, AND ASSISTANCE RELEASED DURING 1983-84. (Rs. Crores).

	Name of the State	Calmity	Amount requested for	Ceilings of Expenditure approved Non-Plan	Plan	Total	Central Assistance released
	1	2	3	4	5	6	7
1.	Andhra Pradesh	Cyclone	330.50	76.16	3.00	76.16	59.88 (includes ARM Rs.4.00 Crs.)
		Flods	75.89	19.54	1.00	20.54	
2.	Assam	Flood	52.00	11.07	-	11.07	-
3.	Gujarat	Cyclone'82 (Spillover)	(included in Demands of 1982-83)	4.45	-	4.45	-
				-	-	-	- @
		Flood and Cyclone 1983	5.43 (Interim)	0.98	-	0.98	-
		Flood'83	161.42	38.24	-	38.24	24.26
4.	Haryana	Flood'83	103.77	15.13	1.94	17.07	9.46
							1.71
							11.17
5.	Himachal Pradesh	Hailstorm, Heavy Rain & Flood	35.23	5.87	-	5.87	
		Flood	37.86	2.42	-	2.42	-5.84
6.	Jammu & Kashmir	Hailstorm excessive rains etc.	1.00	1.00	-	1.00	-
7.	Karnataka	Flood	18.99	3.29	-	3.29	0.13
8.	Madhya Pradesh	Floods'82 (Spillover)	(Included in the Demands for 1982-83	1.00	-	1.00	@
9.	Maharasthra	Floods'83	23.93	5.69	-	5.69	3.35
		Flood, June'83	65.34	14.91	-	14.91	-
		Flood, Sept.'83	40.70	9.78	-	9.78	16.96
10.	Meghalaya	Flood & Cyclone 1983	4.17	0.73	-	0.73	0.21

(Contd.) TABLE-XI-17 : ASSISTANCE SOUGHT, CEILINGS OF EXPENDITURE APPROVED FOR FLOOD, CYCLONE, hAILSTORM ETC, AND ASSISTANCE RELEASED DURING 1983-84.

(Rs. Crores).

	Name of the State	Calmity	Amount requested for	Ceilings of Expenditure approved			Central Assistance released
				Non-Plan	Plan	Total	
	1	2	3	4	5	6	7
11.	Nagaland	-do-	1.62	0.77	-	0.77	
12.	Orissa	Floods'82 (Spillover)	618.40	21.43	1.56	22.98	13.30 1.55 APA
13.	Tripura	Flood	19.43	4.50	-	4.50	14.85
14.	Sikkim	Flood/Land-slides	33.34	1.97	-	1.97	2.25
15.	Tamil Nadu	Flood	129.12	40.15	1.03	41.18	1.00
16.	Rajasthan	Floods	68.00	8.93	-	8.93	22.97, 1.03, 24.00
17.	Uttar Pradesh	Floods	563.76	54.26	3.00	57.26	6.62
18.	West Bengal	Floods/Tornades	-	0.60	-	0.60	32.59 3.00 35.59 @
TOTAL:			2389.90	339.87	11.62	351.99	206.18
Arrears paid for previous years.							
	Orissa	Floods 1981-82					1.95
	Sikkim	Earthquake					0.39
	Uttar Pradesh	Floods					0.63
GRAND TOTAL:			2389.90	339.87	11.62	351.39	209.15

@ Met out of the margin money.

Source: Government of India, Ministry of Finance, 'Statistical Statements on Finances and Plans of States and Union Territories 1985'.

TABLE XI.18 : ASSISTANCE SOUGHT, CEILING OF EXPENDITURE APPROVED AND CENTRAL ASSISTANCE RELEASED FOR RELIEF OF FLOOD, CYCLONES, HAILSTORM ETC. DURING 1984-85.

(Rs. Crores)

STATES	Assistance sought	Ceilings approved	Central Assistance Released
1. Andhra Pradesh			
Heavy Rains	14.64	04.73	18.04
cyclone	115.86	37.90*	
2. Assam (Floods)	151.61	39.12*	26.50
3. Bihar (Floods)	204.94	39.05	15.10
4. Haryana (Cold wave)	33.32	01.55	-
5. Himachal Pradesh	05.30	02.73	02.05
6. Jammu & Kashmir	06.09	03.78	01.86
6a. Karnataka (Floods)	3.73	A	A
7. Kerala	195.15	21.33	14.80
8. Madhya Pradesh	19.10	05.91	03.23
9. Manipur	02.00	00.28	00.03
10.Meghalaya (Spillover)	02.17	01.17	
(Floods)	05.92	01.76	02.16
11. Orissa	161.24	24.43	11.11
12. Rajasthan	22.25	04.99	Met out of MM
13. Sikkim	11.33	06.33	03.82
14. Tamil Nadu			
(Floods 83-84)	-	04.32	
(Floods)	47.00	08.41	
(Cyclone (Nov.1984)	52.23	18.76*	17.27 @
(Cyclone Dec. 1984)	06.55	00.79	
15. Tripura (Floods)	12.44	07.30	05.00
16. Uttar Pradesh			
(Floods83-81)	-	09.35	
(Floods)	264.17	47.89	32.07
17. West Bengal	151.58	48.03	25.00
TOTAL :	1485.89 +3.73	338.81	178.04
Arrears			
18. Karnataka			00.87
			178.91

* Excluding IAFBills on account of evacuation of affected population.

'A' relates to floods which occurred in June /July 1984. memorandum was received on 5th March, 1985. Ministry of Agriculture has not yet taken a decision on sending a Central Team or otherwise.

Source : Government of India, Ministry of Finance Statistical Statements on Finance and Plans of States.

TABLE-XI-19.: FINANCIAL RETURNS FROM MULTLPURPOSE, MAJOR AND MEDIUM IRRIGATION SCHEMES (EXCLUDING FLOOD CONTROL SCHEMES) DURING THE FIVE YEAR PERIOD 1984-85 TO 1988-89. (R.s Lakhs).

	STATE	As given in State forecast			As assessed by the Commission		
		Gross receipts	Working expenses** +	Net receipts	Gross current	Working expenses receipts	Net receipts
1.	Andhra Pradesh	13681*	16063	(-)2382	15485	15659	(-)174
2.	Assam	341	2435	(-)2094	589	638	(-)49
3.	Bihar	5030	33240	(-)28210	12087	12654	(-)567
4.	Gujarat	9181@	8012	(+)1169	4688	5075	(_)387
5.	Haryana	6811	19302	(-)12491	9071	9178	(-)107
6.	Himachal Pradesh	1	227	(-)226	23	33	(-)10
7.	Jammu & Kashmir	197	4716	(-)4519	705	940	(-)235
8.	Karnataka	2500	14274	(-)11774	6233	6247	(-)14
9.	Kerala	851	5803	(-)4952	2667	2681	(-)14
10.	Madhya Pradesh	6545@	11182	(-)4637	7615	8003	(-)388
11.	Maharastra	10156	14986	(-)4830	6343	6930	(-)587
12.	Manipur	33	133	(-)100	121	173	(-)52
13.	Meghalaya	-	-	-	-	-	-
14.	Nagaland	-	-	-	-	-	-
15.	Orissa	3661	9187	(-)5526	7775	7775	-
16.	Punjab	5524	28222	(-)22698	12401	12430	(-)29
17.	Rajasthan	7478	19421	(-)11943	7924	8184	(-)260
18.	Sikkim	-	-	-	-	-	-
19.	Tamil Nadu	4355$	12006	(-)7651	6069	6102	(-)6
20.	Tripura	-	-	-	-	-	-
21.	Uttar Pradesh	34190@	48973	(-)14783	30234	31289	(-)1055
22.	West Bengal	618	12936	(-)12318	7619	7693	(-)74
	TOTAL:	111153	261118	(-)149965	137676	141684	(-)4008

* Includes an estimated amount of Rs. 12860 lakhs attributable to Irrigation but shown under Land Revenue.

$ Includes Rs. 1775 lakhs attributable to Irrigation but shown under Land Revenue.

@ Includes additional yield estimated during 1984-85 from revision of irrigation rates effected in 1983-84 in Gujarat (Rs. 2955 lakhs), Madhya Pradesh (Rs. 2790 lakhs) and Uttar Pradesh (Rs. 6370 lakhs).

** Includes committed expenditure in respect of Plan Schemes completed upto 1983-84 shown separately by the State Government.

Source: Report of the VIII Finance commission.

TABLE-XI-20: CONTRIBUTION OF STATE ROAD TRANSPORT CORPORATIONS (AT 1979-80 RATES). (Rs. Crores).

STATES	1980-81 Actuals	1981-82 Actuals	1982-83 Actuals	1983-84 Actuals	1984-85 (L.E.)	TOTAL 1980-85 (L.E.)
1	2	3	4	5	6	7
I. SPECIAL CATEGORY STATES						
1. Assam	-0.90	-0.90	-2.37	-3.50	-10.61	-18.28
2. Himachal Pradesh	-0.14	-4.61	-6.17	-8.20	-9.63	-28.75
3. Jammu & Kashmir	-2.88	-4.05	-6.34	-5.16	-8.50	-26.93
4. Manipur	-0.34	-0.60	-	-0.75	-1.86	-3.55
5. Meghalaya	-0.26	-0.92	-1.47	-0.44	-1.70	-4.79
6. Nagaland	-	-	-	-	-	-
7. Sikkim	-	-	-	-	-	-
8. Tripura	-0.63	-0.98	-1.19	-1.23	-1.18	-5.21
TOTAL:	-5.15	-12.06	-17.54	-19.28	-33.48	-87.51
II. NON-SPECIAL CATEGORY STATES						
1. Andhra Pradesh	-1.32	-35.88	-43.70	-32.78	-48.28	-161.96
2. Bihar	-0.69	-5.40	-8.50	-10.47	-18.01	-43.07
3. Gujarat	-	7.70	-31.64	-45.97	-81.53	-151.44
4. Haryana	-	-	-	-	-	-
5. Karnataka	-11.69	-28.99	-38.83	-42.79	-76.33	-198.63
6. Kerala	-9.80	-21.85	-29.57	-34.65	-38.59	-134.46
7. Madhya Pradesh	-2.99	-14.92	-21.82	-25.12	-32.74	-97.59
8. Maharastra	4.21	-27.62	-89.75	-100.16	-97.51	-310.83
9. Orissa	-1.76	-2.23	-4.89	-7.02	-14.61	-30.51
10. Punjab	-5.90	-8.60	-11.80	-13.55	-16.72	-56.57
11. Rajasthan	-3.96	-20.12	-27.78	-27.47	-32.08	-111.41
12. Tamil Nadu	1.18	-37.89	-46.75	-52.96	-59.44	-195.86
13. Uttar Pradesh	-3.37	-17.54	-32.15	-46.13	-61.55	-160.74
14. West Bengal	-4.44	-9.01	-9.86	-8.75	-9.25	-41.31
TOTAL:	-40.53	-222.35	-397.04	-447.82	-586.64	-1694.38
GRAND TOTAL:	-45.68	-234.41	-414.58	-467.10	-620.12	-1781.89

Source: Government of India, Ministry of Finance, 'Statistical Statements on Finances and Plans of States and Union Territories 1985'.

TABLE-XI.21: CONTRIIBUTION OF STATE ROAD TRANSPORT CORPORATIONS (AT 1984-85 RATES) (Rs. Crores).

	STATES	1985-90 Plan Estt.	1985-86 Annual Plan Estt.
	1	2	3
I.	**SPECIAL CATEGORY STATES:**		
1.	Assam	-7.06	-1.59
2.	Himachal Pradesh	-11.97	-2.00
3.	Jammu & Kashmir	-7.05	-1.56
4.	Manipur	-6.09	-0.81
5.	Meghalaya	-4.46	-0.71
6.	Nagaland	-	-
7.	Sikkim	-	-
8.	Tripura	-5.21	-0.83
	TOTAL:	-41.84	-7.50
II.	**NON-SPECIAL CATEGORY STATES:**		
1.	Andhra Pradesh	24.85	10.17
2.	Bihar	-45.67	-18.13
3.	Gujarat	-115.60	-8.29
4.	Haryana	-	-
5.	Karnataka	-152.28	-27.67
6.	Kerala	-148.77	-18.50
7.	Madhya Pradesh	-8.40	-4.00
8.	Maharashtra	122.66	27.10
9.	Orissa	-99.72	-9.07
10.	Punjab	-82.54	-12.29
11.	Rajasthan	2.51	1.97
12.	Tamil Nadu	177.63	33.40
13.	Uttar Pradesh	120.59	14.29
14.	West Bengal	-168.79	-23.31
	TOTAL (II)	-373.53	-34.33
	GRAND TOTAL (I+II) :	-415.37	-41.83

Source: Government of India, Ministry of Finance, 'Statistical Statments on Finances and Plans of States and Union Territories 1985'.

TABLE-XI.22: CONTRIBUTION OF STATE ELECTRICITY BOARDS (AT 1979-80 RATES) (Rs. Crores)

	STATES	1980-81 Actuals	1981-82 Actuals	1982-83 Actuals	1983-84 Actuals	1984-85 L.E.	TOTAL 1980-85 (L.E.).
	1	2	3	4	5	6	7
I.	**SPECIAL CATEGORY STATES**						
1.	Assam	-6.78	-7.91	-11.95	-11.15	-35.00	-72.79
2.	Himachal Pradesh	-4.13	-2.51	-6.01	-7.83	-10.80	-31.28
3.	Jammu & Kashmir	-5.35	-10.37	-14.17	-14.08	-20.38	-64.35
4.	Manipur	-	-	-	-	-	-
5.	Meghalaya	-2.96	0.31	-4.59	-6.62	-7.33	-21.19
6.	Nagaland	-	-	-	-	-	-
7.	Sikkim	-	-	-	-		-
8.	Tripura	-	-	-	-	-	-
	TOTAL (I) :	-19.22	-20.48	-36.72	-39.68	-73.51	-189.61
II.	**NON-SPECIAL CATEGORY STATES**						
1.	Andhra Pradesh	15.15	20.76	-18.75	-15.36	-33.32	-31.52
2.	Bihar	-44.01	-61.08	-92.90	-113.04	-82.76	-493.79
3.	Gujarat	-49.67	-68.94	-159.18	214.59	-396.24	-788.62
4.	Haryana	-8.01	3.65	-27.08	-33.76	53.91	-119.11
5.	Karnataka	-15.42	-43.70	-62.22	-69.31	-109.87	-300.52
6.	Kerala	38.42	3.77	-1.63	-4.47	-35.58	0.51
7.	Madhya Pradesh	=9.01	-50.52	-72.09	-83.50	-162.52	-377.64
8.	Maharashtra	67.83	15.10	-79.38	-137.52	-97.05	-231.52
9.	Orissa	0.06	-12.02	-27.47	-31.41	-40.69	-111.53
10.	Punjab	0.50	-29.29	26.68	-53.24	-104.30	-213.01
11.	Rajasthan	-7.53	-25.98	-27.43	-73.05	-97.51	-231.50
12.	Tamil Nadu	-10.98	48.10	-162.71	-215.12	-224.23	-564.94
13.	Uttar Pradesh	-42.71	-61.62	-118.65	-231.66	-215.99	-670.23
14.	West Bengal	-39.10	-75.76	-81.08	-95.95	-82.87	-374.76
	TOTAL (II) :	-104.48	-337.13	-957.25	-1371.98	-1736.84	-4507.68
	GRAND TOTAL (I+II)	-123.70	-357.61	-993.97	-1411.66	-1810.35	-4697.29

Source : Government of India, Ministry of Finance, 'Statistical Statements on Finances and Plans of States : and Union Territories 1985'.

TABLE-XI-23: CONTRIBUTION OF STATE ELECTRICITY BOARDS
(At 1984-85 RATES) (RS. CRORES)

	STATES	1985-90 (Plan Estt.)	1985-86 (Anuual Plan Estt.)
	1	2	3
I.	SPECIAL CATECORY STATES:		
1.	Assam	-137.98	-28.54
2.	Himachal Pradesh	-19.54	-10.52
3.	Jammu & Kashmir	-79.93	-14.04
4.	Manipur	-	-
5.	Meghalaya	-27.21	-3.13
6.	Nagaland	-	-
7.	Sikkim	-	-
8.	Tripura	-	-
	TOTAL (II):	-264.66	-56.23
II.	NON-SPECIAL CATEGORY STATES:		
1.	Andhra Pradesh	380.01	112.60
2.	Bihar	-249.14	-59.60
3.	Gujarat	289.77	44.98
4.	Haryana	55.00	9.00
5.	Karnataka	-1026.83	-84.16
6.	Kerala	96.11	33.18
7.	Madhya Pradesh	667.35	69.75
8.	Maharashtra	-551.76	-7.20
9.	Orises	173.47	24.20
10.	Punjab	-146.04	-12.53
11.	Rajasthan	-404.71	-51.90
12.	Tamil Nadu	-513.18	-97.14
13.	Uttar Pradesh	-131.45	18.36
14.	West Bengal	57.25	7.43
	TOTAL (II):	-1304.15	6.97
	GRAND TOTAL (I+II)	1568.81	-49.26

Source: Government of India, Ministry of Finance, 'Statistical, Statements on Finances and Plans of States and Union Territories 1985

TABLE XI-24. COMMERCIAL LOSSES OF STATE ELECTRICITY BOARDS(AT 1979-80 RATES)

(RS.CRORES)

STATES	1980-85 Orignal Ests.	1980-81 A/c	1981-82 A/c	1982-83 A/c	1983-84 Pre- A/c	1984-85 L.E.	1980-85 L.E.
1	2	3	4	5	6	7	8
1. SPECIAL CATEGORY STATES.							
1. Assam	-269.40	-27.14	-37.06	-56.04	-64.19	-101.88	-286.31
2. Himachal Pr.	-56.09	-11.90	-11.56	-15.68	-18.29	-25.76	-83.83
3. Jammu & Kashmir	-103.74	-15.15	-20.71	-26.29	-33.25	-37.28	132.68
4. Manipur	-	-	-	-	-	-	-
5. Meghalaya	-21.83	-3.31	-2.68	-4.83	-7.45	8.62	-26.89
6. Nagaland	-	-	-	-	-	-	-
7. Sikkim	-	-	-	-	-	-	-
8. Tripura	-	-	-	-	-	-	-
TOTAL (I)	-451.06	-57.50	-72.01	-102.81	-123.82	-173.54	-529.71
II. NON-SPL.CATEGORY STATES:							
1. Andhra Pradesh	23.85	-8.16	-30.46	-59.74	-68.85	-87.30	-254.51
2. Bihar	-450.42	-75.53	-125.70	-157.55	-189.45	-235.21	-783.44
3. Gujarat	-126.00	-59.16	-84.04	-164.08	-208.62	-319.65	-635.55
4. Haryana	-202.52	-40.42	-65.16	(-)87.52	-99.15	-199.07	-411.32
5. Kernataka Board	47.10	-26.72	-38.00	-46.00	-93.05	-122.07	-325.84
K.P.C.	-1[illegible]03						
6. Kerala	-52.11	29.33	-11.34	-7.98	-23.60	-47.29	-60.88
7. Madhya Pradesh	-238.10	-65.77	-114.03	-139.93	-224.47	-262.82	-807.02
8. Maharashtra	-229.37	-44.68	-93.78	-152.50	-181.87	-234.75	-707.58
9. Orissa	-16.86	-[illegible].91	-21.80	-43.03	-39.98	-50.10	-168.82
10. Punjab	-405.36	-78.[illegible]	-82.33	-138.00	-179.83	-231.30	-168.82
11. Rajasthan	-383.25	-43.2[illegible]	-63.07	-71.70	-127.65	-177.73	-710.02
12. Tamil Nadu	-756.74	-113.40	-171.87	-258.10	-337.52	-342.78	-483.38
13. Uttar Pradesh	-817.70	-212.73	-265.27	-340.92	-427.92	-484.11	-1223.67
14. West Bengal	-212.82	-56.27	155.40	-140.65	-151.92	-166.63	-1730.95
15. TOTAL (II)	-3930.33	-809.21	-12[illegible].25	-1807.70	-2353.88	-2880.81	-630.87
GRAND TOTAL (I+II)	-4381.39	-866.71	-1354.26	-1910.54	-2477.70	-3054.35	-9133.85
							-9663.56

Source: Government of India, Ministry of Finance, 'Statistical Statements on Finances and Plans of States and Union Territories 1985'

TABLE XI.25 : COMMERCIAL LOSSES OF STATE ELECTRICITY BOARDS (AT 1984-85 RATES)

(Rs. CRORES)

	STATES	1985-90 Plan Ests.	1985-86 Annual PlanEsts.
	1	2	3
I.	SPECIAL CATEGORY STATES:		
1.	Assam	-687.24	-94.99
2.	Himachal Pradesh	-162.13	-28.59
3.	Jammu & Kashimir	-186.80	-33.09
4.	Manipur	-	-
5.	Meghalaya	-31.37	-4.66
6.	Nagaland	-	-
7.	Sikkim	-	-
8.	Tripura	-	-
	TOTAL (I):	-1067.52	-161.33
II.	NON-SPL. CATEGORY STATES :		
1.	Andhra Pradesh	39.48	63.51
2.	Bihar	-1053.51	-158.15
3.	Gujarat	-8.22	20.82
4.	Haryana	-382.06	-45.10
5.	Karnataka@	-924.13	-95.30
6.	Kerala	-15.46	19.09
7.	Madhya Pradesh	-257.60	-62.88
8.	Maharashtra	-1022.37	-84.84
9.	Orissa	106.07	13.54
10.	Punjab	-1354.24	-163.85
11.	Rajasthan	-1172.56	-124.32
12.	Tamil Nadu	-1414.03	-206.58
13.	Uttar Pradesh*	-2760.35	-319.37
14.	West Bengal	-475.05	-68.05
	TOTAL (II):	-10694.13	-1211.48
	GRAND TOTAL (I+II)	-11761.55	-1372.81

@ Includes K.P.C. * Includes Rajya Vidyut Utpadan Nigam.

Source: Government of Inida, Minsitry of Finance 'Statistical Statements on-Finances and Plans of States and Union Territories 1985'

TABLE XI.26 : PROVISION OF PAYMENT OF SUBSIDIES IN THE CENTRAL BUDGET

(Rs. Crores)

	1	1980-81 Actuals 2	1981-82 Actuals 3	1982-83 Actuals 4	1983-84 Actuals 5	1984-85 R.E. 6	1985-86 R.E. 7	1986-87 R.E 8
1.	Food Subsidy	650	700	710	835	1100	1650	1750
2.	Fertiliser subsidy	505	375	605	1042	1832	2050	1950
3.	Assistance for Export Promotion and Market Development	399	477	477	463	499	605	555
4.	Loss on Sugar Export/Import	-	-	25	83	39	108	-
5.	Loss on Imported Cloth	7	2	-	26	18	-	
6.	Subsidy on Controlled cloth	76	125	56	53	53	52	52
7.	Subsidy to Railways	69	78	97	93	98	119	147
8.	Interest subsidy to Coal India Ltd.	54	58	58	58	58	336	287
9.	Ship Building	4	20	22	10	9	-	-
10.	Other subsidies	148	111	254	223	716	-	-
	TOTAL:	1912	1946	2304	2836	4422	4921	4741

Source: Government of India, Ministry of Finance, "Statistical Statements on Finances and Plans of States and Union Territories' 1985 and the Central Budget for 1986-87.

TABLE XI.27 : INTERST RATES AND OTHER TERMS AND CONDITIONS OF LOANS AND ADVANCES BY THE CENTRAL GOVERNMENT AND THE R.B.I. TO THE STATE GOVERNMENTS

Interest Rates on	Interest rate per cent per annum From 1.6.1984 to 31.5.85	From 1.6.1985
I. Loans and advances by the Central Govt. to State Govts		
i Ways and Means advances recoverable within the year	6. 1/4	6.1/4
ii Loans out of net collections of small savings	10	10.1/2
iii Other loans	7.1/2	8
II.Loans by the Central Govt. to the R.E.C. for relending to State Govts./S.E.Bs. for rural electrification in the State Plan under the M.N.P.		
i From Ist to 10th year of loan	6.1/2	7
ii From 11th to 20th year of loan	6.3/4	7.1/4
iii From 21st to 30th year of loan	7.1/2	8
III.Advances by the RBI to State Govts	Rate of interest (as communicated by the R.B.I. in May,1978) (Effective from 1.5.1976)	
(A) Normal and secured ways and means advances		
i) For the first 90 days	1% below the Bank rate	
ii) Beyond 90 days upto 100 days	1% above the Bank rate	
iii) Beyond 180 days	2% above the Bank rate	
(B). Overdrafts.		
i) upto 7 days	Bank rate	
ii) Beyond 7 days	3% above the Bank rate	

TABLE-XI-27 B

Other terms and conditions:

I. Terms and conditions of W & M advances given to States

The ways and means advances will carry interest at 6 1/2 % per annum (effective from 1.6.1986) and will be recovered by adjustment against the share of Central Taxes duties and grants/Central assistance released to the State during a financial Year

II. Terms and conditions of the loans for Normal Plan and advance Plan astistance for drougt relief

a) The loan will carry interest at 8% annum (effective from 1.6.1985).

b) The loan represents a part of the block loans for State plan schemes and should be consolidated and deemed to have been paid on the Ist October of the financial year.it is repayable in 15 annual equal instalments of principal together with interest on the outstanding principal commencing from the next financial year. The amount annually payable (by way of principal and interest) will be recovered in four instalments on the Ist July, October, January an March each year.

c) A rebate of 1/4% in the interest will be admissible for timely repayment of principal and interest. In the event of default in the repayment of principal and/or interest, interest at the rate of 10 1.2% would be chargeable on all such overdue instalments.

III. Terms and conditions of special medium term non-Plan loan assistance to states during 1985-86

a) The loan will carry interest at 8% per annum.

b) The loan is repayable in four annual equal instalments.

c) A rebate of 1.4% in the interest will be admissible for timely repayment of principal and interest. In the event of default of repayment of principal and/or interest. interest at the rate of 10.1/2% would be chargeable on all such overdue instalments.

Sourcs: Government of India, Ministry of Finance, 'Statistical Statements on Finances and Plans of States and Union Territories 1985.

TABLE XI.28 : TIME SCHEDULE OF RELEASES OF STATUTORY GRANTS, SHARE IN CENTRAL TAXES AND CENTRAL ASSISTANCE ETC.

I. Statutury Grants : Releases made every quarter in April, July, October and January.

II. Share of Central Taxes:

(a) Income Tax: Releases made every month commencing from June each year at 1/12 of the amounts due, the balance being adjusted in March;

(b) Excise Duty: Releases made every month commencing from May at 1/12 of amount due, the balance being adjusted in March.

III. Grants in lieu of Tax on Railway Passenger Fares:

- Releases made every month commencing from may, each year at 1/12 of amounts due, the balance being adjusted in March.

IV. Loans against collection of Small Savings:

- Release are made every month on the basis of amounts of the collection of Small savings.

V. Central assistance for Plan:

(a) Central assistance for State Plan Schemes, Ten instalments each representing 1/12th of the amount allocated for State Plan are released avery month from April to January and the balance is released towards to end of February-March on the basis of the progress of expenditure.

(b) Additional Central Assistance for Externally Aided Projects: Releases are made in four instalments for each quarter ending June, September, December and March.

(c) Advance Plan assistance for expenditure necessitated by the Natural Calamities

- Advance Plan assistance for expenditure necessitated by natural clamities is allocated on the basis of the recommendation of the Central Study Teams and High Level Committee on relief and is released in suitable instalments depending on the progress of expenditure.

(d) Central Assistance for Centrally Sponsorad schemes :-

- Untill the and of 1976-77,the procedure as that eight instalments of ways and means advances, each representing 1/12th of the amount of assistance allocated for Centrally Sponsered Schemes were released by the Ministry of Finance (Plan Finance I Division) every month from April to November toward expenditure on Centrally Sponsored Schemes. There after, regular sanctions were issued by the Administrative Ministries on the basis of the progress of expenditure reported by the State Governments after adjustments of the ways and means advances already sanctioned.

The above procedures was discontinued with effect from ist April, 1977 and since then the Central Ministries themselves have been releasing funds directly to the States Government for the Centrally Sponsered Schemes. As of parent, there is no firm schedule of releases to the State governments by the Central Ministries. However, they have been advised to ensure regular flow of funds to the States by releasing funds each month or quarters on ad-hoc basis and thereafter follow up the requirements of obtaining progress of expenditure etc, so as to enable themselves to make the final releases at the and of the financial year.

Central Assistance for Central Sector Scehems

The administrative are Ministries are responsible for the issue of the sanctions and funds are also relaeased by them after due appraisal moritoring of the schemes, during the course of the finacial year. No specfic schedule of releases is followed for this purpose.

Source: Government of India, Ministry of Finance, 'Statisical Statements on Finances and Plans of States and Union Territories 1985'.

TABLE XI.29 : NOTE ON TRANSFERS TO STATES

NON PLAN:

1. Non-Plan transfers of resources from the Centre to the State consists mainly of States' share of Central taxes and duties. Statutory grants-in-aid, grants in lieu of tax on railway pasenger fares, other non Plan grants for such purposes as relief of distress caused by natural calamities like floods and cyclone (other than drought), development of handloom industry, improvement in the salary scales of University and College teachers and other educational programmes, compensation for loss of revenue due to implementation of prohibition policy, improvement of roads, etc, loans against net collections of small savings, short term loans for distribution of fertilisers and other agricultural inputs and ways and means advances.

2. The shares of States in Central taxes, (Income tax, Excise duty and Estate duty), statutory grants in aid and grant-in-aid in lieu of tax on railway passanger fares, which form the bulk of the non-plan transfers of resources to the States are distributed in accordance with the recommendations of the Finance Commission.

3. Non-Plan grants for relief of distress caused by natural calamities like floods, cyclone, earthquake (other than drought) are given to the States affected by these natural calamities to meet the expenditure on relief and rehabilitation of the affected people and repair and restoration of public works. In accordance with the recommendations of the 8th Finance Commission, the non-Plan grant from the Centre cover 75% of the totalexpenditure in excess of the margin money. Other non-Plan grants, the amount of which is very small, are generally allocated on objective criteria uniformly applicable to all the States.

4. Loans to States against net collections of small savings are given to the extent of 2/3 of the net collections of small savings mobilised in each State. Short term loans for agricultural inputs are disbursed on the basis of the requirements of various States.

5. Ways and Means advances, which are recoverable within the same financial year, are given to the various States to enable them to tide over temporary ways and means difficulties.

PLAN

Central Assistance for State Plans

6. Since the begining of the Fourth Plan period (1969-74), the Central assistnace for the State Plans has been allocated on the basis of the Gadgil Formula which was modified recently by the National Development Council while approving the draft Sixth Five Year Plan 1980-85. Under this modified formula, a lumpsum amount is set apart for meeting the requirements of 8 Special category States which include Assam, Himachal Pradesh, Jammu & Kashmir, Manipur, Meghalaya, Nagal and, Sikkim and Tripura. The balance of the Central assistance is distributed among the remaining 14 States in the following manner "

   i) 60% on the basis of population,

ii) 20% on the basis of per capita income - only to States having per capita income below the national average.

iii) 10% on the basis of tax effort.

iv) 10% for special problems of States.

7. <u>Centrally Sponsored Scheme Central Sector Schemes:</u>

These are schemes for which, because ot their national importance, the Centre takes the intiative. Proposed and formulated by the Ministry involved, approved by the Planing Commission and financed largely by the Centre, the schemes are implemented by the States because they are in the sectore of States' competency. There is little substantive difference between the two types of schemes other than that Centrally Sponsored Schemes are generally financed both by the Centre and the States whereas the Central Sector schomes are finsnced 100% by the Centre.

Source: Government of India, Ministry of Finance, 'Statistical Statements on Finances and Plans of States and Union Territories 1985'